HUMAN WELL-BEING AND
THE NATURAL ENVIRONMENT

D1602795

Praise for Human Well-Being and the Natural Environment

'Dasgupta raises the most challenging moral questions of our age: Is there a utilitarian foundation for trading-off an entire species-habitat for the gratification of the current generation? Are decisions about procreation and the sustenance of ecological systems based strictly on personal morality or based on a broader political ethic? In the process of asking these big questions, he addresses the role of citizenship, civil rights, democracy, and "progress". He explores intergenerational well-being and conflicts. He asks how we do and how we should value goods. He presents a powerful analysis of the evaluation of policies in imperfect economies. Reading this book is the equivalent of a crash course in political economy and moral philosophy. I wholeheartedly recommend it as one of the most important books of the new millennium.'

Professor Elinor Ostrom, Indiana University

'Building on his classic magnum opus . . . Partha Dasgupta has joined this rethink in an intellectually rich, thought-provoking and occasionally metaphysical work. His new book probes many issues beyond those that might be anticipated from the title and confirms his position as one of the most exciting economic thinkers today . . . we can ask why so many feel we need reforms in ethical behaviour to ensure sustainability. Dasgupta touches on some of the framework needed to answer this question. More is needed. If anyone is going to supply it it is likely to be Dasgupta.'

Times Higher Education Supplement

'Professor Dasgupta's latest book is a remarkably comprehensive account of his subject. It seeks out and develops the fundamentals so thoroughly that its methods will have application in many branches of economic evaluation and policy assessment even beyond the environmental aspects that are its primary focus. He moves with ease from deep studies of the meaning of concepts like "sustainability" to detailed empirical accounts of environmental damage. It is a book that will be used and consulted for a long time to come.'

Professor Kenneth J. Arrow, Stanford University

'Partha Dasgupta is one of the deepest thinkers and most powerful analysts in ecological economics. [In this book] he attempts to go beyond measures of current well-being, such as the Human Development Index of the United

Nations Development Programme because, as he puts it, "The present is the past's future". His tightly reasoned and carefully presented effort will enrich the thinking of students and professionals in economics, environmental studies, political science, political philosophy, and population studies.'

Professor Joel E. Cohen, Rockefeller University and Columbia University

'The anthropologist notices that, as a tribe, economists love argument, which means of course that they also love theory and exact measurement. The great economists add to these two loves one more, a passion for justice. Partha Dasgupta adds yet another—compassion. His understandings of the meaning of poverty and of helpless imprisonment in poverty traps provide a common-sense platform for proposing new measurements and challenging professional assumptions. This is how the book transcends its own formidable proficiency as it initiates the non-professional reader into the idea of social cost benefit.'

Professor Mary Douglas, University College London

'Concepts like GDP focus on easily measurable things, whilst omitting ecosystem services and other environmental factors on which life ultimately depends. Partha Dasgupta is a seminal figure in his discipline, taking on the difficult, yet hugely important, task of trying meaningfully to measure "quality of life". This book will, I hope, set the tone for the new millennium, melding conventional economic concepts, ecological and environmental science, and a great deal of plain commonsense. Read it.'

Lord Robert May, University of Oxford

'Ecological systems are essential to sustain life. They contribute to the generation of income and enhance human well being. Their amenities enrich our experience. *Human Well-Being and the Natural Environment* demonstrates that economic analysis must be relevant to all aspects of this sustainable growth trilogy. This volume's *layered* presentation assures access to advanced under-graduates as well as fresh insight to graduate students and scholars. In the process, Dasgupta provides a compelling challenge to all readers to consider how economic analysis can improve the human condition.'

Professor V. Kerry Smith, North Carolina State University

'...The seventy-two page Appendix constitutes an important new textbook for graduate students in resource economics. The economy-wide valuation issues are dealt with in detail, including second-best cases, and the non-convex problems receive a good exposition.'

John Hartwick, Queen's University, Kingston

Human Well-Being and the Natural Environment

PARTHA DASGUPTA

OXFORD
UNIVERSITY PRESS

OXFORD
UNIVERSITY PRESS

Great Clarendon Street, Oxford OX2 6DP

Oxford University Press is a department of the University of Oxford.
It furthers the University's objective of excellence in research, scholarship,
and education by publishing worldwide in

Oxford New York

Auckland Bangkok Buenos Aires Cape Town Chennai
Dar es Salaam Delhi Hong Kong Istanbul Karachi Kolkata
Kuala Lumpur Madrid Melbourne Mexico City Mumbai Nairobi
São Paulo Shanghai Taipei Tokyo Toronto

Oxford is a registered trade mark of Oxford University Press
in the UK and in certain other countries

Published in the United States
by Oxford University Press Inc., New York

© P. Dasgupta, 2001

British Library Cataloguing in Publication Data

Library of Congress Cataloging-in-Publication Data
Dasgupta, Partha.
Human well-being and the natural environment / Partha Dasgupta.
p. cm.
1. Sustainable development. 2. Natural resources—Management. 3. Human ecology. I. Title
HD75.6 .D367 2001 306–dc21 2001036597

ISBN 0–19–924788-9 (hbk.)
ISBN 0–19–926719-7 (pbk.)

1 3 5 7 9 10 8 6 4 2

Typeset by Newgen Imaging Systems (P) Ltd., Chennai, India
Printed in Great Britain
on acid-free paper by
Ashford Colour Press Ltd., Gosport, Hampshire

To Carol
as always

Preface to the Paperback Edition

Since the book was originally published, I have had the pleasure of collaborating with Professors Kenneth Arrow and Karl-Göran Mäler in further developing the welfare economics of imperfect economies. In a pair of articles (cited in the Appendix) we have also applied our findings to gain a better understanding of the links between human well-being and the natural environment. Meanwhile, colleagues from several universities have written to say that they have used the book in their graduate courses in environmental and resource economics. So it seemed to me that, in preparing the paperback edition, I ought to expand the original Appendix to include the new findings. Several colleagues have suggested that, for the sake of completeness, I ought to include an account of intertemporal welfare economics in what we economists refer to as first-best economies. The Appendix that I have prepared for this edition contains all the material of the earlier Appendix, but now also includes applications of the theory to first-best economies and to several imperfect economies. Furthermore, it now contains a far more detailed technical account of the positive feedbacks that would appear to be prevalent in many ecological processes. One of the tasks I undertook in the revised Appendix was to study the way such positive feedbacks affect deliberations on intergenerational well-being. The Appendix also develops approximate formulae for estimating the value of environmental natural resources in various institutional settings.

I am very grateful to Andrew Schuller and the Oxford University Press for permitting me (even encouraging me) to produce the new Appendix. I have taken the opportunity to correct a few misprints that appeared in the original edition.

St John's College   Partha Dasgupta
Cambridge
May 2003

Preface

This essay is on measuring the quality of life, a problem on which I have worked periodically ever since becoming a student in economics. A few passages, from Chapters 6 and 14, have even been lifted from my doctoral dissertation of 1968 (I have worked on the subject that long!). And there are chapters, particularly the Appendix, which report findings only a year or so old. The subject surrounding the problem is a complex one. One way or another, it pervades a number of disciplines. But the problem's relevance extends beyond the academic realm. International organizations routinely publish cross-country estimates of the quality of life, journalists and commentators publicize them, national governments are obliged to take note of them, non-governmental organizations criticize them, and intellectuals reflect upon them. Since much of the purpose of measuring the quality of life is to help search for ways to improve life's quality, the exercise reduces to valuing objects and evaluating policies. Today, quality-of-life indices broker political arguments and together form a coin that even helps purchase economic and social policy.

But the flurry of activity doesn't mean that the subject has progressed evenly. Since people have strong feelings about the matters involved, debates are often acrimonious. Moreover, intellectual training differs across the biological sciences, the social sciences, and the humanities. Findings are often misunderstood and are on occasion even misused. In shaping this essay I have been influenced by such incidents, and I offer illustrations when the occasion demands.

Broadly speaking, there are two ways to attack the problems inherent in valuing and evaluating. One is to start at an abstract level and proceed to concrete problems, as and when abstract considerations yield results that are capable of being applied, or when they refuse to yield results. The other is to start with concrete problems, even mundane problems, and move towards abstraction, so as to check that the findings have general validity. Which route one follows is a matter of taste and ability. Personally, I find the latter route more congenial. The present essay traces that route.

Books are in part autobiographical. Over the years, a good deal of my own research has been to help develop the economics of environmental and natural resources. Much of that too has been in the context of poor regions and the people who inhabit them. Inevitably, I reacted adversely to the fact that the natural environment is absent from national accounts, from quality-of-life indices, and, more generally, from official development economics. I found it puzzling too that, in its turn, official environmental and resource economics have made no contact with poverty in poor countries. The two fields of specializations had passed each other by and had weakened in consequence. Just how much they have suffered will become apparent in the chapters that follow.[1]

In great measure, their detachment from each other continues. For example, in responding to the inadequacies of Gross National Product (GNP) as an index of social well-being, one influential group of development economists seem content to study measures of *current* well-being (expectancy of life, infant survival, public expenditure) when describing the state of the world and devising prescriptions for governments.[2] To many, this has very limited appeal. It appears odd to ecologists, who are trained to study the many slow processes that are influencing long-term development possibilities and so can't help peering into the future. A seemingly natural retort to ecologists is that people come first and that, after all, present anguish should matter most. But that would be to miss the point. The present is the past's future. Moreover, the future has an unnerving habit of becoming the present. An effective response to ecologists would be to work within a framework for valuing and evaluating that combines present and future concerns. Economics has had such a framework in place for several decades. In this essay I draw upon the literature.

But with two significant differences.

First, welfare economics has neglected ecology and, thereby, demography. In this essay I give particular attention to the natural environment and show how it can be brought into economic reasoning in a seamless way. Secondly, intertemporal welfare economics, including the literature on 'green' national accounts, was developed for a society in which the State is not only trustworthy, but also optimizes on behalf of its citizens. Policy prescriptions emerging from the theory are for Utopia or, at worst, for what James Meade called Agathotopia (the 'good-enough society').[3] But they are not directly relevant for the world we have come to know—perhaps, most especially, for today's poor countries, the majority of which are a far cry from Agathotopia. Recently, intertemporal welfare economics has been extended to Kakotopia (today we would call it the 'dysfunctional society', or, at best,

---

[1] I have grumbled about these deficiencies on a number of occasions. See *The Control of Resources* (Cambridge, Mass.: Harvard University Press, 1982); 'The Resource Basis of Economies', Commencement Day Address, *Export–Import Bank of India*, Bombay, 1987; 'Environmental and Resource Economics in the World of the Poor', Forty-fifth Anniversary Lecture, *Resources for the Future*, Washington, 1997; 'The Economics of Poverty in Poor Countries', *Scandinavian Journal of Economics*, 1998, 100: 41–68; and 'Population and Resources: An Exploration of Reproductive and Environmental Externalities', *Population and Development Review*, 2000, 26: 643–89.

[2] The well-known Human Development Index in the annual *Human Development Report* of the United Nations Development Programme is a prominent case in point.

[3] J. E. Meade, *Agathotopia: The Economics of Partnership* (University of Aberdeen Press, 1989).

imperfect society).[4] I am concerned here with valuation and evaluation in Kakotopia.

I pay attention to the ways in which our quality of life is now known to be tied to the natural environment. Methods of valuation and evaluation are developed and are put to work in that context. When the occasion demands and evidence is available, I apply the methods to data on poor countries. The picture that emerges of recent experiences of development processes is sobering and contrasts sharply from the one portrayed in writings that focus on the current quality of life as a measure of economic progress. But it is hard to resist moving from the concrete to the abstract, and I am singularly weak of character. A number of chapters focus on the foundations of reasoning about human well-being. The essay as a whole is an iteration between the concrete and the abstract.

Although the subject of the essay is the domain of several disciplines, the style I adopt reflects my own specialized training. I assume a point of view of the circumstances of living that gives prominence to the allocation of resources— among contemporaries and over time. One hallmark of the viewpoint is to study human well-being in terms of its commodity determinants and the institutions that shape resource allocation. Another is to reason quantitatively. Moreover, because it is subject to empirical discipline, the inquiry encourages approximations. Inevitably, the viewpoint is partial. But increasingly I have come to realize that it is possible to look outward from that partial view to catch a glimpse of the larger enterprise called 'living'. I try to do that regularly in this essay.

I believe it is on each of these scores that moral and political philosophers sometimes misunderstand what we economists are up to. A few years ago, at an evening seminar at the British Academy, a distinguished moral philosopher read a paper attacking economists for inferring human well-being from the choices people actually make. I don't know who had advised my philosopher colleague on what economists actually write, but he was evidently unaware of a huge empirical literature on valuation that goes well beyond what he imagines it does.[5] Nor, it seemed to me, did he appreciate that the short-cuts social scientists resort to are influenced by the scope of the problem they happen to be tackling.

---

[4] P. Dasgupta and K.-G. Mäler, 'Net National Product, Wealth, and Social Well-Being', *Environment and Development Economics*, 2000, 5: 69–93. I am grateful to Prof. Malcolm Schofield, of St John's College, Cambridge, for suggesting that the name 'Kakotopia' best describes the kind of society I study here.

[5] I personally found the accusation ironic, because I had published a treatise only a few years earlier, on destitution and well-being, where well-being was given a wider interpretation than one based exclusively on 'revealed preference', which is what the philosopher was attacking. See *An Inquiry into Well-Being and Destitution* (Oxford: Clarendon Press, 1993).

Consider the following questions, which are representative of the kinds asked of economists:

1. The traffic on a highway is heavy, causing delays. There is a proposal to enlarge the road. Should it be accepted?
2. The State in a poor country has for some decades been subsidizing the use of the country's natural resource base. Should it continue to do so? Should the subsidies be enlarged, or should they be reduced?
3. There are plans among international bodies to help rebuild a poor country, which has been racked by civil strife and corrupt government. What should the mix of government engagement, private enterprise, and civic involvement be?

There is a clear sense in which reasoned responses to the successive questions would be more elaborate, more hesitant, requiring greater sensitivity to life's nuances. People's preferences inferred from past behaviour may well be a reasonable basis for a response to the first question on the list. (How else would we know what the traffic will bear?) Even if it weren't entirely reasonable, I don't believe that Aristotle, whose writings are regarded by philosophers as the touchstone of speculations on the ethical life, could help decide how else one should go about advising what to do. Aristotle does have useful things to say on the third question, but only as a prelude. As matters stand today, substantive responses to the questions would require a good dose of modern economics, with all its technicalities. They would also require inputs from anthropology, ecology, and political science. The present essay reflects this experience.

I have written this book not only for fellow economists, but also for students of economics, environmental studies, political science, and political philosophy. It is intended even more broadly for the general citizen interested in what are among the deepest and most urgent social problems we face today. The reader I have in mind is someone who wants to know if there is a workable language in which to discuss economic policy without ignoring the centrality of the natural environment in our lives. I imagine this reader to be shrewd and (even if an economist) sceptical of economics. I see her demanding intellectual evidence before being convinced of anything. So, I also imagine she doesn't want me to cut corners in my exposition.

I have placed the rigorous argument justifying the text in a lengthy Appendix and a few formal examples that help to illustrate the arguments in four starred chapters. This isn't a relegation; I have done it only because my reader doesn't necessarily know mathematics. However, she appreciates that an easy read can mislead. Most especially, she knows that it is a convenient myth that anything worth knowing can be explained in easy sentences. She also knows that there are readers (for example, economists) who would find the arguments easier to follow if presented in terms of formal models. So she is not put off when the occasional notation appears in the text, as long as it is accompanied by words of interpretation. My reader is someone willing to work hard with me.

The essay originated in my Arrow Lectures at Stanford University in April 1997 and in a Plenary Lecture I delivered at a conference at the World Bank on evaluation and poverty reduction, in June 1999.[6] They were in effect early drafts of Parts I and II of the book. The issues discussed in Parts III and IV were the basis of a lecture delivered at the Annual Conference of the European Association of Environmental and Resource Economists (Crete, June 2000), of my Presidential Address to the Royal Economic Society at its Annual Conference (University of St Andrews, July 2000), the Mullin Lecture at the University of Maryland Baltimore Campus (September 2000), the Wiegand Lectures at Duke University (October 2000), and lectures at the AGORA/SIAS Symposium at the Institute for Advanced Study Berlin and the Collegium Budapest (both in November 2000). Part V is based on a lecture delivered at the conference on Ethics, Economics and Environment, at the Swedish Collegium for Advanced Study in the Social Sciences, Uppsala, in 1995. But the immediate motivation for preparing the essay was an invitation to deliver the Tanner Lecture on Human Values at the University of Michigan, Ann Arbor (October 2000). A condition of the Tanner Foundation is that the lectures be written in advance of the occasion. It was while preparing the Tanner Lecture that I realized I was writing a book. The essay's overall design, however, reflects my attempt to respond to a letter I received from Peter Raven, director of the Missouri Botanical Garden, St Louis, in which he asked why it is that macroeconomic forecasts rarely have the natural environment built into them, and enquired if it is because economics doesn't have a language in which to study ecosystems as capital assets.[7]

My understanding of ecological processes and the way they shape, and are in turn shaped by, human activities has been sharpened over the years through my association with the Beijer International Institute of Ecological Economics in Stockholm, which offers an uncommonly good environment for interdisciplinary exchanges. Over the past several years, the Institute has organized, at the marine field station on the island of Askö in the Trosa archipelago, an annual meeting of ecologists and economists to discuss research problems of mutual interest. The meetings have been administered by Astrid Auraldsson and Christina Leijonhufvud with a touch that has regularly established a mood conducive to intellectual discourse. These meetings have influenced the way I have framed many of the questions raised below. For this I am most grateful to Sara Aniyar, Kenneth Arrow, Bert Bolin, Gretchen Daily, Paul Ehrlich, Carl Folke, C. S. ('Buzz') Holling, AnnMari Jansson, Bengt-Owe Jansson, Simon-Levin, Karl-Göran Mäler, Tore Söderqvist, and Brian Walker, each of whom has been a regular attendant of the occasion.

---

[6] See 'Valuation and Evaluation', in O. Feinstein and R. Picciotto (eds.), *Evaluation and Poverty Reduction* (Washington: World Bank, 2000).   [7] Letter, 19 August 1999.

For more than a decade, Karl-Göran Mäler (director of the Beijer Institute) and I have conducted a teaching and research programme in environmental and resource economics for university teachers of economics in poor countries. My understanding of the subject of this essay has been shaped by the many discussions I have had with participants in this programme, too numerous to mention individually.[8]

My intellectual debts on these matters are, of course, wider still and go back further. Over the years I have benefited from discussions and correspondence with Scott Barrett, Simon Blackburn, John Broome, Gretchen Daily, Carol Dasgupta, Paul David, Jayasri Dutta, Paul Ehrlich, Yehuda Elkana, Jack Goody, Frank Hahn, Geoffrey Heal, Robert Hinde, Bengt Kriström, Wolf Lepenies, Stephen Marglin, Alaknanda Patel, I. G. Patel, Elinor Ostrom, Charles Perrings, Peter Raven, John Rawls, Debraj Ray, Paul Seabright, Amartya Sen, Ismail Serageldin, Robert Solow, Hirofumi Uzawa, Jeff Vincent, and, most especially, Kenneth Arrow, Karl-Göran Mäler, Eric Maskin, and James Mirrlees. Many of the ideas developed here were given to me by them, and they will recognize that.

The Tanner Lecture was followed by a seminar chaired by Stephen Darwall, where the text was subjected to probing questions by Debra Satz, T. N. Srinivasan, Jeremy Waldron, and members of the Department of Philosophy at the University of Michigan, Ann Arbor. Kenneth Arrow, Scott Barrett, Jeremy Edwards, Robert Hinde, Karl-Göran Mäler, Andrew Schuller, Robert Solow, Jeff Vincent, and two readers for Oxford University Press commented on earlier drafts of the essay. The present version reflects the impact of their comments. Louise Cross has helped me in innumerable ways to prepare the essay for publication. Sue Hughes edited the typescript I submitted to Oxford University Press with an understanding that I have now come to anticipate. To all these good people, I am most grateful.

St John's College   Partha Dasgupta
Cambridge
March 2001

---

[8] The programme began in 1989 under the auspices of the World Institute for Development Economics Research (WIDER) in Helsinki, and has been funded since 1994 by the MacArthur Foundation in Chicago and the Swedish International Development Authority (SIDA). Two recent developments of the programme have been the establishment of the South Asian Network for Development and Environmental Economics (SANDEE), based in Kathmandu, Nepal, and the Research Accounting Network for Eastern and Southern Africa (RANESA), based in Pretoria, South Africa. Both SANDEE and RANESA fund teaching and research workshops in environmental and resource economics, and award research grants to enable economists based in South Asia and in Eastern and Southern Africa, respectively, to work on both local and transfrontier environmental problems. These developments would not have been possible but for the encouragement and support given by Lal Jaywardena, previously director of WIDER; Dan Martin, previously of the MacArthur Foundation; and Mikael Stahl of SIDA.

Contents

Summary and Guide

It is today a commonplace that our use of the natural environment ought to enter economic accounts. *How* it should enter isn't a commonplace, though; it isn't even well understood. This may explain why accounting for Nature continues to be a rarity in practical economic reasoning. Since this essay is about measuring the quality of life, the natural environment is viewed here as a source of human well-being, meaning that I am mostly concerned with natural *resources*. So we will regard Nature as an array of capital assets: minerals and fossil fuels, soils, fisheries, sources of water, forests and woodlands, watersheds, the oceans, places of beauty and tranquility, and the atmosphere (as both a source of well-being and a sink for the residuals of human activity). Natural resources are but one kind of capital asset. Other types of asset include manufactured capital (buildings and machinery), human capital (skills), and knowledge (ideas). The quality of life in an economy is determined by the way the portfolio of its assets is managed. How it is managed is determined in great measure by a society's institutions (e.g. property rights to various assets).

There are sensibilities that go beyond the viewpoint adopted here. For example, Nature is seen by some people to be more than a means to human ends. My treatment of the subject is therefore minimalist. As I shall show, economic practice neglects a good portion of the sources of human well-being. So, widening our perception of Nature would reveal that the neglect is even greater and our economic policies even more misguided than are identified in this essay.

The idea is to value states of affairs in terms of the quality of life they sustain. One reason for the valuation exercise is that we could then evaluate policies, in order to choose better. It transpires that practical measures of well-being involve valuing goods and services, among which are those comprising the natural environment.[1] However, as Nature is a stock, no deep study can be made of its role in our lives unless the analysis includes the way services are drawn from it over time in various institutional settings. Valuing states of affairs and evaluating policies involve valuing goods and services over time.

In all this I am assuming, as demographers do when they make population forecasts, that the size of future generations is not influenced by policy. This assumption helps us to define conflicts among generations over the use of the natural environment in a sharp way: it permits us to talk about 'us' and a sequence of 'thems'. But reflections on Humanity's interactions with

---

[1] Throughout, the terms 'quality of life' and 'well-being' will be used interchangeably.

Nature lead to thoughts on Humanity's size, to the question of how we should value potential lives, and to what is ethically justifiable reproductive behaviour. Discussions on Earth's carrying capacity are a response to such questions.

The chain of reasoning just sketched is developed in this essay in five parts.

Part I advances a pluralist conception of personal well-being, which is then used to develop the concept of social well-being. The notion I arrive at is inclusive of human rights. A distinction is drawn between the constituents and determinants of well-being and is put to work in describing quality-of-life indices in use by international agencies. A prerequisite for measuring the quality of life over time is a measure of well-being at a point *in* time. Part II develops an empirically comprehensive measure of social well-being at a point in time and offers quantitative estimates in poor countries. The measure includes not only health, education, and material well-being, but also indices of political and civil liberties. Evidence from the 1970s is then used to show that countries in which citizens enjoyed greater civil and political liberties performed better in the socio-economic sphere. The oft-repeated fear among rulers in poor countries—that there is a trade-off between economic performance and political and civil rights—is belied by what evidence we have.

The fact remains though that *within* democratic countries there are enormous differences among people in the prospects they face. Political scientists have shown that democracy is neither necessary nor sufficient for civic cooperation and the benefits that come with it. Moreover, democracies in poor regions harbour significant proportions of malnourished people. In order to explain the findings, we are led to study institutions and the geography of poverty traps.

Time and generations are introduced in Part III, so it isn't until then that the natural environment enters the picture. We are concerned there with valuing states of affairs. The concept of *sustainable development* is formulated and the sense in which it is related to the protection and promotion of human well-being is identified. *Accounting prices* are introduced. They measure the social worth of goods and services and are shown to depend on substitution possibilities among resources and among resources, labour, and manufactured capital. A study is made of the role of biodiversity in creating and preserving substitution possibilities in economic activities. Accounting prices are shown also to depend on the structure of property rights and the institutional rules guiding the allocation of resources. Illustrations are provided from poor countries of resources that are neither private property nor state-managed, but owned communally. A rationale for the co-existence of various property-rights regimes is offered. I also try to identify reasons why some common-property resources in some locations are managed communally, while others remain unmanaged and result in the 'tragedy of the commons'. Where institutions function badly, accounting prices differ substantially from market prices. Practical methods for estimating accounting prices are discussed.

Part IV begins with a theory of policy evaluation based on accounting prices. This is followed by an analysis of a class of accounting prices that has been the subject of regular controversy: *social discount rates*. The topic is over forty years old, and yet the controversy is about matters that have long been settled, involving as they do technical economics. The framework developed in Parts III and IV is then used to clarify contemporary debates on structural adjustment programmes, freer trade, and global warming.

A key concept in both Parts III and IV is that of a *productive base*, which includes not only an economy's stocks of manufactured and human capital, knowledge, and natural capital, but also its institutions and cultural coordinates. Whether we are interested in valuing a state of affairs or in evaluating policy, the index of interest is shown to be an economy's *wealth*, which is the social worth of its capital assets. The concept of wealth adopted here is a comprehensive one. In Part III and the Appendix it is shown that, adjusting for population change and subject to certain qualifications, an increase in a nation's wealth simultaneously signifies an increase in social well-being and signals that development has been sustainable. We find too that, adjusting for demographic differences and subject to certain qualifications, cross-country differences in wealth reflect differences in social well-being among them.

It is argued that, since wealth changes measure the economic progress of nations, the object of study should be *genuine investment*, which is the social worth of the accumulation of a nation's capital assets. Under current accounting practices, however, recorded investment could be positive, even large, while genuine investment is negative. This can happen because environmental resources are typically underpriced. (In the extreme, they are regarded as free.) Moreover, because the depletion of natural capital doesn't count for much in economic calculations, investment projects judged to be productive can in fact be unproductive owing to their rapacious use of natural resources. The direction of technological change can also be biased against the natural environment. I argue that this is why industrial technology is often environmentally unfriendly.

Investment projects are the simplest examples of policy change. They perturb an economy. In Part IV and the Appendix it is shown that the way to evaluate investment projects is to compare reductions in consumption arising from the investments with the increase in wealth the investments help to create. To put it in slightly different words, projects should be accepted if they add to wealth, but not otherwise. Rules of social cost–benefit analysis, developed several decades ago, are shown to be implied by this finding.

The chain of results in Parts III and IV and the Appendix unify procedures for valuing states of affairs and evaluating policies: *they both involve wealth comparisons.* Given that Adam Smith's inquiry into the wealth of nations is over two hundred years old, the conclusions could appear banal, but for the fact that in recent years the progress of nations has almost invariably been measured with every yardstick *but* wealth. Most common among them have been gross national product (GNP) and such *ad hoc* measures of well-being as the United Nations Development Programmes' Human Development Index, neither of which is related to wealth.

Genuine investment is the social worth of net changes in an economy's capital assets. It is a comprehensive notion, including as it does the social worth of net changes in manufactured and human capital, public knowledge, and natural capital. Ensuring that social well-being is sustainable involves taking care that the economy's assets are managed well.

In the background of Parts III and IV is a puzzle created by the conflicting intuitions that have been derived from two different empirical perspectives concerning the question of whether the character of contemporary economic development is sustainable.[2] On the one hand, if we look at specific resources and services (e.g. fresh water, ecosystem services, and the atmosphere as a carbon sink), there is convincing evidence that the current rates of utilization are unsustainable.[3] On the other hand, if we look at historical trends in the prices of marketed resources or the recorded growth in GNP per capita in countries that are currently rich, resource scarcities would not appear yet to have bitten.[4] The focus of genuine investment helps to resolve the conflict.[5]

The findings are put to work on contemporary data from the poorest countries in the world. The picture that emerges about recent development experiences and the problems poor countries now face is substantially different from the one portrayed in the contemporary literature on economic development. Countries that would be regarded as having performed well if judged on the basis of such indices as GNP per head or the Human Development Index are found to have grown *poorer,* a few alarmingly so. The estimates I offer are rough and ready, but they suggest that the poorest countries of the world have 'developed' by depleting natural capital relative to their high population growth rates. This finding is at variance with current thinking among development

---

[2] For a good illustration of the conflicting intuitions, see the debate between Norman Myers and the late Julian Simon in Myers and Simon (1994).

[3] See e.g. Vitousek *et al.* (1986, 1997) and Postel, Daily, and Ehrlich (1996)

[4] See e.g. Barnett and Morse (1963) and Simon (1990).

[5] Arrow *et al.* (2001) contains a summary of this line of thinking.

economists that in poor countries high population growth has not been a hindrance in the recent past.[6] The theory I advance here identifies circumstances where high fertility, poverty, and malnutrition, illiteracy, and degradation of local resource bases feed on one another, cumulatively, over extended periods of time.[7] However, none is seen in the theory to be the prior cause of the others: over time, each influences, and is in turn influenced by, the others. Thus, it makes no less sense to say that high birth rates cause poverty and illiteracy than to say that poverty and illiteracy cause birth rates to be high. The findings suggest that there is now a need to review our collective thoughts on the processes of development and on the institutions that ought to govern the allocation of natural capital. Since development economics is many decades old, this is a sad conclusion.

In Part V, I extend the framework of Parts III and IV to offer an outline of a theory which enables us to value states of affairs and evaluate policies when future numbers are influenced by policy. Classical–Utilitarian thinking on the subject has been known to recommend what would otherwise be regarded as overly large populations. I offer an outline of a theory that is based on an especially strong conception of personhood. In comparison with Classical Utilitarianism it appears to perform well when put to work in a world facing environmental limits.

I have provided a Prologue for each Part. They break the exposition by offering an idea of what the forthcoming chapters are about. I hope they help. The subject of the essay is not easy, and I don't know how to present the material in a simpler way without the risk of making the analysis superficial.

---

[6] Bauer (1981, 2000), Kelley (1988), Simon (1989, 1990), Sen (1994), and Temple (1999).

[7] The theory is developed in greater detail in Dasgupta (1993, 1995, 1997, 2000b,c).

Introduction: Means and Ends

I.1. MAKING COMPARISONS

In common parlance, we *value* when comparing objects and we *evaluate* when comparing the relative merits of actions. The objects need not be concrete—they can be abstract (ideas)—and evaluation is not restricted to a narrowly construed notion of action. We evaluate strategies, which are conditional actions, be they personal or collective ('I will do this if that happens'; 'We will do that if he does this'; and so forth). We evaluate policies as well, which can also be personal or collective. There is a sense in which valuation is passive, while evaluation signifies more of an active engagement. We frequently value in order to evaluate. But not always. We sometimes value simply because we wish to understand a state of affairs.

This essay is about the quality of life, and the valuing of objects and evaluating of policies is only a means to measure it and to discover ways of improving it. When discussing policies, I shall be thinking of *public* policies, the sorts of policies governments and international agencies are expected to ponder. They involve such matters as the character of public investment, the structure of taxes and transfers, property rights (ownership of firms, land, and resources; environmental legislation), international aid, reproductive-health programmes, and so forth. The examples I will appeal to for purposes of illustration are taken mostly from rural areas of poor countries, and the backdrop will be the natural environment, upon which we depend not only for our livelihood, but, more deeply, for our very existence. This choice in great measure is a reflection of the fact that I have studied poor countries more than rich ones and natural resources more than other types of goods and services. But it is also guided by the experience that many of the issues we will discuss appear in a starker form when the context involves the rural poor in poor countries and the goods and services in question are natural resources.

Notice that in speaking of 'poor' and 'rich' countries I have already engaged in a bit of valuing. I don't suppose there is any harm in anticipating some of our conclusions. By 'poor' countries I mean those that, together, harbour the bulk of the world's poorest people. And we all have an intuitive understanding of 'poor' and 'rich' when applied to people. Although volumes have been written on the concept of poverty, the immediate sense of the term is clear enough: we say someone is poor if they have very limited access to the resources they need to be able to function. Now, this may seem overly rough and ready and aggregative. After all, there are many kinds of resources, and one can be well-off in some (food), but poor in others (health care). Moreover, 'needs' requires elucidation. (It too has elicited book-length inquiries.) And what, after all, should one mean by something being 'very limited' and by someone's 'ability to function'? All these are valid concerns. We will see though that our intuitive sense of the concept of poverty serves us well as a starting point of analysis.

In speaking of the evaluation of public policy, I mean the evaluation of *changes* in public policy. In fact, both valuation and evaluation involve comparisons. When we ask if the standard of living in some country is currently higher than in some other country, we seek a comparison. When we wish to evaluate a public policy, our intention is to compare it with some other policy. That other policy would typically be the existing policy. For example, it could be that the prevailing policy sustains a bad state of affairs. A good government would seek to change the policy; indeed, it would wish to choose the best policy. In order to do that, though, it would need to identify the best *possible* policy. In this essay I want to consider a wider world, where the government may not be good and may even be bad.[1] In the latter case the policy change to be evaluated could be a small shift from the prevailing policy. Whether the government is good, bad, or indifferent, however, evaluation involves thinking about counter-factuals; valuation isn't necessarily so involved.

The qualification 'public', when applied to policy, means two, often related, things. First, choice of one public policy (rather than another) implies one background environment (rather than another) within which the various parties in society act. The choice influences the constraints to which the parties are subject. So, evaluating public policy requires an assessment of the likely responses of the ecological and economic systems to the policy. Secondly, evaluation has to be conducted on behalf of a large, possibly disparate group of people, possessing different preferences, values, and needs. This calls for an acceptable procedure for aggregating the often conflicting claims of the parties. It also requires that we identify those features of the consequences of choices that are to be included in the evaluation exercise, which involves valuing.

I remarked earlier that the need for quality-of-life indices arises not only because policies have to be evaluated, but for a number of other reasons. For example, we often wish to know if a certain group (women, children, the old) is doing as well today as it did in the past, or if one group (a community) enjoys

---

[1] I elaborate on this in Sect. I.3. The idea is formalized in the Appendix.

a higher standard of living than another. In the chapters that follow, I am much concerned with such questions as these. One of my aims is to develop indices which could be used in answering them (Parts II and III, and the Appendix). I also develop criteria, based on quality-of-life measures, that would be suitable for evaluating public policies (Parts IV, V and the Appendix). It will be seen that the most appropriate criteria for policy evaluation are not quality-of-life indices, even though, of course, they are based on such indices.

In a moving discourse on the character of poverty at the 2001 meeting of the Pontifical Academy of Social Science, Justice Nicholas McNally urged us to see poverty as the reflection of a sense of *fatalism* to ever-increasing economic hardships in a changing, and elsewhere an often progressive, world. At that same meeting, the political scientist Wilfrido Villacorta suggested that the term 'poor', when applied to countries, is no longer useful; that countries ought perhaps now to be classified in accordance with some such term as *competitive* (alternatively, *progressive*), thereby directing us to ask if they have the institutions, policies, and civic attitudes in place to enable the poorest to improve their lot. In an earlier study (Dasgupta, 1993) I worked with a pluralist conception of poverty, one part involving descriptions of states of affairs, the other being concerned with identifying pathways (or processes) by which bad states of affairs come about and prevail. In this essay I explore that perspective further. Throughout, I iterate among the different conceptions of poverty. It will help us to see that, though distinct, the various conceptions are related to one another, and that each speaks to an important feature of our world.[2]

I.2. DISAGREEMENTS OVER FACTS AND VALUES

If commentators in earlier periods recorded contemporary phenomena in terms of wars and strife and diplomacy, today they add the state of the economy and (on occasion) environmental destruction. There is an urge, on reading contemporary reports on poverty and environmental degradation (and there is much to read), to say that we have adopted wrong values, that if we could only frame the prevailing state of affairs the right way, we would know what should be done to put the world right. Frequently, we are tempted into thinking that to rename a phenomenon is to explain why and how it occurs. I believe this is what attracts us to the voluminous debate on quality-of-life indices in academic publications and international development reports.[3] Unhappily, as valuation and evaluation

---

[2] Such a pluralist conception of poverty, more generally, of human well-being has been explored in a marvellous essay by Douglas and Ney (1998).

[3] Among the former, see Sen (1999); among the latter, see the annual *Human Development Report* of the United Nations Development Programme (UNDP).

raise passions, writers all too frequently fall prey to the temptation of making sanctimonious pronouncements. It is one thing to criticize the reliance on such indicators of economic development as gross national product on the ground that they neglect intergenerational concerns; it is another to propose alternative descriptors with such captions as 'development with a human face', or 'putting people first', or 'humanizing economics', the suggestion being that those who are not on board with the authors overlook the human race, or regard economic activity as having priority over human interests. The rhetoric can backfire. Making good points with bad arguments can disguise the fact that there are good arguments that would have served the purpose. The following is an example of the kind of mistake one makes when attempting over-kill.

In drawing attention to the enormous inequality in today's world, UNDP (1998: 30) writes: 'New estimates show that the world's 225 richest people have a combined wealth of over 1 trillion US dollars, equal to the annual income of the poorest 47 percent of the world's people (2.5 billion).'

Now, wealth is a stock, while income is a flow. As they differ in dimension, they cannot be compared.[4] The stock has to be converted into an equivalent flow (or vice versa) before comparisons can be made. If we were to pursue UNDP's reasoning, we could follow the standard practice of converting wealth into a figure for permanent income by using a 5 per cent annual interest rate; that is, to divide wealth by 20. When this conversion is made on the data, my calculations, albeit they are very crude, tell me that the world's richest 225 people, having a combined annual income of over 50 billion US dollars, earn more than the combined annual incomes of people in the world's twelve poorest countries, or about 7 per cent of the world's population (385 million). This is still a sobering statistic.

In any event, one may doubt that fundamental differences in ethical thinking are what fuel disagreements on international economic policies. In all my encounters with people from widely differing cultural and occupational backgrounds, I have observed few differences in the way redress, fairness, obligation, and reciprocity are understood. Evolutionary biologists explain this core commonality in terms of the kinds of problems we humans and our ancestors have faced and tried to solve over hundreds of millennia. Our capacity to have such feelings as shame, affection, anger, approval, and jealousy has emerged under selection pressure. No doubt culture helps to shape preferences and expectations (thus, behaviour), which are known to differ widely. But cultural coordinates enable us to identify the locus of points *upon* which shame, fairness, obligations, reciprocity, and approval are put to work: they don't displace the centrality of shame, fairness, obligations, reciprocity, and approval. Moreover, the cultural coordinates themselves demand explanation in terms of the exigencies

---

[4] UNDP (1999) repeats the mistake.

of history. No theory striving for depth and reach would regard culture as an explanatory variable.[5]

It seems to me that disagreement on ethics stems more from our lack of understanding of the ways socio-economic and ecological systems respond to policy than from fundamental differences in ethical thinking. This is at odds with what is otherwise widely held to be true. Economists (and, no doubt, philosophers too), stress that people differ on social goals; that when they agree on them they differ on what are appropriate rates of trade-off among competing social goals. Political differences among people are to be traced to this, or so the assertion goes.[6] My own understanding is otherwise. Differences of opinion about how the world works seem to assume importance in international economic and political debates long before real differences in ethical views manifest themselves. I have yet to read an economics document which doesn't agree that unemployment should be reduced wherever it is extensive, that destitution should be a thing of the past, or that the rate of disappearance of the rainforests is a cause for concern. I have also read many disagreements over what are the most effective means of bringing about desirable changes to such states of affairs.

No doubt people who agree on social goals differ on the rates at which they should be traded off among one another. But economic debates tend to avoid mention of admissible trade-offs. Discussions on the economics of global warming, for example, centre on the costs of reducing carbon emissions and the effects of the phenomenon on future economic productivity. There are disputes over the rates to be used for discounting future costs and benefits, but the disagreements are over which among the many prevailing interest rates one should use to do the discounting.[7]

Similarly, disputes on the desirability of trade liberalization read as though they are about whether it actually brings benefits to most people or whether a substantial number of the poorest of the poor get hurt. Ethical differences may well underlie these debates, but they don't get much of a look in, at least not explicitly. As the philosopher Hilary Putnam has put it (Putnam, 1993: 146), 'It is all well and good to describe hypothetical cases in which two people "agree on the facts and disagree about values", but . . . [w]hen and where did a Nazi

---

[5] See, especially, Barkow, Cosmides, and Tooby (1992); Hinde (1997); Wilson (1998); and Ehrlich (2000). The idea of culture as a coordination device is discussed in Sect. 4.4 and developed further in Dasgupta (2000a).

There is experimental evidence that we are generally unable to reason in accordance with Aristotelian logic. In a bold and controversial essay, Cosmides and Tooby (1992) explain this by arguing that there were no selection advantages in being able to so reason. They argue that there were instead advantages to being able to reason in ways that enable us to identify free-riders in cooperative ventures.

[6] Within economics, the most prominent expositions of this view include Robbins (1932); Samuelson (1947); Graaff (1962); and Robinson (1964); within political theory, see Barry (1965).

[7] Birdsall and Steer (1993); Arrow *et al.* (1996); and Portney and Weyant (1999). See Ch. 11.

and an anti-Nazi, a communist and a social democrat, a fundamentalist and a liberal ... agree on the facts?'

One can argue that the fact–value distinction is not as clear-cut as it is commonly thought to be, that perhaps deep down it is the anti-Nazi's value with which the Nazi disagrees, and that the two filter their perceptions of the way the world works through their distinctive ethical receptors—possibly, too, their distinctive personal interests. But even if they cloak their real differences by arguing about facts, it is facts they argue about and that is the point I am making here.

It can also be argued that, if development policies chosen in poor countries have not infrequently failed, they have failed because of our vastly imperfect understanding of the way economic systems respond to policies, by which I mean the way people respond to policies and the way ecosystems respond to the treatment meted out to them. I know of little evidence that the failures have been due to a wrong view of what constitutes development. To put the matter differently, at a deep level disagreements over the right means to further given ends seem to arise more frequently than disputes over the nature of appropriate ends. This is not to say that disputes over the latter can't, or don't, occur; it is only to say that when they do they seem frequently to be a cover for disagreements on history and the ways in which socio-economic and ecosystem processes work. (Ethnic strifes in themselves are not a counter-example to the interpretation I am offering.)

To take an example, in their influential World Bank monograph on the incidence of undernourishment in poor countries, Reutlinger and Pellekaan (1986: 6) wrote:

... long run economic growth is often slowed by widespread chronic food insecurity. People who lack energy are ill-equipped to take advantage of opportunities for increasing their productivity and output. That is why policymakers in some countries may want to consider interventions that speed up food security for the groups worst affected without waiting for the general effect of long-run growth.

Then there are economists who advocate policies based upon an opposite causal mechanism, such as the one in World Bank (1986: 7): 'The best policies for alleviating malnutrition and poverty are those which increase growth and the competitiveness of the economy, for a growing and competitive economy facilitates a more even distribution of human capital and other assets and ensures higher incomes for the poor. Progress in the battle against malnutrition and poverty can be sustained if, and only if, there is satisfactory economic growth.'

There doesn't appear to me to be a conflict in values in the quotations here. Rather, it reads as though there is disagreement over the most effective means for eliminating destitution. That the publications are from the same institution and from the same year should not cause surprise: we are all still woefully ignorant of the ways in which human societies and the natural environment respond to policies.

I.3. VALUATION AND EVALUATION IN KAKOTOPIA

It has been a tradition in economics to develop the principles of valuation and evaluation for Agathotopia, a 'good-enough society'.[8] Occasionally the principles have been extended to cover Utopia (in modern terminology, the perfect society), an extreme, special place.

Unlike Utopia, Agathotopia suffers from agency problems. Citizens regard it as imprudent to engage in transactions with others merely on verbal assurances that they will keep their word. People look for firmer guarantees before trusting one another to fulfil their commitments. They are wise to do so, because private incentives matter in Agathotopia. In that land people can be trusted to do what they said they would do only if it is in their interest to keep their word when the time comes for them to act. Economic transactions in Agathotopia are undertaken only when the parties are assured that agreements have a firm basis, that is when they are backed by credible guarantees. The guarantees may take the form of contracts enforceable in the courts of law, the penalty for a breach of contract being the necessary deterrence. But contracts are enforceable only if the terms underlying them are verifiable. For example, if the effort labourers exert at work is not verifiable, remuneration cannot be based on effort. A labourer's wage will instead be based on something that can be verified, such as his output, or possibly the hours worked. Now, it may be that output (or the hours worked) are imperfect surrogates for effort. If this is so, mutually beneficial transactions between employers and workers that could have taken place if effort were verifiable will not be undertaken. The quality of life suffers on account of this. Social scientists call it a *transaction cost*.

Just as citizens in Agathotopia face agency problems in their transactions with one another, the State faces an agency problem *vis-à-vis* citizens. The State recognizes that citizens will not divulge private information, even on matters that would help promote social well-being, unless it is in their personal interest to do so. Therefore, the State is unable to help bring about as good a state of affairs as its counterpart in Utopia is capable of. The best that can be hoped for in Agathotopia falls short of the ideal, and can fall well short of it. Economists use the term 'second-best' to identify the best public policies implementable in Agathotopia.[9]

---

[8] The term 'Agathotopia' was introduced by Meade (1989).

[9] Second-best too is an invention of James Meade (see Meade, 1955). Mirrlees (1971) is the seminal and definitive formulation of the way a Utilitarian government would design optimum redistributive taxes in a

However, while the State in Agathotopia faces an agency problem *vis-à-vis* citizens, welfare economics in Agathotopia in large measure presumes that citizens do not face an agency problem *vis-à-vis* the State. The State is trusted by citizens to implement the best set of policies in what is otherwise a second-best world. And the State delivers. Matters of political economy are absent from modern welfare economics.[10]

Political economy has been prominent, however, in positive economics, where much analytical and empirical work is about Kakotopia, or the dysfunctional society (at best a not-so-good society).[11] This essay is about the quality of life and the natural environment in Kakotopia, which, for ease of recognition, I will mostly refer to here as an *imperfect economy*. Except when discussing examples, I will not be explicit about the underlying character of the economy under study, the number of possible imperfect economies being far too many for anyone to attempt a taxonomy. There will be no presumption that the State can be trusted, let alone that it optimizes on behalf of its citizens. It may be that citizens know about institutional failure and take individual or collective action in order to soften the blow that falls on them. (In Parts III and IV, I offer examples of informal institutions that do that.) On the other hand, it may be that institutional failure has reached the stage where cooperation even within local communities has atrophied, or has been destroyed by civil strife.

I take the status quo in such a world to be given, and ask how one should conduct valuation there. I also study changes to the status quo and ask how the changes should be evaluated. We will study ways of evaluating *policy reforms*. The agency engaged in the valuation or evaluation exercise could be an international organization, it could be a bold and enlightened civil servant (possibly even a progressive government department), or it could be concerned citizens reflecting upon the world they inhabit. The analysis that follows extends to Agathotopia, but is not limited to it. I am interested in developing the principles that should inform valuation and evaluation exercises in Kakotopia. The application of the principles to Agathotopia is an agreeable special case.

---

world where citizens' work efforts and earning abilities are not verifiable. For a study of the extent to which the quality of life in such a world falls short of what is realizable in Utopia, see Dasgupta (1982a). National accounting in Agathotopia has been studied by Mirrlees (1969), Dasgupta (1993: ch. *7), and Aronsson and Löfgren (1998a,b; 1999).   [10]See Atkinson and Stiglitz (1980) and Myles (1995).

[11] See Persson and Tabellini (2000) for theoretical work in this area.

PART I

VALUING AND EVALUATING

Prologue

The chapters in Part I advance a pluralist conception of personal well-being. The conception includes the material sources of well-being and the ability of a person to exercise various kinds of freedom. It is argued that social well-being is an aggregate of individual well-beings. In Chapter 1, where these ideas are developed, it is shown that, if undertaken with care, the aggregation exercise doesn't blunt human rights.

Reasons for seeking an index of social well-being are identified in Chapter 2. Four are given prominence: (1) to compare well-being across countries (or communities); (2) to compare well-being across time and generations for the same country (or community); (3) to check if well-being is sustainable; and (4) to derive a criterion for judging if a policy is worth undertaking (e.g. if it is socially beneficial to accept a proposed investment project). There is no *a priori* reason why the same index would be appropriate for the four sets of exercises. One of the tasks in Parts III and IV is to explore this question and determine the answer.

In order to identify usable indices, measures of well-being are classified in Chapter 3 according to whether they are based on well-being's constituents (e.g. health) or their commodity determinants (e.g. food and nutrition). For practical purposes, it is often simpler to construct measures based on well-being's commodity determinants. The indices that are developed in Parts III and IV reflect this fact.

1

The Notion of Well-Being

1.1. PERSONAL TO THE SOCIAL

The term *well-being* will be used to denote the quality of life. We will explore measures of *social* well-being. I take it as understood that the measure is to be built from the ground up. Since the locus of sensation, perception, and feeling is at the individual level, it is appropriate to start there. Not only is the socio-economic personal, the political is personal too: it is the individual that matters. I am setting aside here arguments that have been offered for treating all animals equally.[1] Their acceptance would have far-reaching implications for many of our institutions. For the most part I limit myself to measures of *human* well-being.[2]

The concept of a well-lived life is fraught with difficulties, but its basic features are not controversial. As regards personal growth, most people would place emphasis on being able to realize a certain type of character, one that they themselves can admire, something that is a source of self-respect, for example having a disposition towards honesty and charitability, being able to stand up for one's principles, having the patience to probe and to discover where one's innate gifts lie (and to then develop them), and being capable of displaying and receiving affection. In the related social sphere, most people would place emphasis on a successful family life, warm friendships, a meaningful job, fruitful vocational activities, an occasional trip to see other places and cultures, and at the end of it a reflective and useful old age. The centrality in all this of social organization and its implied role as a basis for resource allocation is clear enough: social life is an expression of a person's sense of social unity, and commodities and an absence of coercion are the means by which people can pursue their own conception of the good. We can curb our desires and needs and thus our commodity requirements. We can as well escape into an inner world of self-sufficiency to accommodate an absence of both types of liberty. Several, what one might call mystical, systems of thought in fact instruct us to do just that. But if the exercise of our natural powers is a leading human good, there is no

---

[1] See especially Singer (1976).   [2] But see Ch. 10.

getting away from commodity requirements and thereby from the economic component of personal well-being.

A not infrequent criticism of the practice of building measures of social well-being on individual well-beings is based on the thought that 'the whole is greater than the sum of the parts'. Taken literally, this view is an acknowledgement that the processes which shape the way individual values and opportunities get translated into social outcomes are non-linear, with positive feedback. Usually, though, the thought is not taken literally, but is regarded more as offering a metaphor for the collective body. Now those who espouse collectivist goals (e.g. national prestige) sometimes offer reasons why such goals are desirable. The ones I have heard mentioned eventually reduce to a concern over the individual members of the collective (e.g. securing pride among members of the collective, thereby enabling them to cooperate and flourish).

Although the framework I adopt here is secular, I doubt if the conclusions that are reached would be unacceptable to someone with religious sensibilities. In any event, disagreements between religious and secular people (and among religious people themselves) are frequently over the interpretation of facts (e.g. whether usury is corrupting). To have a pluralist outlook is to acknowledge that the character of a well-lived life is not uniquely given, but is shaped in part by a person's dispositions and abilities and the contingencies she faces. Religious tolerance encourages people to lead their lives in the light of their own religious perceptions—so long, that is, as they do not infringe on the liberties of others.

1.2. WELFARE AND WELL-BEING

States of affairs are frequently called *social states*. A social state includes in its description the allocation of resources (who gets what, when, where, and why) and anything else deemed to be relevant for personal and social choice. Let us call the value someone attaches to his personal circumstances in a social state his *welfare*. The circumstances include in their description the goods and services he enjoys, his personal relationships, and those other aspects of life that affect him. Much normative economics is based on the idea that when states of affairs are compared their character shouldn't matter directly: what should matter are only individual welfares in those states of affairs. This is called the *neutrality* assumption. No doubt an individual's welfare in a social state depends on the character of the state of affairs; what the neutrality assumption does is to maintain that the social ranking of states of affairs should be arrived at solely on the basis of individual welfares in those states of affairs. Change the names and contents of social states: so long as individual welfares in the renamed social states are the same as they are in the previously named ones, social rankings of the two sets of states of affair would be identical. Neutrality is *anonymity* with respect to social states.[3]

Anonymity with respect to people is the requirement that human beings should be treated equally, that their names, castes, or political or religious or ethnic affiliations should not matter for valuing objects and evaluating policies from the social point of view.[4] But anonymity isn't a compelling assumption if applied to social states. For example, adherence to the demands of human rights can involve violation of the neutrality assumption.[5] Well-being is a wider notion than welfare, including as it does non-welfare characteristics of social states. A person's well-being is inclusive of his welfare and, for example, the rights he enjoys. It includes other characteristics of social states if they are judged to matter.[6]

The centrality of human rights in collective living is a reason why measures of social well-being must include them. However, it has sometimes been suggested that, because the concept of social well-being involves an aggregation exercise, human rights do not sit comfortably with it. In the remainder of the chapter I draw on certain aspects of the literature on rights, to consider how human rights can be accommodated in an aggregation exercise. The moral I draw is that to aggregate over people is not to close the door on human rights. I follow this up in Part II, by putting the theory developed here to use on contemporary data.

1.3. HUMAN RIGHTS AS CONSTITUENTS OF WELL-BEING

Different people know different things and possess different skills and talents, and not all people can observe the same things. These pervasive facts of life offer a powerful justification for the right to individual discretion in thinking, choosing, and acting. Thus, many rights are instrumentally valuable. The legal right to certain kinds of private property is frequently justified on grounds that it enables economies to progress. So too more generally with institutions: they

---

[3] See Arrow (1963a [1951]); May (1952); and Sen (1970).

[4] That people should be treated differently if their needs differ is a different matter. Nutritional and health care needs differ between children and adults, between the young and the old, between women who are pregnant or lactating and those who are neither, and so forth. Differences in treatment among such categories of people do not amount to a violation of anonymity over people.

[5] Sen (1970, 1982) formulated the connection between rights and the neutrality assumption. There are other ways to formulate rights (e.g. Nozick, 1974; and see below in the text). The existence of 'merit goods' is another reason why the neutrality assumption isn't compelling (Ch. 4).

[6] Sen (1982) calls an adherence to the neutrality assumption 'welfarism'.

too have instrumental value. Institutions embody in them the rights, roles, duties, and obligations of members. In Parts III and IV of this essay I consider the role of institutions in protecting and promoting human interest. Here I am concerned with a different pattern of rights: those that have intrinsic worth. Some are called human rights, or *fundamental* rights.

Fundamental rights (henceforth, simply 'rights') are usually seen to provide a basis for protecting and promoting a certain class of human interests, such as agency, independence, choice, and self-determination. An individual has a right when there is a reason for awarding him some liberty, opportunity, or commodity even though mere considerations of his valuation of states of affair would not warrant the award. Rights don't go against interest. They reinforce some interests against the claims of other, less urgent or vital, interests. Specifically, rights distinguish interests from welfare. Rights-based theories violate the neutrality assumption.

Neutrality is a condition imposed on aggregate well-being, or what I am calling here social well-being. To talk of 'neutrality' is to presume that there *is* an aggregate notion in play. However, it hasn't been uncommon to distinguish ethical theories grounded on the idea of social well-being from rights-based theories in terms of their relative concerns for the claims of the individual *vis-à-vis* the aggregate mass of individuals, or, in other contexts, between the individual and the society of individuals.

Some philosophers have gone farther. They have viewed theories of social well-being, seeking as they do to aggregate individual well-beings, as being *goal-based* which are then contrasted with rights-based theories. 'The distinction between rights-based and goal-based theories', writes Waldron (1984: 13), '[lies in the idea] that a requirement is rights-based if it is generated by a concern for some individual interest, goal-based if it is generated by concern for something taken to be an interest of society as a whole.' Rights-based theories, according to this reckoning, shudder at the thought of aggregation exercises, because it is held that in any such exercise the interests of the individual can all too readily get swamped by claims made on behalf of a multitude of others. 'A goal', writes Dworkin (1978: 91), 'is a non-individuated political aim.' Or, to put it bluntly, goal-based theories are collectivist. Worse, they are technocratic, formulaic, and ultimately, 'algorithmic'.[7]

I have never felt I understood the distinction. Rights need to be justified. Even those that are regarded as 'fundamental' have as their basis the thought that they are necessary for human flourishing.[8] Problems of interpretation have been compounded by the claim that fundamental rights are inviolable, or absolute: 'Individuals have rights, and there are things no person or group may do

---

[7] O'Neill (1986).   [8] Scanlon (1978) develops this assertion into an argument.

to them [without violating their rights]' (Nozick, 1974: ix). This means they impose rigid constraints on what people may or may not do. Thus, states of affairs in which Nozickian rights are violated to the slightest extent are rejected in Nozick's scheme of things. Nozickian rights are what have been called 'negative rights' (see below). Only those that are left after this pruning exercise are subject to social choice.[9] But this *is* an aggregation exercise. The presence of rights-based constraints tells us how the aggregation is to be conducted; it doesn't offer an alternative to aggregation. The exercise is influenced in other theories by the suggested hierarchy of rights, as in Rawls (1972), where they are lexicographically ordered.[10]

The brilliance of Professor Nozick's and Professor Rawls's writings has given the impression that rights by definition are inviolable, that rights-based theories do not entertain trade-offs among individual interests, and that they differ from Utilitarian theories most vitally in that the latter are rapacious in their willingness to do so.[11]

I believe this would be a wrong inference.[12] Rights are not all or nothing. There are always degrees to which interests are frustrated and the corresponding rights, if there be corresponding rights, are not met. Moreover, it is all too easy to regard a right as inviolable when no evidence is required on the resource costs involved in protecting that right. So, one must acknowledge the necessity of trade-offs even for fundamental rights. In any event, since inviolability means a zero rate of trade-off, we wouldn't depart from the practical spirit of inviolability (if rights are inviolable) if we allowed trade-offs between rights, and between rights and other goods such as welfare, provided that the trade-off rate is very small in appropriate regions of the space of states of affairs. From such a perspective, what distinguishes rights-based theories from, say, Utilitarianism is not that the former avoid aggregation, nor that the former are incapable of admitting trade-offs where the latter are most eager to admit them. They differ in terms of the kinds of objects that are aggregated. They differ in that the former rejects the neutrality assumption, whereas the latter accepts it. In Part II we explore how these considerations can be put to work in practice.

---

[9] Nozick (1974: 166). [10] See Sect. 4.1.

[11] In what follows I use the terms 'utility' and 'welfare' interchangeably.

[12] 'Collective goals may, but need not, be absolute. The community may pursue different goals at the same time, and it may compromise one goal for the sake of another ... Rights may also be absolute: a political theory which holds a right to freedom of speech as absolute will recognize no reason for not securing the liberty it requires for every individual; no reason, that is, short of impossibility. Rights may also be less than absolute; one principle might have to yield to another ... We may define the weight of a right, assuming it is not absolute, as its power to withstand such competition. It follows from the definition of a right that it cannot be outweighed by all social goals' (Dworkin, 1978: 92). See also Gewirth (1981), who asks if there *are* any absolute rights.

1.4. POSITIVE AND NEGATIVE RIGHTS

In an important and interesting essay, Fried (1978) classified rights in a binary way. We are to think of *positive rights* as a claim *to* something, a share of material goods or some particular commodity, such as education when young and medical attention when in need. It is to the satisfaction of such needs that we have positive rights, and Fried derives them from the primary morality of respecting the integrity of persons as free, rational, but incorporated beings. A *negative right*, on the other hand, is a right that something *not* be done to one, that some particular imposition be withheld. It is a right not to be wronged intentionally in some specified way. This too is derived from the primary morality alluded to above.

Fried observed that positive rights are asserted to scarce goods and that scarcity implies a limit to their claim. He also suggested that negative rights, for example the right not to be interfered with in forbidden ways, do not to have such natural limitations. ('If I am let alone, the commodity I obtain does not appear of its nature to be a scarce or limited one. How can we run out of people not harming each other, not lying to each other, leaving each other alone?' Fried, 1978: 110.) This is not to say that protection against unauthorised violence doesn't involve material resources. But then, the claim to protection from, say, the government against such violence is a positive right, not a negative one.[13]

Fried's distinction is attractive. Indeed, the seeming asymmetry in resource costs could explain the powerful hold that negative rights have on our moral sensibilities. It is always feasible to honour negative rights (there are no direct resource costs, remember), but it may not be feasible to honour positive ones: the economy may simply not have sufficient resources to enable all to enjoy adequate nutrition, for example. It is then possible to entertain the idea that negative rights are inviolable, in a way that positive rights are not. For how can a right be inviolable if it is not always possible to protect it?

The asymmetry also offers an explanation for why we regard all persons to have equal negative rights, even while we eschew the idea of full equality in the distribution of goods to which we have positive rights. Negative rights don't have to be created, they have only to be protected. In contrast, positive rights are produced goods, and in deliberating their distribution we have to care about differences in individual talents to produce, we have to worry about *incentives* and the concomitant notion of *obligations* (to honour agreements, not behave opportunistically, and so forth); we have to worry about *needs*, as well as the related matter of *deserts*. The realization of positive rights involves a resource

---

[13] The agency on which one is making the claim to protection is by hypothesis not the one committing the offence.

allocation problem, with all its attendant difficulties, most especially in the imperfect economies of Kakotopia.

It is doubtful, though, that the protection of negative rights and the protection and promotion of positive rights are as asymmetric as is taken to be the case in Fried's theory.[14] In the field of environmental law and economics, *pollutees' rights* (the right not to be harmed by pollution) are like negative rights. But enforcing pollutees' rights does involve resource costs; it can involve even direct resource costs—for example when the potential polluter is obliged to install expensive, but 'clean', technology.

Negative and positive rights can therefore clash. It has been argued by architects of the East Asian economic miracle that the exercise of civil and political liberties doesn't come without cost. They have been heard to say that citizens of poor countries cannot afford the extensive set of rights that have been won by their counterparts in western industrial nations.

The claim cannot be rejected out of hand, no matter how greatly we wish it weren't true. But statistical exercises conducted on data from poor countries suggest that, where citizens enjoyed greater civil and political rights, the countries performed better in the economic sphere. The findings are at variance with the suggestion that civil and political rights are a luxury poor countries can't afford.[15] The findings are reported in Chapter 5 (Section 5.5).

1.5. AGGREGATION IN THEORY

To speak of social well-being is to speak in aggregate terms. There is, however, a danger that by an 'aggregate' one understands some sort of *average*. This isn't the way I am using the term here. The kind of aggregate I have in mind reflects a comprehensive notion of aggregate well-being, including as it does not only average well-being, but also other features of the distribution of well-being, such as its variance, skewness, and so forth. In common parlance, features other than the average of the distribution of a thing are called the 'distributional features' of that thing. I follow this practice here.

Notice though that social well-being could be sensitive to the distribution of *income* even if the aggregate index of well-being is the average of individual well-beings. This would be so if individual well-being is a non-linear function of personal income and social well-being is the sum of individual well-beings.[16]

---

[14] I owe this observation to Scott Barrett.

[15] For example, the statement, 'Democracy and destitution do not go well together' was attributed to President Houphouet-Boigny of Côte d'Ivoire by President Omar Bongo of Gabon, in an interview reported in the *International Herald Tribune* (5 Sept. 2000, sponsored section, p. 10).

[16] Kolm (1969); Atkinson (1970); Mirrlees (1971).

Classical Utilitarianians were careful to stress this point. They observed that if marginal utility diminishes with increasing income, the sum of individual utilities (or average—it doesn't matter) would increase more if an additional unit of income were at the disposal of someone who is poor than of someone who is rich.

If people differ in their access to basic goods and services (food, health care) owing to systematic inequalities in the distribution of capital assets, there is a case for awarding greater weight to the claims of those who are poor. In recent years, much has been written on such weighting systems. For example, in developing a set of guidelines for evaluating investment projects in poor countries, Dasgupta, Marglin, and Sen (1972) suggested the use of 'income distribution weights', so as to acknowledge that a greater weight should be awarded to project benefits enjoyed by poor people than to the benefits enjoyed by the rich. Weighting systems are, of course, explicit in measures of inequality.[17]

As just noted, social well-being can be equality-seeking in the space of individual incomes even if it happens to be neutral as regards the distribution of well-being. But there are theories of distributive justice that, unlike Classical Utilitarianism or their modern versions (e.g. Harsanyi, 1955), are sensitive to the distribution of well-being. Rawls's theory is the most prominent among them. The conception of social well-being that I adopt here is inclusive of such theories, but it isn't committed to any particular one among them.

1.6. NUMERICAL INDICES: COMPLETE VS. PARTIAL ORDERING

In constructing an index of social well-being, the idea is to award each state of affairs a numerical value—the better the state of affairs, the higher the number awarded to it. As noted earlier, this requires two conceptual presumptions. It requires first that personal well-beings are themselves numerical indices and, secondly, that social well-being is a numerical index of personal well-beings. Social well-being is therefore a numerical index of numerical indices.[18]

To explain what the requirements amount to in formal terms, suppose that X is the set of all possible states of affairs. X consists of elements x, y, z, and so on (i.e. x is one possible state of affairs, y is another, z is still another, and

[17] For example, the well-known Gini index of inequality awards an income group a weight equal to the group's rank on an ascending order of poverty.

[18] The best known example of this is Classical Utilitarianism, which interprets social well-being as the sum of individual well-beings, and individual well-being as a numerical index of personal utility. The modern generalization of this is the welfare economics of Burk (1938); Samuelson (1947); and Arrow (1963a [1951]). In their formulation welfare isn't identified with utility in the sense of the Classical Utilitarians, but is a broader notion. Graaff (1962) is still the outstanding exposition of the subject.

so forth). Imagine there are N people in society, labelled by i. So, i ranges from 1 to N. Let $U_i(x)$ be the index of i's personal well-being in social state x. We are to imagine that U_i is a numerical index. It awards a number to every possible social state—the higher the well-being of person i, the greater is the number. $U_i(x) > U_i(y)$ means that i's personal well-being is greater in x than in y; and so on. We now write social well-being as V. We imagine that it too is a numerical function. It awards a number to every possible social state, and the higher is social well-being, the greater is the number. $V(x) > V(y)$ means that social well-being is greater in x than in y; and so forth.

But social well-being is built on personal well-beings, which means that V is a function of the U_is. We may then write,

$$V(x) = V(U_1(x), U_2(x), \ldots, U_i(x), \ldots, U_N(x)). \tag{1.1}$$

This is the sense in which social well-being is a numerical index of numerical indices. Of course, in writing (1.1) I assume that interpersonal comparisons of well-beings are possible.[19]

Expression (1.1) is too general to be of practical use. We therefore seek special forms of V. The most famous particular form of V is additive:

$$V(x) = U_1(x) + U_2(x) + \cdots + U_N(x). \tag{1.2}$$

In expression (1.2), social well-being is the sum of individual well-beings. As the Classical Utilitarians discovered and as decision theorists subsequently showed, the additive form has intuitive appeal and is also simple to apply to practical problems. In later chapters we will make frequent use of expression (1.2).[20] But the theory of valuation and evaluation I develop in this essay does *not* depend upon the additive form of social well-being.

Now, a numerical index is meaningless unless the system of units in which it is expressed is made explicit. As it happens, there is always a choice of units. The extent of choice determines the kinds of comparisons it is possible to make by means of the index. To illustrate, consider that temperature is measured in some parts of the world in the Fahrenheit scale and in other parts of the world in the Centigrade scale.[21] The two systems of units are related. If the temperature at a place in Fahrenheit is T_f and in Centigrade is T_c, then $T_f = 32 + 9T_c/5$. When comparing temperatures, what are we entitled to say if what we say is to be independent of the scale in which temperature is measured? Obviously, *ordinal* comparisons of temperature ('this object is hotter than that object') are independent of the scale in which temperature is measured. If one object is

---

[19] For a more thorough discussion of interpersonal comparability of well-beings and its links to aggregation possibilities, see Sen (1970), Hammond (1976), and Maskin (1978). [20] See Parts III–V.
[21] There is also the Kelvin scale, but I ignore it here.

hotter than another in the Fahrenheit scale, it is obviously hotter in Centigrade as well.

But we are entitled to make sharper comparisons of temperatures. We are entitled to compare differences in temperatures. We can say, for example, that the difference in the temperatures at sites A and B is three times the difference in the temperatures at sites C and D; and so on. However, it makes no sense to say that one place is twice as hot as another place. (If it is true in Fahrenheit, it won't be true in Centigrade, and if it is true in Centigrade, it won't be true in Fahrenheit!) An index is said to be *cardinal* if the ratios of differences in the index are independent of the scale in which it is measured.

Indices of weight are subject to even greater restriction than those of temperature. There is a natural zero which all scales must observe.[22] As weightlessness is weightlessness, it is independent of the scale in which weight is measured. So, for example, we are entitled to say that an object is twice as heavy as another. The claim is independent of the scale in which weight is measured. We will regard an index to be 'strongly cardinal' if the ratios of the index are independent of the scale in which it is measured.

The measurability of indices is deeply connected to the ways in which they can be aggregated. For example, if personal well-being is at best an ordinal index (well-being can be higher or lower, but nothing more specific can be said), then social well-being cannot take the additive form (1.2). Social well-being can assume the additive form only if personal well-being is cardinal. In Chapter *1 we discuss the measurability of well-being in more formal terms.

1.7. COMPLETE VS. PARTIAL COMPARABILITY OF WELL-BEING

Personal well-being is composed of a variety of objects (health, happiness, associational life, various kinds of freedoms to be and to do). There is an aggregation problem right there. Even in theory, let alone in practice, we are unlikely to arrive at a weighting system with which to do the aggregation, even assuming that there is a 'correct' weighting system. It isn't mere intellectual idleness that prompts people to say that at least some of the constituents of personal well-being are incommensurable. Additionally, there is the aggregation we would be required to conduct on individual well-beings (expression (1.1)), which poses similar problems. Thus, the requirement that social well-being is a numerical index of states of affairs is in all likelihood over-ambitious.

---

[22] There is an absolute zero for temperature too, but it seems not to have prevented the Centigrade and Fahrenheit scales from flourishing.

While it is no doubt possible to say that social well-being is greater in certain states of affairs than in others, there must also be social states that would be non-comparable.[23]

Nevertheless, it pays to assume not only that individual well-being is a numerical index, but that social well-being is one too. There are two, interrelated, reasons why it pays. First, decision-makers should be required to provide reasons for their choices. Even though they will not have in hand such numerical indices as we are discussing here, thinking in their terms when judging alternative courses of action is good discipline. It is tempting to occupy the aesthetic high ground and to say that tragic choices cannot be evaluated. But decisions have to be made, and thinking in terms of numerical indices makes decision-makers face trade-offs explicitly. To start with a sharp but consistent framework and then to allow doubts to enter is better than to begin with doubts and then to make recommendations without knowing if there is a consistent set of judgements underlying the recommendations.

Secondly, thinking in terms of numerical indices enables us to conduct sensitivity analysis when valuing and evaluating. We may not know the correct numerical index of individual well-being, but we may be fairly confident that it lies within a certain range. And similarly for social well-being. We may not know precisely what distributional weights to use when aggregating individual well-beings, but we may be confident that they lie within a certain range. Of course, not having a firm ethical conviction isn't necessarily a reflection of uncertainty: it is not knowing what is right, which isn't the same thing as being uncertain about what is right.

Sensitivity analysis is a useful tool for evaluating policies.[24] It enables the evaluator to discover parameter values for which a policy should be recommended, those for which it should be rejected, and those for which no answer can firmly be given. This in turn helps the evaluator to make choices that are consistent with one another over time.

---

[23] This point is stressed in Sen (1970) and in Dasgupta, Marglin, and Sen (1972).

[24] See the case studies in Dasgupta, Marglin, and Sen (1972) for an illustration of how useful it can be.

★1

Ordering Social States

★1.1. DEFINITIONS

In Chapter 1 personal well-beings were the raw ingredients of social well-being (equations (1.1) and (1.2)). It was presumed that indices of personal well-being have been constructed. The reasoning we followed was that, if someone's index of personal well-being is higher in social state x than in y, we ought to conclude that her personal well-being is higher in x than in y. It was somewhat like inferring that A is hotter than B by noting that A's temperature is higher.

In order to construct an index, however, the move has to be in the reverse direction: A's temperature ought to be higher if in fact A is hotter. Likewise, the reasoning on indices of the quality of life ought to be that, if someone's personal well-being is higher in x than in y, then the index to be constructed of his personal well-being should reflect that fact. The idea underlying indices of well-being is therefore that of an *ordering* of states of affairs. As this is the basic concept in both valuation and evaluation, it will pay to formalize it here in general terms.

As in Chapter 1, let X be the set of all possible social states. Let R be a binary relation among elements of X. In the present context, xRy would be taken to mean that x is *at least as good* (or *at least as desirable*) a state of affairs as y. The judgement 'xRy' is arrived at on the basis of the criteria that are regarded to be relevant for assessing if x is at least as good (or at least as desirable) as y. R reflects the implicit trade-offs that are admitted among the criteria. The construction of R represents an intermediate stage in valuation and evaluation.

R is a *pre-ordering* of the elements of X if, for all x in X, xRx (this is called *reflexivity*) and, for all x, y, and z in X, if xRy and yRz, then xRz (this is called *transitivity*). A pre-ordering, R, is an *ordering* of the elements of X if, for all x and y in X, either xRy or yRx (that is, if all pairs of social states are related to each other by R). A pre-ordering R is a *partial ordering* if there is at least one pair of elements that are not related to each other by R.

We are interested in defining indices on X. Let V be a numerical function on X. This means that V awards a numerical value to each element of X. As in the previous chapter, if x is an element of X, we write $V(x)$ as the numerical value of x. We say that V is a *numerical representation* of an ordering R of the elements of X, if, for all x and y in X, $V(x) \geq V(y)$ if and only if xRy. In this essay V will be taken to denote social well-being. Of course, V would not be uniquely given. We noted this in the previous chapter (Section 1.6). Let us formalize the idea that there is choice in selecting the system of units for measuring V.

An index is said to be ordinal if *any* order-preserving renumbering of the index is also an admissible index. Examples include representing preferences by numerical functions, numbering iso-bars on maps, and many other things besides.[1]

An ordering over states of affairs is cardinal if the indices representing the ordering are related to one another by positive affine transormations; that is if F is an admissible index, then all admissible indices are of the form $aF + b$, where a and b are constants, and $a > 0$. In the previous chapter we noted that indices of temperature are cardinal.

We will call an ordering over states of affairs 'strongly cardinal' if the indices representing the ordering are related to one another by proportional transformations; that is, if F is an admissible index, then all admissible indices are of the form aF, where $a > 0$. Examples include weight and height (a kilogram is 100 grams; a metre is 100 centimetres). Orderings are strongly cardinal when there is a meaningful 'zero' (as in weight or height).

*1.2. EFFICIENT LIBERALISM

In Chapter 1 a distinction was drawn between 'welfare' and 'well-being'. Well-being incorporates welfare, but it includes other things too, such as the enjoyment of rights, *qua* rights. Social well-being was taken to be a function of personal well-beings. In an N-person society, social well-being was expressed in equation (1.1) as $V(U_1, U_2, \ldots U_N)$. What general properties might we wish to impose on V?

One property in wide use in the social sciences is *anonymity*. It holds that V is a symmetric function: permute the U_is, the value of V remains the same. Ethically, it is a compelling restriction on V. Notice that expression (1.2) satisfies anonymity.

Another property in wide use is *efficiency*. To explain, imagine that there are social states x and y with the property that $U_i(x) \geq U_i(y)$ for all i, with strict inequality for at least one i. We then say that x *dominates* y. We say V respects efficiency if $V(U_1(x), U_2(x), \ldots, U_N(x)) > V(U_1(y), U_2(y), \ldots, U_N(y))$ if

---

[1] Economists justifiably regard ordinal utility theory as a major achievement of modern economics. It broke out of the demanding structure of utilitarianism. Among the pioneers were Hicks (1939) and Samuelson (1947).

x dominates y. In this essay we will assume implicitly that social well-being has this property.

Let Y be the set of feasible social states (as opposed to the set of all possible social states, X, which is larger). We say that x is an efficient point in Y if there is nothing in Y that dominates x. Clearly, if V respects efficiency, the optimal social state in Y must be efficient.

Efficiency, as defined above, is a concept that has to do with comparisons of personal well-beings. In contrast, efficiency with respect to welfares is called *Pareto efficiency*. I have heard it suggested in conversation that, because 'liberalism' can be in conflict with Pareto efficiency (Sen, 1970), rights-based theories are non-aggregative. I believe this to be wrong.

For suppose that social well-being in an N-person society is $V(W_1, W_2, \ldots, W_N, R_1, R_2, \ldots, R_M)$, where W_i ($i = 1, 2, \ldots, N$) is i's welfare index and R_j ($j = 1, 2, \ldots M$) is a numerical index of the jth, non-welfare constituent of social well-being (e.g. the right to free speech). So, there are $N + M$ constituents of social well-being. Imagine now that V respects efficiency in this $(N + M)$-dimensional space, which is to say that if $\bar{W}_i \geq \hat{W}_i$ for all i and $\bar{R}_j \geq \hat{R}_j$ for all j, with strict inequality for at least one, then $V(\bar{W}_1, \bar{W}_2, \ldots, \bar{W}_N, \bar{R}_1, \bar{R}_2, \ldots, \bar{R}_M) > V(\hat{W}_1, \hat{W}_2, \ldots, \hat{W}_N, \hat{R}_1, \hat{R}_2, \ldots, \hat{R}_M)$. It must then be that, given any set of feasible social states, Y, the optimum is efficient. Let $(\tilde{W}_1, \tilde{W}_2, \ldots, \tilde{W}_N, \tilde{R}_1, \tilde{R}_2, \ldots, \tilde{R}_M)$ be the optimum in Y. It is a point on a space of $N + M$ dimensions. Now consider the projection of the point onto the N-dimensional space of individual welfares. Unless the R_js are co-linear with the W_is, the projection would *not* be an efficient point of the set that is formed when the set of feasible ingredients of social well-being (of $N + M$ dimension) is projected onto the N-dimensional space of individual welfares. This proves the impossibility of a Paretian liberal. And the proof has assumed not only that an index of social well-being exists (V), but also that V respects efficiency on the space that matters, namely, the entire space of the constituents of social well-being. In short, efficiency is not in conflict with liberalism: what is in conflict with liberalism is a truncated version of efficiency.[2]

---

[2] That 'non-welfarist' social well-being functions are not compatible with the demands of Pareto efficiency was proved in Dasgupta (1993: ch. 3). The result's implications for public policy were explored in Dasgupta (1993: ch. 7). The issue has been revived by Kaplow and Shavell (2001).

2

Why Measure Well-Being?

We need measures of social well-being for at least five reasons.

2.1. MEASURING ECONOMIC ACTIVITY

First, there is a need to measure the scale of economic activity so as to summarize a macroeconomy. The thought arises that economic activity approximates welfare. This is probably why gross national product (GNP) is in wide use today as a welfare index. But it wasn't really designed for that purpose. It was designed to measure current economic activity, and that, too, in a market economy. As conventionally estimated, GNP isn't a good measure of economic activity in economies where large volumes of transactions are undertaken in non-market institutions. Even if we were to leave that aside, we should ask how well GNP can in principle serve as a measure of well-being. Later in this chapter I do this.[1]

2.2. COMPARING GROUPS

Secondly, we need measures of social well-being because we may wish to compare the lives of different groups of people at a given point in time, as well as through time. For example, we may wish to compare the well-beings of men and women, female-headed households and male-headed households, members of a particular denomination and the rest, and so forth.

Other than curiosity, why would we want to make such comparisons? The examples indicate why. We wish to know if there are systematic differences in well-being across identifiable groups in a country. This would help us to determine whether attention needs to be given to those who are revealed to fare badly. A group may fare worse than the rest because its members are denied certain civil liberties or democratic rights. They may be at a disadvantage because they have less access to resources. And so forth. Social cost–benefit

---

[1] See also Sect. 5.8.

analysis offers us a way to determine how the allocation of resources can be improved, what kind of reforms ought to be made.

The character of the links connecting democratic rights, civil liberties, and material resources depends on the level of aggregation. Evidence from poor countries indicates that civil liberties, democratic rights, and access to resources are related at the national level.[2] On the other hand, these virtues are often not connected at lower levels of aggregation. Citizens of a nation may have the right to vote, they may even be exercising their right; but some could be living in extreme poverty, while others enjoy affluence. Economic theory identifies pathways which create poverty traps, into which groups of people can get caught even when an economy is enjoying progress in the aggregate. So we need to evaluate policy reforms for reducing the chance that people will fall into such traps.[3]

These are qualitative observations, of a general nature. They hint at places to look for improvements in the quality of life, but they aren't a direct guide to action. For the latter, we need methods that will help identify desirable reforms, in a quantitative manner. In Parts III and IV, I develop the welfare economics necessary for constructing such methods.[4]

2.3. COMPARING LOCALITIES

The third reason we need measures of social well-being is that we may wish to compare the state of affairs in different places (villages, districts, provinces, countries). Well-being comparisons across regions within a country are useful because they help us to determine in which way the regions differ and what, if anything, needs to be done.[5] In international publications, however, the unit of analysis is usually the nation. Policy analysts frequently ask if a country is doing better today than it did a decade ago (if the poor are fewer in number now than previously, if the status of women has improved, and so on), or if one country is better off than another. These comparisons are made, for example, in the World Bank's annual *World Development Report* and the UNDP's *Human Development Report*, which offer estimates of changes over time in such measures as life expectancy at birth, infant survival rate, and public and private consumption per head in a country. Notice though that these are indices of the current quality of life; they do not measure intergenerational well-being.

---

[2] See Ch. 5.   [3] See Ch. 12.

[4] Social cost–benefit analysis is the subject of Chs. 10 and 11.

[5] Dutt and Ravallion (1998) is a study in this spirit. The authors discuss why reductions in rural poverty have differed widely across the various states in India.

However, the publications in question also use GNP per head to make well-being comparisons. Why?

The intention may be to appeal to a measure that incorporates both current well-being and future prospects. As the sum of consumption and investment, GNP would appear to be adequate for the task. The problem is that, as it doesn't include the depreciation of capital assets, GNP isn't capable of reflecting the future prospects of a nation. It would be wrong to regard a country as rich simply because its GNP per head is high: it could be blowing its capital assets on a consumption binge. As regards future prospects, GNP is neither here nor there and no amount of finessing can rescue it.[6] GNP is a measure of current economic activity, nothing more. It may, in fact, correlate well with *current* well-being (Chapter 5), but that would be an empirical fact, not an analytic truth.

2.4. MEASURING SUSTAINABLE WELL-BEING

The previous two reasons for the need to measure the quality of life have in practice led to the construction of indices that reflect current well-being. So the fourth reason arises from a desire to estimate the quality of life a population is capable of sustaining under alternative policies. Since we think of policies mostly in connection with national policies, the population in question is usually taken to be a nation. Early definitions of *national income* were designed for the purpose of constructing an index of sustainable well-being, and the bulk of recent theoretical explorations in *net* national product (NNP) have returned to it.[7] The idea is as follows.

Although GNP doesn't include the depreciation of capital goods, NNP, especially *green* NNP, does. Being the sum of an economy's consumption and net investment, green NNP includes net additions not only to manufactured capital, human capital, and knowledge, but also to *natural* capital (hence the term of approbation 'green'). As these capital assets together form a part of the productive base of an economy (the other part consists of the economy's laws and institutions; see Chapter 9), green NNP looks plausible as an index of sustainable well-being. Consequently, green NNP has also been referred to as 'comprehensive NNP'.

---

[6] I confirm this in Ch. 9 and the Appendix.

[7] Lindahl (1934), Hicks (1940), and Samuelson (1961) are the classics. The modern literature contains Weitzman (1976, 1998, 2000); Solow (1992); Hartwick (1990, 1994); Lutz (1993); Asheim (1994, 1997, 2000); Aronsson, Johansson, and Löfgren (1997); Aronsson and Löfgren (1998a,b, 1999); and Asheim and Weitzman (2001).

It transpires, however, that green NNP does not measure sustainable well-being, but that *wealth* does. Wealth is also the right index to use for making cross-country comparisons of well-being.[8] Just as a household's wealth measures the worth of its capital assets, so does a village's wealth measure the worth of its capital assets; so too for a district, a province, a nation. Changes in the wealth of a nation measure changes in the social worth of its capital assets.

We shall call a change in wealth *genuine investment*: if genuine investment is positive, wealth increases; if it is negative, wealth declines. Adjusting for demographic and institutional changes, a rise in wealth reflects a rise in intergenerational well-being, and a decline in wealth measures a decline in intergenerational well-being (Chapter 9). This is the sense in which wealth measures social well-being. From this perspective, it may not be a coincidence that Adam Smith's classic was an inquiry into the wealth of nations, not the GNP or NNP of nations, nor the United Nations Development Programme's Human Development Index of nations.

2.5. FINDING CRITERIA FOR POLICY EVALUATION

The fifth reason we seek measures of social well-being is that policies have to be evaluated. This line of work is called *social cost–benefit analysis*. To conduct the analysis, we need criteria by which to judge if a policy is worth undertaking. The criteria themselves are expressed as indices. Criteria for evaluating investment projects, such as their social rate of return, or their present discounted value of the flow of net social profits, are examples.

Social cost–benefit analysis is a huge subject. It is developed in Part IV and the Appendix. There I confirm that the correct index for project evaluation is the present discounted value of the flow of net social profits, or PDV for short. If the PDV of a project is positive, it contributes to social well-being and should therefore be accepted; if it is negative, the project reduces social well-being and should therefore be rejected. It can be shown too that the PDV of a project is its contribution to wealth. So, wealth is the appropriate measure of social well-being even for policy evaluation.

2.6. FOUR SENSES OF PLURALITY

The notion of personal well-being is pluralist. It is based on the recognition that the character of a well-lived life is not uniquely given, but is shaped in

---

[8] These assertions are explained in Ch. 9 and proved in the Appendix (Propositions 3 and 10).

part by a person's inclinations and abilities and the contingencies she faces. The notion is pluralist also in the sense that well-being isn't taken to be a single measure (e.g. happiness), but embodies the idea that we face trade-offs between a plurality of goods (e.g. health, happiness, the ability to be and do). Social well-being is an aggregate of personal well-beings, but in a pluralist conception personal well-being is itself an aggegrate index.

There is a third sense in which the expression 'plurality of measures' can be used. Suppose it were argued that, if we were to seek an index of social well-being, we should measure it directly and not look for a surrogate and give it a different name—present discounted value of the flow of social profits, wealth, or whatever. What should our response be? We would point out that the most *convenient* index of a thing could be something other than the thing itself. Imagine, for example, that we are interested in some object X, but X is especially hard to measure because it involves estimating non-linear functions of observable quantities. Imagine too that X is known to correlate perfectly with Y and that Y is easier to measure than X, say because Y is a *linear* function of observable quantities. Then we would wish to rely on Y, not X, as a matter of convenience. As it happens, wealth is linear in quantities. This is the case also with the present discounted value of the flow of net social profits. They reflect social well-being, in that they correlate with it. This is why they are attractive as measures of social well-being.

There is a fourth reason why we would be well advised to adopt a plurality of measures. It has to do with the character of social institutions, particularly with *agency*, and thereby with delegation and accountability. If it is to be accountable, an agency established for a purpose must be given a clearly defined role and scope. It would be no good if the international community were to have established the World Bank, the International Monetary Fund, the United Nations Environment Programme and the many other international agencies that exist today, and to have asked each to shoulder the world's problems. The organizations would not have been accountable, their duties being far too diffuse. The international community would have been faced with a massive amount of what insurance companies call 'moral hazard'.[9] The organizations would have been guaranteed to perform dismally.

It would have been no good either if, say, the recently instituted Monetary Policy Committee of the Bank of England, whose sole business is to set interest rates that are congruent with the government's inflation targets, were charged instead with improving the well-being of the island's inhabitants: the Committee would have folded almost immediately through incompetence, or would have become a white elephant. Decentralization requires not only that public

---

[9] See Sect. 3.2.

organizations be set their own tasks, but also that they be given their own, clearly defined, objectives. To be sure, the objectives ought to be congruent with one another and with social well-being. But if the organizations are to be effective, their objectives need to be distinct. Plurality of measures arises from a need for effective decentralization.[10]

---

[10] Recall Milton Friedman's stricture (e.g. Friedman, 1962) that private corporations ought to be interested solely in the profits they can legitimately earn for their shareholders, and have no business donating part of their profits to charity. Friedman's argument was that, if capitalism is to be an effective form of decentralization, private corporations should go about their own business, which is to make money for their shareholders. Charities, in this view, ought to be funded only by citizens, as members of civil society.

3

Constituents and Determinants
of Well-Being

3.1. CONSTITUENTS OR DETERMINANTS?

There are two ways to measure social well-being. One is to study the *constituents* of well-being, including health, happiness, freedom to be and do, and, more broadly, basic liberties. The other is to value the commodity *determinants* of well-being, which are commodity inputs in the production of well-being, such as food, clothing, potable water, shelter, access to knowledge and information, and resources devoted to national security. The former procedure measures output (health, the exercise of one's abilities, and civil and political liberties), whereas the latter values and then aggregates the required inputs (expenditure on food, clothing, education, potable water, shelter, and resources deployed for the protection and promotion of civil and political liberties). If undertaken with sufficient precision and care, either one on its own would do the job: changes in a suitable measure of either the constituents or the determinants can serve as a measure of changes in the quality of life in a society.[1] Along the former route, we would measure the constituents directly and aggregate them in a suitable way, using *social weights* to reflect the relative worth of the various constituents. Along the latter route, we would need to estimate the *social worths* of the determinants of well-being in order to arrive at a suitable index for the purpose in hand.[2] Roughly speaking, the constituents and determinants of well-being can be thought of as being ends and means, respectively. Moral and political philosophers regard the constituents as the obvious objects of study, in contrast to economists and statisticians, who gravitate towards the determinants. There is a cultural divide here.

The cultures often clash. Consider education and skills. Are they constituents or are they determinants? They are in fact both. The acquisition of education is partly an end in itself and partly a means to increasing future income by

---

[1] This is shown formally in Dasgupta (1993: ch. *7).

[2] The social worth of a good used often to be called its *social price*. It is customary today to refer to it as the good's *accounting price*. We study them in Ch. 8.

improving skills. Aristotelian ethics emphasizes the former, while the economics of 'human capital' stresses the latter. That education has both flavours doesn't pose problems so long as we are able to track the two and their contributions to well-being. Double-counting is a virtue when a commodity offers joint benefits. Education ought to be counted twice.

Those who pioneered the economics of human capital contributed greatly to our understanding of the process of economic development by drawing attention away from Aristotelian virtues.[3] If governments in today's poor countries were persuaded that education does not increase productivity, but is solely an end in itself, they would have an excuse to neglect it even more than they currently do. Governments could argue that poor countries can't afford luxuries.

3.2. VALUATION, TRUST, AND INSTITUTIONS

Why bother about determinants, when the direct route would be to measure the real thing, namely, the constituents? There are two reasons. First, without an understanding of the ways in which the constituents are determined by their determinants, we wouldn't know which institutions are best able to promote human interests, and which ones are likely to prove disastrous. Should markets be relied upon to produce and allocate food, clothing, shelter, and information? Should the State be involved in the supply of education, public health care, roads, and ports? Should local communities be engaged in the management of local resources? What kinds of institutions should people depend upon for insurance and credit? And so on.

Secondly, it can prove especially hard to observe the constituents. We have all learnt to live with this, and have tailored our activities with it in mind. We exchange objects we can observe jointly; we don't transact on such objects as someone's happiness, which can only be inferred by others, but cannot be observed with confidence. Of course, not all determinants can be observed publicly. So, contracts are based on those states of affairs that can be verified.

Broadly speaking, there are two types of informational problem besetting potential transactors. One involves unobservable actions; the other, hidden information. A group of people face a problem of unobservable actions if some are unable to observe others' actions at the time they choose their own actions, and when what they ought to do depends on the others' actions. (This is sometimes called a problem of 'moral hazard'.) The group faces a problem of hidden information if some know things about themselves or the world that others don't know, and when the appropriate course of action by the latter depends

---

[3] Schultz (1974) and G. Becker (1983).

on what the former know. (This is sometimes called a problem in 'adverse selection'.) Of course, the parties could choose to trust one another to behave honourably. But unless they have the incentives to behave honourably the trust would be blind, and people would know that.[4]

What could be mutually beneficial transactions will not take place unless the interested parties are able to overcome these problems. Creating institutions that economize on losses arising from unobservable actions and hidden information is of vital importance. Trust, born of the right incentives, plays a central role here. Both you and I have confidence in the State to enforce contracts, so I trust you to deliver those goods and services you are to deliver under the terms of the contract the two of us have signed. And so forth. Good institutions create trust and sustain it. They enable people to engage in mutually beneficial transactions. By a similar token, without trust good institutions cannot be established. If your trust (or confidence) in the enforcement agency falters, you will not trust people to fulfil their terms of an agreement. You may therefore choose not to enter into that agreement. By the same token, as democrats have long noted, you should not trust the enforcement agency (e.g. government) to do on balance what is desired of it if the agency does not expect to be thrown out of power if it does not do on balance what is desired of it. It is this interconnectedness that makes trust a fragile commodity. If it erodes in any part of the mosaic, it can bring an awful lot down with it. The enforcement agency could, of course, be 'society at large', rather than the State. Social ostracism, and the sense of shame society can invoke in one, are examples of punishment that can act as a deterrence against malfeasance. There is mutual influence between trust and good institutions.[5]

Decentralization is desirable because it enables private information to be pooled.[6] For decentralization to be effective, it is useful if the indices used by various parties are linear in the quantities of goods and services. Wealth is such an index, as is the present discounted value of the flow of social profits of an investment project or of a small policy change. Both indices are linear in the stocks and flows of goods and services. This is why they will figure prominently in this essay.

However, when in practice we come to value states of affairs, neither the constituents nor the determinants, on their own, will be seen to reflect what

---

[4] The incentives in question depend on the people's characters. Someone of honour would not need much incentive: his word would be enough. Others would have a price. The point, however, is that others wouldn't be expected to know someone's price.

[5] An early, analytical work on the idea of trust is Gambetta (1988). Trust is central to the concept of social capital. On this, see R. D. Putnam (1993); Fukuyama (1995, 1999); and the essays in Dasgupta and Serageldin (2000). The character of trust in non-market institutions is discussed in Ch. 12.

[6] Hayek (1945, 1948) was the early exponent of this. Stiglitz (1994) contains the modern statement, much of which is based on his own pioneering work on the economics of incomplete and asymmetric information.

we wish to see reflected in any defendable conception of the quality of life. The reason is that there would be far too many person-specific social prices to contend with if we were to estimate an overarching measure using only the determinants of social well-being. A study of the determinants alone wouldn't suffice. On the other hand, some of the constituents of well-being are very hard to estimate. Because of this, governments and international agencies pursue both avenues at once, and it is today a commonplace to assess the quality of life by studying a heterodox collection of indicators when investigating how a group is doing compared with another, or whether a community is doing better today than it did yesterday. Some indices reflect determinants, others the constituents.[7] Earlier, we noted several weaknesses in the indices currently in use. In Parts II and III of this essay I explore ways to overcome their limitations.

3.3. HAPPINESS

Although it is a constituent of well-being, happiness has for some time been in bad odour among economists. The word doesn't even appear in textbooks on modern welfare economics. But ethical theories that ignore experiential states are rationally repugnant. It would be peculiar if we were to value the formation of the capacity to prepare life plans, but were indifferent to its realization and the experiential states that go with its realization. Happiness is an experiential state. It is not, however, the same as well-being. One could be in a happy frame of mind under the influence of drugs and yet be in a bad state. It is also hard to quantify experiential states. The problem is that states of mind are involved. Admittedly, other minds are not as inscrutable as they are commonly made out to be: our own experiences provide the right source of information. Placing ourselves sympathetically in possible situations often enables us to obtain the information we seek. But sympathetic considerations offer at best a sketch; they don't offer the real thing.[8]

Among sociologists, who as a profession have remained interested in happiness, the search has been for objective measures. Such indices as a country's divorce or suicide rate have been suggested. But they are seriously deficient. Divorce rates in a society may be low not because marriages are happy, but because the cost of divorce is prohibitively high for women. Similarly, the rate of suicide picks out features of the lower tail of the distribution of mental states. We would wish to know something about the entire distribution.

---

[7] See the World Bank's annual *World Development Report* (e.g. World Bank, 1999) and the United Nations Development Programme's annual *Human Development Report* (e.g. UNDP, 1998).

[8] Davidson (1986) has made the powerful claim that the meaning we attach to interpersonal comparisons of experiential states involves our own judgements on the value of such ingredients.

In making comparisons of the state of mind over time, one could ask people if they are happier now than they were, say, a decade ago. The answers can be unreliable though: recollection is known to be faulty.[9] An obvious alternative is to ask people how they would currently rate their state of mind on a scale of, say, 1 to 10. The responses could be used to create time-series of reported happiness. Of course, whether happiness should be included in discourses on the quality of life depends on the point of the exercise. Contractarian theories of the State, for example, don't see the State's business as being concerned with citizens' happiness. Rather, they see the business of the State as making sure that basic liberties are enjoyed, so that citizens are able to protect and promote their own projects and purposes.[10]

This said, happiness is far too important a constituent of well-being to be bypassed. Fortunately, a small literature now exists. The investigators have sought to discover what is conducive to happiness. The evidence suggests striking differences between the very poor and the rich.

To be very poor and to experience the pain that goes with it is to be a *destitute*, someone who has no command over resources. Destitutes don't even possess labour power: at best they have potential labour power, which is a different thing. The reason destitutes don't possess labour power is that, unless they have access to resources in advance, the quality of work they are able to offer is inadequate for obtaining the food they require if they are to improve their nutritional status.[11] They are prey to poverty traps. They are wasted and stunted if caught in such traps. Destitution brings in its wake the physical pain of undernourishment and the moral pain of having to make tragic choices (e.g. over the allocation of food and health care within the household). To be a destitute is to lack power over one's life and to experience the emotional pain and despair that comes with it. There should be no question that when people are very poor, their state of mind is influenced by their command over resources.[12]

---

[9] Kahneman, Wakker, and Sarin (1997) offer a good account of the problems in measuring experienced utility. [10] Rawls (1972) and Nozick (1974).

[11] This view of destitution is developed further in Sect. 5.7.

[12] This perspective on extreme poverty is advanced in Dasgupta (1993, 1997, 1998a), where various pathways confining people to poverty traps are identified analytically (on which, see Sect. 5.7). A recent World Bank study (Narayan *et al.*, 2000), reporting the experiences, views, and aspirations of more than 60,000 poor people from sixty countries, confirms the perspective advanced by the theoretical work.

Much contemporary ethics assumes at the start of the inquiry that basic commodity needs have been met: 'As for what typically goes on psychologists' lists of what constitutes "positive mental health"—things such as being healthy and confident, having self-esteem, being adaptable, caring—we might specify our subject by supposing such traits are already present. The question then becomes: How should someone live who has reached the ample launching pad these traits provide?' (Nozick, 1990: 22). Lomas (1999) is a reflection on what the psychoanalyst is able to offer people with means seeking help in realizing an answer to that question when they lack the launching pad of 'positive mental health'. Lomas's point is that, provided they have the material means, seeking to realize an answer to the question is itself a way out for someone lacking that launching pad.

But even for someone rich, we should expect health to contribute significantly to happiness: other things remaining the same, healthier people would be expected to be happier than those suffering from ill-health. This has been found to be the case in rich countries as well.[13] Studies in Europe also suggest that unemployment contributes significantly to unhappiness, a sign that social status, measured in as general a way as whether one is 'officially' at work, matters. Interestingly, in their analysis of data collected from the cantons of Switzerland, Frey and Stutzer (1999) report that associational life plays a role too: people who are more engaged in civic activities are happier. Given this finding, it should not surprise that local democracy is conducive to happiness.[14] Similar links have been observed in poor countries.[15]

Assuming that the findings are robust, in poor countries indices of consumption, health, and civic and political liberties could serve as determinants of happiness. If we were to include these indices in our measure of current well-being in poor countries, we would not need to introduce measures of happiness directly. This is the route I follow in Part II for applying the ideas developed here to cross-country data.

3.4. IMITATION AND THE DEMONSTRATION EFFECT

The sample studied in Part II is restricted to poor countries. The reason is that I remain unsure whether to include consumption in measures of current well-being in rich countries. (Should current consumption be included in the reckoning when the quality of life in the United States is compared with that in Italy?) I am unsure because consumption would appear *not* to contribute to happiness among people who have a great deal more than the basic necessities of life. Surveys in a number of rich countries have revealed that the poor in society are less happy than the rich. But, even though income per head grew in the periods covered by the samples, there was no trend in reported happiness, a finding that is at odds with the fundamental premises of welfare economics.[16]

One possible explanation for the finding is that, when income levels are high, what determines someone's state of mind, at the margin, is their income (or expenditure) *relative to* the average income (or expenditure) of their reference group, rather than on its own. If this were so, behaviour would be driven in part by the urge to imitate, a motivation that was postulated by early exchange theorists for understanding primitive societies.

---

[13] Frey and Stutzer (1999).   [14] Frey and Stutzer (2000).   [15] Narayan *et al.* (2000).
[16] This result was found, for example, in the USA, where income per head more than doubled between the mid-1950s and the early 1990s; see Oswald (1997) for a summary of the findings. Easterlin (1974) was an early study on the possible lack of influence of economic growth on personal happiness.

It has proven hard to obtain direct evidence of imitative behaviour. So there isn't much of it. The famous experiments of Sherif and Asch, where subjects were set visual discrimination tasks (the task of comparing lengths without the aid of a measuring rod), showed not only that people are more influenced by others' opinions when the facts in question are more uncertain, but also that people may conform simply to avoid censure, ridicule, and social disapproval.[17] Psychologists have classified the findings in a way that implies that conformity is lower in the 'individualistic' cultures thought to embody North American and North-West European societies than in the 'communitarian' cultures widely taken to represent societies in Africa, Asia, Oceania, and South America.[18] This may appear intuitively plausible to many. To me, however, it hints at how difficult it is to separate various types of conformism, and how problematic it is to talk of conformism unless the domain of behaviour over which conformism is thought to prevail has been specified. The point is that a society could be individualistic in some respects even while it is deeply conformist in others.

People conform in their purchase of such goods as the telephone, the fax machine, and the personal computer because there are interpersonal 'complementarities' in their use-value. (My use for a telephone increases as the number of others who rely on telephones increases, and so on.[19]) But other patterns of conformism could be due to shared disposition.

For example, in a classic study, Duesenberry (1949) postulated imitative behaviour in order to explain aggregate data on short-term, cyclical consumption patterns in the United States. He conjectured that people at each income level try to reach the consumption standards of those at the next higher income level. (This is the shared disposition.) While Duesenberry's explanation of consumption behaviour has fallen by the wayside in current macroeconomics, the term that was christened to denote imitative behaviour in consumption expenditure remains in use. It is the *demonstration effect*.

What is the source of the demonstration effect? There is evidence of cultural pressures for acquisitiveness.[20] The desire for status, based on consumption patterns, could be one. Whatever it is, if people acted in such ways as to increase their personal happiness when they are subject to the demonstration effect, a rat-race can ensue. To see why and how, imagine a world where to begin with people are similar in both endowments and motivations. In a society where it is relatively easy for everyone to earn more (because of, say, technological

[17] Hogg and Vaughan (1995: ch. 6).
[18] See Smith and Bond (1993) for review of a number of such studies. For simplicity, I am using 'imitation' and 'conformity' interchangeably.
[19] For early work on this, see Farrell and Saloner (1985) and Katz and Shapiro (1985).
[20] Ehrlich (2000: 284–90) offers a biologist's explanation of why consumption behaviour is subject to 'peer pressure'.

improvements and greater resource use), the individual urge among reasonably well-off people to beat the Joneses would result in a race in which everyone strives to earn more than the average. So long as growth in labour productivity remains high, the race continues. Some would be ahead for a while, only to be overtaken by others, who in turn would be overtaken by yet others, and so forth.

The above analysis is vastly incomplete, because the urge to initiate techno-logical change isn't explained. But it is suggestive of a process that is capable of feeding upon itself. If, owing to other forms of institutional failure, the nat-ural resource base isn't costed adequately, there would be cumulative pressure brought upon on that base. This is something we will have to consider when we come to value goods and evaluate policies through time.

Economists refer to motivations that are inclusive of others as *social preferences*. We should take care not to pre-judge the character of social preferences, which can reflect the competitive side of our nature (as in the demonstration effect), our cooperative side (our urge to reciprocate; see Section 4.4), or, more widely, our need to connect with others at an emotional level. Consumption, for example, is a hugely complex activity. In their classic work, Douglas and Isherwood (1996 [1979]) showed that consumer goods are more than mere instruments of survival, gratification, or competition: they also help to establish relationships, which themselves are both ends and means. Mary Douglas once remarked that to be poor is not to be able to invite someone home to tea. This isn't all there is to poverty, of course, but it says a great deal. The idea of social capital is related to this aspect of poverty.[21] Eating in a group, for example, is a way of connecting. However, to throw a lavish feast is to display wealth.

Consumer goods serve a number of purposes. They enable us to survive, they satisfy needs, they gratify, they are an instrument for competition, they help to relate and cooperate; more comprehensively, they enable us to attain our humanity. In the process, though, very many things can go wrong. In Parts III and IV we will identify the many pathways by which they can go wrong.

---

[21] See Ch. 9.

PART II

MEASURING CURRENT WELL-BEING

Prologue

A prerequisite for constructing a measure of well-being through time and across generations is a measure of well-being *in* time (current well-being). In the following two chapters we study a comprehensive, but operational, notion of current well-being, developing ways of measuring it (Chapter 4), and illustrating how the concept can be put to work on the contemporary world (Chapter 5). The idea is to take snapshots of societies in motion. Current well-being, which is inferred from the snapshots, is a component of well-being through time.

In order to find a usable measure of current well-being, I appeal to an overarching idea in Chapter 4, that of *citizenship*, with its three constituent spheres: the civil, the political, and the socio-economic. The classification is useful for identifying the constituents of well-being. The idea of citizenship is useful also in that it directs us to study the kinds of institutions that are best suited to protect and promote human interests. Political scientists have shown that democracy is neither necessary nor sufficient for civic cooperation and the benefits that come with it. In Chapter 5 I draw upon evidence from the contemporary world's poorest countries to suggest that, interestingly, the three constituent spheres of citizenship may well be synergistically related to one another. The findings indicate that democracy and civil liberties are not only intrinsically valuable, but may even be instruments for bringing about material progress in poor countries.

The fact remains though that, within democratic countries, there are enormous differences in people's life-chances. Democracies in poor regions harbour malnourished people. It is argued that the malnourished are caught in poverty traps. In order to explain the findings, we are led to study institutions and the role they play in determining the allocation of resources.

4

Theory

4.1. CITIZENSHIP: CIVIL, POLITICAL, AND SOCIO-ECONOMIC

In his classic essay on social and political history, T. H. Marshall (1964) codified the modern concept of citizenship by identifying three social revolutions which took place sequentially in Western Europe: that of civil liberties in the eighteenth century, political liberties in the nineteenth, and socio-economic liberties in the twentieth.[1]

Civil society is the sphere of autonomous institutions, protected by the rule of law, in which people are able to express their opinions and conduct their business freely and independently of the State, or, for that matter, are free of the coercive influence of any other body. The civil element of citizenship consists of the right to justice.

Civil society is an encompassing notion. In itself the concept doesn't identify the types of autonomous institutions citizens would choose to establish, institutions whose character would depend on such features as the circumstances in which people find themselves, the transaction costs they face, the ability and personality of the State, the ecological landscape, and the family and kinship structure, all of which should, in any case, be considered as interconnected. In some dysfunctional economies autonomous institutions may be the only channels available to individuals in their attempt to flourish; in others they may be unable to get off ground because of a violent State, oppressive warlords, coercive mafias, an intrusive kinship structure, or whatever. In still others, the autonomous institutions could be the problem, not the solution, and may even pose an obstacle for the State to be able to realize its proper functions.[2]

---

[1] Marshall's analysis of citizenship is further developed in Marshall (1981). See also Hirschman (1991) for an account of the kinds of doubts expressed by contemporary thinkers against the changes. For ease of exposition, I shall be thinking here of citizenship in the way it is viewed today, namely, citizenship of a nation-state. This isn't to say that non-nationals do not have rights, or that their rights aren't systematically violated in many parts of the world.

[2] Each of these possibilities has been much discussed in recent explorations on the concept of social capital. See the essays in Dasgupta and Serageldin (2000) and Seabright (2000).

By the 'political element' of citizenship, I mean the right of a person to participate in the exercise of political power, as a member of a body invested with political authority, or as an elector of the members of such a body. Political freedom includes the freedom to form parties for the purpose of competing for public office. And by the 'socio-economic element' I mean a range that encompasses the right to a certain share of resources, the right to share to the full the social heritage, and to live the life of a civilized being commensurate with the standards prevailing in the society in question.

The most prominent of modern theories of justice embracing the notion of citizenship is that of Rawls (1972). Among other things, Rawls studied the just distribution of those commodities that are essential to the exercise of freedom. He calls them *primary goods*. His first principle of justice ('Each person is to have an equal right to the most extensive total system of equal basic liberties compatible with a similar system of liberty for all') covers both political and civil liberties; and his second principle ('Social and economic inequalities are to be arranged so that they are (a) to the greatest benefit of the least advantaged, consistent with the just savings principle, and (b) attached to offices and positions open to all under conditions of fair equality of opportunity': Rawls, 1972: 302) addresses in part socio-economic freedom. We should note, though, that some Rawlsian primary goods, such as income and wealth, have only instrumental value. By way of contrast, other primary goods, such as self-respect and basic liberties, have intrinsic worth as well.

4.2. THE NEED FOR PARSIMONY

In empirical work, we have to cut corners and search for surrogates for the constituents of well-being. Even on the determinants of well-being, data are frequently unavailable. When available, they are often unreliable, such as data on income inequality in poor countries. Often enough, one has to rely on crude indices of inequality, for example the proportion of national income at the disposal of the poorest quintile of the population (the lower the figure, the greater the inequality). But even these are not to be trusted.

Why? One reason is that large numbers of transactions in poor countries are unrecorded, owing, among other reasons, to the fact that non-market interactions are a commonplace.[3] Therefore we need to search for indices that can serve more reliably as surrogates for distributional measures.

The aggregate index I construct below is composed of sufficiently diverse aspects of people's lives for us to be able to pick up a range of inequities. For

---

[3] On non-market interactions, see Chs. 10 and 12.

example, if people differ in their access to positions and opportunities owing to differences in their ethnic or religious background, certain consequences would seem to follow, such as the prevalence of communal strife.[4] Since communal strife (in the extreme, civil war) is frequently both a cause and consequence of authoritarianism and corruption at the level of government, indices of civil and political liberties tend also to reflect inequities along ethnic or religious lines.

The problem is to identify a minimal set of indices which would span a reasonable conception of social well-being, be it current or intergenerational well-being. In doing this it is important to avoid double-counting. To give an example, statistics on the proportions in populations not having access to potable water are in frequent use when attempting to determine the quality of life, as are statistics on infant mortality rates. But the two are highly correlated; indeed, one is an important cause of the other. If information on one of them is available, there is no need to include information on the other in a quality-of-life index. We noted earlier that it has become customary to make cross-country and intertemporal comparisons of the quality of life in terms of current well-being. I argued too that, even as measures of current well-being, they are deficient. In this chapter we consider how to improve upon existing measures of current well-being. In the next chapter I shall put such conclusions to work on a data set pertaining to the world's poorest countries. I develop measures of intergenerational well-being in Part III.

Begin with a person. In constructing a measure of her quality of life, a balance has to be struck between the claims of completeness and costs. Leaving aside for the moment the extent of civil and political liberties she enjoys, there would seem to be at least three sorts of indices of current well-being: her disposable income, her health status, and her educational attainments. Now these are different categories of goods. Health and education are both ends and means and would seem to embody aspects of what are sometimes called 'positive freedoms', the 'ability to be a doer'; while disposable income contributes to the enjoyment of freedom.[5]

Someone's disposable income measures the extent to which they are able to obtain private consumption goods, like food and clothing, shelter, legal aid, and general amenities in the market-place. These goods differ from early education and primary health care. When supplied privately, the latter give rise to wide-ranging *externalities*, by which I mean the side-effects that occur when people undertake activities without mutual agreement. The private benefit to someone in becoming literate doesn't include the benefit to others in being able to correspond with her. To be immunized against an infectious disease is to one's

---

[4] On this see Homer-Dixon (1994). Using cross-country data, Collier and Hoeffler (1998) have shown that nations are at greatest risk of communal strife when ethnic diversity is neither too small nor too large.

[5] On both positive and negative freedoms, see Berlin (1959).

own benefit, but it also confers benefit to others, because they are that much less likely to catch an infection. People would choose to purchase less primary education and less primary health care than they would wish collectively to purchase. Market supply of these goods should ideally be allied to an explicit support by the State, so as to correct for externalities in the market-place.

Of course, even nutrition intake can give rise to externalities. Undernourished people are more susceptible to infections than people who enjoy an adequate diet.[6] Food security programmes in part correct for externalities. They should not be directed exclusively at poverty alleviation.

Health and education are at once both constituents and determinants of well-being. In their guise as determinants, they are like capital goods and together comprise 'human capital'.[7] At present we are considering current well-being; so, in this and the following chapter I study health and education in their guises as constituents of well-being. They reflect aspects of the flow of current well-being.

4.3. EXOTIC GOODS AND BASIC NEEDS

There are further reasons why a good State is involved directly in the provision of early education and primary health care.[8] The young don't have the means to acquire primary and secondary education, nor should they be expected to appreciate their value. For this reason, decisions on these matters are taken on their behalf. If the State is not engaged in providing early education, parents and charities would be its sole suppliers. Charities could be few and far between and could be motivated by private agenda. Parents may not have the means. Nor do parents everywhere appreciate the value of modern education, which in many places continues to be an exotic object. Until recently, most people in the world were illiterate. Survival, even economically successful lives, did not depend upon it. Today it is generally held that children should be literate and numerate. Economic structure everywhere has evolved in such a way that to be illiterate is to be at especial economic risk.

A similar consideration applies to primary health care, which also can be undervalued by households. The market-place is thus unlikely to appreciate the worth of early education and primary health care. Appropriately, these commodities are called *merit goods*.[9]

---

[6] Scrimshaw (1970, 1983); Scrimshaw and Wallerstein (1982).   [7] See Ch. 9.

[8] This isn't to say that state education is the only possible route by which people can acquire education. State provision of education is different from state education.

[9] The term 'merit goods' was introduced in Musgrave (1959). Recall the neutrality assumption, which was studied in Ch. 1. To acknowledge that there are merit goods amounts to a rejection of the neutrality assumption in valuing and evaluating allocations of resources.

Relationships between physicians and patients, and between teachers and pupils, have been shaped by the enormous differences in knowledge, information, and expertise among parties. They are a far cry from relationships in the market-place. Physicians and teachers know better than their patients and pupils the latter's needs. This is why they are expected to choose the character of the goods to be supplied. Traditionally, quality assurance has been provided by bodies within the medical and education professions, who do the screening and award the certification. Norms of conduct are instilled into those preparing to be physicians and teachers. This is part of the training process. To regard the medical and teaching professions as suppliers of marketable commodities to 'consumers' is to practise bad economics. Thus also for the legal profession, at least in principle.[10]

Tertiary education is subsidized by the State in most countries, especially in poor ones. But it is questionable whether the extent of subsidies has been a wise use of public resources. Tertiary education is meant for adults, who should be expected to know their own best interests. On average, the move from secondary to tertiary education in such technical subjects as mathematics, science, and engineering yields private returns at least as high as those from other forms of investment.[11] Admittedly, young adults would not be expected to have the collateral required to finance higher education privately. One solution involves student loans. Government loans with guarantees that repayment will be based on the ability to pay would remove the downside risk associated with borrowing. Admittedly, the government would have to subsidize such a scheme, but the subsidy would be far less than current subsidies to higher education in parts of the poor world such as the Indian sub-continent.[12]

Food (by which I mean nutrition), clothing, and shelter are basic needs. Some among them used also to be regarded as merit goods. When household purchase of cereals is subsidised, the point of view is that cereals, in contrast to, say, clothing, are a merit good. When the government issues food stamps to poor households, the thought is that food is both a basic need and a merit good. The tradition in welfare economics, however, has been to link the nutritional status of households to their ability to purchase food in the market-place, where nutrition isn't viewed as a merit good. It may explain why, although nutrition, clothing, and housing increasingly appear in public discourses, when attention is drawn to poverty and inequalities of income, they don't appear on the list of merit goods. The thought may be that, as they are not exotic goods, their value

---

[10] Arrow (1963b) is the economics classic on this.

[11] World Bank (1999). A recent finding from the UK is Dutta, Sefton, and Weale (1999), who have estimated the rate of return from tertiary education in general.

[12] See Dreze and Sen (1995) for a commentary on the neglect in India of early education in comparison with higher education.

would be appreciated by households, who also have information about their own needs and tastes. There is also the question of preserving private incentives to acquire these goods. This then leads to the recommendation that the State should offer supplementary income to poor households, to be spent in any way they choose. This in turn leads to the question of incentives and opportunistic behaviour on the part of citizens.

4.4. CIVIC ATTITUDES, ENTITLEMENTS, AND DEMOCRACY

Although quantitative estimates are sparse, civic virtues would appear to differ enormously across societies. In poor countries, where the State is often viewed by communities as an alien fixture and the public realm an unfamiliar social space, the temptation to free-ride on such state benefits as there are must be particularly strong. Even in a 'well-ordered' society (I am using the term in the sense of Rawls, 1972) free-riding would not be uncommon: separation of the private and public spheres of life is not an easy matter. Living off the State can become a way of life.

Political scientists have puzzled over the fact that in some countries taxpayers comply far more frequently than would be expected if compliance rates in other countries were used as a basis of comparison. Paying taxes is voluntary, in that people choose to comply in situations where they are not directly coerced. But it is only 'quasi-voluntary',[13] in that those who don't comply are subject to coercion if they are caught. One way to interpret differences in compliance across countries is to suppose that people are willing to pay their dues if (i) the government can be expected to keep to its side of the bargain on transfers and public expenditure, and (ii) others pay their dues. Taxpayers are viewed in this interpretation as people who are willing to cooperate on a good cause if a sufficiently large number of others cooperate as well, but not otherwise. The hypothesis is that most people are civic minded when and only when most others are civic minded.

The evidence with which I am familiar (mainly for the United Kingdom) makes interesting reading.[14] Golding and Middleton (1983) studied people's knowledge, attitudes and beliefs about the welfare–benefit system in the United Kingdom. Over half of their working-class respondents regarded welfare benefits as 'embarrassing'. However, the attitudes of potential claimants have been found to vary depending on the type of benefit. Exemptions from prescription charges seem to carry no stigma, but rent rebates do.[15]

---

[13] I am borrowing the term from Levi (1988).
[14] I am grateful to Ray Jobling for the references.　　　[15] Taylor-Gooby (1976).

Why? One possible reason is that health problems are diagnosed by someone else (it is the physician who does the assessing) and are either attributed to bad luck or acknowledged to be associated with verifiable states of affairs (childbirth, old age, accident). But whether one's low earnings are due to bad luck, or lack of effort, or an absence of skills isn't something that is easily verifiable. There are fewer problems of unobservable actions and hidden information associated with health than with employment. The term 'welfare cheat' isn't used against someone who is chronically ill, but it is not uncommon of neighbours to use it to describe someone chronically unemployed. This may be one reason why in the United Kingdom exemptions from prescription charges are seen as a 'right', whereas rent rebates are regarded as a 'benefit'.

There is evidence that people don't merely display reciprocity, they have feelings about reciprocity. As Levi (1988: 53) remarks, nobody likes being a sucker.[16] Findings such as these have been deployed by economists in modelling the attitudes of citizens to work on the one hand, and to the volume of taxes and the character of public transfers on the other.[17] Imagine now that a person's desire to live off the State increases with the proportion of those who live off the State. (There is little stigma or shame when the proportion is large, but a good deal when the proportion is small.) Citizens vote on levels of taxes and transfers, and then choose in the light of the outcome of the votes whether to work. As the two sets of decisions are taken in a sequential manner, the model isn't easy to analyse, but it has been found that, with some additional structure, quantitative conclusions can be reached.[18] The model (and others like it) is attractive because it treats the degree of compliance (more generally, the degree of civic cooperation) as something to be explained; civic behaviour isn't regarded as part of the explanation. A significant feature of the model is that it admits more than one equilibrium pattern of behaviour, each characterized by a particular degree of compliance. Being equilibria, compliance rates, whether high or low, are held together by their own bootstraps, involving circular chains of reasoning. Where compliance rates are high, it is because most people reciprocate by behaving in a civic-minded way when most others are behaving in a civic-minded way. Conversely, where compliance rates are low in a society it is because most people reciprocate by behaving in an opportunistic way when most others are behaving opportunistically. And so on.[19]

---

[16] Evidence that people have preferences that incorporate 'reciprocity' (economists refer to them as *social preferences*) has been found in experimental situations by Fehr, Gächter, and Kirchsteiger (1997) and Fehr, Kirchsteiger, and Riedl (1998). See Sect. 12.2 for a discussion of whether such social perferences can survive under selection pressure.   [17] Lindbeck (1995, 1997); Lindbeck, Nyberg, and Weibull (1999).

[18] Lindbeck, Nyberg, and Weibull (1999).

[19] For pioneering work along these lines, see Granovetter (1978) and Schelling (1978). Formally, social preferences give rise to *coordination games*. Coordination games are littered with multiple equilibria, in sharp contrast to the much-studied *Prisoners' Dilemma* game, where people are assumed not to have social

Which equilibrium prevails could be the consequence of historical accidents rather than conscious design. So it can be that societies that are identical in their innate characteristics display very different civic behaviour. History matters. The model also offers the sobering thought that, under slowly changing circumstances, the degree of civic cooperation can alter imperceptibly over a long period, until a moment is reached when society transforms itself rapidly from one state of affairs (a society where citizens are civic-minded) to another, very different, state (a society where citizens are not civic-minded). The rapid transformation is a transition from one equilibrium compliance rate to another.[20] To me, the model's overall message is enormously important for social scientists.

Democracy and civil liberties, although virtues in themselves, don't ensure that people are civic-minded. The extent to which people are civic-minded is influenced by their perception of how civic-minded others are. Civic behaviour requires coordination among citizens, something democracy cannot guarantee. So, democracy isn't a sure-fire means to a flourishing civil society. It is possible too that democracy weakens when people are not civic-minded. If so, democratic practice and civic virtues would be held together by their precarious bootstraps, a point that is being made increasingly by political scientists in their study of social capital.[21]

These considerations help to explain why government involvement in the provision of primary health care and education could be expected to vary across poor countries, even if they were all democratic. It follows that people could enjoy a higher disposable income in one country and yet suffer from worse health care and education facilities than in another. Conversely, people in one country on average could be better educated and enjoy better health than in another, even while their access to other material goods is more restricted (Chapter 5, Tables 5.1 and 5.4). Disposable income, and indices of health and education, reflect a person's current socio-economic status.

---

preferences, and which in consequence harbours a unique equilibrium in which everyone free-rides. The famous 'Tragedy of the Commons' (Hardin, 1968) is the outcome of a Prisoners' Dilemma game (see Sect. 7.1).

[20] In sociology the phenomenon is called 'tipping'. See Schelling (1978), who used it to explain rapid transformations in the urban landscape in the USA, namely, middle-class white escaping inner cities for suburbia in the 1960s. Pathways leading to the tipping phenomenon have been used also to characterize the recent fall in birth rates in parts of the poor world (Dasgupta, 2000c).

[21] R. D. Putnam (1993). The term 'social capital' isn't entirely suitable. We study the concept further in Sect. 9.2. On the central role of civic virtues for economic prosperity, see Schama (1987) on the 17th-cent. Dutch. We return to these matters in the following chapter and in Ch. 12, when we identify devices that societies have developed to ensure that people comply with agreements they reach among themselves.

4.5. AGGREGATION IN PRACTICE

Data on income inequality within nations come in too crude a form to reflect most of the nuances in the idea of inequality. Among poor countries, life expectancy at birth and literacy pick up some aspects of poverty and inequality. The aggregate measure of current well-being to be estimated in the following chapter is an average over a given population; some of the component measures of the aggregate reflect the distribution of the quality of life among members of a population.

A problem frequently overlooked is the legitimacy of moving from a person's disposable income (when thinking of a person's well-being) to a country's aggregate output per head (when reflecting upon social well-being). Thus, GNP per head continues to be regarded as the quintessential indicator of a country's living standard. An enormously large, on-going literature on the determinants of economic growth testifies to this, as do annual publications from international organizations. Even the United Nations Development Programme, relentless though it has been in its criticism of GNP per head as a measure of social well-being, includes it in its Human Development Index.[22]

Personal income is the return on a person's wealth. But GNP is not the return on a nation's wealth. This will make for complications when, in Part III and the Appendix, we come to develop a measure of intergenerational well-being. But at this point we are interested in measuring current well-being. So I ignore saving and investment. We are then left with consumption, comprising as it does private and government consumption. In poor countries the latter consists mainly of expenditures on health, education, and defence. As we will measure the quality of health and education directly (by two aggregate measures: life expectancy at birth and literacy, respectively), we would be counting health and education twice if we were to include government expenditure on them in our summary index. So I ignore such components of government expenditure.

This leaves us with defence, a central responsibility of government. But in poor countries the machinery for warfare is all too frequently used by governments against their own people. Moreover, what counts for use is our freedom to be and to do, a freedom that is generally compromised if national security is threatened. People in countries fighting wars, be they civil or international wars, are unlikely to be enjoying many political and civil liberties. Since civil and political liberties are prime components of the quality of life, we should in any case include them explicitly. This means that we can ignore defence expenditure, and therefore public expenditure, entirely.

---

[22] See Sect. 5.4.

To sum up, a minimal set of indices for spanning a reasonable conception of current well-being in a poor country includes private consumption per head, life expectancy at birth, literacy, and civil and political liberties.[23]

4.6. CARDINAL OR ORDINAL INDICES

There remains the question of aggregating the five indices. Here we run into a problem. Indices reflecting the economic component of well-being are strongly cardinal (Section 1.6 above). Whether we measure private consumption in dollars or in cents doesn't matter, so long as we remember that the latter is one-hundredth of the former. This enables us to say, for example, that someone consumes twice as much as another person, or that someone today consumes three times as much as he did ten years ago. But indices of civil and political liberties aren't like that. It can make sense to say that the average citizen of some country enjoys greater civil liberties than his counterpart in another country, or that civil liberties have increased in a country. It can also make sense to say that the differences in civil liberties between countries A and B are a lot less than the differences between either of them and country C, but it makes no sense to say that the change in civil liberties in one country over the past decade is four times the change experienced over the past decade by citizens in another country, or that people in some country are now only half as free as they were before the most recent *coup d'état*. Indices of civil and political rights are ordinal. Although there ought to be restrictions on the extent to which they can be represented by order-preserving numbers, the indices are not cardinal.[24]

I have been unable to find an aggregator that accommodates indices that are neither cardinal, nor ordinal, but something in between. To assume that indices of civil and political liberties are ordinal is to err; but then, so is it to err to imagine that they are cardinal. I don't know which is the bigger error. When I first

---

[23] Alternatives for each suggest themselves. For example, infant survival rate (or the under-5 survival rate) could substitute for life expectancy at birth as an index of aggregate health. Refinements also suggest themselves. The average length of life doesn't take account of the concern that the healthy years of someone's life should count for more than the years in which they suffer from bad health. Health economists have devised the concept of quality-adjusted life years (QALYs) (alternatively, that of disability-adjusted life years (DALYs)) to count the burden of diseases; see Moore and Viscusi (1988) and World Bank (1992). I abstract from this. Finally, literacy is not quite a current measure: it is a stock, and so picks up aspects of intertemporal well-being. I am grateful to Pranab Mukhopadhyay for the many discussions we have had on the selection of indices that best serve the purpose of measuring current well-being.

[24] Formally, suppose there are N countries indexed by i. Suppose also that they are so labelled that civil liberties are greater in i than in $i + 1$, for all $i = 1, 2, \ldots, N$. Then $R(i)$ is a numerical index of civil liberties if $R(i) > R(i + 1)$ for all i. If civil liberties were purely ordinal, any order-preserving renumbering of the $R(i)$s would be an equally valid numerical index of civil liberties. In the text I suggest that, while civil liberties aren't cardinal, they aren't purely ordinal either. See Chs. 1 and *1.

worked on ways to include human rights in quality-of-life indices, I regarded measures of civil and political as ordinal without giving the matter thought.[25] Subsequently, economists have interpreted the measures as cardinal, run linear regressions between human rights and economic variables, and obtained somewhat different results from mine.[26] To offer a contrasting approach to the one prevailing in the subsequent literature, I assume without further justification that civil and political rights are ordinal.

We must then search for an *ordinal aggregator*. Of the many we could devise, the one best known and most studied is the Borda Rule. This rule provides a method of rank-order scoring, the procedure being to award each alternative (say, a country) a point equal to its rank in each criterion of ranking (the criteria being (i) private consumption per head, (ii) life expectancy at birth, (iii) literacy, (iv) political liberties, and (v) civil liberties), adding each alternative's scores to obtain its aggregate score, and then ranking alternatives on the basis of their aggregate scores. To illustrate, suppose a country has the ranks i, j, k, l, and m, respectively, for the five criteria. Then its Borda score is $i + j + k + l + m$. The rule invariably yields a complete ranking of alternatives. Since the criteria can be thought of as 'voters', the Borda Rule can be viewed as a *voting rule*. Of Arrow's classic axioms on social choice (Arrow, 1963a [1951]), the Borda Rule violates the one concerning the independence of irrelevant alternatives. The strengths and limitations of the Borda Rule have been much studied.[27] The rule is also familiar, in that 'committees' frequently use it to reach decisions. So I use it to illustrate how one can make cross-country comparisons to the current quality of life. But I cannot emphasize strongly enough that the exercise is simply an illustration.[28]

---

[25] Dasgupta (1990a).　　[26] E.g. Barro (1996).

[27] See Goodman and Markowitz (1952); Fine and Fine (1974).

[28] We could of course, create a cardinal aggregator for the socio-economic indices (private consumption per head, life expectancy at birth, and literacy), and then construct the Borda ranking out of the three resulting rankings, i.e. the rankings based on civil and political liberties and the socio-economic aggregate. This would award equal status to socio-economic, civil, and political rights. I avoid the complications, by working directly with the five rankings.

5

Current Quality of Life in Poor Countries

Quality-of-life indices in use by international organizations measure the extent to which socio-economic rights are respected. The United Nations Development Programme's well-known Human Development Index (HDI) is based on GNP per head, life expectancy at birth, and adult literacy.[1] In contrast, growth economists consider GNP per head to be *the* measure of the standard of living. Contemporary data suggest that, although neither index incorporates civil and political rights, they aren't wildly misleading as measures of current well-being within poor countries. But not much should be read into this. I am able to offer only two sets of data on the subject (Sections 5.1–5.4 below).

Cross-country comparisons of living standards by means of such indices as the HDI and GNP per head are about the current quality of life. Future possibilities are not adequately reflected in them. However, even as measures of current well-being, the published figures should not be trusted beyond an early point. The methods deployed in different countries to estimate the quantities are frequently not comparable. Moreover, GNP estimates can be wildly wrong if rural households are much engaged in non-market activities. The published figures are often mere guesses, borrowed from neighbouring countries. In this chapter I want to show how the theory developed in earlier chapters can in principle be put to work. It is meant to be illustrative, not much more.[2] Sections 5.1–5.3 consider data on poor countries for the year 1980. In Section 5.4 I examine more contemporary data. These offer somewhat contrasting pictures of current well-being in the poor world. And they have a moral to tell.

5.1. THE DATA

Our first laboratory consists of countries that in the early 1970s were among the world's poorest in terms of income per head. The idea is to gain an

[1] See Sect. 5.4.

[2] For an exposure of how unreliable cross-country data on leading socio-economic indicators can be, see the Special Issue on the subject in the *Journal of Development Economics*, Vol. 44, especially the editorial introduction by Srinivasan (1994).

understanding of the way the various components of current well-being are related. Given the context in which international discussions take place, the restriction to the world's poorest countries is both deliberate and right. The period is right too. As we will see presently, most of the poor world had settled into an array of dysfunctional economies.

I consider countries where in 1970 GNP per head was less than $1,500 at 1980 international dollars.[3] The year in question is 1979/80. I was able to obtain data on all five components of current well-being for only forty-six out of more than fifty-five countries that should be on our list. Table 5.1 summarizes the data. Since GNP per head is probably the most familiar international statistic, estimates of this are provided in the first column of figures (but in parentheses, so as to remind ourselves that the country ranking on the basis of GNP per head is not being used in the construction of the Borda index).

The second column in Table 5.1 consists of estimates of private consumption per head in 1980. The third and fourth columns present life expectancy at birth and literacy, respectively, again for the year 1980. The fifth and sixth columns represent indices of political and civil liberties in our sample for the year 1979. They are taken from the valuable compendium of Taylor and Jodice (1983).[4] Rights to political liberty are taken to be the rights of citizens to play a part in determining who governs their country, and what the laws are and will be. Countries are coded with scores ranging from 1 (highest degree of liberty) to 7 (lowest degree of liberty). Values for this index are given in the fifth column of figures in Table 5.1.

Civil rights are different. They are rights the individual has *vis-à-vis* the State. Of particular importance in the construction of the index in Taylor and Jodice (1983) are freedom of the press and other media concerned with the dissemination of information, and the independence of the judiciary. The index measures the extent to which people, because they are protected by an independent judiciary, are openly able to express their opinions without fear of reprisals. Countries are coded with scores ranging from 1 (highest degree of liberty) to 7 (lowest degree of liberty). Values of the index are given in the sixth column of figures.

Even a glance at the last two columns tells us that, for the most part, political and civil liberties were scarce goods in poor countries in the late 1970s. Citizens of thirty-two countries in our sample of forty-six suffered from systems that

---

[3] The data have been taken from Dasgupta and Weale (1992) and Dasgupta (1993). There, per capita GNP was taken to be one of the socio-economic components of the quality of life. As I have just argued in Chs. 3 and 4, this was a mistake. So I have redone the calculations, by replacing per capita GNP by private consumption per head. This makes for some difference in the ranking of poor nations.

[4] Indices of political and civil liberties in Taylor and Jodice (1983) were taken from the annual publications of Freedom House, a non-profit organization.

Table 5.1. *Current Well-Being Indicators, 1980*

	(Y)	C	E	L	R_1	R_2
Bangladesh	(540)	491	48	26	4	4
Benin	(534)	427	47	28	7	7
Bolivia	(1529)	1147	50	63	3	5
Botswana	(1477)	827	55	35	3	2
Burundi	(333)	393	46	25	6	7
Central African Republic	(487)	536	47	33	7	7
Chad	(353)	339	42	15	6	6
China	(1619)	955	67	69	6	6
Ecuador	(2607)	1642	63	81	3	5
Egypt	(995)	657	58	44	5	5
Ethiopia	(325)	260	44	15	7	7
Haiti	(696)	633	52	23	6	7
Honduras	(1075)	720	60	60	3	6
India	(614)	423	54	36	3	2
Indonesia	(1063)	606	53	62	5	5
Jordan	(1885)	1372	62	70	6	6
Kenya	(662)	430	55	47	5	5
Korea	(2369)	1486	67	93	5	5
Lesotho	(694)	1106	52	52	4	5
Liberia	(680)	374	52	25	4	6
Madagascar	(589)	437	51	50	5	5
Malawi	(417)	334	44	25	6	6
Mali	(356)	288	44	10	7	7
Mauritania	(576)	271	43	17	6	6
Mauritius	(1484)	1042	65	85	2	4
Morocco	(1200)	803	57	28	4	3
Nepal	(490)	456	45	19	6	5
Niger	(441)	309	42	10	6	7
Nigeria	(824)	511	48	34	3	5
Pakistan	(990)	821	49	24	5	6
Paraguay	(1979)	1464	66	84	5	5
Philippines	(1551)	1039	61	75	5	5
Rwanda	(379)	322	45	50	5	6
Senegal	(744)	655	45	10	3	4
Sierra Leone	(512)	394	38	15	5	6
Somalia	(415)	324	44	60	7	7
Sri Lanka	(1200)	509	68	85	3	2
Sudan	(652)	554	46	32	5	5
Swaziland	(1079)	550	51	65	6	5
Tanzania	(353)	275	50	79	6	6
Thailand	(1694)	1117	62	86	4	6
Tunisia	(1845)	1107	60	62	6	5
Uganda	(257)	252	46	52	7	7
Zaire	(224)	168	49	55	6	7

Table 5.1. *(Continued)*

	(Y)	C	E	L	R_1	R_2
Zambia	(716)	387	50	44	5	5
Zimbabwe	(930)	586	55	69	5	5

Notes: Y: per capita GNP (international dollars).
C: per capita private consumption (international dollars).
E: life expectancy at birth (years).
L: adult literacy rate (%).
R_1: index of political rights.
R_2: index of civil rights.

Source: World Bank (1982); Dasgupta and Weale (1992).

score 5 or more for political rights, and those of no fewer than thirty-nine countries from systems that score 5 or more for civil rights. This suggests that civil rights can be, and frequently are, curtailed in countries where elections are held. The scores reflect severe deprivation of basic liberties. There were exceptions of course, most notably Botswana, India, Mauritius, and Sri Lanka. But for the most part the columns make for dismal reading. And when they are combined with the columns that reflect the socio-economic sphere of life, the picture that emerges is chilling. There was nothing to commend the state of affairs in a large number of the countries in our sample.

5.2. BORDA RANKING

The first column in Table 5.2 presents the Borda ranking of nations, based on the rankings in the five columns that follow. Countries are listed in accordance with their Borda ranks. The ranking is from the worst (score of 1, with Mali and Ethiopia being the joint losers) to the best (score of 46, with Mauritius being the winner). For completeness, country rankings on the basis of GNP per head is provided in the final column.

The relative positions of China on the Borda ranking (coming in at 17 from the top) and India (coming in six places ahead, at 11) deserve comment. For a long while, China and India have provided commentators with a classic tension: achievements in the economic sphere against those in the arena of political and civil liberties. As Table 5.1 shows, China beat India handsomely in each of the three socio-economic indices on our list (for example, private consumption per head in China in 1980 was more than twice that in India), while India beat China in political and civil liberties.[5] This is consistent with what any

---

[5] This continued to be so in the 1990s; see Table 5.4.

Measuring Current Well-Being

Table 5.2. *Rankings of Countries, 1980*

	BORDA	C	E	L	R_1	R_2	(Y)
Mali	1	6	5	1	1	1	7
Ethiopia	1	3	5	4	1	1	3
Niger	3	7	2	1	7	1	11
Mauritania	4	4	4	7	7	11	17
Chad	5	11	2	4	7	11	5
Uganda	6	2	12	27	1	1	2
Malawi	7	10	5	11	7	11	10
Burundi	8	14	12	11	7	1	4
Somalia	9	9	5	30	1	1	9
Benin	10	17	15	15	1	1	15
Sierra Leone	11	15	1	4	20	11	14
Zaire	12	1	19	29	7	1	1
Central African Republic	13	24	15	18	1	1	12
Nepal	14	20	9	8	7	23	13
Haiti	15	29	26	9	7	1	24
Rwanda	16	8	9	25	20	11	8
Tanzania	17	5	21	40	7	11	5
Liberia	18	12	26	11	33	11	22
Pakistan	19	34	19	10	20	11	29
Sudan	20	26	12	17	20	23	20
Zambia	21	13	21	22	20	23	25
Madagascar	22	19	24	25	20	23	18
Swaziland	23	25	24	35	7	23	33
Kenya	24	18	31	24	20	23	21
Senegal	25	30	9	1	38	40	26
Nigeria	26	23	17	19	38	23	27
Bangladesh	27	21	17	14	33	40	16
Egypt	28	31	35	22	20	23	30
Indonesia	29	28	29	32	20	23	31
China	30	36	44	36	7	11	40
Zimbabwe	31	27	31	36	20	23	28
Jordan	32	43	39	38	7	11	43
Tunisia	32	40	36	32	7	23	42
Honduras	34	32	36	30	38	11	32
Lesotho	35	39	26	27	33	23	23
India	36	16	29	21	38	44	19
Philippines	37	37	38	39	20	23	39
Bolivia	38	42	21	34	38	23	38
Morocco	38	33	34	15	33	43	34
Botswana	40	35	31	20	38	44	36
Thailand	41	41	39	45	33	11	41
Paraguay	42	44	43	42	20	23	44
Korea	43	45	44	46	20	23	45

Table 5.2. *(Continued)*

	BORDA	C	E	L	R_1	R_2	(Y)
Ecuador	44	46	41	41	38	23	46
Sri Lanka	45	22	46	43	38	44	34
Mauritius	46	38	42	43	46	40	37

Notes: BORDA: ranking using Borda Rule.
C: per capita private consumption (international dollars).
E: life expectancy at birth (years).
L: adult literacy rate (%).
R_1: index of political rights.
R_2: index of civil rights.
Y: per capita GNP (international dollars).

newspaper reader knows to be the case. However, the fact that the two finish close in a ranking of forty-six countries means that the *ordinal distance* between them in political and civil liberties is large relative to their distance in terms of the socio-economic indicators. Other things remaining the same, had more countries managed to squeeze themselves in between China and India in the socio-economic indicators, the overall ranking of these two countries would have been reversed. On the other hand, had more countries squeezed themselves in between China and India in the sphere of political and civil liberties, the Borda gap between the two countries would have been greater. The relative placings of China and India are sensitive to the aggregator being used.[6]

It is informative to get a quantitative feel for the relationship between the Borda ranking and each of the rankings based on the five components of social well-being. Statistically, how close then is the Borda ranking to the others, and how close are the others on a pairwise basis? In order to examine this, we look at rank correlations.

Table 5.3 provides the (Spearman) correlation coefficient for each pair of rankings from the seven rankings of nations in Table 5.2. It transpires that the correlation coefficient between the Borda ranking and the others are: 0.84 for private consumption per head; 0.88 for life expectancy at birth; 0.72 for literacy; 0.76 for political rights; and 0.75 for civil rights. I had not expected this. I had no reason to think that life expectancy at birth would be the closest to our measure of the quality of life.

[6] In Dasgupta and Weale (1992) and Dasgupta (1993), where such computations were first undertaken, the socio-economic indices that were included were GNP per head, life expectancy at birth, infant survival rate, and literacy. Since life expectancy at birth is strongly influenced by infant survival, this amounted to counting similar health indices twice. It explains why, using what was essentially the same data-set as Table 5.1, the two earlier studies found China to have a higher Borda score than India, the reverse of the present finding.

Table 5.3. *(Spearman) Correlation Matrix of Rankings of Current Well-Being*

	Borda	C	E	L	R_1	R_2
C	0.84					
E	0.88	0.75				
L	0.72	0.54	0.79			
R_1	0.76	0.51	0.48	0.28		
R_2	0.75	0.47	0.50	0.25	0.76	
Y	0.87	0.91	0.83	0.61	0.55	0.52

5.3. GNP AND CURRENT WELL-BEING

The Borda ranking of countries is strongly correlated with the ranking of countries based on GNP per head, the correlation coefficient being 0.87. The present findings imply that, if we had to choose a single indicator of current well-being, either life expectancy at birth or GNP per head would have sufficed. Recent insistence that GNP per head is a vastly misleading index of current well-being is not borne out by the present exercise. I doubt though if there is a general moral to be drawn from this. In the following section we will find that, for contemporary data, GNP per head is not strongly correlated with the Borda index.[7]

Earlier I argued that private consumption should replace GNP in measures of current social well-being. Not surprisingly, though, the link between GNP and private consumption per head is close: in our sample the correlation coefficient is 0.91. It is customary in studies of economic development to regress GNP per head against other socio-economic indicators, to see how closely they are related. The last row of figures in Table 5.3 presents Spearman rank correlation coefficients between GNP per head and each of the five components of well-being. Ignoring private consumption per head, the highest correlation (0.83) is with life expectancy at birth. Again, I did not expect this. Also, I had no prior notion that correlation with literacy (0.61) would be considerably less.

Richer countries enjoy greater political and civil liberties. But the correlation is not overly high. (The correlation coefficient between private consumption per head and political rights is 0.51 and with civil rights, 0.47.) In a more extensive political theory, neither private consumption per head nor political and civil liberties would be exogenous. So, the correlation between them should be read simply as a correlation, nothing more. No causal relationship should be inferred

---

[7] I argue in Ch. 9 that GNP and its growth are vastly inadequate as measures of social well-being over time.

from the data. Correlation coefficients of 0.51 and 0.47 do however mean that it would be wrong to claim that the circumstances that make for poverty are also those that make it necessary for governments to deny citizens their civil and political liberties. There are countries in the sample that are very poor in terms of private consumption, but enjoy relatively extensive civil and political liberties. However, to see if there is a causal link between political and civil liberties and economic progress, we would first have to see if, over a period of time, there is a link between the time-average values of those liberties and changes in socio-economic indicators over a period of time. I will return to these more complex matters in Section 5.5.

5.4. THE CONTEMPORARY POOR WORLD[8]

Unlike socio-economic variables, the extent of political and civil liberties can be altered rapidly, at the stroke of a pen or at the burst of guns. People in a number of countries in sub-Saharan Africa experienced political change in the decade of the 1990s, many for the better. What does the contemporary poor world look like? Does it have the intellectual tidiness of Tables 5.1–5.3?

It doesn't. My guess is that it doesn't because there hasn't been enough time for the political changes to have the influence on socio-economics we could expect of them. The year on view is 1995–6. Table 5.4 is the counterpart of Table 5.1. I have included countries whose per capita GNP was less than 3,500 international dollars. There are only thirty-six countries on the list because they are the ones for which I have been able to obtain data on all five variables (private consumption per head, life expectancy at birth, literacy, and political and civil liberties). A number of countries on our list for 1980 are missing because they are no longer poor in terms of GNP per head. Countries are listed in alphabetical order.[9]

The first column of Table 5.5 ranks the thirty-six countries on the basis of the Borda index. Sierra Leone scores the lowest (it is pretty much at the bottom, no matter which way you look), while Honduras appears at the top. The relative positions of India and China haven't changed, but they are ordinally closer now.

Table 5.6 lists the Spearman rank-correlation coefficients. GNP per head continues to be about as closely correlated with the Borda ranking as life expectancy at birth. Otherwise, the table suggests that the poor world has

---

[8] I am most grateful to Nicholas Vrousalis, a second-year undergraduate in my department, for the computations I report in this section.

[9] Countries that were part of the former Soviet Union are missing from the list because of incomplete data.

Table 5.4. *Current Well-Being Indicators, 1995–1996*

	(Y)	C	E	L	R_1	R_2
Bangladesh	(1010)	778	58	38	3	4
Benin	(1230)	984	54	38	2	2
Burkina Faso	(950)	740	46	19	5	4
Burundi	(590)	538	47	36	6	7
Cameroon	(1760)	1355	56	64	7	5
Central African Republic	(1430)	1200	48	60	3	4
Chad	(880)	810	49	49	6	5
China	(3330)	1632	69	82	7	7
Congo (Democratic Republic)	(790)	695	52	78	4	4
Congo (Republic)	(1410)	650	52	75	7	6
Côte d'Ivoire	(1580)	1045	54	40	6	5
Ethiopia	(500)	395	49	35	4	5
Ghana	(1790)	1468	59	65	4	4
Guinea	(1720)	1376	46	36	6	5
Guinea-Bissau	(1030)	917	43	55	3	4
Honduras	(2130)	1342	67	73	3	3
India	(1580)	1074	62	52	4	4
Kenya	(1130)	894	58	78	7	6
Lesotho	(2380)	2023	58	72	4	4
Malawi	(690)	545	43	57	2	3
Mali	(710)	525	50	31	2	3
Mozambique	(550)	315	45	41	3	4
Nepal	(1090)	905	57	28	3	4
Nicaragua	(1760)	1478	67	66	4	4
Niger	(920)	782	47	14	3	5
Nigeria	(870)	566	53	57	7	7
Pakistan	(1600)	1168	63	37	3	5
Rwanda	(630)	567	40	61	7	6
Senegal	(1650)	1270	50	33	4	5
Sierra Leone	(510)	505	37	32	7	6
Sri Lanka	(2290)	1649	73	90	4	5
Togo	(1650)	1288	50	52	6	5
Uganda	(1030)	845	43	62	5	4
Vietnam	(1570)	1209	68	93	7	7
Zambia	(860)	697	44	79	3	4
Zimbabwe	(2200)	1320	56	85	5	5

Notes: Y: per capita GNP (international dollars, PPP).
C: per capita private consumption (international dollars, PPP).
E: life expectancy at birth (years).
L: adult literacy rate (%).
R_1: index of political rights.
R_2: index of civil rights.

Sources: Y (World Bank, 1998: table 1.1); C (World Bank, 1999: table 13);
E (World Bank, 1999: table 2); L (World Bank, 1998: table 2); and R_1 and R_2
(Freedom House, 2000).

Table 5.5. *Rankings of Countries, 1995–1996*

	BORDA	C	E	L	R_1	R_2	(Y)
Sierra Leone	1	3	1	5	1	5	3
Burundi	2	5	10	8	9	1	4
Rwanda	3	8	2	22	1	5	5
Ethiopia	4	2	13	7	17	9	1
Nigeria	4	7	20	19	1	1	10
Burkina Faso	6	12	8	2	14	20	13
Niger	7	14	10	1	25	9	12
Chad	8	15	13	15	9	9	11
Congo (Republic)	9	9	18	29	1	5	20
Guinea	10	31	8	8	9	9	28
Mozambique	11	1	7	14	25	20	1
Senegal	12	26	15	6	17	9	26
Côte d'Ivoire	12	21	21	13	9	9	23
Togo	14	27	15	16	9	9	26
Uganda	14	16	3	23	14	20	15
Kenya	16	17	26	30	1	5	18
Guinea-Bissau	17	19	3	18	25	20	15
Cameroon	18	30	23	24	1	9	29
Mali	19	4	15	4	34	33	7
Nepal	20	18	25	3	25	20	17
Zambia	21	11	6	32	25	20	9
Malawi	22	6	3	19	34	33	6
Congo (Democratic Republic)	22	10	18	30	17	20	8
Bangladesh	22	13	26	11	25	20	14
Vietnam	25	25	34	36	1	1	22
Pakistan	26	23	31	10	25	9	25
Central African Republic	27	24	12	21	25	20	21
China	28	34	35	33	1	1	36
India	29	22	30	16	17	20	23
Zimbabwe	30	28	23	34	14	9	33
Benin	31	20	21	11	34	36	19
Ghana	32	32	29	25	17	20	31
Lesotho	33	36	26	27	17	20	35
Nicaragua	34	33	32	26	17	20	29
Sri Lanka	35	35	36	35	17	9	9
Honduras	36	29	32	28	25	33	32

Notes: BORDA: ranking using Borda Rule.
C: per capita private consumption (international dollars).
E: life expectancy at birth (years).
L: adult literacy rate (%).
R_1: index of political rights.
R_2: index of civil rights.
Y: per capita GNP (international dollars).

Table 5.6. *(Spearman) Correlation Matrix of Rankings of*
Current Well-Being

	Borda	C	E	L	R_1	R_2
C	0.69					
E	0.70	0.64				
L	0.54	0.43	0.43			
R_1	0.40	−0.10	−0.09	−0.30*		
R_2	0.48	−0.03	−0.07	−0.12	0.83	
Y	0.69	0.96	0.71	0.45	−0.13	−0.05

*The high negative correlation is due to outliers Cameroon, Vietnam, and China.

changed in curious ways since the late 1970s. For example, the correlation coefficients between GNP per head and political and civil liberties, respectively, are now negative, a consequence of the abrupt changes in political regimes that occurred in sub-Saharan Africa.

5.5. CIVIL RIGHTS, DEMOCRACY, AND ECONOMIC PROGRESS: THEORY

The Borda rankings in Tables 5.2 and 5.5 and the rank-correlation coefficients in Tables 5.3 and 5.6 are just that, nothing more. They don't speak to possible causal links between political and civil liberties on the one hand and economic well-being on the other. Over the years however there has been a persistent idea that the protection and promotion of civil rights, democratic practices, and personal access to material resources go together. Lipset (1959) argued that economic development should be expected to help promote democratic practice. The converse—that democratic practice and civil liberties in poor countries promote economic development—has also been suggested.[10] Democracy and civil liberties, including the existence of a free press ('people have the right to know'), have been seen not only as ends in themselves, but also as means to material prosperity. There are, of course, theoretical reasons for expecting a mutual relationship between the three sets of goods; I am alluding at this point to empirical observations only.[11]

[10] Statistical evidence from the contemporary world was sought by Dasgupta (1990a), Dasgupta and Weale (1992), and Barro (1996). Landes (1998) offers historical evidence in his study of economic progress in the West in the wake of the Enlightenment.

[11] The theory is developed in Schumpeter (1942), Hayek (1948, 1960), and Friedman (1962). For recent explorations of the strengths and limitations of democracy, see the collections of essays in Shapiro and Hacker-Cordon (1999a,b).

In his masterly affirmation of the democratic ideal, Dahl (1989) observed that 'effective participation by citizens' and 'voting equality among citizens' are two features that embody the idea of democratic process. He also observed that participation can be effective only if there are opportunities among people to acquire information. But the converse holds as well, and offers an instrumental justification for democracy and civil rights: participation by citizens in decision-making enables information to be pooled.

It has been said that democracy is the worst system of government, except for the other systems of government. The epithet rings true not only because people have limited information, but also because different people know different things. Recent studies on the management of local common-property resources among rural communities in poor countries suggest that local participatory democracy has instrumental virtues.[12] The State should exercise its authority if the local resource base isn't to be captured by the local elite. However, local governance is desirable, since it permits local information to be pooled. It should not surprise that both seats of decision-making are desirable. In a cross-country analysis, Barrett and Graddy (2000) have shown relatedly that, controlling for income differences, urban air-borne pollutants and several water-borne pollutants are negatively and significantly correlated with the extent to which citizens enjoy political and civil liberties. People have greater voice in more open societies; moreover, voice is able to translate itself into political action.[13]

Economists and political scientists have also drawn attention to the positive influence that civic engagement can have on government performance.[14] Their argument is that government accountability requires not only that citizens have access to pertinent information, but also that they are able to take collective action. A free 'media' (newspapers and magazines, radio, television) is necessary if information is to spread. Systems of checks and balances on the media help to minimize the spread of false information. The role of the State's judicial arm is self-evident here, assuming of course that it is independent of the executive arm of government and of the army. As elsewhere in social life, circular chains of monitors and control are necessary if people are to thrive. Official A keeps an eye on official B, who in turn keeps an eye on official C, . . . , official Y keeps an eye on official Z, who keeps an eye on A; and so on.

---

[12] These matters are discussed further in Chs. 7 and 12. See also Dasgupta and Maskin (1999) and Dasgupta (2000a).

[13] Judith Shapiro's study of ill-conceived economic programmes in Maoist China (Shapiro, 2001) is a convincing account of how suppression of civil and political liberties can contribute to the destruction of a country's natural resource base.

[14] Adelman and Morris (1965, 1967) and R. D. Putnam (1993) are pioneering empirical studies on this. The cognate notion of social capital is discussed in Ch. 9.

However, the mere supply of newspapers and magazines would not ensure that information spreads. There has to be a demand for it. I don't know of any law akin to the one attributed to J. B. Say, to the effect that supply creates its own demand. Literacy and numeracy are necessary if there is to *be* a demand (radio and television don't require them, and are in this respect superior media), but they aren't sufficient; they need to be allied to civic engagement, creating demand via shared experiences and emulation. Collective action requires coordination; it requires that people trust one another enough to coordinate. Civic engagement creates trust by reducing the uncertainties that each party harbours about others' predilections and dispositions. Contrariwise, an absence of such engagement makes trust that much harder to build.[15]

For issues more extensive than local matters, participatory democracy has to give way to representative democracy, and to the concomitant idea of political competition. In his classic study of the nature of democracy, Schumpeter (1942) argued that candidates for political office in democracies compete for votes in the way firms compete for markets under capitalism. Political democracy and civil liberties together are the means by which government can be made accountable.[16] On the other hand, as I noted in the previous chapter, democracy cannot guarantee responsible citizenship. And if citizens free-ride on the State, the State's capability to offer the infrastructure needed for economic progress weakens.

So, then, is democracy associated with economic progress? Are growth in national income per head, or increases in life expectancy at birth and the infant survival rate, or improvements in adult literacy, greater in countries where citizens enjoy less curtailed civil and political liberties?

These questions are enormously hard to answer. Democracy means different things to different people, as does the idea of civil liberties. Some would view majority rule as being more democratic than plurality rule, while others would take the opposite view. The same would apply for the many other democratic voting rules that can be devised. Many see in the simple majority rule the quintessential feature of democracy, while others regard it to be too coarse a rule for converting individual values into social choice. But even if we were to leave such problems aside, empirical investigations into the possible links

---

[15] In his highly original study of milk-producers' cooperatives in South Indian villages, Seabright (1993, 1997) found that prior history of cooperative institutions in the community is a positive predictor of a cooperative's success: cooperation begets further cooperation. He reported too that cooperation among producers was more successful in those villages where members had previously organized *communal* religious festivals, as opposed to festivals segmented by caste. The finding supports the view that social inclusion pays off.

[16] In their editorial introductions, Shapiro and Hacker-Cordon (1998a,b) summarize Schumpeter's theme. Przeworski (1991) and Persson and Tabellini (2000) contain formulations of the idea that periodic electoral contests help make government accountable.

between democracy and economic progress require at their start that the criteria taken to be indicators of democratic practice should be explicit and *independent* of material well-being. The cross-country indices of civil and political liberties, reported in Tables 5.1 and 5.4, satisfy this condition.[17]

So far as I know, at levels of aggregation below that of the nation, there are no consistent sets of indices of democracy and civil liberties that are independent of material well-being. And yet, democratic practice and civic engagement could differ widely among regions within a country. Suppose we wish to inquire if differences in the economic performance of different states or provinces in, say, India or China can be explained, at least in part, in terms of differences in the practice of local democracy. What should we look for? Problems are compounded because most of us want to believe that democracy is allied to the other things that make life good. Empirical investigations are thus vulnerable to what econometricians call the 'warm glow effect', meaning that we are tempted to read signs of democratic practice in precisely those societies that have prospered materially.[18]

For these reasons, it is difficult to resist claiming more than is uncovered when we study the links between democracy, civil liberties, and economic progress. Commentators, in their enthusiasm for democracy, not infrequently read more than is perhaps claimed even by the researchers themselves. Thus, for example, in an engagingly critical essay on John Rawls's recent work on global justice, Kuper (2000: 663) refers to the instrumental value of democracy by saying that it has been 'demonstrated repeatedly that nondemocratic regimes are in fact unfailingly detrimental to human rights and well-being'.

If only the demonstration were in hand. Alas, it isn't. The evidence is fragmentary and qualitative. Below the level of nations, the evidence mostly amounts to citing instances, occasionally dressed up in the form of case studies, that are especially vulnerable to the warm-glow effect. Counter-citings aren't hard to find. Over the years, India and China have been used repeatedly to settle one intellectual score or another.

5.6. CIVIL RIGHTS, DEMOCRACY, AND ECONOMIC PROGRESS: ILLUSTRATION

Case studies have enjoyed a long tradition. An alternative is to conduct statistical analysis. The only systematic statistics on political and civil rights that I am aware

---

[17] Taylor and Jodice (1983) offer a clear account of the basis on which the indices were constructed.

[18] Roemer (1999) makes a similar point about the temptations the political 'left' yielded to in the 1960s and 1970s, to define 'socialism' as the confluence of all good things.

of are cross-country. If we wish to know whether democracy and civil liberties are conducive to material progress, we should seek, as a bare minimum, statistical links between political and civil liberties and changes in socio-economic indices. This was the point of the exercises in Dasgupta (1990a) and Dasgupta and Weale (1992). The studies were restricted to poor countries.

The sample consisted of countries where, in 1970, GNP per head was less than $1,500 at 1980 international dollars. There were fifty-one such countries with populations in excess of 1 million.[19] The period under observation was the decade of the 1970s. Table 5.7 summarizes the data. Since we are involved with a greater range of questions here, I study a larger pool of countries. I vary the sample size as and when we need to.

The first column of Table 5.7 presents the average of the 1970 and 1980 figures for GNP per head. We study this average, rather than GNP per head in a given year during the decade, because growth rates varied across countries during the period. Column (2) provides the percentage change in GNP per head over the decade. It will be noticed that fifteen of the fifty-one countries experienced a decline in real income per head during the 1970s.[20]

Column (3) gives life expectancy at birth in 1970. We need a measure of the change in this index over the decade. This is a delicate matter. Equal increments are possibly of less and less ethical worth as life expectancy rises to 65 or 70 years and more. We should, however, measure performance. So it becomes more and more commendable if, with increasing life expectancy, the index increases at the margin. The idea here is that it becomes more and more difficult to increase life expectancy as life expectancy itself rises. A simple index capturing this feature is the ratio of the increase in life expectancy to the shortfall of the base-year life expectancy from some target, say 80 years.[21] Column (4) of the table gives this index of improvement over the period 1970–80 for fifty-one countries. All but two countries—Rwanda and Uganda—recorded an improvement.

The construction of an index of improvements in literacy rates doesn't pose problems of the kind we faced in connection with life expectancy at birth. It isn't immediately clear why it should be a lot less or a lot more difficult to increase the literacy rate when people are more literate—except, that is, near 0 and 100 per cent. This suggests that we should simply measure increases in adult literacy rates if we want to know what net improvements there have been in this field. Unfortunately, I was unable to locate adult literacy rate figures for a number of

---

[19] Summers and Heston (1988).

[20] For a recent commentary on this fact of sub-Saharan Africa, see Pritchett (1997).

[21] Thus, an increase in life expectancy at birth from 35 to 40 years is less difficult to achieve than an increase from 60 to 65 years. The mathematical representation of the index is given in the key to Table 5.7.

Table 5.7. *Improvements in Living Standards*

	Y (1)	ΔY (2)	E (3)	ΔE (4)	L (5)	ΔL (6)	R_1 (7)	R_2 (8)
Bangladesh	499.0	17.9	45.0	8.6	22.0	4.0	4.9	4.2
Benin	552.5	−6.5	40.0	17.5	5.0	23.0	7.0	6.3
Bolivia	1383.0	23.6	46.0	11.8	39.0	24.0	5.6	4.1
Botswana	1179.0	67.7	50.0	16.7	41.0	**	2.1	3.1
Burundi	324.0	5.7	45.0	2.9	14.0	11.0	7.0	6.4
Cameroon	789.0	24.5	49.0	12.9	19.0	**	6.1	4.4
Central African Republic	499.0	−4.7	42.0	13.2	7.0	26.0	7.0	7.0
Chad	409.5	−24.2	38.0	9.5	6.0	9.0	6.4	6.4
China	1315.5	60.0	59.0	38.1	43.0	26.0	6.7	6.7
Congo	986.5	−1.1	51.0	13.8	16.0	**	5.9	6.1
Ecuador	2005.0	85.8	58.0	22.7	68.0	13.0	6.4	3.7
Egypt	833.0	48.3	51.0	24.1	26.0	18.0	5.6	4.7
Ethiopia	333.0	−4.7	43.0	2.7	4.0	11.0	6.3	6.1
Gambia	561.0	−1.8	36.0	9.1	**	**	2.0	2.0
Ghana	494.5	−25.9	49.0	9.7	27.0	**	6.6	5.1
Haiti	623.0	26.5	48.0	12.5	15.0	8.0	6.4	6.0
Honduras	1001.0	16.0	53.0	25.9	45.0	15.0	6.1	3.0
India	595.0	6.6	48.0	18.8	28.0	8.0	2.1	3.3
Indonesia	811.0	90.2	47.0	18.2	39.0	23.0	5.0	5.0
Jordan	1653.0	32.7	55.0	28.0	32.0	38.0	6.0	6.0
Kenya	607.0	19.9	50.0	16.7	20.0	27.0	5.0	4.6
Korea	1779.0	99.2	60.0	35.0	71.0	22.0	4.9	5.6
Lesotho	527.0	92.8	49.0	9.7	**	**	5.3	3.9
Liberia	694.0	−4.0	47.0	15.2	9.0	16.0	6.0	4.3
Madagascar	631.0	−12.5	45.0	17.1	**	**	5.1	4.4
Malawi	359.0	38.5	40.0	10.0	**	**	6.9	6.0
Mali	336.5	12.3	40.0	10.0	2.0	8.0	7.0	6.6
Mauritania	573.0	1.1	39.0	9.8	5.0	12.0	5.9	6.0
Mauritius	1254.5	44.8	62.4	17.0	**	**	2.7	2.3
Morocco	1037.5	36.9	52.0	17.9	14.0	14.0	4.6	4.4
Nepal	498.0	−3.2	41.6	9.1	9.0	10.0	6.0	5.0
Niger	421.0	10.0	38.0	9.5	1.0	9.0	6.7	6.0
Nigeria	727.0	30.8	44.0	11.1	15.0	19.0	5.7	4.0
Pakistan	893.0	24.1	46.0	8.8	15.0	9.0	4.3	4.9
Paraguay	1584.0	66.4	65.0	6.7	75.0	9.0	4.9	5.4
Philippines	1322.5	41.8	57.0	17.4	72.0	3.0	4.9	5.1
Rwanda	323.5	41.4	48.0	−9.4	16.0	34.0	6.9	5.3
Senegal	752.0	−2.1	43.0	5.4	6.0	4.0	5.6	4.4
Sierra Leone	485.5	11.5	34.0	8.7	7.0	8.0	5.6	5.0
Somalia	394.5	11.0	40.0	10.0	2.0	58.0	7.0	6.4
Sri Lanka	1108.5	17.8	64.0	25.0	75.0	10.0	2.0	3.0
Sudan	667.5	−4.5	42.0	10.5	13.0	19.0	5.9	5.7
Swaziland	911.0	45.2	46.1	16.5	**	**	5.7	3.9

Table 5.7. (Continued)

	Y (1)	ΔY (2)	E (3)	ΔE (4)	L (5)	ΔL (6)	R_1 (7)	R_2 (8)
Tanzania	318.0	24.7	45.0	14.3	10.0	69.0	6.0	6.0
Thailand	1378.5	59.4	58.0	18.2	68.0	18.0	5.4	4.1
Tunisia	1460.5	71.5	53.9	24.9	16.0	46.0	6.0	5.0
Uganda	304.5	−27.0	47.0	−3.0	25.0	27.0	7.0	7.0
Yemen	742.0	81.6	38.6	10.4	3.0	18.0	7.0	7.0
Zaire	291.0	−37.4	45.0	11.4	31.0	24.0	7.0	6.1
Zambia	752.5	−9.3	46.5	10.7	29.0	15.0	5.0	4.9
Zimbabwe	870.0	14.8	50.5	15.3	39.0	30.0	5.9	5.0

Notes: Y: GNP per capita (average of 1970 and 1980 values at 1980 international prices).
ΔY: percentage change in Y over the decade 1970–80.
E: life expectancy at birth in 1970.
ΔE: life expectancy improvement index = ((life expectancy at birth in 1980 − life expectancy in 1970) × 100)/(80 − life expectancy at birth in 1970).
L: adult literacy rate in 1960.
ΔL: adult literacy rate improvement index = (adult literacy rate in 1980 − adult literacy rate in 1960).
R_1: political rights index, averaged over 1973–9 (decreasing with increasing liberty).
R_2: civil rights index, averaged over 1973–9 (decreasing with increasing liberty).

Sources: World Bank (1983, 1989); Taylor and Jodice (1983: tables 2.1 and 2.2).

countries for 1970. I therefore present the figures for 1960 in column (5). The net increase in literacy rates over the period 1960–80 is then given in column (6). All countries recorded an improvement.[22]

Columns (7) and (8) present indices of political and civil rights in the sample of fifty-one countries, averaged over the period 1973–9. The 1970s were a decade of relative stability of political and civil rights indices. With few exceptions, countries that began the decade with appalling political systems remained appalling. Time averages therefore do not mislead.[23]

Table 5.8 consists of the fifteen (Spearman) rank correlation coefficients associated with the six columns of figures we are studying: (1) GNP per head and (2) its percentage growth; (3) improvements in life expectancy at birth and (4) in adult literacy rates; and the extent of (5) political and (6) civil rights enjoyed by citizens. The findings may be summarized as follows.

1. Political and civil rights are positively and significantly correlated with GNP per head and its growth, and with increases in expectancy of life at birth.[24]

---

[22] The coverage here is smaller. Figures for adult literacy rate are not available for a number of countries.
[23] Taylor and Jodice (1983: tables 2.1 and 2.2).
[24] The level of significance is 6.6% for growth in GNP per head. Each of the other figures is at a level of significance less than 5%.

Table 5.8. *Correlation matrix of Indicators of Improvements in Living Standards*

ΔY	0.5883*				
ΔE	0.6578*	0.4113*			
ΔL	−0.0308	0.0660	0.2710*		
R_1	0.5187*	0.2956*	0.2383*	−0.3769*	
R_2	0.4493*	0.2776*	0.2788*	−0.2806*	0.7290*
	Y	ΔY	ΔE	ΔL	R_1

Note: *indicates that a correlation is significant at a 5% level. The correlations are based on 51 observations, except for those for the changes in adult literacy, ΔL, which are based on 42 observations.

2. GNP per head and its growth were positively and significantly correlated, and they in turn were positively and significantly correlated with improvements in life expectancy at birth.
3. Political and civil rights are not the same; but they were strongly correlated.[25]
4. Increases in adult literacy were not related systematically to GNP per head. They are positively and significantly correlated with improvements in expectancy of life. But they were negatively and significantly correlated with political and civil liberties.

These findings suggest that literacy stands somewhat apart from other 'goods', that it doesn't appear to come in tandem with the other constituents and determinants of well-being. Moreover, regimes that had bad records in political and civil rights performed well in literacy. This goes counter to the prevailing wisdom that democracy and literacy go together. I have no explanation for the finding, but it is difficult to resist speculating on the matter. One possibility is that literacy was used by a number of states in the sample to promote the acceptance of established order. This would seem plausible in rural communities, where the classroom provides a relatively cheap means of assembling the young and propagating the wisdom and courage of the political leadership. Education in this case would be a vehicle for ensuring conformity, not critical thinking.

Intellectual fashions in the social sciences swing far too fast for comfort or safety. At the time the research reported here was conducted (Dasgupta, 1990a), the Soviet Union still existed and the Berlin Wall had not fallen. Democracy and civil liberties didn't convey the warm glow they do today almost universally among social commentators. Moreover, political economists were sceptical of cross-country statistics. I have colleagues who, in conversation at the time, argued against the morals I tried to draw from the statistical findings by pointing

[25] I found this to hold as well in Tables 5.3 and 5.6.

to the small number of countries where citizens had their political and civil liberties particularly restricted, and where growth in material well-being had been impressive.[26] But I felt then, and continue to feel now, that it is absurd to advise citizens to establish for themselves a one-party system of government, or to locate for themselves reliable and efficient dictators, on the grounds that there have been a few progressive autocracies. Good authoritarianism can't be willed by citizens, and bad authoritarian regimes are hard to dispose of. A central problem with authoritarianism is its lack of incentives for error correction.[27] A pluralist political system has a chance of providing political competition, a point at the centre of Schumpeter's celebrated defence of democracy. Of course, if civil order and general civic responsibility have broken down pretty much completely, as they have in so many parts of sub-Saharan Africa, there is no prescription to be obtained, one way or the other. Admittedly, too, had the findings gone the other way, there would have been something really urgent to discuss and to think through. As it is, I feel that the evidence from poor countries for the decade of the 1970s gives us no compelling reason to question the instrumental virtues of civil and political liberties.

Subsequent findings on the links between democracy and material progress, as measured by growth in GNP per head, have been more equivocal, I believe for two reasons. First, the samples haven't been restricted to poor countries, where, as we noted, citizens enjoy only low to middle-level democracy and civil liberties. For example, Barro (1996) studied a sample of 100 countries. He found that middle-level democracy is more favourable for growth in living standards than low-level democracy, which is consonant with the finding in Dasgupta (1990a) for poor countries. But Barro also found that middle-level democracy is more favourable for growth in the standard of living than high-level democracy. This is in effect a finding on a sub-sample consisting of moderately rich to rich countries.[28]

Secondly, the studies I have read interpreted indices of political and civil rights as cardinal numbers and conducted multivariate analysis. In the previous

---

[26] Examples that go against statistical findings are not counter-examples. Stern (1991: 429) muses: 'it would be hard to be confident from comparative history that democracy is good for growth. Has it been democracy that has propelled Hong Kong and Singapore?' What I am suggesting in the text is that that isn't the right way to frame the question.

[27] Sen (1999) has observed that famines haven't been experienced in democracies. In the text, however, I am alluding not to extreme events that the State should prevent from happening, but to run-of-the-mill duties, such as instituting and enforcing an efficient system of property rights and establishing primary health-care systems.

[28] Rodrik (2000) reports that economic fluctuations are less prevalent in democracies, the inference being that democracies encourage compromises to be made among political leaders holding extreme viewpoints. Compromises dampen movements from extreme to extreme and so dampen fluctuations.

chapter I argued that 'cardinality' is a questionable assumption. But if the indices of political and civil rights were renumbered in order-preserving ways, the regression results could be wildly different. Methodologically, the two sets of studies differ. The ones reported in Table 5.8 interpret political and civil rights as purely ordinal (a questionable assumption); moreover, the links between them and indices of economic progress are studied in terms of partial correlations. In contrast, subsequent studies by Barro (1996) and others have regarded political and civil rights indices as cardinal (also questionable), and they involve regression analysis.

Statistically, the record of poor countries during the past three decades has been much influenced by the experience of sub-Saharan Africa, a continent comprising many countries, whose citizens have mostly been treated abominably by governments and warlords and who have simultaneously (and relatedly) treated one another miserably. Ethnic strife has been endemic. The region has in consequence suffered from a decline in pretty much any economic index you care to name. Until recently, Singapore and South Korea were routinely identified by social scientists as countries with bad records on civil and political rights, but not much complaint was made against dictatorships in sub-Saharan Africa. Compared with most of sub-Saharan Africa, though, Singapore and South Korea have all along been near-paragons in their human rights records. Thus, it may well be that in the contemporary world, where the conception of a *public* State frequently doesn't exist, civil and political liberties are positively associated with economic performance among countries where the former are brazenly violated, but not among those where they are extensive. Neither theory nor evidence contradicts this possibility.

The correlations I am reporting don't imply causation. Each of the variables would in any case be 'endogenous' in any general political theory. It is possible that democracy is correlated with some omitted features that enhance growth in GNP per head, or life expectancy at birth. The omitted features could be the extent to which the rule of law is exercised and rights to property are secure. It remains a mostly unexplored question whether democratic practice helps bring about the rule of law and security to the right to property or whether the latter two foster democracy. Subject to these obvious qualifications, what the evidence seems to be telling us is that, statistically speaking, of the fifty-one poor countries on observation, those whose citizens enjoyed greater political and civil liberties during the decade of the 1970s also experienced greater improvements in life expectancy at birth and in real income per head. The argument that democracy is a luxury that poor countries cannot afford is belied by the data, such as they are. This seems to me to be eminently worth knowing.

5.7. GEOGRAPHY OF POVERTY TRAPS

The dependence of human well-being on the natural environment is central to the research concerns of geographers. Elementary textbooks on human geography invariably contain chapters explaining why people eat what they eat, wear what they wear, use the materials they use, and, more generally, live the way they live by reference to *where* they live. Economists, in contrast, have moved steadily away from viewing location as a determinant of the human experience.[29] Economic progress itself is seen to be a release from location's grip on life. We economists stress that investment and growth in knowledge have reduced transport costs over the centuries. We observe too the role of industrialization in ironing out the effects of geographical differences on societies, such as differences in climate, soil quality, distance from navigable water, and, concomitantly, local ecosystems. Modern growth theories dismiss geography as being no more than a negligible factor in economic progress.[30] The term 'globalization' is a signal that location *per se* doesn't matter.

In contrast, the ecologist Jared Diamond has argued that Eurasia's east–west orientation enabled agricultural innovations to diffuse over the millennia, contributing to the continent's economic success.[31] He noted too that, in contrast, the Americas and Africa are aligned in a north–south direction. Diamond argued that the latter land-masses were not propitious for the spread of agricultural practices, because they cover too many climatic zones. Diamond also estimated that Eurasia harboured a greater number of animal species suitable for domestication, which meant a greater range of food and animal power for the human population.

Diamond's time horizon was a lengthy 10,000 years, and his unit of analysis was in effect the continental land mass. If we look nearer our own time and use a finer geographical grid, the locations of economic success prove harder to explain. However, as Tables 5.1 and 5.4 show, the majority of the poorest countries today lie in the tropics. In contrast, most of the rich countries are in the temperate zones.[32] If it is hard to imagine that this is a happenstance, it is equally hard to prove that it isn't. In order to explain how this has come about if the period to be explained is only early modern (starting date round AD 1500),

---

[29] Landes (1998) begins his book with an account of the decline of the role of geography in the social sciences. He doesn't defend the decline: he notes it.

[30] See Aghion and Howitt (1996), Romer (1996), and Jones (1998). I discuss further deficiencies of modern growth theory in Part III.   [31] J. Diamond (1997).

[32] See World Bank (1998, Table 1). Jeffery Sachs and his collaborators have codified the extent to which climate can be used to interpret the distribution of per capita GNP in today's world. Sachs, Mellinger, and Gallup (2001) is a summary of their findings.

economic historians have turned elsewhere: to institutional differences.[33] The previous two sections of this chapter were exercises in that spirit.

But there is one environmental fact that can't be swept aside: many infectious diseases are endemic to the tropics and subtropical zones. Mosquitos and parasitic worms spend part of their lives outside the human host. That they are able to do so is itself an eco-climatic feature. Warm climate enables the pathogens to flourish over the entire year, making it that much more difficult to control the diseases.[34]

Today it is argued that, while such impediments make it harder for people in the tropics to improve their material conditions, they don't pose an insurmountable problem.[35] Economic theorists investigating the circumstances of long-run economic growth have gone further. They have argued that, if the institutions are sound, technological transfers should iron out current differences in well-being across countries. Applied growth economists have conducted statistical tests of the thesis that differences in well-being across countries, rich and poor, are in fact narrowing.

The believable results of the tests have been negative (e.g. Pritchett, 1997), a fact that ought not to cause surprise, for, in a literature running parallel to the one on the poverty of nations, a few economists had explored the theoretical possibility that poor people in poor countries are prey to *poverty traps*. The unit of analysis in their investigations was the household, possibly the village, but not much larger. Pathways to be explored first were the physiological links known to exist between undernutrition, infection, and the human capacity to work. The idea is simple enough: someone who is undernourished doesn't have the energy to produce enough to be able to afford adequate nourishment to have the energy to be able to produce enough . . . , and so on, as an equilibrium outcome. Synergism between infection and undernutrition was shown to exacerbate the pathway. In this account undernutrition and infection among the poor in poor countries are both a cause and an effect of acute poverty.[36]

It isn't enough to counter that someone caught in the trap could borrow and escape from it. The theory demonstrates that, if an economy as a whole is not wealthy and if a substantial proportion of people are assetless, the credit

---

[33] North and Thomas (1973), Rosenberg and Birdzell (1986), and Landes (1998). Colonialism has been used as an explanation too, but the colonial experience is itself a consequence of institutional differences among those that became colonial powers and those that became colonies.

[34] Sachs, Mellinger, and Gallup (2001: 66) observe wryly: 'Winter could be considered the world's most effective public health intervention.' J. Diamond (1997) added germs to his account of the failure of tropical Africa to progress materially.

[35] In contrast, the idea that nations could be locked into a vicious circle of poverty was much discussed in the postwar period. The seminal article on this is Rosenstein-Rodan (1943).

[36] See Dasgupta and Ray (1986, 1987), Dasgupta (1993, 1997, 1998a) and Fogel (1994) for elaborations of the thesis. Scrimshaw (1970) is the classic on the synergy between undernutrition and infection.

market will not be able to clear. Credit will be rationed in such a way that, while some of the assetless are able to borrow, not all can do so. Those who obtain credits are able to move ahead, even while those who are excluded are trapped in poverty. They remain undernourished. They are the economically disenfranchised.[37] Poverty traps in this account are due not to a single cause (e.g. credit rationing), but to a number of reinforcing causes, of which a lack of credit is one. Myrdal (1944), who to the best of my knowledge was the earliest social scientist to explore poverty traps within a country, called such positive feed-backs *cumulative causation*.

Undernourishment displays hysteresis. (Stunting and cognitive disability, caused by early malnutrition and infection, can't be erased in later life.) This makes the labour and credit markets discriminate even more against those who are poor. Hysteresis reinforces the trap. The theory I am sketching here identifies the assetless, or those who at best own only a few assets, as being vulnerable. Even a small misfortune (illness, death in the family) is able to tip them into the mire.[38] Hysteresis means that poverty perpetutates down the generations. (Undernourished women give birth to children who have suffered pre-natal nutritional insults and are under-weight at birth.) A parallel literature on education and skill formation in western industrial societies has identified similar forms of hysteresis, where failed families produce low-ability, poorly motivated students who do not succeed in school.[39]

In Part III we will note that the rural poor in poor countries depend hugely on their local natural-resource base. This fact was used to extend the theory of poverty traps to include high fertility and degradation of fragile local environments.[40] The theory identifies circumstances where high fertility, poverty and malnutrition, illiteracy, and degradation of local resource bases feed on one another, cumulatively, over extended periods of time. However, none is seen in the theory to be the prior cause of the others: over time each influences, and is in turn influenced by, the others. Thus, it makes no less sense to say that high birth rates cause poverty and illiteracy than to say that poverty and illiteracy cause birth rates to be high. The key moral to be drawn from this is that to pull people out of poverty traps requires outside help, since those caught in them are not necessarily able to escape by their own bootstraps. Expansion of international trade—more generally, economic policies that accelerate growth in GNP

---

[37] Dasgupta and Ray (1986). See Braverman and Stiglitz (1989) for a different mechanism by which credit is rationed.

[38] By 'assetless', I mean someone who has neither education nor material resources (e.g. productive land). See Dasgupta and Ray (1986, 1987).

[39] Heckman (2000), who offers a succinct account of the process, says (p. 5): 'Early learning begets later learning and early success breeds later success just as early failure breeds later failure.'

[40] Dasgupta and Mäler (1991, 1995) and Dasgupta (1992, 1993, 1995, 1998a, 2000b,c). For empirical studies of the connection, see Cleaver and Schreiber (1994) and Aggarwal, Netanyahu, and Romano (2001).

per head—cannot be relied upon to pull the poorest among the rural poor out of the mire. In Chapter 12 we will discover how certain patterns of economic growth can even be detrimental to the interests of those who depend directly on their natural resource base for their survival. The *character* of growth matters.[41] Good institutions, not only local and national, but increasingly international, would appear to be necessary if the poorest of the poor are to escape.

Working on poverty traps can have a mesmerizing effect. For a long while after I began to develop formal models of them, I could see nothing but 'traps' in social phenomena. It did not escape me, of course, that there are also benign pathways in the world we have come to know, those that smooth differences among people; but it was the processes that accentuate the differences in the prospects they face that came to dominate my perception of social life. Even now, I haven't quite shaken them off.

The study of poverty traps in poor countries is still in its infancy. Policy documents on hunger acknowledge their presence, but they don't use quantitative economic models of poverty traps to determine economic prescriptions. It is a case where a phenomenon (poverty traps) is widely acknowledged, but prescriptions are obtained on the basis of models that don't in fact harbour the phenomenon. Today, mortality statistics (e.g. life expectancy at birth) dominate assessments of regional performances in poor countries. International development organizations and economic commentators view 'human capital' exclusively through statistics on education. The irony is that it isn't difficult to remain alive even when malnourished and weak; today, reducing the infant mortality rate from 130 per thousand to 120 per thousand doesn't require much more than oral rehydration tablets and immunization programmes. The much harder task is to improve nutrition intake. This involves serious changes to the prevailing rules and engagements governing the allocation of food.

Nutrition is both a consumption and an investment good. However, for all its excellent research on the character of poverty and hunger, the World Bank's policy documents have made no essential use of the physiological links that are now known to connect a person's nutritional status to her productivity. Despite the attention that human capital formation receives today, there appears to be no estimate of the rate of return on investment in better nutrition among the poorest in poor countries. There is intellectual dissonance here.[42]

---

[41] See especially Ch. 9.

[42] See e.g. World Bank (2001). Even the excellent recent book on the quality of growth by Thomas *et al.* (2000) has nothing on nutritional status and productivity. I have grumbled about this dissonance earlier in Dasgupta (1991). For an account of the physiological links between nutrition and productivity and the way they can be used to build economic models, see Dasgupta (1993, 1997). Heckman (2000) raises a similar complaint against contemporary education policies in the USA, by noting the importance for skill formation of early preschool years when human ability and motivation are shaped by families and non-institutional environments, such as the character of one's peer group.

The general properties of pathways involving poverty traps bear a resemblance to processes that have been identified by mathematical ecologists in their investigations of the evolution of locally interacting non-linear systems, where spatial differences don't get ironed out.[43] Of course, in ecology a prime motivation is to explain spatial heterogeneity and modularity, for example to identify the niches that are occupied by different species and to explain why and in which ways their characters differ and how the 'clumps' are distributed. Development economists, in contrast, have avoided viewing malnutrition as a cumulatively caused phenomenon. They have instead spent time estimating how many are malnourished today.

The unit of analysis of growth economists is the nation, a vastly larger unit than the household or village. Growth economists have sought to construct theories where initial differences among nations get ironed out over time. It is, of course, possible that within nations household well-beings don't converge, even while the average well-beings in nations do. But this is hard to believe. One would imagine that, if poor countries harbour substantial proportions of their populations in poverty traps, their average prospects would be curtailed. The fact is that in their models modern growth theorists have not accommodated enough heterogeneity within countries to be in a position to explore the issue. It may have been a well intentioned hope that drove their research, but it is hard not to come away with the feeling that it has misled.[44]

5.8. THE HUMAN DEVELOPMENT INDEX: DEVELOPMENT AS WHAT?

Gross national product is known to be more a measure of aggregate economic activity than of social well-being. Nevertheless, it has become the touchstone by which economists, historians, politicians, journalists, and commentators judge the progress of nations. Its use has also been criticized on a regular basis by economists, historians, politicians, journalists, and commentators. While some historians construct time series on GNP and wages, others unearth mortality and anthropometric statistics.[45] Reflecting the same kind of professional schizophrenia, it is routine practice in economics to use growth in GNP per head as the criterion for judging the progress of nations, even while some in the profession complain that GNP is insensitive to the incidence of poverty, and yet others argue that the complaint is unwarranted because growth in GNP

---

[43] Levin (1999) is an excellent, non-technical account.

[44] In contrast, the links between inequality and growth have been much studied; see Aghion, Caroli, and Garcia-Peñalosa (1999).

[45] Pioneers among the others are Fogel *et al.* (1983) and Floud, Wachter, and Gregory (1990).

per head is typically accompanied by a reduction in poverty (the 'trickle down effect'). Despite these differences in perception, GNP has become so much a part of our collective consciousness that, when someone says 'growth' in an economic context, it is understood that they mean growth in GNP. People would seem to be comfortable adopting a stance of critical allegiance to the measure.

The United Nations Development Programme (UNDP) is an exception. Since its inception in 1990, UNDP's annual *Human Development Report* has engaged in a campaign against the use of GNP as an index of the quality of life within nations. In its stead, the organization has proposed what it calls a Human Development Index (HDI). Over the years, however, the *Report's* increasingly overexcited prose has served to detract from what HDI doesn't deliver—so much so that many who find GNP unduly limiting are drawn to HDI for comfort. It will pay to study the index here.[46]

Imagine that countries are assessed on the basis of M attributes (indexed by i), each of which is deemed to be desirable. There are N countries, indexed by j. Let X_{ij} (a cardinal number) be the index of attribute i in country j. UNDP defines country j's 'performance gap' in attribute i to be

$$I_{ij} = [\max_j\{X_{ij}\} - X_{ij}]/[\max_j\{X_{ij}\} - \min_j\{X_{ij}\}].$$

The average performance gap for country j is defined as

$$I_j = \Sigma_i[I_{ij}]/M.$$

UNDP's HDI for country j is then defined to be

$$(HDI)_j = (1 - I_j).$$

Notice that HDI_j is a number lying in the interval [0,1]. The higher is $(HDI)_j$, the better is j in terms of the M attributes. HDI is a simple and seemingly appealing index of the average quality of life in a country.

In practice, HDI has been based on three attributes: life expectancy at birth, GNP per head, and adult literacy. What aspects of life's quality do they reflect?

Life expectancy at birth is the expected length of life of a randomly chosen new-born if the prevailing age-specific mortality rates were to persist. The conditionality is stressed because it reminds us that life expectancy at birth is a constituent of *current* well-being. But life expectancy at birth this year says

---

[46] HDI has been refined in a number of ways. I ignore the refinements here because they don't meet the criticisms that I will make of the index.

nothing about life expectancy at birth next year. It could be that expectancy of life has been rising in recent years but is about to decline, owing to institutional decay and increased resource scarcity. Indicators of current well-being, such as life expectancy at birth, would be unable to signal this. The decline would catch everyone by (unpleasant) surprise.

GNP (in a closed economy) is the sum of aggregate consumption and gross investment. Consumption is a determinant of well-being. But what about investment? As current practice goes, national income statisticians measure investment in manufactured capital with the greatest care, but play fast and loose with economic theory when they come to the other forms of capital, namely, human capital, knowledge, and natural capital. For example, expenditure on school buildings and equipment is recorded as investment, but salaries of teachers are not. Similarly, the construction of scientific laboratories is regarded as investment, but scientists' salaries are not. Moreover, for the most part, natural capital is ignored, a form of capital I shall discuss in the remainder of the essay.

If these lacunae were removed, *net* investment in the overall productive base would measure the social worth of the flow of additional consumption that would become available over time if the investment were made (Appendix, Proposition 7). By 'net' I mean net of depreciation of assets. It is the 'gross' bit that makes GNP wholly unsuitable as a measure of intertemporal well-being, no matter how carefully and extensively one measures it. GNP is a component of neither current well-being nor future well-being. For this reason, GNP per head was not included in the construction of our Borda index of the current quality of life.[47]

Of the three components of the HDI, it is adult literacy that reflects something about future possibilities. Typically, it is defined as the proportion of the adult population that are literate. In this context, adults are frequently defined as people aged 15 or over. Adult literacy is a stock, not a flow. Even though crude, it is measure of human capital.[48] Like other forms of capital, it depreciates. When people die, they take their literacy with them. A country has to invest in it continually to prevent the stock from declining.

Literacy is a constituent and a determinant of well-being. The theory of human capital focuses on literacy's role as a determinant. UNDP (1994) stresses that it is also a constituent. Literacy is a component of both current well-being and well-being through time.

As a measure of social well-being, the HDI is therefore three-thirds current and one-third intertemporal. But because adult literacy is only one type of

---

[47] In Ch. 9 and the Appendix, I show that net national product (NNP) is also not a measure of social well-being.

[48] On this see Ch. 9.

capital asset, the one-third isn't adequate for reflecting intertemporal concerns. If we are interested in both the present and future, neither GNP per head nor the HDI is satisfactory, because neither measure is derivable from a coherent view of human well-being. In Part III we identify a measure that *is* implied by ethical thought.

PART III

MEASURING WELL-BEING
OVER TIME

Prologue

In the following four chapters I build on the ideas advanced in Part II to construct measures of well-being through time and across generations. The passage of time is not the same as the advance of generations. An individual's lifetime well-being is a construct of the flow of current well-being she experiences, while intergenerational well-being is a construct of the lifetime well-beings of all who appear on the scene. It is doubtful that the two constructs have the same functional form. On the other hand, I know of no evidence that suggests we would be way off the mark in assuming they do have the same form. As a matter of practical ethics, it helps enormously to approximate by not distinguishing the functional form of someone's well-being through time from that of intergenerational well-being. In what follows, I take this short-cut.

The chapters in Parts III and IV assume that the demographic profile over time is given. The resource allocation problems we study there are those that arise when we try to strike a balance between the well-being of present and future generations, keeping in mind that there is a corresponding set of allocation problems arising from the need to strike a balance in every person's lifetime well-being. Parfit (1982) christened allocation problems involving the same demographic profile 'Same Numbers Problems'. The thought is not that population size doesn't change, but that the policies being addressed are those that have a negligible effect on reproductive behaviour. Part III is about *valuation* problems involving Same Numbers. Part IV will be about *evaluation* problems involving Same Numbers.

Chapter 6 offers a framework for developing the notion of intergenerational well-being, or 'social well-being' for short. Chapters 7–9 use the framework to construct a usable index of social well-being. The key concept is that of an economy's productive base, which consists of the determinants of well-being. The base itself comprises the economy's institutions and its capital assets, the latter including not only public knowledge and manufactured capital, but also human capital and the natural environment. Institutions are characterized by the property rights they harbour and the management structure they adopt. Three systems of rights to natural resources are studied in Chapter 7: private, communal, and state. Institutional failures are shown to be the cause of inefficiencies and inequities, both in momentary allocations of resources and in the intergenerational transfer of resources. It is argued that in the world we have come to know there is a bias in the use of the natural environment, in that use at any moment is excessive, not insufficient. Since observed prices frequently do not reflect the social worth of natural resources, use should be made of notional prices, called *accounting prices*. Practical problems of estimating accounting prices are discussed in Chapter 8. Their resolution requires attention to ecological matters, such as the role of biodiversity in creating substitution possibilities among various kinds of natural resources. The chapter also summarizes methods for estimating the accounting prices of environmental resources.

Chapter 9 develops the concept of sustainable development and shows how it is related to the maintenance of social well-being through time. It is shown that wealth, estimated in terms of accounting prices, serves admirably as an index of well-being over time and across generations. A country's wealth measures the social worth of its capital assets. The notion of wealth developed in this essay is a comprehensive one, including in it the social worth of manufactured and human capital, public knowledge, and natural capital. It is argued in Chapter 9 (and proved in the Appendix) that, adjusting for demographic differences and differences in the structure of accounting prices arising from differences in their institutional structures, wealth can be used to compare social well-being among communities and nations. It is argued too (and proved in the Appendix) that, correcting for demographic differences, for changes in institutional structure, and for the knowledge that is acquired freely from elsewhere, changes in wealth over time reflect changes in social well-being over time. Sustainable development is interpreted as the maintenance of wealth.

Given that movements in wealth over time measure movements in social well-being, the object of study is then shown to be *genuine investment*, which measures changes in wealth. Genuine investment is the social worth of net changes in an economy's capital assets. It is a comprehensive notion, including as it does the social worth of net changes in manufactured and human capital, public knowledge, and natural capital. Thus, ensuring that social well-being is sustainable involves taking care that the economy's assets are managed well.

In the background of Parts III and IV is a puzzle created by the conflicting intuitions that have been derived from two different empirical perspectives concerning the question of whether the character of contemporary economic development is sustainable.[1] On the one hand, if we look at specific resources and services (e.g. fresh water, ecosystem services, and the atmosphere as a carbon sink), there is convincing evidence that the current rates of utilization are unsustainable.[2] On the other hand, if we look at historical trends in the prices

---

[1] For a good illustration of the conflicting intuitions, see the debate between Norman Myers and the late Julian Simon in Myers and Simon (1994).

[2] See e.g. Vitousek *et al.* (1986, 1997) and Postel, Daily, and Ehrlich (1996).

of marketed resources or the recorded growth in GNP per capita in countries that are currently rich, resource scarcities would not appear yet to have bitten.[3] The focus on genuine investment helps to resolve the conflict.[4]

In Chapter 9 the theory is also put to work on contemporary data from the poorest countries in the world. Movements in the wealth of nations present a vastly different picture from the one gleaned from the two most popular measures of social well-being, namely, gross national product per head and the United Nations Development Programme's Human Development Index. The evidence therefore shows that a substantial reassessment of the postwar development experience among poor countries is now needed if sustainable development is to be anything more than a slogan at national and international conferences. As development economics is now over fifty years old, this is a sad conclusion to reach.

[3] See e.g. Barnett and Morse (1963) and Simon (1990).
[4] Arrow, Dasgupta, Goulder *et al.* (2003) contains a summary of this line of thinking.

6

Intergenerational Well-Being

6.1. THE RAMSEY FORMULATION

How should well-being over time and across generations be measured? In studying this question we confine ourselves to the socio-economic component of well-being, the implicit assumption being that civil and political liberties are given. This isn't a good assumption, but there's not much I can do about it. There is no adequate theory relating economics to political science and back again, no workable model in which future production and consumption possibilities at one end, and civil and political liberties at the other, are determined jointly. So, with hands tied behind the proverbial back, I consider economic possibilities through time, but not civil and political liberties. The apparatus developed below can certainly accommodate the influence of political and civic institutions on economic possibilities; what it leaves one guessing is their mutual interaction.[1]

Intergenerational welfare economics was established in Ramsey (1928), a classic that reads as though it could have been written last week. The problem Ramsey formulated was a particular one: of its total output, how much should a nation save for the future? Ramsey interpreted his theory along the lines of Classical Utilitarianism. (For example, he used the term 'enjoyment' to refer to what I have been calling well-being.) Nevertheless, the framework he developed for analysing the problem of optimum saving has subsequently been found to have wide applicability, regarding both interpretation and issues—so wide, in fact, that within modern economics there is no rival framework for studying the intergenerational distribution of benefits and burdens. This chapter is about Ramsey's theory and its interpretive extensions. I make use of his formulation without having any necessary commitment to Classical Utilitarianism.

Let t denote date. For notational ease, it will help us in this chapter to interpret the period between adjacent dates as the length of a generation. One can imagine that at the end of each period the existing generation is replaced entirely by its

---

[1] Persson and Tabellini (2000) is a masterly treatise on the influence of political arrangements on economic outcomes.

successor. This isn't good demography, but it turns out not to matter. Every ethical consideration that emerges in this model makes an appearance also in worlds where demography is modelled better. Moreover, better models of demography would not raise any ethical issue that doesn't appear here.[2]

Population size is assumed to be constant and the future is taken to be indefinitely long. Later I relax these assumptions. I first consider a deterministic world (but see Section 6.5). We imagine that each generation's well-being (U) depends on the flow of some generalized consumption, which I call C. We imagine, first of all, that the determinants of a person's well-being have been aggregated. This aggregate reflects the person's generalized consumption level. Next, we use distributional weights to aggregate the generalized consumption of all members of a generation. If the demonstration effect matters (Section 3.4), the distributional weights take the effect into account in such a way as to purge it from our account of intergenerational well-being. This yields C. It is an aggregate of the determinants of well-being of the generation. C includes food, clothing, shelter, health care, serenity, leisure activities, legal aid, and various types of public goods (including civil and political liberties and direct amenities from the natural environment). The various components are weighted so as to reflect their distribution among people of each generation.

The procedure I have just sketched involves a heroic aggregation exercise. It hides matters of importance. In Section A.14 of the Appendix we will see how the analysis can be conducted in a disaggregated manner. As population is assumed to be constant, I shall ignore its size and regard a generation's aggregate consumption as the determinant of that generation's well-being. So, C does all the work in representing the determinants of *intra*generational well-being. The move makes for expositional ease. It enables me to concentrate on intergenerational matters.

Denote generation t's well-being as $U(C_t)$. It is assumed that U is an increasing function of C, but that it increases at a diminishing rate. *Intergenerational well-being*, or *social well-being* for short, is taken to be the sum of each generation's well-being.[3]

---

[2] Later we will regard the unit of time to be a year, and later still we will regard time to be a continuous variable. These are mere tactical moves, to keep in line with accounting conventions and to exploit mathematical conveniences.

[3] It is an elegant feature of Ramsey's formulation that he avoided specifying a subsistence rate. For technical reasons, he assumed that U has a least upper bound (lub), but that the lub is beyond reach no matter how high is consumption. He called the lub 'bliss'! (See Ch. *14.) U is assumed not to depend explicitly on time. This looks odd until we ask in which ways it is likely to change. The fact is, we don't know. Certain obvious thoughts—for example that the baskets of consumption goods and services that are needed today to attain a given level of well-being differ from those needed to attain the same level of well-being a hundred years ago—offer little reason for thinking that U depends explicitly on time. Admittedly, today's necessities are different from necessities a hundred years ago. But the change could have come about because of shifts in the technology of consumption (e.g. if all others communicate over the telephone, one loses out in not using

Let $(C_t, C_{t+1}, \dots)$ be a *consumption stream*, which is a sequence of aggregate consumption from t onward. Denoting social well-being at t by V_t, Ramsey's theory has it that

$$V_t = U(C_t) + U(C_{t+1}) + \cdots,$$

which I write succinctly as[4]

$$V_t = \sum_{t}^{\infty} U(C_\tau), \qquad \text{for } t \geq 0. \tag{6.1}$$

The present is taken to be $t = 0$. Ramsey's problem was to identify, within the set of feasible consumption streams, the one that maximizes V_0. The account in its entirety is as follows.

Generation 0 has inherited from its predecessors a wide range of capital assets, including natural resources and knowledge. Given this inheritance, the generation is able to select from a set of feasible consumption streams. Call this feasible set Ξ_0. Imagine now that $(\hat{C}_0, \hat{C}_1, \dots, \hat{C}_t, \dots)$ is that member of Ξ_0 which maximizes V_0. Ramsey's theory calls upon generation 0 to consume $\hat{C}_0$. This simultaneously leads to an investment decision, which in turn determines the technological possibilities that are open to generation 1. Denote the feasible set of consumption streams for generation 1 to be Ξ_1. A typical member of Ξ_1 can be written as $(C_1, C_2, \dots, C_t, \dots)$. The problem facing generation 1 would be to identify that element of Ξ_1 that maximizes V_1. It is an interesting and important feature of expression (6.1) that generation 1 would identify the optimum consumption stream to be $(\hat{C}_1, \hat{C}_2, \dots, \hat{C}_t, \dots)$. Plainly, then, generation 1 would consume $\hat{C}_1$, invest accordingly, and pass on the optimum stocks of capital assets to generation 2. And so on. The ethical viewpoints of the succeeding generations are congruent with one another. Each generation chooses the policy it deems optimum, aware that succeeding generations will choose in accordance with what it had planned for them.

Ramsey's assumption that the future is infinite feels odd. We know that the world will cease to exist at some date in the future. So it would seem realistic to stipulate a finite horizon, say T periods, where the chosen T is large. The problem is that, no matter how large T is, there is some chance that the world will survive beyond T. An alternative to Ramsey suggests itself: specify the capital stocks that are to remain at T for generations still to appear, and interpret social well-being to be the T-period sum of current well-beings and the size of the capital base remaining at T.

---

the telephone). They could also be due to the demonstration effect. The simplest hypothesis to maintain is that U is not an explicit function of time.

[4] $\sum_{t}^{\infty}$ is the summation sign, from t to infinity. Compare (6.1) with (1.2) in Ch. 1.

There is a problem even with this formulation. If T and the capital base that remains at T are chosen arbitrarily, the consumption stream deemed the best could be sensitive to the choice. This means that T and the capital stocks at T should not be chosen arbitrarily, but should be based on our understanding of what lies beyond T (for example, the needs of those who may appear after T). But then, why not include their claims in the planning exercise to begin with; why truncate the future into two bits? The route Ramsey followed, of regarding the future to be indefinitely long, is logically unavoidable; for, although we know that the world will not exist for ever, we don't know when it will cease to exist.[5]

I want to leave aside for the moment the question whether V_t is well defined. (The infinite sum may not, after all, exist.) The point to which I want to draw attention is that in Ramsey's formulation future values of U are *undiscounted*. (Formally, V_t is symmetric in its arguments.) More than any other feature of his theory, it is this that has provoked debate among economists and philosophers. Ramsey himself wrote (1928: 261) that to discount later Us in comparison with earlier ones is 'ethically indefensible and arises merely from the weakness of the imagination.' Harrod (1948: 40) followed suit by calling the practice a 'polite expression for rapacity and the conquest of reason by passion.'[6]

To some economists Ramsey's stricture reads like a Sunday pronouncement. Solow (1974a: 9) expressed this feeling when he wrote: 'In solemn conclave assembled, so to speak, we ought to act as if the [discount rate on future well-beings] were zero.' But there is a deeper problem with the stance. In such complex exercises as those involving the use of resources over a very long time horizon, it is unsafe to regard any ethical judgement as sacrosanct. This is because one can never know in advance what it may run up against. A more judicious tactic than Ramsey's would be to play off one set of ethical assumptions against another in non-implausible worlds, see what their implications are for the distribution of well-being across generations, and then appeal to our intuitive senses before arguing over policy.

Consider, for example, the following ethical tension.

A: Low rates of consumption by generations sufficiently far into the future would not be seen to be a bad thing by the current generation if future well-beings were discounted at a positive rate. This suggests we should follow Ramsey in not discounting future well-beings.

---

[5] Chakravarty (1969) is a fine exploration of both finite- and infinite-horizon formulations of intergenerational well-being. In Sect. 6.4 we will see how uncertainty in the date of extinction can be built into the formulation.

[6] Their position has been re-examined and endorsed by a number of modern philosophers; see Feinberg (1980), Parfit (1984), Goodin (1986), and Broome (1992).

B: As there are to be a lot of future generations in a world with an indefinite future, not to discount future well-beings could mean that the present generation would be required to do too much for the future; that is, they would have to save at too high a rate. This suggests we should abandon Ramsey and discount future well-beings at a positive rate.

The force of each consideration has been demonstrated in the economics literature. For example, it has been shown that in an economy with exhaustible resources and 'low' productive potentials, optimum consumption declines to zero in the long run if the future is discounted at a positive rate, no matter how low the chosen rate (Dasgupta and Heal, 1974), but increases indefinitely if we follow Ramsey (Solow, 1974b).[7] This finding was the substance of Solow's remark (1974a) that, in the economics of exhaustible resources, whether future well-beings are discounted can be a matter of considerable moment. In recent years, environmental and resource economists writing on sustainable development have taken this possibility as their starting point.[8]

On the other hand, it has been observed that Ramsey's ethical theory, when applied to the model economy he studied in his paper, can recommend that every generation save at a very high rate. For classroom parametrizations, the optimum saving rate has been calculated to be in excess of 60 per cent of gross national product.[9] In a poor country such a figure would be unacceptably high, requiring the present generation to sacrifice beyond the call of duty. The real problem is that we don't know in advance how to formulate the problem of intergenerational saving. The issues are far too complex. Unaided intuition is suspect. However, another way to interpret Ramsey's finding would be to acknowledge that we don't know the correct way to formulate the ethics of intergenerational saving, but that Ramsey's formulation is *a priori* plausible. If, on putting it through its paces in plausible economic models, it is found to prescribe acts that are too demanding for the current generation, the formulation ought to be rejected on grounds that it doesn't capture the right balance between the claims of the present generation and those of future ones. The insight one obtains from quantitative exercises is that the long-run features of optimum consumption policies depend on the relative magnitudes of the rate at which future well-beings are discounted and the long-term productivity of capital assets.

This said, it is not clear why philosophers and economists have interpreted intergenerational equity almost exclusively in terms of the rate at which the

---

[7] By 'discounting the future', I mean the same thing as 'discounting future well-beings'.

[8] We study the concept of sustainable development in Ch. 9. I shall also argue subsequently that the possibility envisaged in consideration A above has been much exaggerated in the literature.

[9] In the Appendix (Sect. A.2) I illustrate this possibility.

future is discounted.[10] The literature on the measurement of intragenerational inequality has revealed that a more sensitive way to reflect equity considerations would be to apply a transformation to U so as to make social well-being more sensitive to distributive issues.[11] Classical Utilitarianism would not permit this move, but many other theories do. So, one way to make the Ramsey framework more equity-conscious without introducing time discounting is to have V_t assume the form

$$V_t = \sum_{t}^{\infty} G(U(C_\tau)), \qquad \text{for } t \geq 0, \tag{6.2}$$

where G makes the resulting V_t in (6.2) more equity-conscious.[12]

6.2. DISCOUNTING THE FUTURE

It transpires though that even this reformulation can't be guaranteed to avoid the problem raised by consideration B. In a remarkable series of articles, Koopmans (1960, 1965, 1967, 1972) showed that B can overwhelm the Ramsey–Harrod stricture and render even expression (6.2) incoherent.[13] The stricture can imply that there is no best policy; that, no matter how high is the rate of saving, saving a bit more would be better. To see how and why, imagine a world where goods are completely perishable. Consider an economic programme where consumption is the same at every date. Now imagine that an investment opportunity presents itself in which, if the present generation were to forgo a unit of consumption, a perpetual streams of additional consumption μ (>0) would be generated.[14] Suppose social well-being is represented by expression (6.2). Then, no matter how small μ is, future generations, taken together, would experience an infinite increase in well-being as a consequence of the investment. (μ 'multiplied' by infinity is infinity.) So, for any level of consumption, no matter how low, a further reduction in consumption (possibly short of a reduction that brings consumption down to zero) would be desirable. Most people would regard this as unacceptable.

---

[10] Parfit (1984) and Broome (1992) are one set of examples, the essays in Portney and Weyant (1999) are another.

[11] Formally, the idea is to apply a concave transformation to U. See Kolm (1969), Atkinson (1970), and Dasgupta, Sen and Starrett (1973).

[12] In this formulation, the greater is the curvature of G, the more does intergenerational equity matter. This is demonstrated in the context of a formal economic model in Dasgupta and Heal (1979: ch. 10). It is demonstrated also in the Appendix (Sect. A.13).

[13] For a simple account of Koopmans's theory, see Dasgupta and Heal (1979: ch. 9). The exposition that follows in the text is taken from an even simpler account in Arrow (1999).

[14] This means that the rate of return on investment is μ.

In consequence of this kind of paradox, Koopmans adopted a different research tactic from Ramsey. Social well-being in Ramsey's theory is the sum of utilities (equation (6.1)). The Ramsey ordering of consumption streams is derived from the sum of utilities. In contrast, the primitive concept in Koopmans's theory is that of an ordering of consumption streams.[15] Koopmans's tactic was to impose ethical conditions on such orderings and to determine, if possible, their numerical representations.[16] Social well-being in Koopmans's theory is a numerical representation of an ordering of consumption streams.

Koopmans (1960, 1972), and in a related manner P. A. Diamond (1965), showed that, if an ordering over well-being streams satisfies two minimal ethical properties, it must involve positive discounting.[17] Koopmans also identified a set of additional ethical conditions on consumption streams which imply that their numerical representations are of the form

$$V_t = \sum_t^\infty \beta^{(\tau-t)} U(C_\tau), \quad \text{for } t \geq 0, \quad \text{where } \beta \equiv \frac{1}{(1+\delta)}, \quad \text{with } \delta > 0.$$

(6.3)

In (6.3) U is interpretable as current well-being; $\beta^{(\tau-t)}$ is the discount factor and δ the corresponding discount rate; δ is often called the 'rate of pure time preference'.[18]

While (6.3) looks like Classical Utilitarianism with discounting, it is not. U doesn't necessarily have the interpretation of utility, in the sense of the Classical Utilitarians. Koopmans's axioms lend themselves to a broader range of interpretations, which is an attraction.

It is an agreeable feature of Koopmans's theory that, as in Ramsey's theory, the ethical viewpoints of the succeeding generations are congruent with one another. Each generation chooses that policy it deems optimum, aware that succeeding generations will choose in accordance with what it had planned for them.

---

[15] The formal definition of an ordering was provided in Ch. 1 (Sect. 1.6).

[16] The formal definition of a numerical representation of orderings was given in Ch. 1 (Sect. 1.6.).

[17] The two properties are *continuity* and *Paretianism*. An ordering is said to be continuous if, in an appropriate mathematical sense, consumption streams that don't differ much are close to one another in the ordering. For an ordering to be Paretian, I mean that a given consumption programme is judged to be better than another if at each date current well-being is no less along the former than along the latter, and if there is at least one date at which it is greater. See Dasgupta and Heal (1979: ch.9) for an exposition of the Koopmans–Diamond result.

[18] In some formulations of intergenerational well-being, δ is taken to be probability of extinction in any period, conditional on humankind surviving until that period; see Mirrlees (1967). I return to this interpretation in Sect. 6.6.

6.3. PUBLIC AND PRIVATE ETHICS

The problem with expression (6.3) is that it is vulnerable to consideration A. It is easy to construct possible worlds where Koopmans's ethical axioms regard as best those consumption streams that decline to zero. So, then, what is to be done?

One possible way out of the dilemma posed by considerations A and B is for the present generation to award equal weight to the well-beings of every future generation, but to award its own well-being a higher weight than that of any future generation. Arrow (1999) has explored this route by appealing to agent-relative ethics. Both Kantian ethics and Classical Utilitarianism regard *impartiality* as a defining character of moral reasoning. In contrast, agent-relative ethics sees both the 'universal other' and the 'self' as creating obligations on an agent. In the intergenerational context, the 'agent' in each generation is that generation itself. So Arrow takes V_t to be of the form

$$V_t = U(C_t) + a \left[\sum_{t+1}^{\infty} U(C_\tau) \right], \qquad \text{where } 0 < a < 1. \tag{6.4}$$

In words, generation t's valuation of social well-being is a weighted sum of its own well-being and the sum of the well-beings of all future generations, with less weight awarded to the latter.[19]

There is an awkwardness in social values embodied in expression (6.4). It can be shown that the ethical viewpoints of succeeding generations are incongruent with one another. A consumption stream deemed best by one generation would be less than best by the generation that follows. The latter generation would therefore have no incentive to implement what its predecessor had regarded to be the most worthy economic programme. Their ethical viewpoints being incongruent with one another, the generations would be involved in a *game*. How should they play the game?

Generations separated greatly in time are incapable of making binding agreements. Consider the current generation. Since it cannot enforce its choice on future generations, it would be unwise to set in motion the consumption stream it deems optimal. The argument generalizes to all generations. They would all realize though that the best any of them can do is to anticipate correctly the rates at which succeeding generations will save and then choose its own consumption level in the light of its conception of intergenerational well-being. If this strategy were followed by all, the resulting consumption stream would

---

[19] Agent-relative ethics in the intergenerational context was introduced in a classic paper by Phelps and Pollak (1968). Expression (6.4) is a special case of the Phelps–Pollak formulation.

be an equilibrium: no generation would have an incentive to deviate unilaterally from it. Such a consumption stream is called a *Nash equilibrium*. The rational thing for each generation to do would be to identify Nash equilibrium consumption rules and act upon them.

But there is a prior problem with expression (6.4). It is questionable whether, as a piece of *ethics*, (6.4) is a persuasive formulation of social well-being. Agent-relative ethics is appealing at the personal level; to many it would be even compelling at that level. Such ethics explain the basis of rules concerning what we, as individuals, should be expected to do and what type of constraints should limit the government's sphere of activities. We can't be expected to spend our time constantly seeking to do good to others, nor should the body collective be permitted to busy itself by constantly peering into our personal sphere. To act in such a way would not only be hopelessly inefficient, but would also devalue our 'selves'. This it would do by undermining our personal projects and purposes.[20]

In trying to construct a measure of social well-being, we are engaged in an exercise in the public sphere. Arrow's agent is, after all, a generation, and we are talking here of public ethics. It can be argued that, when measuring its own well-being, Arrow's agent should purge from consideration the interests of the generations that are to follow. In the language we have been using here, generation t's public business ought to be to estimate its current well-being $(U(C_t))$ and that of future generations. Public impartiality then demands that the ethical ordering over consumption streams should be the same no matter which generation peers into the future. Even though there is a tension between them regarding considerations A and B, the formulations of Ramsey and Koopmans fulfil the requirement of this particular form of intergenerational impartiality.

To be sure, parents care about their children. Considerate parents take into account the well-being of their children when deciding how much to save. If, in addition, they are thoughtful parents, they know that the well-being of their children will depend upon the well-being of their grandchildren; that the well-being of their grandchildren will in turn depend upon the well-being of their great grandchildren, and so on, down the generations. There is a natural recursion along each family line. Thoughtful parents can be expected to take account of the interests of their distant descendants indirectly, even if they are directly interested only in their own children.

This however involves the private concerns of people, as parents. It accommodates agent-relative concerns on the part of people as parents. Just institutions are those that enable such concerns to be acted upon by the individuals themselves. However, it is also the business of just institutions to mediate among different generations, in case private acts lead to outcomes that are less than

---

[20] Williams (1976, 1985) has developed this line of argument in his critique of Kantian ethics.

publicly just (owing to myopia, imperfect institutions, or whatever). But in order for just institutions to function justly, a criterion for social well-being is needed. Even if the prevailing institutions are unjust, as they are in Kakotopia, the evaluation of policy reforms ought to be founded on a criterion based on justice.

Imagine that we adopted Koopmans's formulation of intergenerational well-being (equation (6.3)), applied it to a deterministic model of production and consumption possibilities, and discovered that, if the rate of pure time preference (δ) is positive, optimum consumption will decline to zero in the long run, no matter how small δ is. Suppose it is also discovered that, if δ is sufficiently small—but not zero—the decline in consumption will begin only in the distant future: the smaller is δ, the farther is the date at which consumption will begin to decline.[21] Should Koopmans's formulation be rejected on the ground that it recommends an eventual decline in consumption?

Many would indeed reject it on that very ground.[22] But I have never understood why. Models of a deterministic world with an infinite horizon are mathematical artefacts. They are meant to train our intuitions about economic possibilities in a world with a long, but finite, horizon, when we are loath to specify the termination date, and are also loath to acknowledge that it is an uncertain date. The models must not be taken literally, because Earth will not last for ever. We cannot, of course, know now when Earth will cease to exist, but we do know that it will cease to exist *by* some date, say 10^{12} years. (That's 1 trillion years; and Earth is a mere 4 billion years old.) Suppose, for example, that we were to set δ equal to 10^{-n} per year and were to choose n sufficiently large, so that optimum consumption in the kind of deterministic model I have been considering would have a turning point in, say, year 10^{30} (that's a billion billion trillion years). Should we care that consumption in the model will decline from year 10^{30}? I know of no reason why we should. On the contrary, justice would be ill-served if all generations were asked to save for a vacuous posterity. As an articulation of the concept of intergenerational well-being, Koopmans's theory is compelling. Since Ramsey's formulation, (6.1), is an extreme special case of that of Koopmans, I shall, for brevity, refer to (6.3) as the Ramsey–Koopmans formulation of intergenerational well-being.

6.4. POPULATION GROWTH

Since Earth is finite, changes in the size of population when averaged over time will be zero over the very long run. The base case we have been considering so

---

[21] This has been shown to be the case in simple economic models involving exhaustible resources. See Dasgupta and Heal (1979: ch. 10).   [22] For example, Heal (1998). Earlier, I called it consideration A.

far, that population size remains constant, is thus valid when the reckoning is the very long run. But for the not-so-very long run, population can be expected to change. How should the notion of intergenerational well-being be formulated when population size changes over time?

Two alternatives have been much discussed in the literature. Both reduce to the Ramsey–Koopmans formulation if population is constant. After presenting them I introduce a third formulation, which will be shown to be the natural one to use when we come in Chapter 9 to formulate the concept to sustainable development. It too reduces to the Ramsey–Koopmans formulation if population is constant.

One alternative is to regard the well-being of a generation to be the per capita well-being of that generation (with no allowance for the numbers involved) and sum the per capita well-beings of all generations, possibly using a discount rate. To formalize, let y_t be the index of aggregate consumption per head at t, and let $U(y_t)$ denote well-being per head of generation t. We then have[24]

$$V_t = \sum_t^\infty U(y_\tau)\beta^{(\tau-t)}, \quad \text{for } t \geq 0, \qquad \text{where } \beta \equiv \frac{1}{(1+\delta)}, \quad \text{and } \delta \geq 0.$$

$$(6.5)$$

The other view is to interpret social well-being as the sum of the discounted flow of each generation's well-being. Specifically, if N_t is the size of generation t, and y_{it} the consumption level of person i of generation t, then[25]

$$V_t = \sum_t^\infty \left[\sum_{i=1}^{N\tau} U(y_{i\tau}) \right] \beta^{(\tau-t)}, \qquad \text{for } t \geq 0,$$

$$\text{where } \beta \equiv \frac{1}{(1+\delta)}, \qquad \text{and } \delta \geq 0.$$

$$(6.6)$$

Non-additive forms of V_t suggest themselves, but yield no insights beyond those to be gained from the Ramsey–Koopmans theory. So I focus on (6.5) and (6.6) and compare their merits.

Expression (6.6) regards people, not generations, to be the subject. In contrast, expression (6.5) regards generations, not people, to be the subject. To see in which ways their recommendations differ, imagine an economy in Utopia consisting of two islands, with populations $\tilde{N}$ and $\hat{N}$. People in Utopia are identical. A person's well-being is denoted by U, which increases with consumption, but at a diminishing rate. There is a fixed amount of consumption services, $\bar{C}$, that

[23] See Cass (1965) and Koopmans (1965).
[24] See Meade (1955), Mirrless (1967), and Arrow and Kurz (1970).

the government has to distribute.[25] Let $\tilde{C}$ and $\hat{C}$ be the amounts distributed to the two islands. As the economy is in Utopia, it is to be expected that, no matter how much is awarded to each island, the distribution of consumption *within* each will be equal. The economy is timeless.

If numbers count, then analogous to (6.6), social well-being would be $[\tilde{N}U(\tilde{C}/\tilde{N}) + \hat{N}U(\hat{C}/\hat{N})]$ and the government would distribute in such a way that consumption is equalized among all citizens.[26] This is obviously the right allocation, because geographical differences are an artefact for the problem in hand. On the other hand, if numbers don't count, so that social well-being is taken to be $[U(\tilde{C}/\tilde{N}) + U(\hat{C}/\hat{N})]$, the Utopian government would distribute less to each person in the more populous island.[27] Analogously, the use of (6.5) discriminates against more numerous generations. This simply cannot be right. Of (6.5) and (6.6), the latter reflects the notion of intergenerational well-being more adequately.

Expression (6.6) measures *total* well-being. It is of the same functional form as Classical Utilitarianism. But there is yet another way to formulate the concept of intergenerational well-being: it reflects the *average* well-being of all who are to appear on the scene. This has an attractive ethical basis: choice under uncertainty.

The idea is to regard an economy at t to be a different economy from that same economy at $t+1$. Now suppose you were asked which of the two economies you would choose to inhabit if you did not know which person's shoes you would occupy in either, but attributed 'equi-probability' to each position.[28] Imagine next that in this thought experiment your choice is based on your *expected well-being* in the two economies. Expected well-being in the economy commencing at t is

$$V_t = \left\{ \sum_t^\infty \left[\sum_{i=1}^{N\tau} U(y_{i\tau}) \right] \beta^{(\tau-t)} \right\} \bigg/ \left\{ \sum_t^\infty N_\tau \beta^{(\tau-t)} \right\}, \qquad \text{for } t \geq 0,$$

$$(6.7)$$

where $\beta \equiv 1/(1+\delta)$, and $\delta \geq 0$.[29]

---

[25] The example is taken from Meade (1955: 87–9) and Arrow and Kurz (1970: 13–14).

[26] To prove this, simply maximize $[\tilde{N}U(\tilde{C}/\tilde{N}) + \hat{N}U(\hat{C}/\hat{N})]$ by suitable choice of $\tilde{C}$ and $\hat{C}$, subject to the constraint $\tilde{C} + \hat{C} = \bar{C}$.

[27] To prove this, simply maximize $[U(\tilde{C}/\tilde{N}) + U(\hat{C}/\hat{N})]$ by suitable choice of $\tilde{C}$ and $\hat{C}$, subject to the constraint $\tilde{C} + \hat{C} = \bar{C}$.

[28] See Harsanyi (1955). I have qualified equi-probability in the text because it makes no sense when the future has no termination. To give it sense, we must suppose that the probability of extinction over the indefinite future is unity. We may then talk of equi-probability of the conditionals. We discuss this in the following section. See also Dasgupta and Heal (1979: ch. 9).

[29] Notice that in $t + 1$ the only shoes you will not have to consider are the ones that belonged to those of generation t.

Notice that V_{t+1} is of the same form as V_t, with τ commencing at $t+1$ in (6.7). You would choose between the two economies on the basis of V_t and V_{t+1}. This is the ethical justification of expression (6.7).

We will find (6.7) to be the natural one to use when we come to formulate the notion of sustainable development (Chapter 9 and the Appendix). Notice though that, once we are given the population forecast, the denominator in (6.7) is independent of the policies that could be chosen at t. This means that a policy deemed to be *optimal* if (6.6) were used as the criterion of choice would also be judged to be optimal if instead (6.7) were used as the criterion of choice. For Ramsey the two expressions would amount to the same. However, they would be seen to differ if we wished to determine whether a policy is *sustainable*. Optimality and sustainability are different concepts, serving different purposes.[30]

6.5. UNCERTAINTY

How do we introduce uncertainty into the Ramsey–Koopmans formulation of social well-being? The theory of choice under uncertainty, in its normative guise, is called the *expected-utility theory*. There is a large and still-growing experimental literature attesting to the fact that in laboratory conditions people don't choose in accordance with the theory.[31] But here we are concerned with normative questions. That the choices we make in the laboratory don't conform to expected utility theory doesn't mean that the theory is not the correct ethical basis for valuing and evaluating.

When applied to the valuation of uncertain consumption streams $(\tilde{C}_t)$, the theory directs us to estimate expected social well-being. Probabilities are imputed to future events. The probabilities are taken to be subjective, such as those involving long-range climate, although there can be objective components, such as those involving the weather. Let E_t denote generation t's expectation. For simplicity, imagine that the population remains constant. Expected social well-being (or 'social well-being', for short) can then be

---

[30] Notice that V_t is *linear* in the Us in (6.5)–(6.7). U is therefore a cardinal index (Ch. 1, Sect. 1.6 and Ch. *1). The ethical ordering over consumption streams remains the same if, rather than $U(C)$, current well-being of a person were measured as $aU(C) + b$, where a and b are arbitrary constants and $a > 0$. That b can be arbitrarily chosen (it can have either sign) has a curious implication for the theory: there is no room for saying that a consumption stream is deplorable (even that it is bad), or that it is good. Terms like 'good' and 'bad' have no operational role in a Ramsey–Koopmans theory. Later, when we come to formulate the idea of desirable population size (Ch. 14–15), we will discover that certain questions regarding human well-being invite us to say whether a state of affairs is good or bad. (The index to be constructed will be strongly cardinal.) The theory to which we will be led will be shown to have an operational role for those absolute concepts. [31] See e.g. Bell, Raiffa, and Tversky (1988).

expressed as

$$V_t = E_t \left[\sum_{t}^{\infty} \beta^{(\tau - t)} U(\tilde{C}_\tau) \right], \qquad \text{for } t \geq 0,$$

$$\text{where } \beta \equiv \frac{1}{(1 + \delta)}, \qquad \text{with } \delta \geq 0. \tag{6.8}$$

Expression (6.8) says that the social worth of an uncertain consumption stream is the expected value of intergenerational well-being.

The discount factor β can be given a new interpretation. The time horizon has so far been taken to be infinity. But we know that Earth will become uninhabitable some time in the future, even though we do not know when that will be. Consider those causes of extinction that are beyond our control. The simplest way (though not the most plausible) to formulate this uncertainty is to suppose that the date of extinction is subject to a *Poisson process*, which is to say that the probability of extinction at any particular date, given that extinction hasn't occured until that date, is constant. The constant is called the Poisson rate. It can be shown that choice under uncertainty governed by a Poisson process is equivalent to choice in a world where there is no chance of extinction, but where future well-beings are discounted at the Poisson rate.[32] For example, suppose that at each date t, conditional on Earth surviving until t, the probability of extinction is 0.001 per cent. Then, in valuing consumption streams, one may pretend that extinction won't occur and add a premium of 0.001 per period to the pure rate of time preference. In (6.8) uncertainty in the date of extinction is included in β. Extinction at some unpredictable date offers a reason why the future should be discounted.

That the possible exogenous causes of Earth's extinction are subject to a Poisson process really does stretch the imagination. The probability of extinction at date t, conditional on Earth surviving until t, would presumably be zero for many centuries, rising only in the very long run. The Poisson process is often invoked by economists because of its simplicity (a large asteroid hitting Earth is a possible interpretation), but there is little else to commend it.

Uncertainties regarding events in the very distant future are sometimes called *deep uncertainties*, the qualifier taken to mean that it may not be possible to assign subjective probabilities to those events. This is another way of saying that when there are deep uncertainties it is difficult to know what one should choose, or how one should organise one's thoughts regarding what to choose. Examples frequently mentioned involve environmental risks. People observe that it may not be possible today to estimate the risks of environmental catastrophies in the

---

[32] Yarri (1965).

distant future, let alone to enumerate what they may consist of. Bewley (1989) has developed an account of uncertainty that offers a reason why we ought to be reluctant to undertake activities involving inestimable risks. He offers a reason why the status quo should assume a favoured status, which is the hallmark of what many refer to as the *precautionary principle*.[33] Bewley's theory would appeal to someone who feels that it is easier to prevent environmental damage than to repair it subsequently. The theory gives expression to the demand that, in evaluating radically new technology (e.g. biotechnology), the burden of proof ought to shift away from those who advocate protection from environmental damage, towards those supporting the new technology.

But these are early days for such theories as Bewley's. The problem is that they can be supremely conservative. Admittedly, even the expected utility theory can be made ultra-conservative if we adopt an infinite aversion to risk and imagine that the worst that can happen under any change in policy is worse than the worst that can happen under the status quo. But it is difficult to justify such an attitude: we wouldn't adopt it even in our personal lives. At the moment we don't have a theory, normative or otherwise, that covers long-term environmental uncertainties in a satisfactory way.

These are some reasons why the expected utility theory remains a popular framework for valuing and evaluating. In practical decision-making, though, short-cuts have to be made. Simple rules-of-thumb are often followed in the choice of public policy, for example setting interest rates so as to keep the rate of inflation from exceeding α per cent per year. But the expected utility theory remains the anchor for reasoning about economic policies. If the probability of disasters under radically new processes and products are non-negligible, the expected utility theory recommends caution (see Appendix, Section A.18). The theory stresses trade-offs; it asks us to articulate our attitude to risk; and it forces us to deliberate on the likelihood of various outcomes. For the moment, it is the only plausible game in town.[34]

---

[33] Appell (2001).

[34] Alternatives to the expected utility theory were much explored during the 1950s. See Luce and Raiffa (1957, Ch.13) for an axiomatic classification of such theories.

Intergenerational Conflicts

In formulating the concept of intergenerational well-being, we noted a pair of considerations (dubbed A and B in the previous chapter—Section 6.1) that brought intergenerational conflicts into sharp relief. We explored agent-relative ethics as a way out of the dilemma and found it to harbour problems of its own. In recent years economists have studied further ways to avoid the dilemma posed by considerations A and B. This chapter is about two such explorations. The chapter is starred because the exposition is technical and it can be skipped if wished.

We return to a deterministic world. Population is assumed to be constant.

*6.1. PRESENT VERSUS THE FUTURE

Koopmans's theory avoids the problem raised by consideration B, but consideration A could gnaw. One way to weaken the force of A is to regard social well-being as a weighted sum of expression (6.3) and the time-average of the well-beings of generations in the very distant future.

Formally, let k be a number between 0 and 1. Write V_t as[1]

$$V_t = k \sum_t^\infty \left[\beta^{(\tau - t)} U(C_\tau) \right] + (1 - k) \lim_{T \to \infty} \inf \left[U(C_T) \right], \qquad (^\star 6.1)$$

where $\beta \equiv 1/(1 + \delta)$ and $1 > k > 0$.

The second term in (*6.1) is the *asymptotic part*. It gives prominence to the well-being of distant generations (literally, generations at an infinite distance), something that could be masked in the first term (the *series part*), owing to the fact that δ is positive.[2] Expression (*6.1) tries to formalize the way in which the claims of the present and near-future generations are traded off against the claims of generations in the distant future.

---

[1] I am assuming that the consumption programme is such that the long-run average exists. If it doesn't, the 'inferior' limit is used to define the second term.

[2] The ethical underpinnings of (*6.1) have been studied by Radner (1967) and Chichilnisky (1994). Heal (1998) contains a fine exposition of the theory.

But there are two problems with this formulation, one technical, the other conceptual. First, it yields no answer to the question of optimum saving in plausible economic models. In fact, (*6.1) doesn't reflect the trade-off it says it reflects: there is a way in which all generations can almost have their cake and eat it too. To see how, let the current generation (i.e. the one at $t = 0$) select a consumption stream that maximizes only the 'series' part. Subsequent generations are asked to follow it. However, it is announced that the chosen stream will be abandoned at some date in the distant future, the intention being to switch to a consumption stream that then maximizes only the asymptotic part. Notice that, the farther is the planned switching date, the more nearly would the series part be maximized. But regardless of how distant is that date, there will remain an infinite number of subsequent dates. So long as capital remains productive, no matter how low the capital base may have been run down by the switching date, it will be possible to make up and maximize the asymptotic part alone. But this means that it is always possible to increase (*6.1) by postponing the switching date. Expression (*6.1) is unable to prescribe a best policy.[3]

Non-existence of an optimum consumption stream is a problem, but not a serious problem. It is possible to get as close to the optimum level of social well-being as is desired by postponing the switching date. But then, why bother introducing the asymptotic part at all; why not simply concentrate on the series part and leave it to a generation in the distant future to make the switch if it is so minded? Since the series part is Koopmans's formulation, we would seem to have returned to it. Expression (*6.1) offers no extra ethical mileage.

This leads me to the second problem with (*6.1), and it is far more serious. We may not know when the world will cease to exist, but we do know that it will cease to exist at some date. But the asymptotic part in (*6.1) gives full weight to well-being at infinity, a curious thing to do when we know that the world will not exist for ever.

*6.2. DECLINING DISCOUNT RATES

There is yet another way to strike a balance between the claims of current and future generations. It is to discount the future, not at a constant rate, but at a rate that declines with time and tends to zero. Imagine then that the rate at which well-being at $t + 1$ is discounted back to t is δ_t (>0), where $\delta_t > \delta_{t+1}$ and δ_t tends to 0 as t tends to ∞. The discount factor to be applied at $t = 0$ to

---

[3] I learnt this argument from Kenneth Arrow, who attributed it to Kenneth Judd.

well-being at date T is then, by definition,[4]

$$\beta_T \equiv [(1 + \delta_0)(1 + \delta_1)(1 + \delta_2) \ldots (1 + \delta_{T-1})]^{-1} \quad \text{for} \quad T \geq 1;$$

$$\text{and} \quad \beta_0 = 1. \tag{*6.2}$$

Let V_t take the form

$$V_t = \sum_{t}^{\infty} \beta_\tau U(C_\tau). \tag{*6.3}$$

If β_t tends to zero slowly enough, the interests of generations in the distant future will not be in jeopardy.[5]

Notice that (*6.3) generalizes expression (6.5) in Chapter 6. Thus, if we set $\beta_t = 1$ and $\beta_\tau = a$ ($0 < a < 1$) for $\tau > t$, (*6.3) reduces to (6.5). So we should not be surprised that (*6.3) raises the same problem as the one we discussed in connection with (6.5): intergenerational incongruence. The reservations I expressed earlier about agent-relative ethics in the public context hold here too.

---

[4] This means that the discount rate for any period is the percentage rate of decline of the discount factor between the period preceding it and the period in question:

$$\delta_t \equiv -\frac{\beta_{t+1} - \beta_t}{\beta_t}, \quad \text{for } t \geq 0.$$

[5] Declining discount rates have been widely studied in recent years. See Loewenstein and Prelec (1992), Cropper, Aydede and Portney (1994), Laibson (1997), Heal (1998), and Barro (1999). It has been common to work with the functional form, $\delta_t = t^{-m}$, where $m > 0$. This is 'hyperbolic discounting'. The limiting case, $m = 0$, yields a constant discount rate.

7

Economic Institutions and
the Natural Environment

7.1. MARKETS

If you were to browse among leading Western journals on environmental and resource economics, you would discover that a recurrent activity in the field has been devising valuation methods. A question that would occur to you is, why? Why should there be a special need to determine the worth of natural resources; why not rely on market prices? You might also wonder why markets aren't an adequate set of institutions for our dealings with Nature.

The answer is that for many natural resources markets simply do not exist. In some cases they don't exist because the costs of negotiation and monitoring are too high. Economic activities affected by ecological interactions involving long geographical distances (the effects of uplands deforestation on downstream activities hundreds of miles away) form one class of examples. There are also interactions separated by large temporal distances (the effect of carbon emission on climate in the distant future, in a world where forward markets don't exist because future generations are not present today to negotiate with us). Then there are cases (the atmosphere, aquifers, the open seas) where the nature of the physical situation (the migratory nature of the resource) makes private property rights impossible and so keeps markets from existing; while in others, ill-specified or unprotected property rights prevent markets from being formed (as is the case frequently with mangroves and coral reefs), or make them function wrongly even when they do get formed. Economists have a special name for the side-effects of human activities when they are undertaken without mutual agreement: *externalities*. Not surprisingly, the study of externalities has loomed large in environmental economics.[1] In elementary economics textbooks, it is

---

This chapter is based on Dasgupta and Mäler (1991, 1995) and Dasgupta (1993, 1996).

[1] See e.g. Pigou (1920), Lindahl (1958), Coase (1960), Kneese and Bower (1968), Arrow (1971), Meade (1973), Mäler (1974), and Baumol and Oates (1975). Sandmo (2000) contains a fine overview of environmental externalities. Optimal public instruments for the preservation of amenities and the control of pollution have been the focus of attention in the USA, influenced considerably by the tasks facing the US Environmental

not uncommon to read that externalities lead to market failure. The way I have defined the term here, externalities are a form of institutional failure. One can go on to say that environmental problems are frequently symptoms of institutional failure, of which market failure is but one example.

It is convenient to classify externalities into two categories: unidirectional and reciprocal.[2] Damage inflicted by upstream deforestation on downstream farmers without compensation is an example of the former. The famous 'tragedy of the commons' is a metaphor for the latter (see below). Carbon emissions into the atmosphere is one example of the tragedy; other examples are unregulated fishing in the open sea and groundwater withdrawal under free access.[3]

We will study unidirectional externalities in Chapter 12 (Section 12.4), where we identify certain weaknesses in the structural adjustment programmes that indebted countries were encouraged to put in place during the 1980s. Here I want to illustrate reciprocal externalities by discussing a mechanism that leads to the tragedy of the commons.

Consider a group of farmers who draw water from an underground basin. Although this isn't an example of open access to a resource base, it does harbour reciprocal externalities.[4] While farmers may have titles to the land they cultivate, they can't have titles to the water below, for water is migratory. In view of this, communities have often instituted the doctrine, under which farmers have the right to extract as much water as they wish without regard to the effect of their withdrawals on others.

The problem with the doctrine is that it provides no protection to a well-owner from the lowering of the water table under his land caused by his neighbour's action. In the absence of some form of collective action (say, a charge on water; see Section 10.2), the doctrine encourages farmers to extract at too fast a rate. Admittedly, if the farms are small, no single farmer can affect the water table significantly. But if there are many farmers, the aggregate effect can

---

Protection Agency (EPA); see Cropper and Oates (1992). Morgenstern (1997) is a collection of studies on regulatory work undertaken at EPA. On the theory of transboundary pollution, see Mäler and de Zeeuw (1998), Folmer and von Mouche (2000), and Folmer and de Zeeuw (2000), and on transnational commons, see the essays in Dasgupta, Mäler, and Vercelli (1997).

² Dasgupta (1982b).

³ Gordon (1954) was the first to analyse the implications of open access to a resource base. Scott (1955) is an original study on the effects of open access to fisheries, and Milliman (1956) is another on the effects on groundwater. Garrett Hardin's invention of the admirable metaphor, 'the tragedy of the commons' (Hardin, 1968), has done much to create public understanding of the problems that arise when property rights to resources are inadequate. On the impact of agriculture on groundwater, see Giacomelli, Giupponi, and Paniconi (2001).

⁴ Dasgupta and Heal (1979: ch. 3) developed a formal, game-theoretic model of reciprocal externalities. They showed that, even when there isn't open access, there can be a tragedy of the commons if those enjoying rights of use do not act with restraint.

be substantial. In extreme cases, over-extraction ruins the basin, because, for example, of salt water intrusion.

Intergenerational externalities have a different structure. Because of the arrow of time, they are unidirectional. No doubt such externalities are to an extent ameliorated by the fact that we care about our children's well-being and know that they, in turn, will care about theirs, and so on, in an intergenerational sequence. But because of institutional failure in other spheres of economic activity (borrowing, lending, purchasing insurance), our implicit concern for generations in the distant future may be inadequate. These considerations, among others, offer reasons why market rates of interest do not reflect social discount rates.[5] So, market failure involves not only misallocation of resources in the present, but also misallocation across time. Even *laissez-faire* economies aren't all that good at producing publicly observable signals of environmental scarcities. If there is open access to a fishery, for example, its market price, *in situ*, is zero. Being in limited supply, though, the scarcity value that ought to be attributed to it would be positive.[6] There is a directional bias in environmental externalities: market failure usually leads to an excessive use of natural resources, not an insufficient one.

There is another reason why markets shouldn't be expected to function well for environmental resources. A major achievement of modern economics has been to show that prices in well-functioning markets reflect social scarcities, but that markets are able to function well only if the processes governing the transformation of goods and services into further goods and services are 'linear'. However, when someone talks of 'ecosystem stress' or 'ecological thresholds', as ecologists frequently do, they mean states of affair in systems governed by non-linear processes.[7] Such processes can be a feature not only of global ecosystems, but also of local ones. Even if a large-scale ecosystem did not show signs of stress, local ones could, and often do, display signs, observable only by local inhabitants. Markets can't be expected to function well in such environments. For example, market prices may be unable to signal the impending collapse of a local resource base. This isn't to advocate command-and-control systems of management, but simply to say that markets need to be supplemented in such ways as to ensure there are additional public signals to accompany prices. Later we shall consider the kinds of supplements that would help matters.

---

[5] See Lind (1982), Arrow *et al.* (1996), and Portney and Weyant (1999).

[6] I am assuming here that there are no external disbenefits inflicted on others when fishermen fish. In Sect. 8.1 I discuss cases where there are external disbenefits associated with the exploitation of natural resources under open access.

[7] Strictly, they are 'non-convex' processes. A process is said to be *convex* if, given any two time paths that are feasible under the process, all time paths that are weighted averages of the two (with positive weights) are also feasible. Non-convex processes are therefore non-linear. Koopmans (1957) is the classic reference on the subject.

7.2. THE LOCAL COMMUNITY

In an oft-quoted passage, Arrow (1974: 33) expressed the view that organizations are a means of achieving the benefits of collective action in situations
where the price system fails. If interpreted literally, this formulation gets the
historical chronology backward, but Arrow's intention was clear enough: there
are institutions serving an economic purpose that are neither the market system
nor the State.

Spatially localized resources are frequently neither private nor state property,
but *common property*. In poor countries communal property rights to resources
are most often based on custom and tradition: they aren't backed by the kinds
of deeds that would pass scrutiny in courts of law. Therefore, tenure isn't
secure, a vital problem, to which I return below.[8] In poor countries the local
commons include grazing lands, threshing grounds, swidden fallows, inland
and coastal fisheries, rivers and canals, woodlands, forests, village tanks, and
ponds. Being spatially localized, their use can be monitored by members of the
community. This makes their management an easier matter than, say, fisheries
in the open seas.

Are the local commons extensive? As a proportion of aggregate assets, their
presence ranges widely across ecological zones. There is a rationale for this,
based on the human desire to reduce risk. Communal property rights enable
members of a group to reduce individual risks by pooling their risks. Moreover,
the incentive to pool risks that are associated with the use of any particular
resource depends on the other risks people face; it depends on their remaining
sources of income, on transaction possibilities in other spheres of life, and
so forth. An almost immediate empirical corollary is that the local commons
are most prominent in arid regions, mountain regions, and unirrigated areas,
and least prominent in humid regions and river valleys.[9] Another corollary is
that income inequalities are less in those locations where common-property
resources are more prominent. Aggregate income is a different matter, though;
it is the arid and mountain regions and unirrigated areas that are the poorest.[10]
This needs to be borne in mind when public policy is devised. However, the
dependence on common-property resources even within dry regions declines
with increasing wealth across households. Theory predicts this and case studies
confirm it.[11]

Jodha (1986, 1995) studied evidence from over eighty villages in twenty-one
dry districts in India to conclude that, among poor families, the proportion of

---

[8] See also Ch. 12.
[9] This has been confirmed in the case of India by Agarwal and Narain (1989) and by Chopra, Kadekodi,
and Murty (1990).   [10] See Agarwal and Narain (1989) and Chopra, Kadekodi, and Murty (1990).
[11] Jodha (1986, 1995) and Cavendish (2000).

income based directly on the local commons is in the range of 15–25 per cent. Moreover, as sources of income, they often complement private property (i.e. labour, milch and draft animals, agricultural land, and tools). Common-property resources offer the rural poor some protection in times of unusual economic stress. For landless people they may be the only non-human asset at their disposal. A number of resources, such as water and minor forest products (fuelwood and fodder, berries and nuts, herbs and spices, resin and gum) are the responsibility of women and children.

In a study of twenty-nine villages in south-eastern Zimbabwe, Cavendish (1998, 1999) has arrived at even larger estimates: the proportion of income based directly on the commons is 35 per cent, the figure for the poorest quintile being 40 per cent. A similar picture emerges from Hecht, Anderson, and May (1988), who offered qualitative descriptions of the importance of babassu products among the landless in Maranhão, Brazil. The products support the poorest of the poor, most especially the women among them. They are an important source of cash income in the period between agricultural crop harvests.[12]

Such evidence as Jodha and Cavendish have unearthed does not, of course, prove that the local commons in their samples were well managed, but it does show that rural households would have strong incentives to devise arrangements whereby they *would* be communally managed.

Are the local commons managed communally? Not invariably, but in many cases they are, or have been in the past. Where they are managed, the commons aren't open to all, but only to those having historical rights, through kinship ties and community membership. In short, the local commons usually aren't open to all; they aren't open access. Communal management of local resources makes connection with *social capital*, viewed as a complex of interpersonal networks and hints at the basis upon which cooperation has traditionally been built.[13] A large empirical literature has confirmed that resource users in many cases cooperate, on occasion through democratic means. Case studies have shown that communal property-rights and management have prevented rural and coastal communities from experiencing the tragedy of the commons. In his work on South Indian villages, Seabright (1997) has shown that milk producers' cooperatives are more prevalent in the drier districts. But the local commons are also more prevalent in drier districts. So, one way to interpret Seabright's finding is that cooperation in one sphere of life (managing the commons) makes cooperation in other spheres (marketing milk) that much easier. Cooperation begets cooperation. The literature on the local commons is valuable because it

---

[12] For a similar picture in the West African forest zone, see Falconer (1990).

[13] I provide a brief account of the idea of social capital in Chs. 9 and 12. For a more extensive account, see Dasgupta (2000a).

has unearthed how institutions that are neither part of the market system, nor of the State, nor of the household, develop organically to cope with resource allocation problems.[14]

This is the good news. There are, however, two pieces of bad news. First, a general finding from studies on the management of common-property resources is that entitlements to products of the commons is, and was, frequently based on private holdings: richer households enjoy a greater proportion of the benefits from the commons.[15] This is consonant with cooperative game theory. In his classic formulation of the way rational people could be expected to bargain, Nash (1950) showed that those who enjoy better outside options would enjoy a greater share of the benefits of cooperation.[16]

The second piece of bad news is that the local commons have degraded in recent years in many parts of the poor world.[17] Why should this happen now if the commons have previously been managed in a sustainable manner? A recent intellectual tradition goes something like this: the reason the poor degrade their local resource base is that, at the margin, income today is of the utmost urgency, meaning that poverty leads poor people to discount future incomes at unusually high rates relative to today's income.[18]

I don't know of many empirical studies testifying to this, but there are some. High rates of discount have been reported among the rural poor in a sample of villages in Indonesia and sub-Saharan Africa. Rates as high as 100 per cent per year were inferred from responses to questionnaires the authors distributed among villagers.[19]

These findings are not easy to interpret. One would imagine that, if discount rates were as high as have been inferred, the local commons in those regions would have been depleted at a faster rate than the evidence, such as it is, suggests.[20] Admittedly, limits on the availability of effective labour could be a reason why depletion rates can be low even when people discount the future at rates far higher than the natural rates at which the resource base regenerates. But

[14] See Feeny *et al.* (1990), Ostrom (1990), Somanathan (1991), Bromley *et al.* (1992), Acheson (1993), and Baland and Platteau (1996). The economic theory underlying communal management was developed in Dasgupta and Heal (1979: ch. 3). Ostrom (1990: ch. 3) ranges over a number of long-enduring common-property resources in Nepal, the youngest of which has been found to be 100 years old, the oldest more than 500 years old.

[15] McKean (1992) and Ostrom and Gardner (1993). See also Molians (1998), who has identified differences based on gender. In India caste also plays a role in segregating access to the commons. For example, people belonging to 'scheduled castes' are frequently not permitted to draw water from the wells in use by caste Hindus.

[16] Banerjee *et al.* (2001) have uncovered similar phenomenon in agro-industrial cooperatives. Their theory is broader and doesn't rely on the bargaining model of Nash.

[17] B. Agarwal (1989) and Baland and Platteau (1996) provide examples.   [18] Bardhan (1996).

[19] Holden, Shiferaw, and Wik (1998).

[20] For estimates of annual rates of deforestation in sub-Saharan Africa, see Cleaver and Schreiber (1994).

depleting the local commons doesn't require much capital equipment. Farmers in some of the regions in question until recently practised swidden agriculture, some practise it even today. Nor is a lack of people a notable problem in Indonesia and sub-Saharan Africa. Moreover, poverty is not a recent phenomenon. If the thesis were correct, the local commons would have disappeared long ago. The matter remains a puzzle. So I consider a different explanation. It is based on the thought that *institutional failure can mean that private returns on investment in the resource base are low*. In the world as we know it, this is probably a common occurrence.

There are many ways in which institutional failure manifests itself. Uncertain property rights are a prime example. You may think that you own the land your forefathers cultivated and passed on to you, but if you do not possess a deed to the land, your rights to it are insecure. Political instability (at the extreme, civil war) is another source of uncertainty: your property could be taken away from you by force. In fact, political instability is a direct cause of environmental degradation: civil disturbance all too frequently expresses itself through the destruction of physical capital.

When people are uncertain of their rights to a piece of property, they are reluctant to make the investments necessary to protect and improve it, the expected returns being low. Often enough, the investments have to be of a collective kind, for example building irrigation ditches, terraces, and structures for controlling floods. If the probity of communitarian institutions is uncertain, the private returns expected from collective work are low. The influence would be expected to run the other way too, with growing resource scarcity contributing to political instability, as rival groups battle over resources. The feedback could be positive, exacerbating the problem for a time, reducing private returns on investment further. Groups fighting over spatially localized resources are a common occurrence.[21]

Rapid population growth can trigger resource depletion if institutional practices are unable to adapt to changing economic circumstances. In Côte d'Ivoire, for example, growth in rural population has been accompanied by increased deforestation and reduced fallows. Biomass production has declined, as has agricultural productivity.[22]

Management of the local commons has often relied on social norms of behaviour, which are founded on *reciprocity*. But institutions based on reciprocity are fragile in the face of growing markets. When traditional systems of

---

[21] Homer-Dixon, Boutwell, and Rathjens (1993), Homer-Dixon (1994), and Collier and Hoeffler (1998). In a study comprising 120 countries, Deacon (1994) has offered suggestive statistical evidence of a positive link between political instability and forest depletion. On poverty and degradation of the local environment, see B. Agarwal (1986, 1989), CSE (1990), Dasgupta (1993, 1995, 2000b,c), and Cleaver and Schreiber (1994).

[22] Lopez (1998) estimates that income at the village level has declined by some 15%.

management collapse, and aren't replaced, the use of the local commons becomes unrestrained. The commons then deteriorate, leading to the proverbial 'tragedy'. Later (Chapter 12) we will see why reciprocity is fragile.

7.3. THE STATE

The State is often the culprit. There are cases where state appropriation of communal property (forests) removed the local population's incentives to protect the resource base. Less directly, management practices at the local level have been overturned by central fiat. A number of states in the Sahel imposed rules that in effect destroyed communal management practices in the forests. Villages ceased to have the authority to enforce sanctions on those who violated locally instituted rules. State authority damaged local institutions and turned the local commons into open-access resources.[23] There have also been cases where the ability of the State to enforce environmental laws diminished under structural adjustment programmes. As this was frequently not accompanied by the emergence of communal management systems, the resource base in effect became open to access by one and all.[24]

Recently, environmental degradation has been traced to government tax policy. In a notable paper, Binswanger (1991) argued that in Brazil the exemption from taxation of virtually all agricultural income, allied to the fact that logging is regarded as proof of land occupancy, has provided incentives to the rich to acquire forests and then to deforest the land.[25] He argued that the subsidy enjoyed by the private sector has been so large that a reduction in deforestation by the removal of subsidies is in Brazil's own interests, let alone that of the rest of the world. This has implications for international negotiations. The current consensus is that Brazil has much to lose from reducing the rate of the deforestation it has been engaged in. If this is true, there would be a case for the rest of the world to subsidize Brazil, as compensation for losses the country would sustain if it were to exercise restraint. Binswanger's account shows that it is by no means clear that the consensus is correct.

Alston, Libecap, and Mueller (1999a,b) have taken the analysis farther. They have shown that accelerated deforestation in the Brazilian Amazon, followed by violent conflicts between landowners and squatters, has also occurred because of legal inconsistencies between the civil law, which supports the title held by landowners, and the constitutional law, which supports the right of squatters to claim land not in 'beneficial use' (e.g. farming or ranching). Ironically, the

---

[23] See Thomson, Feeny, and Oakerson (1986) and Baland and Platteau (1996). [24] Reed (1996).

[25] Heath and Binswanger (1996) have extended their basic argument to a number of other countries.

latter right reflects the government's stated desire for land reform. The authors have shown that the vagueness of the 'use' criteria, and the uncertainty as to when a landowner's claim to a piece of land or a squatter's counter-claim to it is enforced, are together an explosive force.[26]

I have stressed weaknesses in the workings of the State in poor countries for two reasons. First, if the natural environment had been managed well in such countries, I wouldn't be writing this book. Secondly, the State is of the utmost importance for environmental management. If markets are to work well, property rights must be clearly defined and protected and contracts have to be enforced. This only the State can do. If communitarian allocations are to be equitable, there has to be an assurance that the benefits from the local commons aren't expropriated by the more powerful within the community. This only the State can assure. If the rights to the benefits of investment in a resource base of those who invest in it are to be protected and promoted, the State is the agency to which they must turn. Moreover, there are infra-structural investments (sewage systems, water purification plants) that in poor countries only the State is capable of financing. In urban centres, where communitarian systems are unlikely to get off ground (e.g. on air pollution), the State, with its powers to tax and regulate, is the pivotal agency of reform. Environmental economics in the North (I am using the term in its current geo-political sense) has for the most part been developed as a branch of public economics, with its emphasis on optimal instruments for pollution control (e.g. taxes, tradable permits; see Chapter 10). On each such matter, the State has a key role to play.

State ownership of wells and mines is a commonplace in poor countries. Fossil fuels and minerals are a source of government revenue, used for development purposes in some countries and the accumulation of the rulers' personal wealth in others. Forests are often state property. They too are resources of commercial value. But there is a category of resources that, even though they may be perceived as state property, are actually *public property*. The State doesn't 'own' them: instead, it acts as a trustee on behalf of all generations. National parks and cultural monuments are examples of public goods whose preservation is the responsibility of the State as trustee.

---

[26] In a wider discussion of the conversion of forests into ranches in the Amazon basin, Schneider (1995) has shown that the construction of roads through the forests has also been a potent force. Other examples of policy-induced environmental deterioration are the massive agricultural subsidies in the European Union. These are known to have encouraged agricultural practices harmful to aquatic ecosystems. In their estimate of world-wide subsidies for the use of natural resources, both visible and hidden, Myers and Kent (2000) suggest an annual figure of 2 trillion US dollars, which is about 10% of the world's output of goods and services.

7.4. PROPERTY RIGHTS AND MANAGEMENT: A SCHEMATA

Property-rights to a resource are the rights, restrictions, and privileges with regard to its use.[27] *Management* of a resource base is a different, though related, matter. Property rights may be well defined, but a resource could nevertheless be managed badly, owing to disagreements among those holding the rights on how it ought to be used, corrupt practices regarding its use, a lack of understanding of ecosystem functions, and so forth.[28] *Ownership* is yet another matter. Someone owns a resource by law, but transfers their right of use to another person for a limited period. Ownership doesn't change, but the right-of-use does.

Private, communal, and state property rights to resources were discussed in the previous three sections. Table 7.1 presents the classification. We can think of a property rights regime and the associated management structure as defining the institution governing the use of a resource base. In practice, every institution harbours externalities, but some harbour more than others. The relative efficiency of institutions depends on the character of the resource base (e.g. if its productivity is subject to especial risk, if the resource base is lumpy, if its use by someone is observable by other relevant parties); it depends on the efficiency of institutions governing the production and allocation of other goods and services (e.g. credit and insurance); it depends on the extent to which the returns from investment in it can be appropriated by the investor; and so forth. The interplay of market and non-market institutions is a crucial determinant of well-being. The performance of one depends on the performances of the others. Nor are institutions given and fixed. They evolve. For example, Ensminger (1990) has narrated how common grazing lands among the Orma

Table 7.1. *Property Rights to Natural Resources*

Ownership	Resources
Private	Cultivated land, cattle, oil and minerals
Communal (common-property)	Grazing land, threshing grounds, ponds, local forests, inland and coastal fisheries
Open access	Atmosphere, international waters
State	Commercial forests, oil and minerals
State as trustee	National parks, cultural monuments

[27] See Bromley (1991) for a wide-ranging discussion.
[28] Ostrom and Schlager (1996) contains an account of the conditions necessary for effective communitarian management.

in north-eastern Kenya became segmented into private land. She showed that the transformation took place with the consent of the elders of the tribe, and attributed this to changing transaction costs brought about by cheaper transportation and widening markets. The elders were, not surprisingly, from the stronger families, and it did not go unnoted by Ensminger that privatization accentuated inequalities.

Institutions can also be created or destroyed by design and legislation. What was once a relatively efficient institution for a resource base may cease being so when circumstances change. Nostalgia for communitarian solutions is an undependable emotion.

7.5. GLOBAL AND LOCAL ENVIRONMENTAL PROBLEMS

The links between rural poverty and the state of the local resource base in poor countries offer a possible pathway by which poverty, resource degradation, and even high fertility feed upon one another in a synergistic manner.[29] Recent experiences in sub-Saharan Africa and the Indian sub-continent are not inconsistent with this possibility. An erosion of the local resource base can make certain categories of people destitute even while the economy's gross national product (GNP) increases. The thought that entire populations can always be relied upon to make the shift from resource based, subsistence existence to a high-income, industrial one is belied both by theory and by contemporary experiences.[30]

Rural poverty, resource degradation, and institutional failure pull in different directions and are together not unrelated to an intellectual tension between the concerns people share about global warming and acid rains, which sweep across regions, nations and continents, and about those matters (such as the decline in firewood or water sources) that are specific to the needs and concerns of the poor in as small a group as a village community. Environmental problems present themselves differently to different people. In part, this is a reflection of the tension just noted and is a source of misunderstanding of people's attitudes. Some identify environmental problems with poverty and unprecedented population growth in the South, while others identify them with wealth and unprecedented expenditure patterns in the North. (I am using the geographical terms in their current geo-political sense.) Even though debates between

---

[29] See Sect. 5.7.

[30] Cleaver and Schreiber (1994), Filmer and Pritchett (1996), and Aggarwal, Netanyahu, and Romano (2001), among others, offer suggestive evidence. In their study of the effects of stabilization and structural adjustment programmes in the Philippines, Cruz and Repetto (1992) offer evidence in support of a positive feedback between poverty, population growth, and soil degradation. These matters are further discussed in Chs. 9 (Table 9.2) and 12.

the two groups often become shrill, each vision is partly correct. There is no single environmental problem. Consequently, there is no single valuation or evaluation problem: rather, there is a large collection of them.[31] Thus, growth in industrial wastes and resource use have come in tandem with increased economic activity. In the former Socialist block neither preventive nor curative measures kept pace with the production of waste. Moreover, the scale of the human enterprise, by virtue of both unprecedented increases in the size of the world's population and the extent of economic activity, has so extended our use of natural resources that humankind is today Earth's dominant species. During the twentieth century, world population grew by a factor of four to more than 6 billion, industrial output increased by a factor of 40, energy use by a factor of 16, methane-producing cattle population grew in pace with human population, fish catch grew by a multiple of 35, and carbon and sulfur dioxide emissions by a factor of 10. The supply of nitrogen to the environment from the use of fertilizers and from burning fossil fuels is now of the same order of magnitude as biological nitrogen fixation. Vitousek *et al.* (1986) estimated that 40 per cent of the net energy created by terrestrial photosynthesis (i.e. net primary production of the biosphere) is currently being appropriated for human use. This is of course a rough-and-ready figure. Moreover, net terrestrial primary production isn't given and fixed: it depends in part on human activity. Nevertheless, the figure does put the scale of the human presence on Earth in perspective. The figures also give us an idea of the unprecedented disturbance to the natural environment that has been created by human activity in a short space of time.[32]

If the demonstration effect is a powerful force behind consumer demand (Section 3.4), a substantial portion of our use of the natural resource base should be seen as a collective waste. The waste occurs not because of inadequate property rights to the resource base, but because preferences are interdependent.[33] In principle, the demonstration effect can give rise to any one of a number of patterns of resource use. For example, each household would desire high levels of consumption (despite the hard work involved in earning the incomes necessary for high levels of consumption) if other households were to attain high levels of consumption, but would desire moderate levels of consumption if other households were to attain moderate levels of consumption.[34] It could even

---

[31] Dasgupta and Mäler (1991, 1995), Dasgupta (1993), Reardon and Vosti (1995), and Vincent and Ali (1997) go into these distinctions in greater detail.

[32] This was the theme of a special symposium in *Science*, 1997, 277 (see especially the article by Vitousek *et al.*). See also McNeill (2000) for global statistics on changes in the magnitude of the perturbations that were made to the natural environment during the 20th century.

[33] Technically put, there are demand externalities.

[34] This is an example of multiple equilibria. We encountered the possibility of multiple equilibria in Sect. 4.4.

be that people would be happier under the latter circumstances. Consumption taxes would be a policy implication.

The reference group giving rise to the demonstration effect can expand, because newspapers, radio, television (now also the internet) transmit information about other life-styles.[35] The media are then a vehicle by which conformism increasingly becomes based on the behaviour of a wider population than the local community: the reference group widens. This pathway helps explain recent trends in reproductive behaviour in a number of poor countries, where fertility rates displayed little to no trend in the past, but have declined in recent years.[36] The presumption is that the poor are prone to imitating the rich, but the rich aren't prone to imitating the poor.

It would seem, then, that the enlargement of the reference group has two broad effects: a downward trend in fertility rates, and an upward trend in acquisitiveness and economic growth. Other things being the same, the former would reduce human expropriation of the products of nature, while the latter would increase it.

On the other hand, economic growth itself has brought with it improvements in the quality of a number of natural resources. The large-scale availability of potable water and the increased protection of human populations against both water- and air-borne diseases in industrial countries have in great measure come in the wake of growth in national income these countries have enjoyed over the past two hundred years or so. Moreover, the physical environment inside the home has improved beyond measure with economic growth. For example, cooking in South Asia continues to be a central route to respiratory illnesses among women. Such positive links between economic growth and environmental quality often go unnoted by environmentalists in the North. I would guess that this lacuna is yet another reflection of the fact that it is all too easy to overlook the enormous heterogeneity of the natural environment, ranging as it does from the atmosphere, oceans, and landscapes to water-holes, grazing fields, and sources of fuelwood. Both this heterogeneity and the diversity of the human condition need to be kept in mind.

7.6. TECHNOLOGICAL BIASES

In earlier chapters it was noted that estimates of socio-economic indicators currently in use are biased because they don't incorporate changes in the natural environment. The price of natural resources on site is frequently zero, even

---

[35] Freedman (1995), Bongaarts and Watkins (1996), and Iyer (2000).   [36] Dasgupta (2000b,c).

though they are scarce goods. Commercial rates of return on investments relying on such resources are higher than their social rates of return. Resource-intensive projects appear better looking than they actually are. Over time, an entire sequence of resource-intensive technologies is installed. Moreover, people learn by doing and learn by using, not only in installed technology, but also in research and development. The development and use of technology reflect processes that are path-dependent. The conclusion is depressing: it may require a big push to move us away from the current profligacy in our use of natural resources.

These arguments imply that modern technologies are not always appropriate technologies, but instead are often unfriendly towards those who depend directly on their local resource base. This is likely to be especially true in poor countries, where environmental legislations are usually neither strong nor effectively enforced. The arguments help explain why the poorest in poor countries, when permitted, have been known to protest against the installation of modern technology. The transfer of technology from advanced countries can be inappropriate even when that same body of technology is appropriate in the country of origin. This is because the social scarcity of natural resources, especially local resources, varies from country to country.[37] A project design that is socially profitable in one country may be socially unprofitable in another. This may be why environmental groups in poor countries not infrequently appear to be backward-looking, trying to unearth traditional technologies for soil conservation, water management, forest protection, medical treatment, and so forth. To do so isn't to assume an anti-science stance: it could be to infer that wrong prices can tilt the technological agenda in a wrong direction.[38]

The bias towards resource-intensive technologies extends to the prior stage of research and development. When natural resources are underpriced, the incentives to develop technologies that would economize on their use are lower than what they should be. Often enough, once it is perceived that past choices have been damaging to the environment, cures are sought, whereas prevention would have been the better choice. Chichilnisky and Heal (1998), for example, in an *ex post* study of political choice over improving water quality, compared the costs of restoring the ecological functioning of the Catskill Watershed in New York State to the costs of replacing the natural water purification and filtration services the ecosystem had been known to provide in the past by building a water purification plant costing 8 billion US dollars. Their figures reflect the advantages of the choice that was in fact made: preservation over construction. Independent of the other service the Catskill watershed provides, and ignoring the annual running costs of 300 million US dollars for a filtration

---

[37] This is proved formally in the Appendix.

[38] Agarwal and Narain (1996) is an interesting recent study in this vein.

plant, the capital costs alone showed a more than six-fold advantage for investing in the ecosystem. Their investigation offers a rough estimate of the social worth of the watershed itself.

But customary habits of economic thinking are hard to overcome. Accounting for the natural environment, if it comes into the calculus at all, is an afterthought to the real business of 'doing economics'. A recent issue of *The Economist* (25 September 1999) carried a 38-page Survey of the World Economy in which the natural resource base made no appearance in the authors' assessment of what lies ahead. I doubt though that many readers will have noticed this. Even today the natural environment has not entered the common lexicon of economic reasoning. In Chapter 9 we will see that assessments of economic performance can be very misleading when the natural resource base is neglected in the calculus.

8

Valuing Goods

8.1. ACCOUNTING PRICES

Valuing goods and services involves comparisons of a world with and without their availability (at the margin). In developing the idea of the social worth of goods and services, we addressed a number of conceptual issues. There are in addition practical problems of estimation. Their resolution requires a greater attention to ecological matters than I have so far given them. This chapter is a sketch of the literature that has grown in response to the need to make the concept of social worth usable.

Economists call the social worth of a good its *accounting price*. The accounting price of something is the improvement in the quality of life that would be brought about if a tiny bit more of that thing were made available cost-lessly. Alternatively, it may be defined as the deterioration in the quality of life that would be brought about if a tiny bit less of that thing were available. If social well-being is a smooth function of its determinants, the two definitions yield the same numerical figure. If it isn't, they won't, but this will not matter, because, of the two figures, the one that is relevant would be identified by the context in which accounting prices are put to use. Accounting prices reflect the social scarcity of goods and services. Pathological circumstances apart, the social worth of a good or service is the same as its social scarcity-value.[1]

In the above definition, the unit of account is well-being. In practice, it is customary to choose some good or service or some basket of goods and services as the unit of account. Accounting prices are then defined in terms of the chosen unit of account. The good that has been chosen as the unit of

The material in this chapter appeared originally in Dasgupta, Levin, and Lubchenco (2000) and Dasgupta (2001a).

[1] The latter is also called the good's *social opportunity cost*. An alternative name for accounting prices is *shadow prices* (Dasgupta, Marglin, and Sen, 1972). The term 'accounting price' was introduced by Tinbergen (1954). It is sometimes thought, mistakenly, that to call the social worth of a good its accounting *price* implies that the good has been 'commodified'. Accounting prices should not be confused with market prices.

account is called *numeraire*. Since valuation and evaluation involve comparisons, the choice of numeraire affects neither the assessments of states of affairs, nor decisions regarding what should be done to improve the prevailing state of affairs. Accounting prices are significant only in the way they are related to one another: their absolute values are of no significance. To illustrate, it doesn't matter if we express prices in dollars or cents: the choice only reflects a judgement about what is convenient. Shifting the unit of account from dollars to cents requires only that everything is repriced by dividing dollar prices by the dollar price of a cent (1 by 100), which is another way of saying that the dollar prices should be multiplied by one hundred to express them in cents.

In what follows, well-being is taken to be the unit of account. If we wanted to reprice everything in terms of some tangible and easily identifiable commodity, we would divide well-being accounting prices by the well-being accounting price of the commodity in question.[2]

It should be apparent from their definition that accounting prices depend upon four, related factors: (a) the conception of social well-being, (b) the size and composition of existing stocks of assets, (c) production and substitution possibilities among goods and services, and (d) the way resources are allocated in the economy. Their precise influences are determined in the Appendix. But it is as well to illustrate them here.[3]

Consider first factor (a). If special weight is placed on, say, species preservation (e.g. if constraints are imposed on what we can or cannot do to other species when they are endangered), the accounting prices of species will be high, other things remaining the same.[4] To illustrate (b), imagine that, because of overuse in the past, very little of a distinctive resource remains. Assume too that the resource is useful in production. Then, other things remaining the same, it is valuable. So its accounting price is high. Suppose next that a particular resource has no near-substitutes in either production or consumption. Then, other things remaining the same, it is valuable. Its accounting price is high. On the other hand, if a resource has substitutes in large quantities, then, even if it were dwindling, its accounting price will be low. These are illustrations of (c).

In order to illustrate (d), imagine that the social institutions in a country are dysfunctional, so that a number of resources are put to use very inefficiently. Then, other things remaining the same, the accounting prices of those resources will be low, relative to the goods and services that are used more effectively. As this could seem paradoxical, it requires an explanation.

---

[2] *The Economist* has for many years used the basic McDonald hamburger ('Big Mac') as the numeraire for making international comparisons of the cost of living, an ingenious choice.

[3] Notice that (b) and (c) are closely related.   [4] I return to this point in Chs. 10 and 11.

If a commodity is wasted and the prevailing institutions are unlikely to change, the social worth of an additional unit of the good will be low. So its accounting price will be low. Of course, if the prevailing institutions are dysfunctional, there is a strong case for establishing better ones. Similarly, if current policies are wrong-headed, they ought to be revised. If the project being evaluated is an institutional reform under which the resources in question would be better used, their accounting prices will not be low. Accounting prices do a lot of work for us in summarizing information about an economy.

If the good isn't a 'good', but is instead a 'bad' (sulfur emission), its accounting price is negative. But even if a good is a 'good', its accounting price could be negative if the economy's institutions are bad: offering an extra unit of the good to someone could be a bad thing. Examples include common-property resources suffering from the tragedy of the commons. Consider that carbon is emitted into the atmosphere when fossil fuels are burnt. The use of fossil fuels by motorists yields private benefits to them, but they lead to collective losses (enhanced greenhouse effect). If emissions are untaxed, private benefits would be impervious to the collective damage caused by the combustion of fossil fuels. Imagine now that the collective damage arising from a small increase in the use of fossil fuels exceeds private benefits. An additional unit of fossil fuels awarded to a motorist will then lower social well-being. The accounting price of fossil fuels in a motorist's vehicle will be negative.

8.2. NECESSITIES VS. LUXURIES

Natural resources are of direct use in consumption (fisheries), of indirect use as inputs in production (oil and natural gas; the wide array of ecosystem services), and of use in both (air and water). The value of a resource may be *utilitarian* (as a source of food, or as a keystone species)—economists call this its *use-value*; it may be *aesthetic* (places of scenic beauty), or it may be *intrinsic* (primates).[5] In fact, it may be all these things (biodiversity). Their worth to us could be from extraction (timber) or from their presence as a stock (forest cover), or from both (forests).

Interpreting natural resources in a broad way, as we are doing here, enables us to consider a number of substantive issues. Included on our list of resources are assets that provide the many and varied ecosystem services upon which life is based. We should also add minerals and fossil fuels. Note too that environmental pollutants are the reverse side of natural resources. In some cases the emission of pollutants amounts directly to a degradation of ecosystems (the effect of acid rains on forests). In others, it means a reduction in environmental quality

---

[5] Krutilla (1967) explored the idea of intrinsic value.

(deterioration of water quality), which also amounts to degradation of ecosystems (watersheds). Thus, for analytical purposes there is no reason to distinguish resource economics from environmental economics, or resource management problems from pollution management problems. Roughly speaking, 'resources' are 'goods', while 'pollutants' (the degrader of resources) are 'bads'. In this sense, pollution is the reverse of conservation.[6]

The mirror-symmetry between conservation and pollution is well illustrated by the atmosphere, which serves as both a source of nourishment and a sink for pollutants. The atmosphere is a *public good*. (If air quality is improved, we all enjoy the benefits, and none can be excluded from enjoying the benefits.) It is also a common pool for pollution. That it is a public good means that the private benefit from improving air quality is less than the social benefit.[7] Without collective action, there is underinvestment in air quality. On the other hand, as the atmosphere is a common pool into which pollutants can be deposited, the private cost of pollution is less than the social cost.[8] Without collective action, there is an excessive use of the pool as a sink for pollutants. Either way, the atmosphere suffers from the tragedy of the commons.

A resource of prime importance is *biodiversity*, which not only possesses value as an amenity, but also has functional worth, as a 'repository' of genetic information and for the ecosystem services it helps to provide. But scratch an economist and you are likely to find someone who regards the natural environment pretty much as an amenity. It is even today commonly thought that, to quote an editorial in the UK's *Independent* (4 December 1999), '[economic] growth is good for the environment because countries need to put poverty behind them in order to care'; or, to quote *The Economist* (4 December, 1999: 17), 'trade improves the environment, because it raises incomes, and the richer people are, the more willing they are to devote resources to cleaning up their living space'.

These passages reflect the view that the natural environment is a luxury. It is a detached view, observed from Olympian heights.[9] Closer to home, matters look different. Producing as it does a multitude of ecosystem services, a large part of what the natural environment offers us is a necessity. The services include

---

[6] This taxonomy was explored in Dasgupta (1982b).   [7] This was noted in Ch. 7.

[8] This too was noted in Ch. 7.

[9] The view's origin can be traced to World Bank (1992), which reported that in cross-country studies the emission of sulfur oxides has been found to be related to GNP per head in the form of an inverse-U (see also Cropper and Griffiths, 1994; Grossman and Krueger, 1995). It is tempting, but wrong, to extrapolate from this an inverse-U relationship between the use of all natural resources and GNP per head. See the comments in Arrow *et al.* (1995) on the inverse-U relationship, and the responses it elicited in symposia built round the article in *Ecological Economics*, 1995, 15(1); *Ecological Applications*, 1996, 6(1); and *Environment and Development Economics*, 1996, 1(1). See also the special issue of *Environment and Development Economics*, 1997, 2(4).

maintaining a genetic library, preserving and regenerating soil, fixing nitrogen and carbon, recycling nutrients, controlling floods, filtering pollutants, assimilating waste, pollinating crops, operating the hydrological cycle, and maintaining the gaseous composition of the atmosphere. A number of services filter into a global context, but many are local.[10]

A resource can be a luxury for others even while it is a necessity for some. Nowhere is this possibility more poignant than regarding *watersheds*, which harbour commercial timber, agricultural land, recreational opportunities, and non-marketed products (gums, resin, honey, fodder, drinking water, and fuelwood for home use). Watershed forests purify water and protect downstream farmers and fishermen from floods, droughts, and sediments. In tropical watersheds, forests house a significant quantity of carbon and are the major location of biodiversity. A forest canopy can house several thousand species of living forms in a single hectare.

Some of the products of watersheds are necessities for local inhabitants (forest dwellers, downstream farmers, fishermen), some are sources of revenue for commercial firms (timber companies), while others are luxuries for outsiders (eco-tourists). Some of the benefits accrue to nationals (from agricultural goods), while others spill over as transboundary externalities (from carbon sequestration). Watersheds offer joint products (protection of biodiversity, flood control, household goods), but they also offer services that compete against one another (commercial timber, agricultural land, biodiversity). Competition among rival services has been a prime force behind the transformations of watersheds. Politically, commercial demand can easily outrank local needs, especially under non-democratic regimes. If local biodiversity is lost, eco-tourists can go where it still exists. International public opinion, not to mention pressure from the country's elite, is often at best tepid. Local needs are frequently trumped by outsiders' demands.

When wetlands, forests, and woodlands are destroyed (for agriculture, urban extension, or whatever), traditional dwellers suffer. For them, and they are among the poorest in society, there are no substitutes. For others there is something else, often somewhere else, which means there are substitutes. The range between a need and a luxury is enormous and context-ridden. Macroeconomic reasoning glosses over the heterogeneity of Earth's resources and the diverse uses to which they are put—by people residing at the site and by those elsewhere. In Part IV we will identify pathways by which official economic activity (GNP) can grow at the expense of the lives of the poorest. Poverty and degradation of the local natural-resource base are tied to each other by politics and economics. We should not have expected it to be otherwise.

---

[10] For succinct accounts, see Ehrlich and Ehrlich (1997) and Daily and S. Dasgupta (2001).

8.3. BIODIVERSITY AND SUBSTITUTION POSSIBILITIES

Frequently environmental debates are about the extent to which people are able to substitute one thing for another. Many believe that problems arising from the depletion of natural resources can be overcome by the accumulation of knowledge and manufactured and human capital. Others believe there are limits to substitution possibilities.

Four kinds of substitution help to ease resource constraints, be they local or global. First, there can be substitution of one thing for another in consumption (nylon and rayon substituting for cotton and wool, pulses substituting for meat, and so forth). Secondly, manufactured capital can substitute for labour and natural resources in production. (The wheel and double-glazing are two extreme examples.) Thirdly, novel production techniques can substitute for old ones.[11] Fourthly, and for us here most importantly, natural resources themselves can substitute for one another. (Renewable resources may substitute for non-renewable ones as sources of energy.) All this involves the more general idea that, as each resource is depleted, there are close substitutes lying in wait, either at the same site or elsewhere. If this were true, then, even as constraints increasingly bite on any one resource base, humanity should be able to move to other resource bases, either at the same site or elsewhere. The enormous additions to the sources of industrial energy that have been realized (successively, human and animal power, wind, timber, water, coal, oil and natural gas, and, most recently, nuclear power) are a prime historical illustration of this possibility.[12]

Humanity has been substituting one thing for another since time immemorial. Even the final conversion of forests into agricultural land in England in the Middle Ages was a form of substitution: large ecosystems were transformed to produce more food.[13] But the pace and scale of substitution in recent centuries have been unprecedented. Landes (1998) has argued that the discovery of vast numbers of ways of substituting resources among one another resulted in the Industrial Revolution in the eighteenth century. The extraordinary economic progress experienced in Western Europe and North America since then, and in East Asia more recently, has been another consequence of finding new ways to substitute goods and services among one another, and then bring about the

---

[11] For example, the discovery of effective ways to replace the piston by the steam turbine (i.e. converting from reciprocating to rotary motion) was introduced into power plants and ships a little over 100 years ago. The innovation was an enormous energy saver in engines.

[12] But these shifts have not been without unanticipated collective costs. Global warming, associated with the burning of fossil fuels, did not feature in economic calculations in earlier decades.

[13] Forests in England had been denuded earlier, by Neolithic Britons and the Romans.

substitutions.[14] Spatial dispersion of ecosystems has enabled this to happen. The ecological transformation of rural England in the Middle Ages probably reduced the nation's biodiversity, but it increased income without any direct effect on global productivity.

But that was then, and we are in the here and now. The question is whether it is possible for the scale of human activity to increase substantially beyond what it is today without placing undue stress on the major ecosystems that remain. The cost of substituting manufactured capital for natural resources can be high. Low-cost substitutes could turn out to be not so low-cost if accounting prices are used in the costing rather than market prices. Depleting certain types of natural capital and substituting it with manufactured capital can be socially uneconomic.

Degradation of a natural resource base (destruction of native populations of flora and fauna) not only affects the volume and quality of ecosystem services, but also challenges the system's resilience, which is its capacity to absorb disturbances without undergoing fundamental changes in its functional characteristics. To interpret an ecosystem's loss of resilience, one needs to view it as having moved to a different stability domain. Sudden changes in the character of shallow lakes (from clear to eutrophied water) resulting from increases in nutrients, and the transformation of grasslands into shrublands consequent upon bad cattle management practices are examples.[15] Human societies have on occasions been unable to avoid suffering from unexpected flips in their local ecosystems because of this. Fishermen on Lake Victoria and nomads in the new shrublands of Southern Africa are examples from recent years; the inhabitants of the Mayan states in the early ninth century and those of Easter Island in the eighteenth century are examples from earlier eras.[16]

Determining the functional value of biodiversity is a delicate matter. When ecologists speak favourably of biodiversity, which they do in unison and with regularity, there is an implicit assumption that the diverse species have co-evolved under selection pressure. They never mean a simple head-count of 'objects'

---

[14] During the past two centuries gross domestic product per head in Western Europe has increased some twelve-fold.

[15] See Holling (1973), R. M. May (1977), Peterman (1977), Ludwig, Jones, and Holling (1978), Roughgarden, May, and Levin (1989), Dublin, Sinclair, and McGlade (1990), Laycock (1991), Knowlton (1992), Perrings and Walker (1995), Rahmstorf (1995), Scheffer (1997), Levin *et al.* (1998), Carpenter, Ludwig, and Brock (1999), Levin (1999), Brock, Mäler, and Perrings (1999), Mäler (2000), Mäler, Xepapadeus, and de Zeeuw (2000), and Carpenter (2001) for examples. To put the matter technically, one set of circumstances in which flips occur is when a system crosses a bifurcation point; another is when the system is nudged across a separatrix. Murray (1993) is an excellent treatise on the non-linear dynamics of biological systems.

[16] The decay of Mayan civilization has been traced to an overuse of agricultural land. Soil degradation made Mayan populations more vulnerable to crop failure in times of low rainfall. Martin and Grube (2000) have offered evidence that the collapse of a number of Mayan cities occurred in the remarkably short interval of AD 800–30. The death of Easter Island has been the subject of much recent debate. Brander and Taylor (1998) offer a short historical account and a formal mechanism by which a seemingly sophisticated island economy could collapse over a short period of time.

constituting the diversity. When the Nile perch was introduced into Lake Victoria, the diversity of species increased, but not for long. The lake, as a fishery, was devastated.

Biodiversity, appropriately defined, would seem to be a key to ecosystem productivity. By 'productivity' I mean the production of biomass, termed 'primary productivity'. It has been found in experiments in field stations that species-rich plots yield greater biomass than species-poor ones, which would indicate that the total productivity of a population of species is greater than the sum of the productivities of any individual species grown in isolation. This reflects a form of synergy.[17]

The index of biodiversity in these experiments was rough and ready, being simply the number of species; it wasn't based on the functional attributes of the various species in each plot. However, a recent study of several functional attributes of plant species in a lightly grazed site and a heavily grazed site in the Australian rangeland uses a more wide-ranging index.[18] The study sought to test the thesis that biodiversity makes ecosystems resilient. The authors report that the majority of plant species in the lightly grazed site occur in low abundance, with only a few making the bulk of the biomass. The dominant species were functionally dissimilar (they 'complement' one another), while species that were functionally similar to them were those in low abundance. (They would be the 'competitors' and, therefore, the potential 'substitutes'.) The authors also report that a few of the minor species in the lightly grazed site were dominant at the site that had been heavily grazed, indicating that biodiversity plays a role in making ecosystems resilient to changes in the circumstances they experience. The minor species at the lightly grazed site could be regarded as 'waiting in the wings' to take over, if required to do so. The thought here is that species abundance in ecosystems is like spare capacity: it offers an insurance device for ecosystems. These are early days in what is an important research programme, but the findings are suggestive.

It remains a popular belief though that the utilitarian value of biodiversity is located primarily in the potential uses of the genetic material it harbours (e.g. for pharmaceutical purposes). Preserving biodiversity is seen as a way of holding a diverse portfolio of assets with uncertain payoff. But biodiversity is essential for the maintenance of a wide variety of services on which humans depend for survival. (Species complementarities are involved.) This has the corollary that to invoke the idea of substitutability among natural resources in order

---

[17] In plots of up to 32 species, biomass was found to increase with diversity; see Hector *et al.* (1999). Earlier, it had been found that species-rich plots are more drought-resistant than species-poor ones (Tilman and Downing, 1994; Tilman, 1997). See also Loreau and Hector (2001), who have found evidence that the biodiversity–productivity link is due to greater species complementarity in plots containing greater biodiversity; the link is not due to the fact that plots harbouring a greater number of species are likely to contain a few that are especially productive.   [18] Walker, Kinzig, and Langridge (1999).

to play down the usefulness of biodiversity is a wrong intellectual move. The point is this: if biodiversity is necessary for an ecosystem to continue providing services, the importance of that same biodiversity cannot be downplayed by the mere hope that for every species there are substitute species lying in wait within that same ecosystem. Recall the famous analogy in Ehrlich and Ehrlich (1981) relating species in an ecosystem to rivets in an airplane. One by one, perhaps, species may disappear and not be missed. (There is spare capacity, meaning 'species substitutibility'.) Eventually, though, the cumulative effect of biodiversity loss will lead to the crash of ecosystem functioning ('species complementarity' will kick in), just as the cumulative loss of redundant rivets will lead to the crash of an airplane.[19]

The currently dominant literature on economic growth has bypassed these issues. Growth economists point to new ideas as a source of progress. It is mostly supposed that the growth of ideas is capable of circumventing any constraint the natural environment may impose on the ability of economies to grow indefinitely.[20] It is noted too that research and development enjoy cumulative returns, because the benefits are durable and can be shared collectively. The models assume that growth in population leads to an increase in the demand for goods and services. There are models in which an expansion in the demand and supply of ideas implies that, in the long run, output per head can be expected to grow at a rate that is itself an increasing function of the rate of growth of population. (It is only when population growth is nil that the long run rate of growth of output per head is nil.) These models regard indefinite growth in population to be beneficial.[21]

The nature of new products in contemporary growth theory isn't modelled explicitly. One can only assume that the theory imagines future innovations to be of such character that indefinite growth in output would make no more than a finite additional demand on the natural resource base. The assumption is all-too-easily questionable: essential goods and services, such as fresh water, ecosystem services, and the atmosphere as a sink, have increasingly come under 'stress'.[22] In any event, we should be sceptical of visions that place such an enormous burden on an economic regime not much more than 250 years old

---

[19] It is difficult to overstate the significance of biodiversity, its role in the functioning of ecosystems, more generally its place in the evolution of life. Wilson (1992) is a deep meditation on the subject. Levin (2001), which will prove to be *the* source book on the subject for some time to come, is a five-volume encyclopedia. Beattie and Ehrlich (2001) is a lively introduction to the bewildering variety of roles and niches found to be occupied by life forms. For studies on the economics of biodiversity, see Barbier, Burgess, and Folke (1994), Pearce and Moran (1994), Perrings *et al.* (1994, 1995), and Perrings (2000).

[20] There are growth models that incorporate natural resources (Aghion and Howitt, 1996; Beltratti, 1996, 1997), but I have in mind the bulk of the literature, which may be presumed to reflect the mental models that shape economic policy.   [21] Jones (1998) contains a summary of contemporary growth theory.

[22] Vitousek *et al.* (1986, 1997); Postel, Daily and Ehrlich (1996); Levin (2001).

(Fogel, 1994; Johnson, 2000). Extrapolation into the past is a sobering exercise: over the long haul of history (say 2000 years), economic growth was for most of the time not much more than zero until about AD 1700, even in regions that are currently very rich. The study of possible feedback loops between poverty, demographic behaviour, and the character and performance of both human institutions and the natural resource base is not yet on the research agenda of most modern growth theorists. There is a cultural divide between growth economists and those who see the natural environment as playing an essential role in our lives.[23]

8.4. ESTIMATING ACCOUNTING PRICES

A commodity's accounting price reflects the social worth of the overall change to the economy that would be brought about by a small increase in its availability, or, alternatively, by the social loss suffered if there is a small reduction in its availability. We have studied a variety of factors that determine accounting prices. How should the prices themselves be estimated?

There is a Utopian scenario where market prices equal accounting prices. Economists call that state of affairs a 'full optimum'. Elsewhere, depending on the circumstances, market prices are reasonable approximations of some goods and services, while for others they are not. The theoretically valid procedure for estimating accounting prices is to put their definition directly to use. The Appendix shows how in principle this can be done. A Platonic decision-maker is needed. In practice, the procedure is followed when governments consider the preservation of cultural monuments and the funding of the arts. More generally, though, the method can mislead, a fact leaders of the former Eastern Bloc discovered all too slowly and painfully. Democratic procedures involve indirect methods.

One possible way to estimate accounting prices is by discovering people's *willingness-to-pay* for small changes in the flow of goods and services. Frequently, though, willingness-to-pay has been estimated for discrete changes which could be a reasonable approximation of accounting prices in some circumstances, but not in others. For irrigation water, fisheries, timber, and agricultural and grazing

[23] Here is a rough calculation: world per capita output today is about 5000 US dollars. The World Bank regards one dollar a day to be about as bad as it can be. People wouldn't be able to survive on anything substantially less than that. It would then be reasonable to suppose that 2000 years ago per capita income was not much less than a dollar a day. So, let us assume that it was a dollar a day. This would mean that per capita income 2000 years ago was about 350 dollars a year. Rounding off numbers, this means, very roughly speaking, that per capita income has risen about 16 times since then. This in turn means that world income per head has doubled every 500 years, which in its turn means that the average annual rate of growth has been about 0.14 per cent per year, a figure not much in excess of zero, which is what I have alluded to in the text.

land, the idea is to estimate their use-value, using market prices as approximate measures. The accounting price of a fishery would be the present discounted value of the flow of profits it is expected to generate from harvests.[24] Of course, if the fishery is located at a coral reef, matters are more problematic. The damage to the reef caused by fishing will have to be deducted from profits. Ways have to be found to estimate the accounting price of the coral forest; this would include the forest's role in nurturing the fishery, its worth as a tourist site, and as a buffer to the coastal area against storms, and so on.

Losses resulting from water-logging and overgrazing would be the present discounted value of the flow of profits lost because of the water-logging and over-grazing. The value of a piece of agricultural land, *qua* agricultural land, would be the present discounted value of the flow of profits it is expected to generate from cultivation (a not-so-difficult matter to assess), minus the environmental damages caused by the pesticides and herbicides used in cultivation (a difficult matter to assess). And so forth.[25]

One problem with using market prices even for such resources as those just mentioned is that, in an imperfect economy, they don't account for the consumption externalities coming under the general heading of the 'demonstration effect'.[26] Even short-term fads and fashions in consumption behaviour can devastate local resource bases. At least a portion of the demand for goods and services needs to be purged when estimating the contribution of consumption to human well-being. But environmental and resource economists haven't yet taken demonstration effects seriously enough to find ways of making the necessary purge.

Firewood and drinking and cooking water are inputs in household production. In poor countries they are frequently obtained not in the market, but from forests and water-holes. For this reason household production processes need to be studied. To take an example, transportation costs (in particular energy costs, measured in calories) for women and children would be less if the sources of fuelwood and water were not far away and receding. As a very first approximation, the value of water or fuelwood for household production can be estimated from these energy needs. However, this would be an underestimate, because the social worth of the resource on site would not have been included. In some situations (as on occasion with fuelwood), the resource is a substitute for a tradable

[24] See Ch. 9 for an elaboration.

[25] The literature is huge. See e.g. Carson and Mitchell (1993) for water in recreational use; G. Brown and McGuire (1967), Howitt (1995), and N. Becker, Zeitouni, and Shecter (1997) for irrigation water; R. Cooper (1977) and Bjorndal (1988) for fisheries; Magrath and Arens (1989) and Repetto *et al.* (1989) for soil fertility; Bockstael and Irwin (2000) for land use; Anderson (1987), Newcombe (1989), Hassan (2000), Seroa da Motta and Ferraz (2000) for forestry; Vincent and Ali (1987) for minerals and timber; Dixon and Lal (1997) for coastal wetlands; and Pearce and Moran (1994) for biodiversity.

[26] Sect. 3.4 above.

input (paraffin or kerosene); in others (as with cooking water) it is a complement to tradable inputs (food grain). These features make it possible to estimate the accounting prices of non-marketed goods in terms of the accounting prices of marketed goods.[27]

Estimating the worth of tropical rainforests poses intriguing problems. Not only do rain forests preserve biodiversity (and are in turn preserved by it), they also influence regional climate and sequester carbon from the atmosphere. Under one set of calculations, based on a number of models of global warming, the social cost of the emission of a tonne of carbon has been found to be about 20 US dollars. From this it is possible to deduce that conversion of a hectare of primary rain forest into agriculture and cattle ranching causes damage worth 4000 US dollars. In the Amazon region of Brazil, the market value 2 hectare of land is 300 US dollars. (The soil isn't productive for agriculture.) The conversion of rain forests into ranches is a striking case of policy failure.[28]

Benefits from amenities are usually diffused among people. They are frequently public goods. Some are global public goods (the atmosphere). Because market prices aren't even a crude approximation, estimating the accounting prices of public goods is especially difficult. Special methods have to be deployed.[29]

One popular method involves asking representative samples of people hypothetical questions about their willingness-to-pay for preserving the amenity in its current form, rather than allowing it to deteriorate to some specified state. The idea is to add up the responses and so to magnify the sum to arrive at an estimate of the willingnesses-to-pay of the whole population. An alternative is to ask people how much they would be willing to accept as compensation for permitting the amenity to deteriorate from its present state to some other, specified, state. The idea here, again, is to add the responses and magnify the sum so as to arrive at an estimate of the sum of the willingnesses-to-accept by the whole population. The two alternatives taken together is called the *contingent-valuation method*, or CVM for short.[30]

CVM is attractive because it appeals to our democratic instinct that people should be asked for their opinion on matters that may be of concern to them.

---

[27] Mäler (1974) has a good discussion of this.

[28] These estimates, based on Schneider (1992) and Fankhauser (1994), are offered by Pearce and Moran (1994). Among early articles that drew attention to the misuse of the Amazon forests were Feder (1977, 1979).

[29] There is now a huge literature for the case of amenities. Mäler (1974) is the pioneering theoretical work of willingness-to-pay as a way of measuring the accounting price of amenities. For applications, see Krutilla and Fisher (1975), Lynne, Conroy, and Prochaska (1981), McConnell (1985), V. K. Smith and Desvousges (1986), Boyle and Bishop (1987), Hazilla and Kopp (1990), Braden and Kolstad (1991), Englin and Mendelsohn (1991), Viscusi, Magat, and Huber (1991), Kopp and Smith (1993), and K. Brown and Pearce (1994). Freeman (1993) is an excellent treatise on both the theory and the empirics of valuing environmental amenities. Ledyard (1995) surveys various experimental methods for eliciting the willingness-to-pay for public goods.

[30] Mitchell and Carson (1989) and Freeman (1993) contain fine expositions on CVM.

The method is attractive too because in principle it can reveal not only an amenity's use-value, but also the respondents' sense of its intrinsic worth. It is known, for example, that people derive satisfaction from the mere knowledge that the large primates in the forests of Uganda exist—they don't feel they have to go on safari to take pleasure in the thought that the primates are there. CVM is in principle capable of coaxing such information from respondents.[31] People are often willing to pay more to prevent an amenity from deteriorating to some specified level if they are informed that others will contribute as well than if they assumed that others were not contributing anything. A good questionnaire would be sensitive to this possibility.

An interesting application of CVM is to value small reductions in mortality risks, the idea being to estimate the value of a 'statistical life' (or the value of avoiding a 'statistical death'). To illustrate, suppose there are a thousand people, each of whom has a probability of 0.004 of dying during the next year. Imagine that a pollution control would reduce that probability to 0.003. Imagine also that each person in the group is willing to pay £1000 for this policy. The total willingness-to-pay is then £1 million. Since on average there would be one less death during the year if the policy were adopted, £1 million would be reckoned to be the value of a statistical life.[32]

For the most part, though, CVM hasn't been used to estimate accounting prices, which, as will be recalled, are the social worth of small increases in the supply of goods and services, or the social loss from small declines. Instead, the method has been applied to determine someone's willingness-to-pay for discrete changes in the quality of amenities, or, alternatively, their willingness to accept income for discrete changes. It has been found that people are often willing to pay more to prevent an amenity from deteriorating to some specified level than to accept compensation for permitting the amenity to deteriorate to that same level. There are social scientists who interpret this to mean that people don't have a consistent set of preferences. But this is to misinterpret the finding.[33] Someone could have a consistent set of preferences and yet respond differently to questions about their willingness-to-pay and their willingness-to-accept discrete changes in the bundles of goods and services they enjoy.[34]

---

[31] A method commonly in use for places of scenic beauty and game parks involves estimating from sample surveys the distribution of costs that visitors from different locations incur to view the site. This is called the *travel-cost method* (see e.g. Englin and Mendelsohn, 1991). In contrast to CVM, the travel-cost method does not elicit someone's assessment of a resource's intrinsic value.

[32] This and other examples are studied in Freeman (1993), who also summarizes a lively debate that has taken place on basing the value of reductions in the probability of death on statistical lives and their worth. Viscusi and Gayer (2000) is an excellent survey on methods for valuing environmental health risks.

[33] The discussion that follows is based on Mäler (1974), Hanemann (1991, 1994) and P. A. Diamond (1996).

[34] The point is that, if a preference ordering is all that can be obtained by the investigator, there isn't a unique way to represent a preference ordering numerically: if a numerical function represents an ordering, so does any monotonically increasing function of that function represent it (Sect. 1.6). Consider someone who has a

CVM has unravelled interesting features about people's stated values. On preservation, respondents have been discovered to provide answers that are independent of the scale of operation. Willingness-to-pay has been discovered to be the same regardless of whether, say, 100 or 10,000 cranes are saved. This is called the 'embedding problem'. It is almost as though people are willing to put aside so much for preserving populations from extinction, regardless of the size of the population, or even the number of species being preserved.

More problematically, respondents have been known to give different answers to the same question if it is put differently.[35] This means that investigators can elicit the kind of answers they would like to hear by framing the questionnaire in suitable ways. As CVM is not infrequently used in environmental litigations, the method has proved to be hugely controversial, despite its continuing popularity among academic environmental economists.[36] Vast sums of money can be involved. Investigators have been known to obtain responses consonant with their own financial interests. The court cases haven't been the seemliest of occasions for the practice of economics.

The application of CVM ought to have been more circumspect. It is all well and good to ask people for their opinion, but if they are uninformed of the functional attributes of the resources about which their opinion is sought, the point of the exercise is questionable. It is not unoften that we say, 'I don't know enough: tell me more that is known about the matter before I can give you a reasoned response.' It is possible, for example, that the embedding problem unearthed in CVM studies arises because people aren't provided with enough information about the functional attributes of the populations they are asked to value. It would surely be of relevance to respondents if, for example, they were informed that a resource on which their opinion is sought is subject to 'threshold effects' (i.e. that the resource base will collapse if it is drawn down below a certain level).

In democracies, citizens delegate responsibilities in the public domain to elected representatives. We are not uncomfortable that political decisions some-times go against what would have been our collective 'will' had we been asked

---

consistent set of preferences over bundles of goods and services; that is, she can order the alternatives. In asking her to state her willingness-to-pay for discrete changes in the quality of an amenity, the questioner is implicitly seeking to calibrate her preferences by means of one particular functional representation (the amounts of income she is willing to pay to prevent an amenity from deteriorating to various levels); whereas, in asking her to state her willingness to accept income for discrete changes in the quality of an amenity, the questioner seeks to calibrate her preferences by means of a different, but equally valid, functional representation (the amounts of income she is willing to accept for permitting the amenity to deteriorate to various levels). Note though that in neither case is the questioner attempting to estimate the amenity's accounting price.

[35] This is called the 'framing problem'; see Tversky and Kahneman (1988).

[36] E.g. in the *Exxon Valdes* case, where the state of Alaska sued Exxon after one of its oil tankers crashed off the state's coast. For an assessment of the strengths and weaknesses of CVM, see the report on the NOAA Panel on Contingent Valuation (co-chaired by K. J. Arrow and R. M. Solow) in Arrow and Solow *et al.* (1993).

to vote directly on those matters.[37] Limits on the scope of CVM ought to be guided by this fact. It would be dubious at best if CVM were deployed to value biodiversity in tropical rainforests. Normal precautions should have alerted caution before the forests were converted to agricultural land. But the prevailing institutions were not appropriate for the practice of the principles. The structure of incentives was wrong. And they continue to be wrong. Altering institutions is ultimately a political choice. Preserving biodiversity is thereby a political choice. One can imagine circumstances where CVM could help in reaching political decisions. But its role would at most be peripheral.[38]

In contrast to CVM, which asks people how much they value something, the *hedonic price method* involves inferring how much people value something (say, an amenity) from the commercial value of land at sites that offer that something, compared with similar land at sites that don't offer it. The hedonic price method can be used also to infer the value of a statistical life from the way people buy and sell health risks in the market place, for example from differences in wages among groups facing different levels of risk.[39]

Accounting prices have been estimated mostly on the basis of their use-value for resources that are consumed or serve as factors of production. But what is the point of this when we know that resources often possess intrinsic value as well? The answer is that it provides us with *biased* estimates of accounting prices, and this can be useful information. In a beautiful paper on the optimum rate of harvest of blue whales, Spence (1974) took the accounting price of the creatures to be the market value of their flesh, a seemingly absurd and repugnant move. But he showed that, under a wide range of plausible parameter values, it was most profitable for the international whaling industry to agree on a moratorium until the desired long-run population size was reached, and for the industry to then harvest the creatures at a rate equal to the population's (optimum) sustainable yield. Spence's analysis recommended preservation solely on commercial ground. But if preservation is the right policy when the accounting price of blue whales is estimated from their market price when dead, the recommendation would obviously be reinforced if their intrinsic worth, as stock, were added. This was the point of Spence's exercise.

Natural resources often possess yet another kind of value, one that is more amenable to quantification than their intrinsic value. It arises from a combination of two things: uncertainty in their future use-values, and irreversibility in their use. Genetic material in tropical forests provides a prime example. The twin presence of uncertainty and irreversibility implies that preservation of its

---

[37] In the UK, capital punishment is often cited as an example.

[38] I have gained much from discussions on the scope of CVM with Scott Barrett and Karl-Göran Mäler.

[39] Reductions in air and water quality have an additional value, in that they lower the depreciation of physical structures. Mäler and Wyzga (1976) and World Bank (1992) have accounts of this line of analysis.

stock has an additional value: the value of extending society's set of future options. Future options have an additional worth because, with the passage of time, more information should be forthcoming about the resource's use-value. This additional worth is often called an *option value*. The accounting price of a resource is, at the very least, the sum of its use-value and its option value.[40]

The valuation techniques I have just enumerated are built round the idea that preferences and demands, as they stand, should be respected. There is an enormous amount to be said for this, reflecting as it does a democratic viewpoint. But even when commending it, we shouldn't play down the strictures of those social thinkers who have urged the rich, be they in rich countries or in poor ones, to curb their material demands, to alter their ways so as to better husband Earth's limited resources. Their thought is that we deplete resources without trying to determine the consequences of depleting them, sometimes because we haven't the time to find out, but sometimes because we may not wish to know, since the answer may prove to be unpalatable to us. Being sensitive to ecological processes requires investment in early education on the connection between human well-being and the natural environment. If such strictures as I am alluding to seem quaint today, it may be because we are psychologically uncomfortable with the vocabulary. But that isn't an argument for not taking them seriously.[41]

Let me sum up. The social worth of natural resources can be decomposed into three parts: use-value, option value, and intrinsic value. The proportions differ. Oil and natural gas aren't usually thought to possess intrinsic value, nor perhaps an option value, but they do have use value. The great apes are intrinsically valuable; some would say they should have no other value, that they are an end in themselves, not a means to anything. Biodiversity possesses all three types of value. And so on.

8.5. TOTAL VS. INCREMENTAL VALUES

The purpose of estimating accounting prices of environmental resources isn't to value the entire natural environment. It is to evaluate the benefits and costs arising from *changes* to the environment. Valuation and evaluation involve comparisons. Prices, whether actual or accounting, have significance only when there are potential exchanges to be made, as when selecting projects. The statement that an investment can be expected to degrade the environment by, say, 1 million dollars annually has meaning, because it says, among other things,

---

[40] The pioneering works on option values are Weisbrod (1964), Arrow and Fisher (1974), and Henry (1974).

[41] A. Dasgupta (1975) offers a compelling argument for addressing these matters.

that if the investment is not made humanity will enjoy an additional 1 million dollars of benefits in the form of environmental services. The statement also has operational significance: the estimate could (and should) be used to calculate the investment's social profits. The value of an incremental change to the natural environment is meaningful because it presumes that humanity will survive the change to experience it.

Contrast such an estimate with one that says that world-wide the flow of environmental services is currently worth, *in total*, 33 trillion US dollars annually (Costanza *et al.*, 1997). The authors calculated the figure so as to show how vital these resources are.[42] However, there is a problem with the exercise itself: it is meaningless. The reason the estimate is meaningless is that, if environmental services were to cease, life would not exist. But then who would be there to receive 33 trillion US dollars of annual benefits if humanity were to exchange its very existence for them? Economics, when used with care, is meant to serve our ethical values. The language it provides helps us to choose in accordance with those values. Life is precious and is the reason why the natural environment is valuable. Costanza *et al.* (1997) want to persuade us that the natural environment is valuable because it can be imputed a large monetary value. This is to get things backward.[43]

---

[42] The figure is comparable to the world's gross annual output.

[43] Formally, we have a case where the value of an entire something has no meaning, and is therefore of no use, even though the value of incremental changes to that same thing not only has meaning, but also has use. Examples abound in economics (utility) and physics (potential field).

9

Wealth and Well-Being

9.1. SUSTAINABLE DEVELOPMENT

The phrase 'sustainable development' was introduced by the International Union for the Conservation of Nature and Natural Resources (IUCN).[1] The publication drew attention to the role played by the natural environment in our economic life. But the phrase became a commonplace only after the publication of a report by the World Commission on Environment and Development (WCED), widely known as the Brundtland Commission Report, where sustainable development was defined as 'development that meets the needs of the present without compromising the ability of future generations to meet their own needs'.[2] The idea is that, relative to their respective demographic bases, each generation should bequeath to its successor at least as large a *productive base* as it inherited from its predecessor. If it were to do so, the economic possibilities facing the successor would be no worse than those it faced when inheriting productive assets from its predecessor.

Talk of 'productive base', and we are confronted immediately with a problem of aggregation over a myriad of ill-assorted assets. The base in question consists of such disparate objects as buildings and machines; watersheds and the open seas; the differential calculus and the latest software; education and skills; interpersonal networks and the legal system; and so on. I will have much to say about aggregation over assets later in this chapter. Notice though that, in seeking to define sustainable development in terms of an economy's productive base, we are searching for a measure that is based on the determinants of well-being.

What would the corresponding idea be if sustainable development were viewed instead in terms of the constituents of well-being? Several possibilities suggest themselves.[3] The one I explore here is prompted by the discussion in Chapter 6.

---

[1] IUCN (1980).   [2] World Commission (1987: 43).

[3] See Pearce, Markandya, and Barbier (1989) and Pezzey (1992). It should be noted that asking if economic development is sustainable is different from asking if a given level of consumption is sustainable. See below in the text.

Assume, for expositional ease, that population is constant and the world is deterministic. The present is $t = 0$. Denote current well-being at date t by U_t. Let C_t be an aggregate index of the determinants of U_t. Thus, $U_t = U(C_t)$, where U increases with C. Social well-being at t (≥ 0) is taken to be

$$V_t = \sum_{t}^{\infty} \beta^{(\tau-t)} U(C_\tau), \qquad \text{where } \beta \equiv \frac{1}{(1+\delta)}, \quad \text{and } \delta \geq 0.$$

For notational simplicity, I write the consumption stream, $(C_0, C_1, \ldots, C_t, \ldots)$ as $\{C_t\}_0^{\infty}$.

Consider the following definitions:

(X): The consumption stream $\{C_t\}_0^{\infty}$ corresponds to a sustainable-development path if $U(C_{t+1}) \geq U(C_t)$, for $t \geq 0$, that is if $C_{t+1} \geq C_t$, for $t \geq 0$.

(Y): The consumption stream $\{C_t\}_0^{\infty}$ corresponds to a sustainable-development path if $V_{t+1} \geq V_t$, for $t \geq 0$.

In contrast to X, which looks at well-being *in* time (U), the focus of Y is well-being *through* time (V). While criterion X requires that U should never decline, criterion Y requires that V should never decline. While X implies Y, Y does not imply X. So, Y is more general.[4]

Criteria X and Y offer contrasting ideas of what a consumption stream must look like if it corresponds to a path of sustainable development. Both involve conditions that must be satisfied at *every* future date, a phenomenally strict requirement. If the notion of sustainability is to have practical force, it has to be less ambitious. It should be enough for decision-makers at t if they knew that the choices they made would not compromise the prospects open to decision-makers at date $t + 1$. Never mind dates far in the future: decision-makers at t would justifiably feel satisfied if they were to do their own job satisfactorily. After all, or so they could argue, they will have no say over what will be chosen by decision-makers in the distant future.

Consider then the following definitions:

(X'): The consumption stream $\{C_t\}_0^{\infty}$ corresponds to a sustainable-development path *at t* if $U(C_{t+1}) \geq U(C_t)$, that is if $C_{t+1} \geq C_t$.

(Y'): The consumption stream $\{C_t\}_0^{\infty}$ corresponds to a sustainable-development path *at t* if $V_{t+1} \geq V_t$.

It is clear that Y' nails the idea of sustainable development, while X' fails to do so. Being concerned only with comparisons of current well-being (U),

---

[4] If economic policies were arbitrarily given, this would be a trivial matter to confirm. Interestingly, Asheim (1994) has identified cases where even an optimum consumption stream may satisfy Y, while violating X.

criterion X′ could be satisfied at *t* even as the economy's productive base is allowed to shrink, jeopardizing life in the future. It could even be that current well-being increases between *t* and *t* + 1 only because prevailing policies discourage the accumulation of manufactured capital and are also rapacious in the use of the natural environment. Criterion X′ would be unable to detect this. Such measures of the quality of life as the Human Development Index of the United Nations Development Programme suffer from this weakness.[5] In contrast, criterion Y′ is able to detect whether existing policies are myopic, precisely because it involves a comparison of intergenerational well-beings (*V*). So I adopt Y′ as the definition of sustainable development and refer to V_t as *social well-being*, or *well-being* for short.

How can one judge whether an economy is pursuing a sustainable development path at *t*? In principle, we could produce a forecast of future consumption services, measure V_t and V_{t+1} directly, and check to see if $V_{t+1} \geq V_t$. But as with social cost–benefit analysis, a subject we explore in Chapter 10, it proves easier if we are able to use a linear index of the determinants of well-being. Towards this, the social worth of the economy's capital assets suggests itself.

Let us call the social worth of an economy's capital assets its *wealth*. We are interested in an index that is linear in the stocks of the assets. What weights should we use to value them? It transpires that accounting prices are the weights to use. So, by 'wealth' I mean the accounting value of the economy's capital assets.[6] If we were to adopt wealth as the index of well-being, sustainable development would mean the creation of wealth (or, at worst, the non-destruction of wealth).

But wealth creation isn't self-evidently the same as sustainable development in the sense the term is defined in criterion Y′. For example, it could be that, being dysfunctional, an economy expands its capital base even while refusing to enjoy the fruits of that increase, to an extent that consumption declines over time. (The country is on a capital-accumulation spree, with no regard for consumption.) It could be thought that this is a scenario where wealth increases even while the quality of life declines, but in fact this cannot happen. An asset's accounting price is the increase in well-being that would occur if a tiny bit more of the asset were made available costlessly (or, alternatively, it is the decrease in well-being that would be brought about if a tiny bit less were made available). In the case being considered, the accounting prices of some of the capital assets would be negative: shoring them would cause a further decline in consumption. The accumulation spree in question would make the economy grow poorer, not wealthier.

---

[5] Sect. 5.8.   [6] We study the concept of wealth more formally in Sects. 9.2–9.3 and the Appendix.

One can say more. Qualifications apart (I discuss them later in the chapter), the intuitive notion of sustainable development offered by the Brundtland Commission Report, interpreted here as wealth creation, is equivalent to the notion formalized in criterion Y′. But an economy's wealth is an aggregate of the determinants of well-being, while criterion Y′ works with its constituents. Once again, we have an equivalence between a measure of the quality of life based on its constituents and one based on its determinants. Although a formal proof of the equivalence is provided only in the Appendix (Proposition 3), I offer an intuitive understanding of the result in the following two sections.

Equivalence results are just that: equivalence results. Sustainable development as defined in criterion Y′ is the same as the requirement that an economy's wealth must not decline. But the equivalence doesn't mean that sustainable development is *possible*. Whether it is possible depends upon demographic behaviour, consumption patterns, and production and substitution possibilities among the myriad forms of capital assets.[7]

9.2. CAPITAL ASSETS AND INSTITUTIONS

An economy's *productive base* includes not only manufactured capital, human capital, natural capital, and knowledge, but also its institutions. Together they determine the production, distribution, and use of goods and services. A society's productive base is the source of its well-being.

The productive base is a diverse collection of durable objects, some tangible and alienable (buildings and machinery, land and animals, trees and shrubs), some tangible but non-alienable (human beings, the oceans), some intangible but alienable (codified pieces of knowledge, such as patentable ideas), some intangible and non-alienable (air, skills, the legal framework, and cultural coordinates), and some that are yet to be defined in an acceptable way (social capital).[8] This heterogeneity poses a problem. No doubt it serves heuristic purposes to refer to all but people as 'capital goods' and then to say that output is produced by people and capital goods, but explaining that to economic statisticians is not much use. They will ask how all the bits and pieces called 'capital goods' are to be measured and valued. They will also ask how accounting prices are to be estimated. Moreover, economists observe that to say someone is accumulating capital is to suggest that they are sacrificing something now for future benefit. They also note that some of the items on the list (for example, social capital

---

[7] Dasgupta and Heal (1979: chs. 7 and 10).

[8] On social capital and the difficulties surrounding its definition, see the essays in Dasgupta and Serageldin (2000).

in the form of communal festivities) do not involve sacrifice, but rather, seem more like pleasurable activities.[9]

Conceptually, social capital has proved to be problematic and economists have come down hard on the concept.[10] In his work on Italy, R. D. Putnam (1993) pursued an interesting route for measuring social capital. Putnam's unit of analysis was a province, and in cross-provincial data he found a strong positive relationship between economic performance and measures of 'civic engagement', such as membership in unions and choral societies.[11] From this finding to the thought that civic engagement matters for economic performance is a natural step. It is a step Putnam took with relish.

I don't believe economists question that move. What bothers them is a measurement problem. The form of civic engagement evolves over time. Even when choral societies are hard-pressed to attract new recruits, it could be that citizens are discovering new ways to connect with one another (e.g. via the internet), which itself could be the reason why choral societies are hard-pressed. Measurement problems abound in the search for social capital. Nor did it help that Putnam defined social capital to be 'features of social organization, such as trust, norms, and networks that can improve the efficiency of society by facilitating coordinated actions'.[12] As a characterization this appears beguiling, but it suffers from a weakness: it encourages us to amalgamate in turn beliefs, behavioural rules, and such forms of capital assets as interpersonal networks, without offering a hint as to how they are to be aggregated.

A large contemporary literature on social capital interprets the concept as an economy's institutions.[13] Admittedly, a name is but a name, but some names can mislead. To call a society's institutions 'capital' is less helpful than may seem. Institutions are distinct from capital assets, in that they *guide* the allocation of resources (among which are capital assets!). This is why it isn't useful to regard institutions as simply another form of capital. Institutions are better seen as *resource allocation mechanisms*. In the Appendix, I formalize the idea and show how institutions shape valuation and evaluation exercises.

James Coleman's original advocacy of the concept of social capital was based on a different model.[14] He took it to be an input in the production of human capital. Social capital in this view is an aggregate of interpersonal networks. Establishing networks involves time and effort. Much of the effort is pleasurable,

---

[9] See Arrow (2000). In his critique of the concept of social capital, Solow (2000) produces a list of questions economists and statisticians would ask of it, to which there are currently no satisfactory answers.

[10] See, especially, Arrow (2000) and Solow (2000).

[11] Inter-village data from poor countries have revealed similar relationships; see e.g. Narayan and Pritchett (1999).   [12] R. D. Putnam (1993: 167).

[13] See e.g. the Special Issue of the *Journal of Interdisciplinary History*, 1999, 29(3), on 'Patterns of Social Capital, Part I'.   [14] Coleman (1988).

some not. Even so, just as academics are paid for what they mostly like doing anyway, as a return on investment in their education, networking would be expected to pay dividends even when maintaining networks is a pleasurable activity.

Empirical work bears this out. Among business firms in the United States, it has been found that, controlling for age, education, and experience, employees enjoying strategic positions in social networks receive higher emoluments than those who are not.[15] The findings confirm that at least some of the returns from investment in network creation are captured by the investor. This should have been expected. If firms pay employees on the basis of what they contribute to profitability, they would look not only at the conventional human capital employees bring with them (education, experience, personality), but also at the personal contacts they possess. Estimates of human capital should include the privately captured reward for investment in personal networks. In short, part of social capital would be expected to be embodied in human capital. It would be informative to untangle networks from the rest of human capital and the amount of social capital not embodied in human capital. This would reveal the extent to which returns from investment in networks are captured by the investor. But measurement problems abound. They may even be insurmountable. There are pervasive externalities to which network formation gives rise. When I invest in a productive relationship, not only do I benefit, the other party does too, as do those others who are connected to that other party. And so on. It is best therefore to partition an economy's productive base into its institutions and its capital base. The latter consists of stocks of manufactured capital, human capital, knowledge, and natural capital.

How should an asset's accounting price be estimated? There are standard techniques for estimating the accounting prices of manufactured capital. The cost of production can be a reasonable estimate under certain circumstances. The problem is that the inputs in the production of manufactured assets also include unmeasurable and unpriced objects, such as many environmental resources. Recorded production costs are at best a first approximation of what we are after.

In the previous chapter I reviewed a number of methods that have been devised for estimating the accounting prices of natural resources. While some are relatively easy to estimate, others were found to be impossibly difficult. I shall now sketch how the accounting prices of certain intangible assets can be estimated.

Human capital, created by investment in education and skills, is measurable up to a point. Expenditure on formal education (less depreciation when people die) is an approximation of net investment in human capital. However,

---

[15] Burt (1992) and Burt, Hogarth, and Michaud (1998).

national accounting systems regard much of the expenditure on children's education (teachers' salaries) to be a consumption item, a practice that can only be viewed as a relic of the Aristotelian conceit that the acquisition of even primary education is a pleasurable experience. Under current international accounting practices, less than 10 per cent of expenditure on education is classified as investment. In fact, expenditure on education is a significant part of investment. In the United States, it is more than five times the amount of investment in manufactured capital.[16] This doesn't include the time and effort parents put into their children's development, but since most of that affords pleasure to parents, only a portion of it should be called investment.[17]

Expenditures on research and development (R&D) are regarded in accounting systems as investment, which is as it should be. R&D produces knowledge. On the other hand, nutrition intake and health care are regarded as consumption items, even though they affect the future productivity of labour. They are at once both consumption and investment activities. This dual role does not pose a conceptual problem, but it does give rise to practical problems of measurement.[18]

We can appreciate why economic statisticians left social capital out of their accounting scheme. But they didn't have to neglect as much of natural capital as they did do. Current accounting practices have been shaped partly by developments in economic theory and partly by internal dynamics in accounting. For example, while the value of agricultural land is included in accounting systems, watersheds aren't valued in their entirety. Of course, bits of watersheds are valued, namely those supplying commercial products. However, most of the myriad of non-commercial services they provide are excluded. Nor are the commercial benefits bestowed on enterprises outside a watershed included. Earlier, we noted how this biased valuation affects our perception of the natural environment, in particular, how it dulls our capacity to appreciate what it does for us.

One explanation for the bias is that until recently there was little theory to guide economic statisticians in the direction of the natural environment. But the necessary theory is now in hand.[19] In the previous chapter I reviewed a number of approaches for estimating the accounting prices of amenities. In the next

---

[16] Jorgenson and Fraumeni (1989, 1992a,b). In national income accounts, expenditure on school buildings and equipment is regarded as investment, but teachers' salaries are typically not. The exclusion is a mistake.
[17] See Part V.   [18] Dasgupta (1993, 1997).
[19] Lutz (1993), World Bank (1997), and Dasgupta and Mäler (2000a,b). However, it has had little influence on applied development economists. A special issue of the *World Bank Research Observer* (2000, 14(3)) has been devoted to highly sophisticated econometric estimates of trends in private saving in poor countries. None of the contributors offered any comment on how far off the mark their estimates are likely to be in view of the fact that many items involving investment in natural capital were missing from the data.

section I discuss some of the items that accounting frameworks should include if the quality of life is to be measured less misleadingly.

9.3. GENUINE INVESTMENT: THEORY

Taken together, investment in manufactured capital, human capital, the natural environment, and expenditure on research and development change the capital base of an economy.[20] It is in the nature of things that the mix of the base varies across space, time, and circumstances. Possibilities of substituting one type of capital good for another in production affects the way the mix changes. Although seemingly innocuous, enlarging our conception of an economy's capital base has significant implications for the way development processes are viewed. We confirm this below.

UNDP (1994: 14–15) castigates those who regard GNP to be an index of social well-being on the grounds that it is a measure of a country's *opulence*. The criticism is faulty in two ways. First, opulence is a stock concept, and GNP is not a return on any index of opulence that I am aware of.[21] Secondly, and more importantly, the connection drawn in Chapter 3 between the constituents and determinants of well-being tells us that it isn't a mistake to seek to measure a society's well-being in terms of an index of opulence. The point isn't that opulence misleads, but rather that we should search for the *right measure* of opulence.

A country's wealth is the social worth of its capital assets. It is a measure of the nation's opulence. We confirm below that, subject to a well-defined set of qualifications, it is simultaneously a measure of social well-being.

At date t, let K_{it} be the quantity of the ith manufactured asset, H_{jt} the quantity of the jth form of human capital, S_{kt} the quantity of the kth natural capital, and Z_{mt} the stock of the mth type of knowledge.[22] Next, let well-being at t (V_t) be the unit of account, and let p_{it}, h_{jt}, r_{kt}, and q_{mt}, respectively, denote their accounting prices. They are spot prices. The economy's wealth at t can then be expressed as

$$W_t = \sum_i (p_{it}K_{it}) + \sum_j (h_{jt}H_{jt}) + \sum_k (r_{kt}S_{kt}) + \sum_m (q_{mt}Z_{mt}). \qquad (9.1)$$

---

[20] In their monograph on the character of economic growth, Thomas *et al.* (2000) have this as their opening point.

[21] One can even argue that, because it doesn't take note of capital depreciation, GNP *cannot* be a measure of opulence.

[22] It may appear contrived to talk of a measurable stock of knowledge, but, as we will see presently, we don't need to measure stocks, only the social worth of *changes* in stocks.

The notion of wealth advanced here is a comprehensive one, being the social worth of an economy's entire capital base. But what do we mean by the *i*th manufactured asset or the *k*th natural capital at *t*? How should we decide that a pair of assets should be regarded as distinct, rather than the same? We should of course include physical and chemical properties in an asset's attributes. But we should include more. For example, transport costs for traditional manufactured goods are a reason why location matters. Transport costs can assume an extreme form in the case of natural capital. The ecological role of a species of plants is site-specific. Populations are where innovation within a species takes place. A species in one location is a different asset from that same species elsewhere. This is why economists ought to be interested particularly in populations.

In imperfect economies the institutions governing the use of an asset matter too. Even if they possess similar ecological properties, a private fishery is a different asset from a fishery to which there is free access. For classifying assets, ownership matters.[23]

A country's wealth is the sum of the social worth of all the bits and pieces of manufactured capital, human capital, natural capital, and knowledge. Of course, a figure for wealth is meaningless in itself, but *difference* in wealth is meaningful. We may ask, for example, if, correcting for demographic differences, a country is wealthier now than it was earlier. It is useful to ask the question because, as we shall see, wealth can be used as a measure of a society's well-being.

As an index of well-being, wealth has the merit of being linear in assets, the accounting price of an asset being the weight awarded to a unit of the asset. A country's wealth in a given period is its wealth in the previous period plus net investment made during the previous period. *Wealth increases if, and only if, there is net investment in the capital base.*

It helps to formalize this. For convenience, regard time as continuous. We then define net investment at time *t* to be

$$I_t = \sum_i (p_{it} dK_{it}/dt) + \sum_j (h_{jt} dH_{jt}/dt) + \sum_k (r_{kt} dS_{kt}/dt)$$
$$+ \sum_m (q_{mt} dZ_{mt}/dt). \tag{9.2}$$

We will call I_t *genuine investment* at *t*. I_t is the social worth of the change in the capital base at *t*. I_t measures the change in wealth at *t* in spot prices.

Let us continue to assume that population remains constant. Assume too that the acquisition of knowledge is not costless. Imagine also that, being an imperfect economy, there are no significant institutional changes under way.[24] It

---

[23] Thus for theory. In practice, refined partitioning isn't feasible. Economic statisticians are compelled to lump together what are often different assets. [24] We will explore these assumptions in Sect. 9.4.

can be shown that under these circumstances genuine investment is equal to the rate of change in social well-being. This means that the quality of life improves if genuine investment is positive, but not otherwise. To put it formally,[25]

$$I_t = dV_t/dt. \tag{9.3}$$

Equation (9.3) says that genuine investment measures change in social well-being. Moreover, if genuine investment is positive, a country becomes wealthier; conversely, if it is negative, the country becomes poorer (equation (9.2)). So the accumulation of wealth amounts to an increase in social well-being.[26] Adam Smith may have had other reasons for choosing to discuss the creation of wealth, but, whatever they were, he was right to do so.

Of course, if the population is too large and the natural environment overly depleted, it may not be possible to increase wealth. The finding I am describing here is of the 'if and only if' kind: it does not say whether substitution possibilities between the natural environment and other forms of capital are sufficiently large for wealth to increase at the expense of Nature.[27] Imagine, for example, that substitution possibilities are limited, and the economy's institutions are profligate in the use of natural resources. The quality of life will then not be sustainable. This would be signalled by the fact that at some future date accounting prices would assume such values as to make it impossible for genuine investment to be positive: natural capital would have to be run down if there is to be any consumption. Social well-being declines when genuine investment is negative. So, movements in social well-being and genuine investment are two sides of the same ethical coin.

The assumption that the size of the population is constant is wrong. Suppose then that population is projected to increase (or, for that matter, decrease). Since numbers should matter, an adjustment needs to be made to estimates of genuine investment. Earlier we noted that when numbers change in an exogenous manner there are two formulations of intergenerational well-being that are attractive: total and average well-beings of all who ever come into being from the date in question.[28] The formulations don't differ when it comes to ordering consumption streams from an ethical point of view at a given point in time, but they do differ when it comes to comparing social well-being at different points in time. Theories of optimum development focus on the former

[25] See the Appendix (Proposition 4).
[26] Dasgupta and Mäler (2000a,b). These ideas have recently been put to use in assessing various long-term forecasts of world food production; see Dasgupta (1998a) and Daily *et al.* (1998).
[27] See Ch. 11. Dasgupta and Heal (1979: chs. 8 and 10) offer a technical account of substitution possibilities.
[28] Ch. 6, expressions (6.6) and (6.7), respectively.

type of comparison (we observed this when posing Frank Ramsey's question in Chapter 6), whereas theories of sustainable development focus on the latter (we observed this earlier in Section 9.1 above). In the Appendix (Section A.14) it is shown how population change should enter the accounting if we wish to check whether development is sustainable. The Appendix identifies situations where changes in wealth per head measure changes in social well-being: *If genuine investment per head is positive, social well-being increases, whereas if it is negative social well-being declines.* In those situations, the criterion for sustainability is genuine investment per head.

In general, though, genuine investment per head is merely an approximation. So an adjustment needs to be made to it if it is to serve as a criterion for sustainability. However, until economists develop simple ways to estimate the adjustment term, we will have to make do with genuine investment per head. In applying the theory to data on genuine investment in poor countries, this is what is done in Section 9.6.

Costless accumulation of public knowledge creates another wedge between wealth and social well-being: an adjustment needs to be made to wealth if it is to serve as an index of social well-being. It is simple to see why it would be needed. Costless accumulation of public knowledge is like manna from heaven, contributing to an increase in the 'productivity' of wealth. If wealth's productivity were to increase sufficiently fast, a decline in wealth wouldn't matter: the quality of life could improve even if wealth were to shrink. In Section 9.5 and the Appendix we look into this possibility and ask how plausible is the idea that knowledge can increase free of charge.

9.4. WHY NOT NNP?

GNP is insensitive to the depreciation of capital assets, while wealth is the social worth of those very assets. So there is little reason to expect movements in GNP to parallel those in wealth. But, subject to the qualifications made earlier, wealth and social well-being are equivalent. It is then possible that GNP increases for a time even while the country becomes poorer and social well-being declines. The moral is banal: GNP is not a measure of the quality of life.

What about net national product (NNP)? What ethical significance does NNP have?

NNP looks promising because it is consumption plus genuine investment. To formalize, let us return to the base case, where population is constant. Let v_t be the accounting price of consumption.[29] On using equation (9.2), we may

---

[29] Well-being is the unit of account.

express NNP at date t as

$$NNP_t = v_t C_t + I_t = v_t C_t + \sum_i (p_{it}\,dK_{it}/dt) + \sum_j (h_{jt}\,dH_{jt}/dt)$$

$$+ \sum_k (r_{kt}\,dS_{kt}/dt) + \sum_m (q_{mt}\,dZ_{mt}/dt). \tag{9.4}$$

Equation (9.4) says that genuine investment would be positive if the value of consumption were less than NNP, but that it would be negative if it exceeded NNP. If wealth is to increase, consumption must not exceed NNP. This is the ethical significance of NNP, a fact noted by those who originally explored the concept of NNP.[30]

In recent years, though, far more has been claimed on behalf of NNP. It has been said that NNP is the 'interest' on social well-being.[31] If δ is the rate at which future well-being is discounted, the claim would read[32]

$$NNP_t = \delta V_t. \tag{9.5}$$

Solow (1992: 17) has gone further. He has suggested that NNP is the return on wealth: 'Properly defined and properly calculated, this year's net national product can always be regarded as this year's interest on society's total stock of capital.'

As I understand it, this interpretation would read as follows:

$$NNP_t = \left[\sum_i (\rho_{it} p_{it} K_{it}) + \sum_j (\rho_{jt} h_{jt} H_{jt}) + \sum_k (\rho_{kt} r_{kt} S_{kt}) + \sum_m (\rho_{mt} q_{mt} Z_{mt}) \right],$$
$$\tag{9.6}$$

where ρ_{it}, ρ_{jt}, ρ_{kt}, and ρ_{mt} are the own rates of return at t on assets i, j, k, and m, respectively (i.e., $\rho_{it} = \delta - (dp_{it}/dt)/p_{it}$, etc.).

But (9.5) and (9.6) are true only under very restrictive circumstances. Equation (9.5) holds if well-being is linear in the flow of consumption goods and services, but not otherwise, while (9.6) is true if well-being is linear and the transformation possibilities among goods and services are constant returns to scale, but not otherwise.[33] We found reasons for rejecting the former condition in Chapter 6 (see also Chapter 11). The latter condition—that accounting prices are constant over time—holds only if the flow of goods and services, relative to one another, remains the same, year in and year out. In the world as we know it, neither assumption should be acceptable.

[30] Lindahl (1934), Hicks (1940), and Samuelson (1961).
[31] Weitzman (1976, 1998). In their important early work on green accounting, Repetto *et al.* (1989) also interpreted NNP to be an index of well-being, while observing that genuine investment must be positive if consumption is to be sustainable.
[32] Although (9.5) dosen't require it, I am assuming that δ is constant over time. In Ch. 6 a justification was offered for doing so.   [33] See Appendix.

What is the intuition behind these results? Why *isn't* NNP adequate? The problem lies in price changes. It can be shown that[34]

$$dV_t/dt = v_t dC_t/dt + dI_t/dt. \tag{9.7}$$

Using (9.2) in (9.7), we may conclude that social well-being increases during a brief interval of time if, and only if, the value of changes in consumption services plus the change in the value of net changes in capital assets is positive.

Notice the transposition of 'change in' and 'value of' in the previous sentence. The requirement is that the change in consumption is valued at its current accounting price, but changes in the structure of capital assets are not so valued; *movements* in the assets' accounting prices are also included. It is possible for NNP to grow for a time even while a country becomes poorer and the quality of life declines. As an index of social well-being, not only GNP, but also NNP is inadequate.[35]

9.5. WHAT DOES PRODUCTIVITY GROWTH MEASURE?

Some have located signs of economic progress in a statistic very different from either GNP or NNP. In seeking to interpret the expansion of the US economy during the decade of the 1990s, *The Economist* has recently exclaimed: 'In judging an economy's prospects, what is the most important measure? Growth in GDP? Inflation? The size of the budget surplus? The level of the stockmarket? None of the above. Far more important is growth in productivity, which is crucial in itself and which affects all of those things and more.'[36]

The idea underlying 'productivity', which is also called the *total factor productivity*, is as follows.[37] The aggregate output of an economy is produced by various factors of production, including labour inputs, the services of manufactured capital, knowledge, and natural resources. We can therefore decompose observed changes in output over time into its sources: how much can be

---

[34] Appendix (Proposition 11).

[35] NNP comparisons over time can be made to reflect changes in social well-being by a sort of *deus ex machina*. One way to do this is to make use of the changes in the structure of accounting prices over time to re-estimate consumption and genuine investment, and to re-estimate them in such ways that comparisons of the re-estimated NNP correspond to changes in social well-being. Asheim and Weitzman (2001) have explored this route and have found a way of doing this that makes the re-estimated NNP proportional to social well-being. The problem is that their device is dependent on the numeraire they construct. In the text, I am talking of properties of indices that do not depend on the numeraire, because those that do are in effect contrivances: they don't reflect deep underlying properties.

[36] *The Economist* (10–16 February 2001: 22).　　　[37] A formal account is given in the Appendix, Sect. A.14.

attributed to changes in labour force participation, how much to accumulation of manufactured capital and human capital, how much to the accumulation of knowledge brought about by expenditure in research and development, how much to changes in the use of natural resources, and so on? If a portion of the observed change in output cannot be credited to any of the above factors of production, that portion is called the change in total factor productivity. Growth in total factor productivity is also known as the *residual*, to indicate that it is that bit of growth in output which cannot be explained.[38]

What does the residual measure? The passage quoted above implies that it reflects an economy's prospects. But does it?

Traditionally, labour force participation, manufactured capital, and marketed natural resources have been the recorded factors of production. In recent years human capital has been added. Attempts have been made also to correct for changes in the quality of manufactured capital resulting from research and development. But most national accounts still don't include the use of non-marketed natural resources—nor, for that matter, non-marketed labour effort. They don't, for the understandable reason that accounting prices of non-marketed natural resources are extremely hard to estimate.[39] Moreover, how do you estimate unrecorded labour effort? Now imagine that over a period of time the economy makes increasing use of the natural resource base, or of unrecorded labour effort. The residual would be overestimated. In fact, a simple way to increase the residual would be to 'mine' the natural resource base at an increasing rate. But this would be a perverse thing to do if we seek to measure economic prospects.

What if it is possible to decompose the growth of an economy's aggregate output in a comprehensive manner, by tracing the growth to the sources originating in all the factors of production? To assume that over the long run the residual could still be positive is to imagine that the country enjoys a 'free lunch' (like manna from heaven). Is the latter a possibility? One way to enjoy a free lunch, for poor countries at least, is to use technological advances made in other countries without paying for them. The residual then reflects increases in freely available knowledge. However, adaptation is not without cost. To meet local conditions, adjustments need to be made to product design and to the processes involved in production.

For rich countries, the residual could reflect serendipitous growth in knowledge. It has been observed by historians of science though that serendipity is the good fortune of prepared minds. As preparation involves engagement, time, and resources, we are led back to the factors involved in the production of knowledge. Once we take into account the contribution of those factors of production, the residual could well be negligible.

---

[38] See the Appendix (Sect. A.14) for a formulation.   [39] In Ch. 8 we have seen why.

Leaving aside these doubts, imagine that serendipity can be reliably expected to be the source of the residual. It is still only one component of the sources of growth in GNP. Moreover, GNP is not a measure of social well-being. These are reasons why the residual should not be viewed as an indicator of an economy's prospects. It is all too possible for country A to record a higher residual than country B, even as social well-being in B increases while that in country A declines.

Total factor productivity can have short bursts in imperfect economies. Imagine that a government reduces economic inefficiencies by improving the enforcement of property rights, or by reducing centralized regulations (import quotas, price controls, and so forth). We would expect the factors of production to find a better use. As factors realign in a more productive fashion, total factor productivity would increase.

In the opposite vein, the residual could become negative for a period. Increased government corruption could be a cause, or civil strife, which destroys capital assets and damages a country's institutions. When institutions deteriorate, assets are used even more inefficiently than previously. The residual declines. This would appear to have happened in sub-Saharan Africa over the past forty years.

As the name suggests, the residual reflects our ignorance of the sources of change in aggregate output, be that change positive or negative. The originators of the concept didn't interpret it as a measure of an economy's prospects, and they certainly didn't mean it as a measure of prospects over the long run.[40] They were right not to have done so.

Table 9.1, taken from Collins and Bosworth (1996), gives estimates of the annual rate of growth of GNP per head and its breakdown among two factors of production (manufactured and human capital) in various regions of the world. The estimates are given in the first three columns. The period was 1960–94. The fourth column represents the residual in each region. This is simply the difference between figures in the first column and the sum of the figures in the second and third columns.[41] Collins and Bosworth did not include natural capital as a factor of production. If the use of environmental services has grown during the period in question (a most likely possibility), we should conclude that the residual is an overestimate. Even so, the residual in Africa was negative (−0.6 per cent annually). The true residual was in all probability even lower. The residual in South Asia, the other really poor region of the world, was 0.8 per cent annually, but as this is undoubtedly an overestimate I am unclear about whether there has been any growth in total factor productivity in that part of the world. One can but conclude that two of the poorest regions of the

---

[40] Abramovitz (1956) and Solow (1957).   [41] Subject to rounding-off errors.

Table **9.1.** *Sources of Economic Growth, 1960–1994*

	$g(Y/L)$	$g(K)$	$g(H)$	$g(A)$
East Asia	4.2	2.5	0.6	1.1
South Asia	2.3	1.1	0.3	0.8
Africa	0.3	0.8	0.2	−0.6
Middle East	1.6	1.5	0.5	−0.3
Latin America	1.5	0.9	0.4	0.2
United States	1.1	0.4	0.4	0.4
Other industrial countries	2.9	1.5	0.4	1.1

Notes: $g(Y/L)$: annual percentage rate of change in GNP per head.
$g(K)$: share of GNP attributable to manufactured capital multiplied by annual percentage rate of change in manufactured capital.
$g(H)$: share of GNP attributable to human capital multiplied by annual percentage rate of change in human capital.
$g(A)$: percentage rate of change in total factor productivity (residual).

Source: Collins and Bosworth (1996).

world (the Indian subcontinent and sub-Saharan Africa) haven't improved their institutional capabilities over four decades, nor have they been able to improve productivity by making free use of knowledge acquired in advanced industrial nations.

9.6. ACCOUNTING FOR THE ENVIRONMENT

Measuring the quality of life is a different exercise from preparing socio-economic accounts.[42] Making national accounts *green* is an admirable idea, but an even more admirable idea is to be clear in advance about what the accounts are meant to tell us. Much has been written in recent years by theoretical economists on the ethical significance of green NNP. In fact, however, they haven't actually studied green NNP, but instead have studied the *green Hamiltonian*, a mathematical concept useful in optimum control theory for identifying best policies.[43] If, as I have just argued, the critical variable is genuine investment, how should the environment be counted in it? In the previous chapter it was noted that severe practical problems arise when we try to value changes in environmental quality. Understandably, national income accountants ignore them. But it is useful to

---

[42] Ch. 2.

[43] Hartwick (1990, 1994), Lutz (1993), Asheim (1994, 1997, 2000), Aronsson, Johansson, and Löfgren (1997), Aronsson and Löfgren (1998a,b, 1999), and Weitzman (1998, 2000). We will come across the Hamiltonian in the Appendix. But, as we are not studying optimum economic policies, except as extreme special cases, we will not find much use for the Hamiltonian.

know what is being missed in not including them and what surrogates one could use in their stead. Consider the following examples.

1. Industry and transport emit sulfur oxides, which corrode buildings and structures. Maintenance, repair, and replacement costs arising from corrosion amount to £10 million annually. This represents current defensive expenditure. It is customary to include the item in final demand. But it should not be included.[44]

   The reason lies in the first term on the right-hand side of (9.2). Suppose that, if nothing were spent on maintenance, repair, and replacement, the rate of depreciation of manufactured capital would be 7 per cent per year, but that the annual £10 million expenditure reduces that rate to 5 per cent per year. Obviously, when estimating dK_t/dt, we would be using the 5 per cent depreciation figure. It would be double-counting if we were in addition to include the expenditure that reduces the depreciation rate.

2. Urban pollution causes discomfort; even worse, it causes health problems. To obtain relief, inhabitants seek medical care. The practice in accounting is to regard expenditure on health as part of consumption! But it is current defensive expenditure, against a loss of health. The case is similar to the previous example, but the practical implication differs. The expenditure on health should be included in genuine investment as a surrogate (albeit, an imperfect surrogate) for a missing item in national accounts: namely, health as a part of human capital.

3. Global warming is expected to bring in its wake extreme weather events (storms and floods) in places that were not earlier subjected to them. Expenditure on flood-control structures are now being undertaken. As they are a form of defensive capital, the expenditure is part of genuine investment.

   However, changes in the quality of the atmosphere should also be included in genuine investment. If, as is likely, it isn't feasible to include the accounting value of climate change in national accounting systems, an adjustment should be made to expenditure on defensive capital. The aim in doing so would be to reduce the error that is committed in not including the quality of the atmosphere in national accounts.[45]

4. A village's source of drinking water has been exhausted because of growth in demand. To obtain the necessary supply, villagers have now to walk longer distances each day. As currently practised, national accounts would not record the change unless output were to decline because of labour displacement. Imagine that villagers work harder each day to prevent output from falling. In estimating genuine investment, the additional toil should be deducted from

---

[44] Dasgupta and Mäler (1991: 125). See Appendix, Sect. A.16 for a proof.   [45] See Appendix, Sect. A.16.

conventional estimates of investment so as to account for the fact that water quality in regard to location has deteriorated.

5. Profligate use of agricultural land has led to a loss of soil nutrients. In order to maintain yield, farmers have now to spend an additional £1,000 per hectare. As it is current defensive expenditure against deterioration of natural capital, the example resembles (1). The same prescription holds.[46]

6. The government spends £1 billion annually on oil and natural gas exploration. But £10 billion worth of additional reserves were discovered this year. Since the £10 billion is an addition to the economy's natural capital, it ought to be included in genuine investment. But what about exploration costs? If the size of discoveries depends on past exploration costs, it should be included. The reason is that current exploration costs in this case are a form of investment. However, the £1 billion ought not to be included if current discoveries depend not on past exploration costs, but only on current exploration expenditure. The reason is that exploration costs are in that case akin to current production costs.

9.7. GENUINE INVESTMENT: APPLICATIONS[47]

Reporting studies undertaken at the World Bank, Hamilton and Clemens (1999) have provided estimates of genuine investment in a number of countries. They call it 'genuine saving'. The authors included in the list of a country's assets its manufactured, human, and natural capital. There is a certain awkwardness in many of the steps they took to estimate genuine investment. For example, investment in human capital in a given year was taken to be public expenditure on education. It is an overestimate, because each year people die and take their human capital with them. This is depreciation, and should have been deducted.

Among the resources making up natural capital, only commercial forests, oil and minerals, and the atmosphere as a sink for carbon dioxide were included. (Not included were water resources, forests as agents of carbon sequestration, fisheries, air and water pollutants, soil, and biodiversity.) So there is an

---

[46] Soil loss can be substantial. Annual losses from soil erosion on the island of Java have been estimated to be 0.5% of GNP. Over 95% of this are on-site costs of declining soil productivity, affecting millions of farmers. See McGrath and Arens (1989).

[47] That an economy needs to raise the worth of its productive base if social well-being is to increase was the topic of discussion, starting in 1993, among members of an Advisory Council created by Ismail Serageldin, then vice president for environmentally sustainable development at the World Bank. Serageldin (1995) provides an outline of empirical work on genuine investment that was initiated in his vice presidency. For estimates of the depreciation of natural capital on a regional basis, see Pearce, Hamilton, and Atkinson (1996), and World Bank (1997).

undercount, possibly a serious one. Nevertheless, one has to start somewhere, and theirs is a useful compendium of estimates.

Being a global commons, Earth's atmosphere poses an intriguing problem. When a country adds to the atmosphere's carbon content, it damages the commons. In calculating the value of the change in the country's capital assets, how much of the reduction should we include?

Two possibilities suggest themselves.[48] One is to attribute to each country the fraction of Earth's atmosphere that reflects the country's size relative to the world as a whole, using population as a means of comparison (or GNP, or whatever). The other is to regard the global commons as every country's asset. In that case, the entire cost of global warming inflicted by a country would be regarded as that country's loss. Hamilton and Clemens (1999) follow the latter route.[49] They use 20 US dollars as the figure for damages caused by a tonne of emitted carbon dioxide.[50]

The accounting value of forest depletion is taken to be the stumpage value (price minus logging costs) of the quantity of commercial timber and fuelwood harvested in excess of natural regeneration rates. This is an awkward move, since Hamilton and Clemens don't say what is intended to happen to the land that is being deforested. For example, if the deforested land is converted into an urban sprawl, the new investment in the sprawl would be accounted for in conventional accounting statistics; but if it is intended to be transformed into farmland, matters are different: the social worth of the land as a farm should be included as an addition to the economy's productive base.

Despite these limitations in the data, it is instructive to put the theory we have developed to work in the context of the world's poorest regions. Table 9.2 does just that. The account that follows covers sub-Saharan Africa, the Indian subcontinent, and China. Taken together, they contain nearly half the world's population. They also comprise pretty much all the world's poorest countries.

The first column of figures in Table 9.2 contains estimates of genuine investment, as a proportion of GNP, in Bangladesh, India, Nepal, Pakistan, China, and sub-Saharan Africa, over the period 1970–93. Notice that Bangladesh and Nepal have disinvested: their capital assets shrank during the period in question. In contrast, genuine investment was positive in China, India, Pakistan, and sub-Saharan Africa. This could suggest that the latter countries were wealthier at the end of the period than at the beginning. But when population growth is taken into account, the picture changes.

---

[48] Dasgupta, Kriström, and Mäler (1995).

[49] Under optimum global management, the country would be required to pay the total cost in the form of an international tax. The tax is Pigovian (Ch. 8).

[50] See Sect. 8.4. The estimate is due to Fankhauser (1994).

Table 9.2. *Genuine Investment and Capital Deepening in Selected Regions, 1970–1993*

	I/Y (1)	$g(L)$ (2)	$g(W/L)$ (3)	$g(Y/L)$ (4)	$\Delta(HDI)$ (5)
Bangladesh	−0.013	2.3	−2.60	1.0	+
India	0.080	2.1	−0.10	2.3	+
Nepal	−0.024	2.4	−3.00	1.0	+
Pakistan	0.040	2.9	−1.90	2.7	+
Sub-Saharan Africa	0.014	2.7	−2.30	−0.2	+
China	0.113	1.7	1.12	6.7	+

Notes: I/Y: genuine investment as proportion of GNP.
  (*Source*: Hamilton and Clemens, 1999: table 3.)
$g(L)$: average annual percentage rate of growth of population, 1965–96.
  (*Source*: World Bank, 1998: table 1.4.)
$g(W/L)$: average annual percentage rate of change in per capita wealth at constant prices.
$g(Y/L)$: average annual percentage rate of change in per capita GNP, 1965–96.
  (*Source*: World Bank, 1998: table 1.4.)
$\Delta(HDI)$: sign of change in UNDP's Human
  Development Index, 1987–97.
  (*Source*: UNDP, 1990, 1999.)
Assumed output–capital ratio: 0.25.

The second column contains the annual percentage rate of growth of population in the various places over the period 1965–96. All but China have experienced rates of growth in excess of 2 per cent per year, sub-Saharan Africa and Pakistan having grown in numbers at nearly 3 per cent per year. We now want to estimate the average annual change in wealth per capita during 1970–93. To do this, we should multiply genuine investment as a proportion of GNP by the average output–wealth ratio of an economy to arrive at the (genuine) investment–wealth ratio, and then compare changes in the latter ratio to changes in population size.

Since a wide variety of natural assets (human capital and various forms of natural capital) are unaccounted for in national accounts, there is an upward bias in published estimates of output–wealth ratios, which traditionally have been taken to be something like 0.30. In what follows I use 0.25 as a check against the upward bias in traditional estimates. This is almost certainly still a conservatively high figure.

The third column in Table 9.2 contains estimates of the annual percentage rate of change in wealth per head. The procedure for this has been to multiply genuine investment as a proportion of GNP by 0.25, and to substract the annual percentage rate of growth of population from the product. This is a crude way to adjust for population change, but more accurate adjustments would involve greater computation.[51]

---

[51] See the Appendix, Sect. A.17.

The striking message of the third column is that all but China have *decumulated* their capital assets on a per capita basis during the past thirty years or so. Earlier we noted that total factor productivity has declined in sub-Saharan Africa over the past four decades (Table 9.1). Taken together, the evidence is that, relative to its population, the region's productive base has shrunk considerably. This may not cause surprise, since sub-Saharan Africa is widely known to have regressed in terms of most socio-economic indicators. But the figures in Table 9.2 for Bangladesh, India, Nepal, and Pakistan should cause surprise. They have all decumulated their capital assets on a per capita basis. Earlier we noted that there has probably not been any growth in total factor productivity in South Asia as a whole. Taken together, the evidence is that, relative to its population, the region's productive base has shrunk.

How do changes in wealth per head compare with changes in conventional measures of the quality of life? The fourth column of the table contains estimates of the annual percentage rate of change in per capita GNP during 1965–96; and in the fifth column I have compiled changes in UNDP's Human Development Index (HDI) over the period 1987–97.[52]

Notice how misleading our retrospective assessment of long-term economic development in the Indian subcontinent would be if we were to look at growth rates in GNP per head. Pakistan, for example, would be seen as a country where GNP per head grew at a healthy 2.7 per cent per year, implying that the index doubled in value between 1965 and 1993. In fact, the average Pakistani became poorer by a factor of nearly 2 during that same period.

Bangladesh too has disinvested in her capital assets. The country is recorded as having grown in terms of GNP per head at a rate of 1 per cent per year during 1965–96. In fact, at the end of the period the average Bangladeshi was less than half as wealthy as she was at the beginning.

The case of sub-Saharan Africa is, of course, especially sad. At an annual rate of decline of per capita wealth of 2.3 per cent, the average person in the region becomes poorer by a factor of 2 every thirty years. And this doesn't include the decline in total factor productivity. The ills of sub-Saharan Africa are routine reading in today's newspapers and magazines. But they aren't depicted in terms of a decline in wealth. Table 9.2 shows that sub-Saharan Africa has experienced an enormous decline in its capital base over the past three decades. As total factor productivity in the region has fallen too, its entire productive base has shrunk. It will take years for the region to recover, if it is able to do so at all.

India can be said to have avoided a steep decline in its capital base. But it has been at the thin edge of economic development, having managed not quite to maintain its capital assets relative to population size. Total factor productivity

---

[52] HDI was defined in Ch. 5.

in India has risen during the past decade, but, as I argued earlier, the estimates have an upward bias. If the figures in Table 9.2 are taken literally, the average Indian was slightly poorer in 1993 than in 1970.

Even China, so greatly vaunted for its progressive economic policies, has just managed to accumulate wealth in advance of population increase. For a poor country, a growth rate of 1.12 per cent per year in wealth per head isn't something about which one gets too excited. In any event, a more accurate figure for the output–wealth ratio would almost surely be considerably lower than 0.25. Moreover, the estimates of genuine investment don't include soil erosion or urban pollution, both of which are thought to be especially problematic in China.[53]

What of the HDI?[54] In fact, it misleads even more than GNP per head. As the third and fifth columns show, HDI offers almost the opposite picture of the one we should obtain when judging the performance of countries. It has, however, been suggested to me by a colleague that, as HDI has been so constructed that it can assume values only between 0 and 1, it should not be used for intertemporal comparisons. He reminded me also that the United Nations Development Programme has used HDI mostly for cross-country comparisons. But an index that purports to reflect average well-being in a group cannot arbitrarily be limited to group comparisons at a point in time. If the index is deemed suitable for the purposes of such comparisons, it simply has to be made available for the purposes of well-being comparisons among groups separated by time; otherwise, the index isn't a measure of well-being. Furthermore, the fact that HDI lies in the interval [0,1] is no reason why it must not be used for intertemporal comparisons. That well-known measure of income inequality, the Gini coefficient, also lies in the interval [0,1]; but it is routinely asked whether the Gini coefficient of income (or wealth) distribution in a country has worsened or improved over time. I don't have an intuitive feel for what may or may not be a healthy growth rate for HDI in today's poor countries, but for sub-Saharan Africa the index improved during the 1990s. Bangladesh and Nepal have been exemplary in terms of HDI. However, both countries have decumulated their assets at a high rate.

These are all rough and ready figures, but they show how accounting for human and natural capital can make for substantial differences in our conception

---

[53] Hussain, Stern, and Stiglitz (2000) contains an analysis of why China has been the economic success it is widely judged to have been in recent years. However, there is no mention of what may have been happening to China's natural resource base in the process of the country's economic development.

[54] I am grateful to Sriya Iyer for suggesting that I should check to see what HDI says about the progress of the poorest nations.

of the development process. The implication should be heart-breaking: over the past three decades, the Indian subcontinent and sub-Saharan Africa, two of the poorest regions of the world, comprising something like a third of the world's population, have become even poorer. In fact, some of the countries in these regions have become a good deal poorer.

Citizens of imperfect economies typically suffer injustice. They are also subjected to resource allocation mechanisms that are inefficient. In an inefficient economy there is room for raising the levels of both consumption and genuine investment. Table 9.2 suggests that people in the poorest countries today may well be consuming and (genuinely!) investing too little.

EVALUATING POLICIES IN IMPERFECT ECONOMIES

Prologue

The essay so far has been about valuing states of affairs. Part IV develops methods for evaluating policy change. Investment projects are brief changes in economic policy. They alter the mix of consumption and investment. The theory of project evaluation is developed in Chapters 10–11. But the theory's reach is broader. It can be used to evaluate more general policies (e.g. changes in the structure of taxes), which is the theme of Chapter 12. Policy evaluation is called *social cost–benefit analysis*.

The problem is to find a way to judge whether an investment project ('project' for short) raises or lowers social well-being. Accountants have long advocated that commercial firms adopt the present discounted value of the flow of commercial profits as the criterion for selecting projects.[1] In Chapter 10 it is shown that the correct way to evaluate a public project is to compare reductions in consumption arising from the investment outlay with the increase in wealth that the investment helps to create. Putting it in other words, projects should be accepted if they add to wealth, but not otherwise. It is also shown that for public projects this amounts to estimating the present discounted value (PDV) of the flow of the project's social profits. A project whose PDV is positive should be accepted; one whose PDV is negative should be rejected. The correct measure of social well-being, even for purposes of project evaluation, is wealth. The finding unifies valuation and evaluation.

In Chapter 11 we scrutinize a class of accounting prices that has been the object of regular misunderstanding: *social discount rates*. The topic is over forty years old, and yet controversy rages over matters that have long been settled, involving as they do technical economics. Many who express views on social discount rates overlook the literature and make incorrect claims. I point to a few as the occasions warrant.

Chapter 12 is about policy change in the midst of markets and non-market institutions. Accounting prices are particularly difficult to estimate in non-market institutions because of an absence of market prices to serve as guide. Moreover, changes in public policy (e.g. changes in the structure of taxes

---

[1] Selecting projects on the basis of their rates of return is a nearly-equivalent exercise. See Dasgupta, Marglin, and Sen (1972).

and trade) frequently affect the macroeconomy. Involving as they do large changes to an economy, their evaluation requires more complex estimation procedures. Accounting prices don't suffice. By means of three examples, I offer a sketch of how social cost–benefit analysis is useful for identifying what the evaluator ought to try to measure and why. The first example is a miniature, involving communal management of irrigation systems in Nepal; the latter two are altogether more grand, illustrating some of the environmental implications for poor countries of structural adjustment programmes and trade liberalization.

10

Policy Reforms

10.1. POLICY CHANGE AS PERTURBATION

Policy change is a perturbation to the prevailing state of affairs. How should we evaluate the perturbation? I shall illustrate how, by considering the evaluation of investment projects. The subject is called *social cost–benefit analysis*.

Investment projects are policy changes. Building a dam and a system of canals perturbs an economy. Whether the dam should be built can only be judged by comparing life with and without it. Counterfactuals are involved in the exercise. One way to make the comparison is to estimate the changes the dam and canals would bring about to the constituents of well-being. There are considerable advantages though in estimating instead the dam's impact on the determinants of well-being and valuing that impact. We noted earlier that it helps enormously if the index measuring the impact is linear in the determinants' quantities.

It is possible to construct a linear index only if the project is small.[1] Admittedly, what constitutes smallness is a delicate matter and the person doing the evaluation should be sensitive to it. A project may be small in terms of a country's overall economic activity and yet have a big impact on the lives of some very poor people, in which case it wouldn't be small for *them*.

There are evaluation techniques covering such cases. They involve measuring changes in what are called consumer and producer 'surpluses'. The idea is to assess the impact of a project partly in terms of the changes it would bring about to the constituents of well-being and partly in terms of changes to the determinants. An alternative procedure would be to use distributional weights that favour the poor. The losses suffered by them on account of the project would then count for more in the calculus. In what follows, I leave aside this sort of case. I go into a few of the issues that arise in Chapter 12.

Imagine that, even in the imperfect economies being studied here, a project appears on a project evaluator's desk only when backed by a feasibility report. The report contains quantitative estimates of the project's inputs and outputs.

---

[1] In the Appendix it is shown why.

The estimates include the project's requirement in each period of capital equipment, labour of various kinds, intermediate goods, and raw materials. They also include the project's output(s) in each period.

A project's feasibility report enumerates its inputs and outputs quantitatively. But the inputs and outputs are not the same as the perturbation to the economy. By making water available for irrigation, a dam and its canal system should be expected to increase crop output. But the dam would also have significant ecological impacts (loss of forest cover, the creation of a sanctuary for birds) and could involve the displacement of populations. They are part of the perturbation caused by the dam, and it is the perturbation that has to be valued. This means that the 'indirect' effects have also to be enumerated and listed as the project's inputs and outputs. In social cost–benefit analysis the trick is to estimate the value of the perturbation by aggregating the social scarcity values of the project's inputs and outputs in a suitable way. Remarkably, the scarcity values are none other than our now-familiar friends, accounting prices. Remarkably too, the required aggregate is the present discounted value of the flow of the project's social profits, which reflects the change the project makes to the economy's wealth. Let us see why and how.

10.2. PROJECT EVALUATION CRITERION

There is an ideal world (Utopia) where market prices of goods and services equal their accounting prices.[2] Barring well understood exceptions (projects supplying public goods, or requiring significant fixed costs), the commercial profitability of investment projects in Utopia reflects their social worth. Aside from such exceptions, there is no reason to resort to social cost–benefit analysis in Utopia: private incentives suffice. But in the world as we know it, for many goods and services market prices are not good approximations of accounting prices.[3] The basics of social cost–benefit analysis were developed over forty years ago for projects involving the supply of environmental public goods (water resources, amenities).[4] Since formal markets are relatively underdeveloped in poor countries, and governments there are much involved in production activity, the theory in its generality was devised subsequently for public-sector projects involving the production of any kind of good, not just public goods.[5] Significantly, the natural environment did not figure in

[2] We noted this in Chs. 7 and 8.   [3] We noted this as well in Chs. 7 and 8.

[4] Eckstein (1958) and Herfindahl and Kneese (1965) were notable studies.

[5] For the theory, see Little and Mirrlees (1968, 1974) and Dasgupta, Marglin, and Sen (1972). For an account of similarities and differences between the two sets of studies, see Dasgupta (1972). For case studies, see Lal (1972) and Scott, MacArthur, and Newbery (1976).

them, even though social cost–benefit analysis was initiated by environmental concerns.[6]

Assuming that accounting prices have been estimated, how should they be used in social cost–benefit analysis? The idea is to calculate a project's *social profit* in each period of its planned life. Social profit in a given period (usually taken to be a year) is estimated by multiplying the project's inputs and outputs during the period by their corresponding accounting prices and adding them. (Outputs are taken to be positive, inputs negative.) Social profit is a linear index of quantities, the weights awarded to the various inputs and outputs being their corresponding accounting prices.

There is never sufficient knowledge to make precise estimates of inputs and outputs and their accounting prices. Recourse is therefore taken to the language of probabilities. For projects whose social profits are uncorrelated with the performance of the rest of the economy, 'expected values' suffice. However, if a project's social profits are positively correlated with current well-being, the cost of risk ought to be deducted from expected values. Conversely, if social profits are negatively correlated with current well-being, a bonus should be awarded to the project's expected values, the reasoning being that the project is forecast to generate greater benefits in precisely those circumstances where there is a greater need for them.

Accounting prices are useful because they enable us to evaluate the perturbation caused by a project by estimating the project's social profit. The usefulness of the move may be best appreciated when one notes that in each year in the life of an economy large numbers of projects are evaluated. Clearly, it would be simpler if, instead of estimating the perturbation caused by each project, use were made of models to estimate accounting prices for use in all the projects that come up for scrutiny.

Social profits in different periods are like different commodities. If they are to be compared, they need to be priced relative to one another. This calls for yet another set of accounting prices. In social cost–benefit analysis those prices are called *social discount factors*. They are related to a corresponding set of *social discount rates* in the manner shown below. In Chapter 6 the concept of social discount rates was introduced (equation (6.3)). The rates were those appropriate for discounting future well-being. However, the unit of account chosen in applied studies is mostly not well-being, but something else, such as aggregate consumption or government income. Except under special circumstances, social discount rates depend on the unit of account, or what we called the numeraire in Chapter 8.[7] As was noted earlier, the unit of account doesn't affect project

---

[6] Dasgupta (1982b) was an attempt to extend the theory by including environmental natural resources.
[7] This is shown in Ch.11.

choice. Shifting from one unit of account to another is like moving from one currency to another when making purchases. If the project is socially profitable under one numeraire, it will be profitable under any other numeraire.[8]

Consider a project whose expected life is T years. Assume that the unit of account has been chosen, say, aggregate consumption. Let Π_t be a project's estimated social profit and ρ_t the social rate of discount in year t. In the following chapter we discuss the logic of consumption discount rates in detail. For the moment I take them as given to the project evaluator. Let K_T be the expected scrap value of the project at T, evaluated in terms of accounting prices. The present is taken to be $t = 0$. We now denote the social discount factor for net profits at t as β_t and define it to be

$$\beta_t \equiv [(1 + \rho_0)(1 + \rho_1)(1 + \rho_2)\ldots(1 + \rho_{t-1})]^{-1} \quad \text{for } t \geq 1; \text{ and } \beta_0 = 1.$$

(10.1)

The *present discounted value* of the stream of social profits (PDV) is then

$$PDV = \sum_{0}^{T} (\beta_t \Pi_t) + \beta_T K_T.$$

(10.2)

In the Appendix it is shown that a project whose PDV is positive increases social well-being, while one whose PDV is negative reduces it (Proposition 2). Expression (10.2) is therefore the criterion for project evaluation: if the present discounted value of a project's social profits is positive, it should be accepted; if it is negative, the project should be rejected. It is also proved in the Appendix (Proposition 4) that genuine investment measures the present discounted value of the changes to consumption services that are brought about by the investment. Taken together, the two propositions mean that, if a project's PDV is positive, the reductions in consumption resulting from the investment are less in value than the increase in wealth that the investment helps to create. To put it differently, projects should be accepted if they add to wealth, but not otherwise.[9]

---

[8] It has been conventional to choose as numeraire an aggregate commodity index, drawn from a macroeconomic model. Little and Mirrlees (1968, 1974) call social discount rates 'accounting rates of interest'. Their chosen numeraire was government income. Dasgupta, Marglin, and Sen (1972) used aggregate consumption as the unit of account, which is what I am doing here. In Utopia the accounting price of one relative to the other is unity; elsewhere it isn't. Ultimately, it's pretty much a matter of taste and convenience which commodity is chosen as the unit of account.

[9] Dasgupta and Mäler (1991, 2000a) and Mäler (1991) proved that small investment projects may be evaluated on the basis of their contribution to NNP, provided they are of very short duration. Since investment projects are rarely of very short duration, the result is of little interest. The intuition behind the requirement that projects be of short duration is that accounting prices remain constant over the lifetime of projects. So the result extends to long-lasting projects, provided accounting prices remain constant over time. But the new requirement isn't believable either. See the corresponding remarks in Sect. 9.4, on NNP as an index of social well-being.

We now have the required connection between the indices that are useful for intertemporal comparisons of social well-being and those that are useful for project evaluation: they are the same, the index being *wealth*. The finding unifies valuation and evaluation, and brings us, full circle, to Chapter 1, where we asked why we should wish to measure the quality of life and how we should go about it. We now have an answer to the latter also, which is that, whether we wish to measure the quality of life so as to track it over time or to choose among policies, the way we should measure the quality of life is the same: it is by the social worth of an economy's capital assets. The weights that should be used to value assets for estimating changes in an economy's wealth are the same as the ones that we ought to use to value goods and services for evaluating projects. In both cases they are the economy's accounting prices.

I have known this chain of results for some time, but still find it a remarkable fact of life. I can't think of any *a priori* reason why we should have expected the same set of weights to be appropriate for valuing the determinants of social well-being and the same aggregate index—wealth—to serve two seemingly different purposes. There is a deep connection between valuing objects and evaluating policies. It is one of those beautiful facts that social scientists are fortunate in unearthing from time to time.

When done well, social cost–benefit analysis enables us to estimate the gap between a project's commercial profits and its social profits. The gap in part measures the size of externalities.[10] Frequently, though, there is a certain awkwardness in the way externalities are estimated. In a study of alternative methods of disposing of waste water from a geothermal power plant in the Philippines, it was found that the revenue losses to a marine fishery and rice farmers that would be incurred if the waste was untreated were nearly 50 per cent of the commercial costs of the power plant.[11] Presumably, though, losses in profits would be a smaller fraction. (Labour costs and the cost of nets, for example, should be deducted from revenue.) On the other hand, losses to riverine fisheries and the costs to human health were not taken into account in the study. So we are left uncertain about the size of externalities involving the discharge of untreated water. Despite the years that have passed since social cost–benefit analysis was developed and environmental and resource economics came of age, there have been only a few comprehensive case-studies in the literature.[12]

---

[10] The other part would involve the wedge created by monopoly, monopsony, and tax distortions.

[11] Dixon *et al.* (1994).

[12] Among the few are Freeman (1982), Anderson (1987), and Ruitenbeek (1989) for projects involving air and water pollution control, afforestation, and forest protection, respectively. Dixon and Hufschmidt (1986), Pearce and Moran (1994), Weiss (1994), and Abeygunawardena *et al.* (1999) are collections of case studies on forests, watersheds, and, more generally, biodiversity.

10.3. TWO APPLICATIONS

What does the theory of social cost–benefit analysis tell us when put to work on current concerns facing international institutions? I can cite two examples of the theory's use in practical ethics.

The President of the World Bank has recently observed that:

The success of most projects is dependent on many assumptions extraneous to the project itself. Building new schools is of no use without roads to get the children to the schools and without trained teachers, books and equipment . . . Initiatives to make progress creating equal opportunities for women make no sense if women have to spend many hours each day carrying clean water, or finding and gathering fuel for cooking. Seeking universal primary education without prenatal and postnatal health care means that children get to school mentally and physically damaged. Establishing a health system but doing nothing about clean water and sewerage diminishes enormously the impact of any effort. (Wolfensohn, 1999: 8)

The author is pointing to the need to understand an economic system's response to projects (the perturbation!). His examples are about *complementarities*. Just as a shoe for the left foot is useless without the corresponding shoe for the right foot, establishing a health system, but doing nothing about clean water, would not amount to much. The accounting price of an object whose complements are unavailable is low. In the extreme, it is nil. A project producing one when its output's complements are unavailable would register a negative PDV (all costs, no benefits). A comprehensive project could pass the test even when its components, each on its own, does not.

My second example addresses biases in environmental research and development, a phenomenon that was discussed in Section 7.5 above. When resources are underpriced in the market, firms have less than adequate incentives to develop processes and products which would economize their use. Recently the argument has been put to work in the context of public health in poor countries.

Infectious diseases are locally interacting. (Neighbours are more likely to catch an infectious disease than people far away, be it because the disease is contagious or because the pathogens thrive in the locality.) So they involve spatially localized externalities. We noted in Chapters 4 and 5 that private benefits from protection against infectious diseases fall short of social benefits. We noted too that people in the tropics, where the world's poorest live, are particularly vulnerable to infectious diseases (malaria, tuberculosis). Since public health programmes in poor countries are severely limited in scope, demand for vaccines is far less than the need for vaccines. Pharmaceutical companies have little incentive to develop vaccines. The proposal has recently been made that international aid should involve guaranteed purchase of tropical vaccines at guaranteed prices.[13] If accepted, the policy would amount to an issue of contracts stipulating that, if firms are successful in developing acceptable vaccines, specified quantities will be purchased at stipulated prices. Companies would, of course, receive nothing if they were unable to develop the vaccines. What the contracts would do would be to shore up demand in the event that firms are successful in their search. Such forms of guarantees are called *contingent contracts*, involving as they do accounting prices to be paid to firms for each unit of vaccine purchased if, and only if, they are successful in their research and development. The underlying idea is to offer contracts that would provide pharmaceutical companies with greater incentives to develop tropical vaccines. It is a case of creating contingent markets in a world where they currently don't exist.[14]

But in all likelihood, more draconian measures will be needed to counter contemporary epidemiological problems. In a wide-ranging essay, Daily and Ehrlich (1996) explored the mutual influences of population growth, increases in human mobility, growth in the size of human settlements, and the epidemiological environment. They stressed that pathogens and their vectors evolve and resurge as threats to human life in ways that overcome the technologies that were developed to eliminate the threat they posed in the first place. Examples include the Ebola virus and the antibiotic-resistant strains of malarial parasites. Co-evolution between humans and pathogens involve different speeds of change. Under contemporary patterns of economic change 'arms-races' often develop. Dampening the races would involve not only the development of vaccines and antibiotics, but also old-fashioned remedies, such as finding ways to blunt the vectors themselves (e.g. sewage facilities, the availability of clean water, sparser human settlements).

10.4. TAXES AND REGULATIONS AS POLICIES

One way to improve the use of a resource base is to impose regulations on resource users (restrictions on effluent discharges, quotas on fish harvests, a ban on logging). Another is to introduce a system of taxes, known as *Pigovian taxes* (pollution charges, taxes on the amount of fish harvested, and stumpage fees on logging).[15] The idea underlying Pigovian taxes is to bring market prices,

---

[13] See Sachs (1999), who has called for the creation of an international Millennium Vaccine Fund along the lines being outlined here.

[14] Kremmer (2000a,b) has provided quantitative estimates of the required contingent contracts and the Fund.

[15] The term 'Pigovian taxes' honours the economist A. C. Pigou, who first discussed the difference between private and social costs in the context of environmental pollution (Pigou, 1920). The basis of Pigovian taxes on pollution is called the 'polluter-pays principle'. For comprehensive accounts of Pigovian taxes, see Mäler (1974) and Baumol and Oates (1975).

inclusive of taxes or subsidies, in line with accounting prices. A tax or subsidy on a commodity can be thought of as the difference between the commodity's accounting price and its market price. A resource can be said to be subsidized in the market place if its market price is less than its accounting price, a common feature of environmental services.

There are many instances where the government pays the subsidy via general taxation, for example when it supplies free irrigation water. Interestingly, there are innumerable cases where the subsidy is implicit and hidden from the accounting system, being paid by groups that don't even know they are paying. In Chapter 12 we will examine a common mechanism in which implicit subsidies are paid by some of the poorest in society. They involve environmental externalities. For the State to impose Pigovian taxes on those who are causing environmental damage, and to compensate those who are adversely affected, is in effect to remove hidden subsidies.

Each of the two schemes for improving the way we use the natural environment—quotas and taxes—has its advantages and disadvantages relative to the other. Some of the differences between the two become salient when it is recognized that ecological processes are stochastic, and that individuals and state agencies don't have the same information about technology (e.g. about the cost of waste disposal). Typically, we would expect the firm to know more about technology than the state regulator. Under a tax scheme, the government selects the tax rate, say on the waste a firm discharges. In response, the firm chooses its activity level, and so the amount of waste. Since the firm knows more about its abatement technology than the government, society faces uncertainty about the amount of waste the firm will discharge. This is the weakness of a Pigovian tax. Its strength lies in the fact that the firm is able to make use of its privately held information about costs of abatement. In contrast, society doesn't face uncertainty in the level of waste discharged under a quota (the quota would typically be taken up!), which is a good thing; but in setting the quota the regulator doesn't have access to the firm's private information about abatement costs, which is a bad thing. As regards incentives, the two schemes are not equivalent.[16]

There are three additional points worth noting. First, the two schemes are distributionally not equivalent: under a quota, resource rents are captured by harvesters and polluters, whereas under a tax system they are collected by the tax authority. Secondly, Pigovian taxes and quotas provide different incentives to firms to explore technological improvements. If resource-users are taxed,

---

[16] Meade (1973) and Weitzman (1974) offer clear accounts. Quotas are an extreme form of non-linear taxes. For an analysis of non-linear taxes on the use of environmental resources, see Dasgupta, Hammond, and Maskin (1980).

they pay more than they would have done had they been issued quotas instead. This may suggest that the incentives to improve technology are greater under a tax regime, but it depends on the resource. Consider ambient air quality. Pollution taxes certainly provide an incentive for firms to develop cleaner technologies. Both abatement costs and tax payments are lowered. But so does environmental regulation provide incentives: with cleaner technology, firms would be able to produce more of their products while complying with emission standards.

Thirdly, environmental taxes, when properly designed, remove market distortions. There is also a presumption that tax revenues enable the government to reduce distortionary taxes (e.g. taxes on earned income) while meeting budgetary requirements. So Pigovian taxes could yield a 'double dividend', a rhetorical phrase that has been much used in recent years to persuade governments to impose green taxes.[17]

A hybrid policy instrument, which involves the government issuing a fixed number of licences that can be traded in the open market, combines features of quotas and Pigovian taxes. The scheme resembles quotas in that, unless the government sells the licences, resource rents are not captured by government; it resembles Pigovian taxes in that, at the margin licence-holders pay the accounting price. Transferable licences to pollute convert the emission of pollutants into a market activity by offering private property rights to the sink into which the pollutant is deposited. Such licences have been put to use in a wide range of contexts, including industrial emissions of gaseous waste and in the management of fisheries.[18]

The above account views quantity restrictions as *policy instruments*. (Thus the question, should there be taxes or quotas for environmental protection?) But sometimes it is convenient to include quantity restrictions in the way the evaluation problem itself is posed. In his early work on the economics of global warming, Nordhaus (1977) chose a planning horizon of two hundred years and a discount rate of 10 per cent a year, while seeking to discover the most cost–effective way of ensuring that carbon concentration in the atmosphere never exceeds twice the level prevailing in the 1970s. Quantity restriction in Nordhaus's model was an objective, not a means for implementing an objective.

---

[17] See Bovenberg and van der Ploeg (1994), Goulder (1995), Bovenberg and Goulder (1996), and Bohm (1996), among others.

[18] See Tietenberg (1988) on transferable licences in the context of ambient air quality. See also Bjorndal and Munroe (1998) for their use in fisheries. Matters of public finance have been a recurrent theme in environmental and resources economics; see especially Baumol and Oates (1975), Cropper and Oates (1992), and Carraro and Siniscalco (1996). Transferable licences were first proposed by Dales (1968). The intellectual source of the idea that the establishment of well-defined and enforceable property rights to resources, not Pigovian taxes, is the cure for environmental problems is the classic by Coase (1960).

Similarly, in a recent study of the costs and benefits of reducing the discharge of nitrogen and phosphorus into the Baltic Sea, the authors took as a goal that the total nutrient load to the sea should be halved.[19] I don't believe the authors were making a philosophical point, though. I think that specifying targets in the two studies was merely a tactical move, to avoid having to quantify the damage suffered on account of pollution.

On the other hand, environmental pollution has been likened to torture, and lasting pollution to 'a kind of calculable oppression of the future generation'.[20] Now, torture is regarded as an absolute evil in all societies. It violates negative rights (Chapter 2). States inflicting it don't usually question that it is an evil: they claim instead that it is a necessary evil (for the purposes of national security, for safe-guarding the masses from anti-social elements, or for whatever other greater good that comes to mind). In liberal societies torture is prohibited. People found inflicting it on others are incarcerated. If the analogy between pollution and torture is valid (although there may be many who would question the analogy), pollution quotas would be an objective, rather than a policy instrument (an efficient means to some other objective). In such a formulation, 'super-consumption' would be prohibited by quotas, because it amounts to torturing people.

It is not unknown to have quantity restrictions imposed on resources possessing intrinsic value. As objects of agreeable contemplation, they are public goods: we can all derive pleasure and comfort from the knowledge that they are safe. But their publicness makes them vulnerable. Urban development, for example, destroys the markers upon which migratory birds rely. Entire populations of them are then placed at risk. The extinction of species is frequently a consequence of habitat destruction.[21] Cooperation to protect endangered species is difficult at the best of times. When the sites are far away and under different jurisdiction, they assume the status of global public goods. They are then truly vulnerable.

One way societies in the past protected fragile resources was by instituting taboos.[22] Today we don't follow that route, at least not consciously. Instead, interested groups keep an eye on such resources and initiate public debates when a species is threatened with extinction. If the public can be persuaded that the threat is real, government legislation and international agreements sometimes follow. Acute problems arise in the design of policy when a resource

---

[19] Gren, Turner, and Wulff (2000). It was found that the transition economies in the Baltic drainage basin would lose if the reduction were enforced, but that Sweden, Germany, Finland, and Denmark would gain sufficiently to be able to compensate the losers.   [20] Sen (1982: 346).

[21] Examples abound. Among exotic populations, the great apes are a case in point, as are the Bengal tigers, which were facing extinction a few decades ago and continue to be an endangered population.

[22] Gadgil and Guha (1992) offer an account of this in the context of ancient and classical India.

is of worth to us as an extracted commodity, but is slow-growing. Redwood and juniper trees are cases in point. Legislation to create national parks is a way to protect them. Such legislation is a reminder that the stocks of such trees have intrinsic worth.[23]

Cultural monuments pose similar problems. Artefacts can yield private value. If they are removed, the integrity of the monuments is affected. International efforts to preserve them are an acknowledgement that cultural monuments are global public goods. The United Nations Educational, Social, and Cultural Organization (UNESCO) was in part created for this purpose.

Sometimes resources are mistakenly thought to have worth when extracted. Various aphrodisiacs are a testimony to this. If an animal population is mobile and in the wild, it is hard to establish and protect property rights to it. People then enjoy free access to the population. That's when it becomes endangered. The African rhinos are a well-known case. It is easier to legislate than to implement a ban on hunting. As always, private incentives matter. The search should be for systems of property rights under which preservation is in the interest of local populations. Local people are better able to monitor the population and keep poachers at bay. Local populations need to have a stake in the matter. Profit-sharing is a way to give them a stake. It also encourages community involvement, which is valuable in itself.[24]

10.5. HARD AND SOFT PRICES

Accounting prices are conceptually different from market prices. The latter are hard objects, being the terms of actual trade. In contrast, accounting prices are soft; their magnitudes depend on such matters as distributive justice, some of which may be hard to articulate. The discussion in Chapter 5 (Section 5.5) is relevant here. Since it must be impossible to have a fully articulated conception of social well-being, accounting prices can be estimated only within bounds. The thing to do then is to conduct sensitivity analysis of investment projects, by applying an admissible range of figures for prices.[25]

I have colleagues in the humanities who find accounting prices a techno-cratic, even chilling, apparatus with which to deliberate matters of practical ethics. They say that accounting prices are too precise to be of use in delibera-tions that are in their very nature imprecise. They go further and say accounting prices should not be used, as they are too narrow; that instead we should engage

---

[23] See Ch. 11 for further discussion.

[24] Barbier *et al.* (1990) is a study on ways to preserve the African elephant.

[25] See e.g. the case studies in Dasgupta, Marglin, and Sen (1972).

in qualitative considerations, which have a wider reach. An aphorism they often use to justify the position is that 'it is better to be vaguely right than precisely wrong'.[26] What this misses, however, is that you won't even know that you are vaguely right if you operate within a framework in which you cannot be precisely wrong. There is no way to controvert a vague statement. Reliance on the intuitions of influential people, or on the hunches of men regarded as having sound, practical sense, has proved disastrous all too often.

I also have colleagues, in international organizations, who say that evaluation criteria based on accounting prices are too elaborate and overly time-consuming. Some say that the procedures have been tried and found wanting. Far better, they say, if projects are chosen on the basis of their commercial profitability—subject, of course, to being screened on the basis of an assessment of their environmental impacts and their contribution to poverty alleviation. In practice, this may be the best that can be done in the case of some projects. But it is dangerous to think that this is anything more than a very short cut to what is a difficult problem. Social cost–benefit analysis, like the reasonings giving rise to decision-making in other spheres of life, is as much an art as a science. It is necessary to have a tight, analytically sound framework from which to proceed to practical decisions. Along the way, corners have to be cut and qualitative judgements have to be made. But having the correct framework at the back of one's practical mind is good practice. It enables the evaluator to recognize when a corner has to be cut and it forces him to search for good ways to do it. The danger is to dismiss the framework with the shrug of one's practical shoulders. If one does that, all sorts of *ad hoc* considerations can be expected to creep in, such as the interests of powerful groups in society. Following the prescriptions of welfare economic theory is a way to keep oneself honest and clean.

If we use them sensibly, accounting prices can do an enormous amount of work for us. The prices can't be plucked from air: we have to estimate those that can be estimated by working with defendable economic models. We should never be confident that we know what they are, but we would be wrong to pretend that we have no means of knowing the bounds within which they lie.

---

[26] The aphorism appeared originally in Shove (1942: 323) and was attributed by him to a Professor Wildon Carr.

11

Discounting Future Consumption

11.1. WHY

The discounting of future benefits and costs has been the subject of discussion for over four decades. And yet it continues to be misunderstood. (I give three examples later in this chapter.) Its underlying logic is a source of tension between ecologists and economists, and among economists themselves. It will prove useful to review the basic ideas.

Let us recall first that social discount rates are required because they enable the project evaluator to estimate *social discount factors*, which are accounting prices of a project's future social profits relative to its social profit today.[1] In the previous chapter we noted that in social cost–benefit analysis the unit of account (the numeraire) is usually an economic commodity, such as aggregate consumption, or government income. The unit of time is usually a year. For the moment, assume that population is constant. As earlier, I denote the consumption forecast as $(C_0, C_1, \ldots, C_t, \ldots)$. In Chapter 6 the unit of time was taken to be the length of a generation and C_t was interpreted as an index of generation t's consumption level. Here we interpret generation t to be all who are alive in year t. C_t is therefore the index of aggregate consumption at t.

Let $U(C)$ be the measure of current well-being. Assume that well-being increases with consumption, but at a diminishing rate. Intergenerational well-being (or social well-being) at t is taken to be

$$V_t = \sum_{t}^{\infty} \beta^{(\tau - t)} U(C_\tau), \quad \text{for } t \geq 0, \qquad \text{where } \beta \equiv \frac{1}{(1 + \delta)}, \text{ and } \delta > 0.$$

$$(11.1)$$

Expression (11.1) looks similar to (6.3) in Chapter 6, but it is different. Being a measure of current well-being at t, $U(C_t)$ is an aggregate of the current well-being of all who are alive at t. Since generations co-exist, C_t is an index of the

---

[1] See (10.1) and (10.2) above.

determinants of well-being at t of people who are at different stages of life in that year.

Well-being is the numeraire in (11.1) and δ is the social rate of discount in that unit of account. (In Chapter 6, δ was called the rate of pure time preference.) What should discount rates be if instead aggregate consumption were chosen as the unit of account?[2]

It helps to consider first a numerical example, so as to understand what discounting means. Suppose it is claimed that the social discount rate on future consumption is 5 per cent per year. This would mean that 1 unit of additional consumption today has the same social worth as 1.05 units of additional consumption next year. Generalizing from this, we say that the rate of discount to be applied to a small change in next year's consumption is the percentage rate at which next year's consumption can be substituted for today's consumption without affecting social well-being. Generalizing still further, we say that the rate that should be applied in year t to discount a small change in consumption in year $t+1$ is the percentage rate at which consumption at the margin can be substituted between the two years without affecting social well-being. Social rates of discount in consumption numeraire are called *consumption rates of interest*.[3]

There are then two reasons why a small additional amount of consumption to be made available at some future year could be socially less valuable than that same additional amount made available today (i.e., why the consumption rate of interest could be positive): (1) impatience, and the chance that there may not *be* a future year, and (2) the forecast that consumption will be greater in the future than it is today, which means that the benefit from additional consumption in the future will be less. I return to these two considerations below.

11.2. HOW

How may consumption rates of interest be derived from macroeconomic forecasts?[4] To see how they may be derived, let us continue with the base case we have been studying, namely, one where population is constant and the world is deterministic. Denote the change in well-being consequent upon a marginal increase in consumption as $U'(C)$, and the change in marginal well-being consequent upon a marginal increase in consumption as $U''(C)$. Continue to assume

---

[2] In what follows, I frequently refer to 'aggregate consumption' as 'consumption'.

[3] Little and Mirrlees (1974).

[4] The exposition that follows is taken from Little and Mirrlees (1968, 1974), Arrow and Kurz (1970), and Dasgupta, Marglin, and Sen (1972). The former three publications were about optimizing economies, the latter about reformist economies in imperfect societies.

that well-being increases with consumption ($U'(C) > 0$), but at a diminishing rate ($U''(C) < 0$). Now define

$$\eta(C) \equiv -U''(C)C/U'(C) > 0. \tag{11.2}$$

$\eta(C)$ is the percentage increase in marginal well-being consequent upon a percentage increase in consumption. It is called the *elasticity* of marginal well-being and is a measure of the curvature of U. $\eta(C)$ is also a measure of the extent to which intertemporal equality is valued.[5] The greater is $\eta(C)$, the more even would desirable consumption streams be, other things being the same. Given our assumptions about U, $\eta(C)$ is a positive number.

Let ρ_t be the consumption interest rate at t. It assumes an ugly form when time is discrete, as we have assumed it to be.[6] So for expositional ease I simplify by imagining time to be continuous. This is a limiting perspective of short time intervals. On using the continuous-time counterpart of (11.1), it is simple to show that

$$\rho_t = \delta + \eta(C_t)\,(dC_t/dt)/C_t, \tag{11.3}$$

where dC_t/dt denotes the rate of change of C_t and $(dC_t/dt)/C_t$ the percentage rate of change of C_t.

Equation (11.3) is both fundamental and well known. The first term on the right-hand side, δ, reflects consideration (1), while the second term, $\eta(C_t)\,(dC_t/dt)/C_t$, reflects consideration (2). The former is the rate at which future well-being is discounted. The latter term is straightforward as well. The reasoning that led us to consideration (2) suggests that, if consumption is expected to increase over time, $\eta(C_t)\,(dC_t/dt)/C_t$ should have a positive sign. It does.[7] Equation (11.3) says that consideration (2) is the product of the elasticity of marginal well-being and the (percentage) rate of change in consumption: the greater is the product, the higher is the rate of discount. To illustrate, suppose $\delta = 0.001$ per year, $\eta(C_t) = 2$, and $(dC_t/dt)/C_t = 0.02$ per year. The consumption interest rate is then 4.1 per cent per year. Social profits from investment projects should be discounted at 4.1 per cent per year.

A number of points follow from this. Eight are particularly salient.

---

[5] Equation (6.2).

[6] Using the definition of δ_t in expression (11.1), it is easy to check that

$$\rho_t = \{[U'(C_t)/(1+\delta)^t] - [U'(C_{t+1})/(1+\delta)^{t+1}]\}/\{U'(C_{t+1})/(1+\delta)^{t+1}\}.$$

This is an ugly expression: it isn't transparent. But it becomes transparent if time is regarded as a continuous variable.

[7] In applied work it is frequently assumed that $\eta(C_t)$ is a constant (i.e. is independent of C_t). When illustrating the theory, I shall assume that η is constant. Empirical estimates of η, when U is inferred from observed behaviour, are of the order of 2.

First, social discount rates in consumption numeraire are not a primary ethical concept: they are derived jointly from an overall conception of social well-being and the economic forecast. Second, and this follows from the first, discount rates can't be plucked from air: they have to be derived from such considerations as those that are formalized in equation (11.3). Third, just as growing consumption provides a reason why discount rates in use in social cost–benefit analysis should be positive, declining consumption would be a reason why they might be negative. To illustrate again, suppose $\delta = 0.001$ per year, $\eta(C_t) = 2$ and $(dC_t/dt)/C_t = -0.01$ per year. The consumption rate of interest is then -1.9 per cent per year. Fourth (following from the previous two observations), if the external disbenefits from production and consumption are substantial, consumption rates of interest could be negative even while private and social rates of return on investment are positive.[8] Fifth, unless the forecast is a stationary economic programme, social discount rates depend on the numeraire ($\rho_t = \delta$ only if $dC_t/dt = 0$).

Sixth, consumption rates of interest are not necessarily constant over time. For example, suppose long-run economic forecasts indicate that growth in consumption is not sustainable, but rather that its growth is expected to decline at a constant rate of 1 per cent per year, from the current figure of 2 per cent per year to zero. Assume that $\delta = 0$ and $\eta = 2$. In such circumstances, the consumption rate of interest will *decline* over time at 1 per cent per year, from a current high of 4 per cent per year to zero.[9] This means that costs and benefits over the very near future should be discounted at 4 per cent per year, but those, say, seventy years hence should be discounted at 2 per cent per year. And so forth. Note however that, even when consumption rates of interest are time-dependent, the PDV criterion enables us to choose projects in a consistent way over time.

Seventh, in an imperfect economy consumption rates of interest are not equal to private rates of return on investment. They differ because of imperfect capital markets and corporate income taxes. And eighth, if government policies are imperfect, consumption rates of interest are not equal to social rates of return on investment.[10]

The assumption that in the long run population remains constant is clearly correct. There will be fluctuations in numbers, of course, but over time average population must remain constant because Earth is a finite resource. Meanwhile, in the near future population will grow in most countries. How should consumption rates of interest be estimated there?

---

[8] This parallels the conclusion reached in Sect. 8.1, that, if the external disbenefits arising from someone's use of a commodity are large enough, the accounting price of the commodity will be negative even if its market price is positive.   [9] I return to this point in Sect. 11.4.

[10] See Lind (1982) and Arrow *et al.* (1996).

Denote by N_t the population size and by n_t its percentage rate of change at t. Let $y_t(= C_t/N_t)$ be per capita consumption, and $U(y_t)$ current well-being per head. As in Chapter 6 (equation (6.7)), we write social well-being as

$$V_t = \frac{\sum_t^\infty N_\tau U(y_\tau)\beta^{(\tau-t)}}{\sum_t^\infty N_\tau \beta^{(\tau-t)}}, \quad \text{for } t \geq 0,$$

$$\text{where } \beta \equiv \frac{1}{(1+\delta)}, \text{ and } \delta \geq 0. \tag{11.4}$$

Imagine that today's forecast of consumption per head is the stream $(y_0, y_1, \ldots, y_t, \ldots)$. Let the unit of account be consumption *per head*. Denote the consumption rate of interest as ρ_t. Using the continuous-time counterpart of (11.4), it is simple to show that[11]

$$\rho_t = (\delta - n_t) + \eta(y_t)(dy_t/dt)/y_t. \tag{11.5}$$

We conclude from (11.5) that, other things the same, consumption rates of interest are lower if population grows. This is as it should be. Numbers count in the ethical reckoning. If population grows, the greater numbers in the future should count for a bit more than those alive now. A comparison of (11.3) and (11.5) tells us that the appropriate adjustment is remarkably simple: the consumption interest rate is lower by n_t—the population growth rate.

If, instead, aggregate consumption is the unit of account, it is simple to show that

$$\rho_t = \delta + \eta(y_t)(dy_t/dt)/y_t. \tag{11.6}$$

This too is intuitively clear. Admittedly, numbers count in the ethical reckoning. If, say, population grows, the greater numbers in the future would count for a bit more than those alive now. On the other hand, those greater numbers would share the small increase in consumption. The two effects cancel and the population growth rate does not appear in the expression for the consumption rate of interest.

11.3. GLOBAL WARMING AND DISCOUNTING

I believe these findings can help mediate the often acrimonious debate that has taken place over the years on the welfare economics of global warming. In an original and influential body of work, Nordhaus (1977, 1994) concluded

---

[11] Expression (11.5) for the consumption interest rate at t holds even if social well-being were taken to be the sum of the well-beings of all who are ever to come into being from t onward (see (6.6)).

that for the next several decades not much should be done to curb carbon emissions; he has argued that serious restrictions will be required only from the second half of the twenty-first century. Projects that curb emissions significantly don't pass the cost–benefit test in Nordhaus's models because they are costly, and because the rates used to discount future benefits are non-negligible.[12] The rates are non-negligible because in Nordhaus's models, even if nothing is done to curb emissions, consumption would be expected to grow during the twenty-first century and beyond, which is the time horizon assumed in the computer runs.[13] Growth in world output is curbed by global warming, but the models assume that world output will continue to grow. For example, Nordhaus's most favoured specification has it that total factor productivity (see Chapter 9 above) increases over time, albeit at a declining rate. (The rate halves every seventy years.) This assumption, among others, implies that the effect of global warming on world output will be small: a doubling of carbon dioxide concentration (corresponding something like a three-degree Celsius increase in average global temperature) would result in a mere 1.33 per cent loss in world output of goods and services.

Now consider someone who is persuaded that, if nothing substantial is done today to curb carbon emissions, there is a sizeable chance that world output, suitably weighted across regions and income groups, will decline (owing, say, to an increase in the frequency of extreme weather events). To that person, Nordhaus's conclusions would appear puzzling, possibly even bizarre. I have friends among climatologists and ecologists who feel there is something wrong with a discipline that is able to foster complacency about global warming. And I have friends within my own profession who are convinced that ecologists must be innumerate if they can't grasp the logic of discounting.

But the disagreement isn't about economics, nor about social cost–benefit analysis, nor even about the numeracy of fellow scientists. Nor is it about ethical values. It is about the likely effects of future carbon emissions. If world output is firmly expected to grow in the long run even if business is permitted to be conducted as usual, the use of positive, possibly substantial, discount rates in social cost–benefit analysis is justified. But if there is a sizeable chance that world output will decline in the long run if nothing is done now, then (11.5) could well imply the use of positive discount rates for the immediate future, but negative

---

[12] In Nordhaus (1977) the discount rate used was 10% per year, a rate that halves benefits and costs every 7 years.

[13] In the base case, Nordhaus (1994) assumes a decline in the rate of *growth* of total factor productivity by only 1% per year. Nordhaus and Yang (1996) have developed a more refined, inter-regional model in which the losses from global warming, if business is carried on 'as usual', is assumed to be about 1–2 per cent of global incomes over the next century. Globally efficient carbon taxes are estimated to be a mere 6 US dollars per tonne in 2000, rising to 27 US dollars per tonne in 2100.

rates for the distant future.[14] Whereas positive discount rates shrink future losses when viewed from the present, negative discount rates amplify future consumption losses relative to current costs. Economics *per se* says nothing about the sign or magnitude of social discount rates: it is what you put into economics that determines it.

Cline (1992) reached a different conclusion from Nordhaus. The computer runs in his optimization model recommended more urgent action on global warming. But Cline used a significantly lower rate than Nordhaus to discount perturbations to future benefits and losses. (His most preferred figure was 2 per cent a year.[15]) It has been argued against Cline that, if the rates of discount used in social cost–benefit analysis were to be lower than the return on investment in international capital markets (as Cline's preferred discount rate clearly was), weak projects would pass the test: they would register positive social profits and drive out good projects.[16] The criticism is faulty. More productive projects would be ranked even higher under the cost–benefit test than Cline's project and would signal that they too ought to be accepted.

Ultimately, the criticism is a case of misplaced application of economic theory. In Utopia consumption interest rates equal private rates of return on investment, which in turn equal social rates of return on investment. In the imperfect economies we inhabit, there are wedges between each pair. It is one thing to urge that an imperfect economy should be improved, quite another to pretend that the imperfect economies we inhabit are Utopia. The accounting prices that would prevail in Utopia would differ from the accounting prices in imperfect economies. Investment projects are perturbations to an economy. A part of a project's investment outlay typically comes from displaced consumption (partly public, partly private), the remaining portion from displaced investment (partly public, partly private). In an imperfect economy the accounting price of public investment, relative to consumption, is different from that of private investment, which in turn is different from the accounting prices of private and public consumptions. The perturbation to consumption arising from a project should be estimated on the basis of the accounting values of each of those displacements.[17] If, on using the discount rates in (11.5), the social profitability of a project is found to be large and positive, it is a clear signal that there are further projects to be uncovered which would also be desirable. Of course, institutional constraints may prevent other such projects from being uncovered and undertaken.

[14] It doesn't guarantee it, because (11.3) is valid only in a deterministic world. The probabilistic counterpart of the equation would yield negative discount rates if the chance that world output will decline is large enough.

[15] The computer runs in Roughgarden and Schneider (1999) also recommend urgency. In their model there is a non-negligible chance that global warming will have significantly deleterious effects on aggregate output.

[16] Birdsall and Steer (1993).

[17] See in particular Dasgupta, Marglin, and Sen (1972: ch. 14 and case-studies).

But their possible discovery is no reason for tinkering with consumption interest rates and discarding projects that ought to be undertaken.

None of this is a defence of Cline's simulations. I don't in any case have the necessary expertise to judge them. The points I am making are not about the workings of global warming models, but about the way discount rates ought to be estimated.[18]

The studies on global warming I have cited are exercises in intertemporal optimization. They enable one to estimate the magnitude of gains that could in principle be realized from international cooperation. But the gains are realizable provided transfer payments are implementable, and it is in the interest of those nations that sign a treaty to abide by it when they come to implement it. Sanctions, to be imposed on rogue nations, have to be credible if the treaty is to be effective. Put in formal terms, the treaty must be *self-enforcing*, which is to say that it must involve equilibrium behaviour: it should be in the interest of all who have signed the treaty to abide by it on the assumption that all others who have signed it abide by it.

In an interesting and important body of work, Scott Barrett has shown, among other things, that self-enforcing treaties may involve some nations, but not all.[19] Those who do not sign a treaty would in effect be free-riders, but nevertheless it would pay the others to sign it. It can be equilibrium behaviour for some to free-ride but others to cooperate and abide by the treaty. Barrett's analysis implies that, generally speaking, one should expect globally inclusive treaties to be agreed upon only if the number of countries is small. Seeking treaties involving nearly two hundred nations, for example, could be a futile exercise. From this perspective, the failure of the Kyoto Protocol on global warming shouldn't cause surprise. The Protocol itself was recognized not to be self-enforcing. Subsequent behaviour of the signatories confirms it.

On the other hand, the Montreal Protocol on the emission of chlorofluorocarbons (CFCs) has been a success. Why? Barrett's work suggests that if, relative to the costs of curbing emissions, the perceived benefits are large, agreements can be reached among large numbers of nations. In effect, very little in the way of side-payments needs to be made in order for signatories to enjoy the benefits. This was the case with curbing CFCs. Carbon emissions are a problem of a different order of magnitude. The costs of controlling emissions to any significant degree are huge, while the benefits of controlling them are likely to be diffuse: unlike radiation arriving through holes in the ozone layer, global

---

[18] The discount rate frequently used in the literature on global warming is the inflation-adjusted interest rate on long-term US Treasury bonds, the reasoning being that it reflects the risk-free rate of return on investment. In imperfect economies even the latter isn't equal to the consumption interest rate.

[19] Barret (1990, 1996, 1997, 1999).

warming doesn't kill in a direct, identifiable way. It is easy to go into denial over global warming.[20]

Barrett has for the most part modelled international cooperation in the context of repeated interactions among nations. In an illuminating pair of parallel research programmes, Carlo Carraro and Domenico Siniscalco, and Michael Hoel, respectively, have modelled international cooperation in non-repeated settings, but with a stress on the question whether a country chooses to negotiate at all.[21] The results they have obtained are consonant with Barrett's, which suggests that the insights from this body of work are robust.

11.4. GAMMA DISCOUNTING

In poor countries, feasibility reports on investment projects typically assume project lives to be thirty to forty years. It is common practice to choose aggregate consumption as the unit of account and to use a constant discount rate for the cost–benefit exercise. Sensitivity analysis is then conducted with a menu of discount rates (usually, numbers in the range 4–10 per cent per year).

In most of the many case studies I have read over the years, no justification was offered for the choice of a constant rate to discount social profits. One can only assume that the practice is a habit, nothing more. In any case, no one would seem to question the move. Quite the contrary: evaluators would have some explaining to do if they were to use *non*-constant rates. So, the habit persists. If asked to explain the use of fixed discount rates, evaluators versed in economic theory could always invoke equation (11.5) and report their belief that consumption per head will grow at a constant rate during the lifetime of the projects being evaluated. It is a case of convenience winning over such considerations as that consumption interest rates ought to be derived from plausible economic forecasts, that they ought not to be chosen to equal current rates of return on equities, government bonds, or whatever.

The economist Martin Weitzman has offered a new defence of the practice of considering only fixed rates to discount future consumption: namely, that it is the only language policy-makers understand. Or so he invited some 2,800 economists to assume in a questionnaire in which respondents were asked to submit a *single* number as their 'best estimate of the appropriate real discount rate to be used for evaluating environmental projects over a long time horizon'.[22] The list included a 'balanced blue-ribbon panel' of fifty 'leading

---

[20] Pearson (2000) is a recent textbook on the economics of the global environment. Kopp and Thatcher (2000) is a reader on the basic economics and political history of international climate agreements.

[21] Carraro and Siniscalco (1997, 1998); Hoel (1997a,b); and Carraro (2000).

[22] Weitzman (2001: 271).

economists'. (The editors regarded it in taste to permit the author to publish the economists' names with these descriptions.) Weitzman went on in the questionnaire to explain his motive: 'What I am after here is the relevant interest rate for discounting real-dollar changes in future goods and services—as opposed to the rate of pure time preference on [well-being].' In short, Weitzman asked economists to submit their best estimate of consumption rates of interest, while insisting (even 'hectoring' unsure respondents, to quote him—p. 268) that they submit a single number.

As I felt unable to respond, I didn't send in a number. The stipulation puzzled me then and it puzzles me even now. The horizon that Professor Weitzman wished to consider is 300 years or more. Why should it be insisted that my estimate of consumption interest rates over such a long period should be a constant? Suppose, as a crude approximation, that the world is partitioned into two groups: North (where consumption per head is high) and South (where consumption per head is low). We may choose consumption in either region as numeraire. The social discount rate will depend on that choice, because the rates at which consumption in the two regions change over time would be expected to differ. Furthermore, I can think of no reason why changes in consumption per head in either region should be expected to remain constant over the next 300 years. It follows that, no matter which of the two groups we choose to anchor the consumption rate of interest, the rate itself will not be a constant.

In order to draw out this point more succinctly, suppose as a very crude approximation that world well-being is taken to be a function of world consumption per head, where the latter is a weighted average of consumption per head across countries. It is most plausible to assume that in the foreseeable future population will continue to grow faster in poor countries than in rich ones. Even if per capita consumption were to increase in every country (note though that the recent evidence belies this presumption: see Table 5.7), world consumption per head could decline. However, leaving aside this possibility, it would not be unreasonable to imagine growth in world consumption per head as being unsustainable over such a long time horizon as 300 years. The growth experience itself is about 300 years old. Growth in consumption per head over the previous 300 years had been not much more than zero. It has, of course, been argued by many that the world has since invented the magic societal bullet, namely, capitalism. But technological innovations, even under capitalism, can't circumvent deep ecological processes. Why should it be unnatural to imagine that environmental constraints could act as limits on growth in consumption per head over the very long run, in a world inhabited by 10 billion people or more? If growth in per capita consumption were to decline, the consumption interest rate would decline; it would not remain constant.[23] Moreover, the interest rate could be negative in the distant future if there is a real possibility that world consumption per head will have to decline in the long run if the natural resource base is not to be destroyed beyond repair. The correct procedure would be to formalize the uncertainty regarding economic forecasts (some cheerful, some gloomy, and so forth), to calculate consumption interest rates for each sample path, and then to evaluate projects in accordance with the expected present discounted value of the flow of social profits.[24]

However, even if *I* felt unable to respond to Professor Weitzman's questionnaire, 2,160 economists from forty-nine countries did feel able to do so. Each supplied a number, of which all but three were non-negative. Forty-six respondents gave zero as their best estimate, while the rest supplied positive numbers (Weitzman, 2001: Table 1). Weitzman found that, if one were to ignore the forty-nine non-positive numbers, the responses had the shape of a gamma distribution.[25] He interpreted the responses as draws from an urn by a policy maker who is uncertain of what fixed rate to use for discounting social profits. Being uncertain, Weitzman's policy maker selects projects on the basis of the expected present discounted value (PDV) of the flow of social profits. Now, if the uncertain, but fixed, discount rate is governed by a gamma distribution, then the expected PDV of a project is proportional to a sure PDV of that same project, where the rate used to discount future social profits is taken not to be a constant, but is taken to decline over time, starting as a positive number and declining to zero in the long run. Weitzman's recommendation is to use a positive, but declining, rate to discount social profits of long-term investment projects.

What are we to make of the exercise? It seems to me that Professor Weitzman is saying something like the following to his policy maker: 'Look, I know you don't understand anything beyond a constant rate to discount future profits in social cost–benefit analysis. So I asked nearly three thousand PhD economists to tell me what they regard as their best estimate of a fixed rate. More than two thousand of them responded. But they were divided on what rate you

---

[23] That the consumption rate of interest may decline along optimum economic programmes, even in economic models without natural resource constraints, was shown by Cass (1965) and Koopmans (1965).

[24] See Sect. 6.4. In an interesting paper, Newell and Pizer (2001) have explored this route by assuming directly that the consumption interest rate evolves in accordance with an auto-correlated stochastic process. Their simulations demonstrate that under such forms of uncertainty, net benefits in the distant future should be discounted at (certainty-equivalent) rates that decline over time and are lower than the expected rate of interest in initial years. Thus, future uncertainty (say, about climate change) offers a reason for precautionary behaviour. Recall, however, the arguments in Sects. 11.2–11.3 that identified deterministic economic forecasts for which the consumption interest rate declines over time in a manner similar to the certainty equivalent interest rates in the Newell–Pizer paper.

[25] If $f(\rho)$ is the probability density function of ρ (≥ 0), it is of the gamma-form if $f(\rho) = A\rho^{\alpha-1}e^{-\beta\rho}$, where $\alpha > 1$, $\beta > 0$, and A (>0) is the constant that normalizes the distribution. The distribution has a single peak, starts at zero, and tails off to zero. The extreme special case, $\alpha = 1$, yields the exponential distribution.

should use. Now I have proved mathematically that, if you award the view of each economist an equal weight, and interpret their responses as draws from an urn representing your uncertainty about what constant discount rate to use, then in fact you should use a rate that isn't constant, but a variable rate that starts as a positive number and declines to zero in the long run. By the way, you *do* understand expected utility theory and certainty equivalence results, don't you?'

The advice economists offer policy makers takes this form only when their research is prompted by mathematical curiosities, not economics.

11.5. PROJECT-SPECIFIC DISCOUNTING

Considerations of risks apart, all projects that come up for scrutiny should be evaluated with the same discount rates. In recent years, however, it has been argued that projects protecting increasingly rare species ought to be discounted at a lower rate than other projects in the same risk category. What is the logic behind the suggestion?

Slow-growing species are doomed if valued solely for the harvest they are capable of yielding. Economic theory predicts it and experience confirms it. If the rate at which the yield is discounted exceeds the rate at which the stock grows, it is uneconomic to preserve the species.[26] It is not difficult to think of commercial species that are so slow-growing that probably no amount of doctoring rates of discount can save them from extinction. Redwood and juniper trees come to mind. So environmentalists often suggest that an adjustment should be made to discount rates when projects involving the extraction of slow-growing species are evaluated. The idea is to have something like an affirmative action plan for slow-growing species.[27]

The suggestion is appealing, but it is misconceived. The thing not to do is to play willy-nilly with consumption rates of interest. All sorts of ethical contradictions would follow if we were to do so (for example, the ranking of economic programmes would be intransitive). Discount rates in social cost–benefit analysis are not primitive ethical objects. Once the numeraire is chosen and the economic forecast made, they are a given: they are not project-specific.[28]

So, then, how can social cost–benefit analysis be used to justify the protection of slow-growing species, such as the giant redwoods or the junipers? Such justification would be provided if we acknowledged that the worth of the redwoods doesn't lie exclusively in the wood they can supply as building material: they also have intrinsic value as a *stock*. If threatened with extinction, that intrinsic value

---

[26] See Clark (1976) and Brander and Taylor (1998).   [27] See e.g. C. Cooper (1981).

[28] If future risk is discounted, consumption interest rates can be specific to projects in different risk categories. I abstract from this in the text.

(itself an accounting price) will grow. If it grows fast enough, projects designed to protect the remaining redwoods would show large social profits.[29]

What, it may be asked, if the accounting price reflecting the intrinsic value doesn't grow fast enough? This means that social cost–benefit analysis would not recommend preservation. But that wouldn't be a fault of the analysis: it would be a weakness in the prevailing ethics that, even when the redwoods are threatened with extinction, we don't value them sufficiently. Social cost–benefit analysis is a tool for practical ethics, but it cannot be expected to supply the ethics.

11.6. TOTAL OR INCREMENTAL OUTPUT?

Social cost–benefit analysis involves evaluating perturbations to economic forecasts. It mostly presumes that the perturbations are small relative to the size of the economy (although it is not necessary to assume this). It always assumes that humanity will survive the perturbation. I remarked on this when arguing that the well-known estimates in Costanza *et al.* (1997) of the value of the world's entire natural environment are meaningless.

A reasoning similar to that of Costanza *et al.* appeared in a Focus article in *The Economist* (26 June 1999: 128). In observing the disturbing tendency of compound interest to make large figures in the distant future look very small today, the correspondent remarked:

Suppose a long-term discount rate of 7 per cent (after inflation) is used ... Suppose also that the project's benefits arrive 200 years from now ... If global GDP grows by 3 per cent a year during those two centuries, the value of the world's output in 2200 will be 8 quadrillion US dollars (a 16-figure number). But in present-value terms, that stupendous sum would be worth just 10 billion US dollars. In other words, it would not make sense for the world to spend any more than 10 billion US dollars (under 2 US dollars a person) today on a measure that would prevent the loss of the planet's entire output 200 years from now.

I will not belabour the point that humanity would cease to exist if world output were zero. Where the author gets things wrong, even after posing the problem, is in assuming that the rates to be used for discounting future income losses are independent of the economic forecast. The underlying assumption in the passage is the Ultimate Perturbation (zero world output in year 2200). This would involve a sharp secular decline in output from some point in time. Consumption interest rates would then be negative. So, where does the 7 per cent a year discount rate come from? Discounting future incomes produces paradoxes only when it isn't recognized that, as discount rates are themselves accounting prices, they should be determined from the analysis and not plucked from air.

---

[29] Uzawa (1974a,b) was the first to explore this reasoning.

12

Institutional Responses to Policy Change

12.1. NON-MARKET INTERACTIONS

Policy reforms cause perturbations to an economy. It is easy enough to say this, but altogether more difficult to identify the perturbations. Any system, human or otherwise, responds when perturbed. A policy change can create all sorts of effects rippling through unnoticed by those who are unaffected, because there may be no public signals accompanying them. Evaluating reforms involves, among other things, valuing the ripples.

How is it that there can be no public signals to accompany economic interactions? It is possible if the interactions take place via non-market channels. The terms of trade, even when set in cash, would not be publicly broadcast. In non-monetary exchanges they could even be implicit, and thus difficult to unravel. Tracing the ripples would require an understanding of non-market interactions and of their interplay with market interactions.[1] Examples of non-market interactions include those in which environmental and ecosystem services are involved. Communitarian management practices have protected people from the 'tragedy of the commons' in many places, in many periods. In other places and at other times, such practices have failed to take off, or have broken down in the face of changing circumstances. Every such management regime has harboured non-market interactions.[2] On occasion the 'ripples' take the form of distress migration out of villages. These are public signals and should be seen as such. People have been known to leave their villages in numbers when their local common-property resources degrade to the point where life at home is impossible.[3]

In poor countries non-market transactions are undertaken over numerous other commodities, including labour, credit, and insurance. For example,

---

This chapter is based on Dasgupta (2001b).

[1] The subject has been at the heart of economic anthropology.

[2] Ch. 7.   [3] See Chopra and Gulati (1998, 2001).

Udry (1994) has reported that as recently as the late 1980s more than 90 per cent of the value of all loans in Nigeria were obtained from what in the development literature is called the 'informal sector', which includes not only informal money lenders, but also the family and kinship. Udry presents findings from a survey conducted on 400 households in four Nigerian villages. He found that nearly all credit transactions were either between relatives or between households in the same village. No written contracts were involved, nor did the agreements specify the date of repayment or the amount to be repaid. The same data showed that repayment of loans depends on the debtors' ability to pay, suggesting that 'credit' can assume the form of 'insurance'.[4]

In recent years non-market institutions have been studied by economists and political scientists with the same care and rigour they used to invest in the study of markets and the State.[5] There is now an extensive body of work on ways in which people cope with resource scarcity when there are no formal markets for exchanging goods and services across time, space, and circumstances, and when the State is ineffective. The literature also offers a way to understand how people, both individually and collectively, respond to policy changes when they transact in non-market institutions.[6]

Common-property resources illustrate that a key aspect of institutions is the system of property rights. Other ingredients of institutions include roles, rights, responsibilities, and obligations. The goods and services include not only such assets as land, cattle, and water, but also such finely honed objects as fruit and berries, branches of trees and cow dung at particular places, at particular times.[7] Our understanding of the role played by property rights in the way institutions function is now substantially better than it was even twenty years ago.

Institutions are overarching entities. People interact with one another *in* institutions. A more refined concept is that of interactions among people, the term I have been using here. Of particular interest are cooperative ventures, which require that the parties trust one another to do what they said they would do under the terms of their agreements. People cooperate for mutual benefit in both market and non-market institutions. Now, market interactions are sustained by the legal power of the State. How are non-market interactions sustained?

---

[4] Udry (1993). See also Siamwalla *et al.* (1989) for a study of non-market credit institutions in Thailand that have stood in place of formal credit markets.

[5] See the pioneering work of Rudra (1982, 1984) on rural West Bengal and the essays in Hoff, Braverman, and Stiglitz (1993) and Dasgupta and Serageldin (2000).

[6] At a recent workshop organised by the Beijer International Institute of Ecological Economics (BIIEE), Stockholm, young academic economists from India and sub-Saharan Africa presented papers on a remarkably wide variety of non-market relationships over the use of local resources, such as land, water, and fisheries. The articles are collected in BIIEE (2001).

[7] See e.g. Feder and Noronha (1987) and Feder and Feeny (1991).

Four pathways come to mind. First, innumerable transactions occur because the people involved care about one another and trust one another to carry out their obligations. The household best exemplifies institutions based on care and affection. Second, people trust one another to keep agreements if they are sanguine that most others are disposed to be trustworthy and to keep agreements.[8] An extreme form of such social preferences is the disposition to be honest always in one's dealings with others, but to punish those who break our trust in them (e.g. by shunning them). Thus, we not only have a disposition for such behaviour as paying our dues, helping others at some cost to ourselves, and returning a favour, but also practise such norms as those that prescribe that we punish people who have hurt us intentionally; and even such meta-norms as shunning people who break agreements with others, (on occasion) frowning on those who socialize with people who have broken agreements with others, and so forth. By internalizing such norms of reciprocity, a person enables the springs of his actions to include them. He therefore feels shame or guilt in violating the norm, and this prevents him from doing so, or at the very least puts a brake on him, unless he finds other considerations to be overriding. In short, his upbringing helps to ensure that he has a disposition to obey the norm. When he does violate it, neither guilt nor shame will typically be absent, but frequently the act will have been rationalized by him. For such a person, making a promise is a commitment, and it is essential for him that others recognize it to be so. In an important and interesting paper, Sethi and Somanathan (1996) have shown that the disposition to reciprocate and punish those who 'free ride' is stable under selection pressure, provided the personal cost to free riders from being punished is large. If the proportion of those who cooperate (but enforce agreements by punishing those who free ride) is sufficiently large, free riding becomes too costly, and the trait disappears. Formally, cooperative behaviour is evolutionary-stable. [9] Evidence that people have such 'social preferences' has been found in experimental situations.[10]

The third pathway helping to sustain cooperation invokes an external enforcer. An agreement is translated into an explicit contract and enforced by an established structure of power and authority. This may be the State, as in the case of contracts in the large numbers of markets operating throughout the world. But it need not be the State, and this is why I cite the mechanism here. In rural communities the structure of power and authority are in some cases

---

[8] Such social preferences were discussed in Sect. 4.4.

[9] Of course, other things the same, if there is a sufficiently large proportion of free-riders to begin with in the Sethi-Somanathan model, their proportion increases, and cooperation breaks down completely. Free riding is evolutionary-stable too. For wider explorations of the evolutionary stability of traits, see Maynard Smith (1982) and Weibull (1995).   [10] See Chs. 1 and 4.

vested in tribal elders (as in nomadic tribes in sub-Saharan Africa), in others in dominant landowners, feudal lords, chieftains, and priests.

On occasion there have been attempts to make rural communities mini-republics in certain spheres of life. Village Panchayats in India try to assume that form. The idea is to elect offices, the officials being entrusted with the power to settle disputes, enforce contracts (be they codified or only tacit), communicate with higher levels of state authority, and so forth.[11]

The question of why the local authority is accepted by people is a higher-order one, akin to the question of why people accept the authority of the State. The answer is that general acceptance itself is self-enforcing behaviour: when a sufficiently large number of others accept the structure of authority, each has an incentive to accept it, the personal cost of non-compliance (a stiff gaol sentence) being too high.[12]

Recent work on communitarian management of local common-property resources has identified a different enforcement mechanism. The mechanism operates best where people encounter one another repeatedly in similar circumstances. Agreements can be honoured in such situations even if people aren't disposed to be honest, even if they don't necessarily care for one another personally, and even if an authority isn't available to enforce agreements. This pathway, where people are engaged in *long-term relationships*, is an ingredient in theories of social capital. It is the fourth mechanism by which cooperation is sustained.[13]

There are many interactions, however, that involve non-cooperation, while being harmful to the parties involved. Of particular interest are those that occur because of weak property rights. The theory of economic externalities is about such interactions. Recall that externalities are the side-effects that occur when people engage in activities without mutual agreement. Externalities are a form of institutional failure. Earlier we noted that environmental problems are frequently symptoms of institutional failure. Traditionally, environmental and resource economists studied ways to eliminate externalities in circumstances where agreements are enforcible by the State. The theory and practice of environmental legislation and regulation is a development of that perspective.[14]

---

[11] Robert Wade's account of local enforcement of water allocation in rural South India describes such a mechanism in detail (Wade, 1988). Forty-one villages were studied, and it was found that downstream villages (those facing an acute scarcity of water) had an elaborate set of rules, enforced by fines, for regulating the use of water from irrigation canals. Most villages had similar arrangements for the use of grazing land. Wade reports that elected village councils (*Panchayats*) appoint agents who allocate water among farmers' fields, protect crops from grazing animals, collect levies, and impose fines. Baland and Platteau (1996: 217) write about 'water masters' in fishing groups in the Niger River delta who regulated the use of the local fisheries.

[12] A similar analysis was presented in Sect. 4.4 to explain civic compliance.

[13] The enforcement mechanism underlying such relationships involves credible threats of non-cooperation to those who break an agreement; see Sect. 12.5.

[14] Cropper and Oates (1995) and Morgenstern (1997).

Policy reforms are typically aimed at macroeconomic variables (tax rates, the reach of primary education, environmental legislation, price-support programmes, reproductive health care). Since reforms perturb the economy, evaluating a reform involves identifying the perturbation consequent upon it and valuing it. This means asking who benefits, who loses, and how great are the benefits and losses. But that is the subject of social cost–benefit analysis. Since non-market transactions are extensive in poor countries, accounting prices should be particularly useful in policy evaluation there. As of now, though, they are infrequently used in policy documents. This is because it is technically very difficult to estimate accounting prices in non-market institutions. In an implicit way, however, they are used, because there is no way to avoid them. When someone says a reform would hurt one group more than it would help another, they are in effect using the language of accounting prices. It is presumed that the person making the claim knows something about the reasons why those likely to be hurt would be hurt and those likely to benefit would benefit. This in turn presumes that the speaker has an understanding of the economic processes at work, which is to say that she understands the workings of the prevailing institutions and the perturbation that would be created by the reform. All this is the stuff of social cost–benefit analysis.

Invariably, certain portions of the perturbations created by policy reforms are ignored. I am referring not to the fact that policy evaluation requires approximations to be made, but to the fact that portions whose size is not known are ignored. The ignored bits typically include people involved in non-market interactions. In Sections 12.3–12.5 I present three examples of this by pointing more generally to the comparative neglect of non-market interactions in economic policy discussions. All involve international economic policy. They also involve poor people in poor countries in an essential way. My idea is not to offer a detailed account of any of the examples, but rather, to use the apparatus developed in this book to interpret the reactions the policies have elicited from commentators and non-governmental organizations. It will prove useful first to frame the discussion in the way the debates themselves have been conducted. I do that in the following section.

12.2. GROWTH OR REDISTRIBUTION?

In Section 5.7 the idea was developed that poor people in poor countries are vulnerable to poverty traps. By poor people I mean those possessing little to no assets. Lack of wealth is a sign that someone is at especial risk.

Although applied development economists frequently don't acknowledge their debt, theory does direct their investigation. Taking theory's lead, the natural question to ask is this: who are likely to be the assetless? In India, where some of the best empirical work on poverty has been done, it would most likely be landless households. Among them are members of what are euphemistically called 'scheduled tribes' (whose communal assets may have been stripped over the years; Section 12.4), widows, and female-headed households. The latter are likely to be vulnerable everywhere in the poor world, not just India. Empirical findings are consistent with theory.[15]

The direct route for reducing poverty is asset redistribution. Understandably, this arouses passions everywhere. Land redistribution without adequate compensation is otherwise known as state robbery: it violates the civil liberties of those from whom land is taken by government fiat. If the land had been acquired by its current owner by force, it would be a different matter, but most frequently it hasn't been so acquired. Righting wrongs of the distant past without adequate reflection can entail the committing of new wrongs.

One category of policy reforms that avoids these treacherous measures is the public provision of early education, public health programmes, and targeted food subsidies. This kind of reform redistributes assets, because education and health are aspects of human capital and because state aid is financed by general taxation. Today, such policies are not viewed as acts of robbery.[16] Another set of policy reforms is the enforcement of good laws of property and a reduction in corruption, both of which are likely to aid the poor.[17]

Comparisons of well-being among groups have given rise to debates on growth versus redistribution of income, a recurrent theme in development thinking.[18] Now, redistribution makes one think of the present, whereas growth encourages us to peer into the future. Loosely speaking, growth-oriented economic policies are directed at improving future well-being, while redistributive policies aim to improve current well-being. The 'versus' in the refrain suggests a tension between the two. Advocates of one are not infrequently made to appear opposed to the other, or at best uncaring about the other. Someone's political position is called 'right' or 'left', depending on whether they advocate growth or redistribution. Publications, even Reports from international organizations, assume a sophomoric tone of moral superiority when they decry policies their authors oppose.

But it isn't clear that in today's poor countries reforms that would realize faster growth are opposed to those that are directly redistributive.[19] For example,

---

[15] See e.g. Buvinic and Gupta (1997), Dreze and Srinivasan (1997), and Meenakshi, Ray, and Gupta (2000).

[16] But not all would agree that taxes collected above and beyond the needs of common security are justifiable. Nozick (1974) contains an engaging account of why anything beyond taxation for, roughly speaking, the supply of collective security and guarding property rights amounts to robbery.

[17] Thomas *et al.* (2000) elaborates this line of thought.

[18] Chenery *et al.* (1975) contains a pioneering set of essays on the subject.

[19] Adelman (1979) and Dasgupta and Ray (1987).

people of both right and left political persuasions favour effective state provision of early education with universal coverage. Creation of human capital spurs growth in gross national product (GNP), but it also redistributes wealth. Theory suggests that there are other redistributive measures (e.g. judicious land reform) that bring about growth. Recent empirical work offers tentative support of the thesis.[20]

The other side of the theoretical coin are patterns of growth that reduce poverty over time, via what is colloquially called the *trickle-down effect*. There is evidence of that too.[21] The two sets of empirical studies co-exist comfortably because, for one thing, causality is nearly impossible to establish; for another, the variables studied are a number of imperfect surrogates (e.g. GNP per head) for what we should really be after. The studies aren't quite comparable. Recall the passages quoted in the Introduction (Section I.2), both of which were from World Bank documents, published in the same year. One recommended asset redistribution in the form of food security as an engine for economic growth, while the other saw growth in GNP as the most effective route for poverty reduction.[22]

The debate on growth versus redistribution can be expected to continue. The problem is that it has been conducted in terms of growth versus distribution of *GNP*, a singularly inappropriate measure over which to do battle. In Chapter 9 I explained why GNP misleads. It is as well to recall the reason why it misdirects the debate on growth versus distribution.

In focusing on growth in GNP, protagonists have ignored the state of the natural resource base, a recurring concern of this essay. In poor countries, the poorest depend directly on the local resource base for their livelihood and in great measure transact in them through non-market channels. Statistics bypassing that base are misleading. But it is easy to bypass them because they aren't publicly observable. It is no good being triumphant over high growth rates of GNP if the resource base declines simultaneously. It is also a case of misplaced concern to focus on the distribution of GNP if what hurts the poorest as much as low income is a declining non-marketed resource base.

I believe, however, that among those who have worried about slow growth in the poorest countries, a few have had something else in mind, namely, an efficient allocation of resources. My impression is that they used GNP growth as a surrogate for what they were really advocating: namely, policy reforms to

---

[20] Deininger and Squire (1997), Besley and Burgess (2000), and Thomas *et al.* (2000).

[21] Recently they have been called the 'pulling-up' effect. The industrial West provides one broad class of examples of the trickle-down effect. Dollar and Kraay (2000) have studied recent cross-country data for the poor world and have found evidence of the effect. Later in this chapter I comment on what the Dollar–Kraay study misses.   [22] Reutlinger and Pellekaan (1986) and World Bank (1986).

reduce economic waste. For me, the subtler part of the debate has been about efficiency versus equity.[23]

It is possible to argue though that in poor countries the tension between efficiency and equity is less pronounced than is suspected in the theoretical literature. The point is that public economics was developed mostly for Agathotopia. The State there is both benevolent and wise. Owing to agency problems, however, the State in Agathotopia has to strike a balance between efficiency and equity.[24] The classic papers of Diamond and Mirrlees (1971) and Mirrlees (1971) formulated the choice in a precise manner. But here we are talking of policy reforms in the imperfect economies of Kakotopia. Resource allocation in imperfect economies can be so deplorable that it is possible to devise reforms that reduce both economic waste and inequity, and possibly also the extent of poverty.[25] We have identified a class of reforms in poor countries that would seem to have these virtues: a judicious increase in public expenditures on early education and public health. Instead of creating a list of further examples, I want to consider the reverse perspective. The examples that follow illustrate how public policy can go awry if non-market interactions are neglected in economic modelling. When they are neglected, the possibility of reducing both waste and poverty is missed. Of the examples, the first is a local miniature, while the other two are altogether grander and near-global.

12.3. MANAGING LOCAL IRRIGATION SYSTEMS

For many years, the political scientist Elinor Ostrom has been studying the management of common-property resources in various parts of the world.[26] In her work on collectively managed irrigation systems in Nepal, she has accounted for differences in rights and responsibilities among users (who gets how much water and when, who is responsible for which maintenance task of the canal system, and so forth) in terms of the fact that some farmers are head-enders, while others are tail-enders. Head-enders have a built-in advantage, in that they can prevent tail-enders from receiving water. On the other hand, head-enders need the tail-enders' labour for repair and maintenance of traditional canal systems, which are composed of headworks made of stone, trees, and mud.

---

[23] Meade (1964) and Bhagwati (1988). Efficiency was defined in Ch.*1.

[24] In Utopia there isn't a conflict between the two: both are attainable.

[25] See R. Cooper (1977) and Dasgupta (1982b) for explorations of this possibility. World Bank (1992) christened the possibility 'win–win'.

[26] Ostrom (1990, 1996), Ostrom and Gardner (1993), and Ostrom and Schlager (1996).

Both sets of parties can in principle gain from cooperation. Because their fortunes would differ greatly if they did not cooperate, cooperative arrangements would be expected to display asymmetries, and they do.

In Ostrom (1996), the author reported that a number of communities in her sample had been given well-meaning aid by donors, in that the canals had been improved by the construction of permanent headworks. What could be better, you might ask. But she observed that those canal systems that had been improved were frequently in worse repair at the tail end and were delivering less water to tail-enders than previously. Ostrom also reported that water allocation was more equitable in traditional farm management systems than in modern systems managed by external agencies, such as government and foreign donors. She estimated from her sample that agricultural productivity is higher in traditional systems.

Ostrom has an explanation for this. She argues that, unless it is accompanied by counter-measures, the construction of permanent headworks alters the relative bargaining positions of the head- and tail-enders. Head-enders now don't need the labour of tail-enders to maintain the canal system. So the new sharing scheme involves even less water for tail-enders. Head-enders gain from the permanent structures, but tail-enders lose disproportionately. This is an example of how well-meaning aid can go wrong if the nature of the institution receiving the aid is not understood by the donor.

12.4. STRUCTURAL ADJUSTMENT PROGRAMMES AND THE NATURAL ENVIRONMENT

My second example is altogether more grand and fiercely debated. So, of course, I will be a lot more tentative in what I say. It has to do with the experience people in poor countries have had with structural adjustment programmes, under which a plethora of taxes, subsidies, and direct controls introduced by governments over decades were reduced under pressure from the World Bank and the International Monetary Fund. The programmes were designed to encourage a more efficient allocation of resources.

Many have criticized the way structural adjustment programmes were implemented. Some have pointed to the additional hardship that many of the poor have experienced in their wake. Others have argued that, in order to reduce deficits, governments embarked on economic programmes that were particularly harsh on the natural resource base. Still others have argued that the two effects have come in tandem, that structural adjustment programmes encouraged countries to raise export revenue by depleting natural capital in a rapacious manner.

It is, however, possible to argue that structural adjustment programmes, facilitating as they did the growth of markets and the reduction in government deficits in poor countries, were necessary. And it has been so argued by proponents of the programmes.

I want to suggest that both proponents and opponents of the programmes may be right. The growth of markets and the reduction in government deficits benefit many, but simultaneously they can make vulnerable people face additional economic hardship occasioned by environmental degradation. It is possible that the economic gains from structural adjustment were in principle large enough to compensate the losers, but losers are frequently not compensated; they may even remain undetected. There are a number of pathways by which this can happen. Here I sketch one.

An easy way for the State to earn revenue in countries endowed with forests is to issue timber concessions. The State can exercise its rights to forests that are public property by a judicious use of force to evict long-term dwellers. Timber concessions can then be sold to favoured firms, reducing government deficit while simultaneously enlarging the private bank balances of officials. Forests are an easy target of usurpation by the State because there tend to be no legal documents proving ownership.[27]

I leave aside the losses incurred by those evicted, because there is nothing really to say on the matter other than platitudes. I want to think instead about concessions made on forests in the uplands of a watershed so as to consider the ecological pathways by which deforestation inflicts damage on people in the lowlands (siltation, increased incidence of flooding, and so forth).[28] It pays to study them in terms of the assignment of property rights. The common law in many poor countries, if we are permitted to use this expression in a universal context, in principle recognizes pollutees' rights. So it is the timber merchant who, in principle, would have to pay compensation to downstream farmers for the right to inflict the damage that goes with deforestation. However, even if the law sees the matter in this light, there is a gulf between the 'written' law and the enforcement of law. When the cause of damage is hundreds of

---

[27] Colchester (1995) has recounted that political representatives of forest-dwellers in Sarawak, Malaysia, have routinely given logging licences to members of the state legislature. Primary forests in Sarawak are expected to be depleted within the next decade or so. Cruz and Repetto (1992), Reed (1996), and Seymour and Dubash (2000) describe other pathways by which structural adjustment programmes have been unfriendly to the natural environment.

[28] The example is taken from Dasgupta (1990b). Hodgson and Dixon (1992) is a case study on logging and its impact on fisheries and tourism, in Palawan, the Philippines, that illustrates the example well. Chichilnisky (1994) has developed the argument in the text in a more general context.

miles away, when the timber concession has been awarded to public land by the State, and when the victims are a scattered group of poor farmers or fishermen, the issue of a negotiated outcome doesn't usually arise. But when the timber merchant isn't required to compensate downstream farmers and fishermen, the private cost of logging is less than its social cost. From the social point of view, we would expect excessive deforestation of the uplands. We would also expect that resource based goods would be underpriced in the market (say, in export markets). The less roundabout is the production of the final good, the greater would this underpricing be, in percentage terms. Put another way, the lower is the value that is added to the resource in the course of production, the larger is the extent of this underpricing of the final product. The accounting price of timber being greater than its market price, there is an implicit subsidy on primary forest products, possibly on a massive scale. Moreover, the (export) subsidy is paid not by the general public via taxation, but by some of the most disadvantaged members of society (the sharecropper, the small landholder or tenant farmer, the fisherman). The subsidy is hidden from public scrutiny, which is why its isn't acknowledged officially. But it is almost certainly there. We should be in a position to estimate such subsidies. As of now, we have very few official estimates.

12.5. POVERTY AND FREER TRADE

The demonstrations in Seattle at the end of 1999 and the response of those who regard free trade as being good for everyone offer an example similar to that concerning structural adjustment programmes. Public discussions on the appropriate role of the World Trade Organization (WTO) are now routinely conducted in terms of an alleged battle between multinational companies and hapless governments in poor countries. But the poor in poor countries are not the same as the governments that rule over them.[29] There should be no question today that increased international trade has benefited many and arbitrary restrictions on trade have harmed many. But freeing trade in the presence of externalities can be predicted to hurt segments of the population. Externalities are particularly rampant in poor countries, where markets and non-market institutions co-exist and support similar types of transaction (insurance and credit).

All societies rely on a mix of market and non-market institutions. The mix shifts through changing circumstances, as people find ways to circumvent difficulties in realizing mutually beneficial transactions. Arnott and Stiglitz (1991)

---

[29] Ch. 5.

have developed a formal account of the externalities that prevail when market and non-market institutions supply the same commodity. Their purpose was to show how the presence of non-market institutions can prevent people from transacting as much in the market as they should for their collective good. In what follows, I present a case offering the opposite moral: namely, that an expansion of markets can destroy non-market institutions and make certain vulnerable groups worse off. Economic analysis can identify the kinds of people who would get hurt when trade expansion occurs in the absence of appropriate safety nets or compensations. Here is a pathway that may well be powerful.[30]

In rural communities in poor countries non-market interactions are often founded on long-term relationships, which are sustained by *social norms*, such as norms of reciprocity. Social norms are behaviour patterns (strategies) that are subscribed to by most members of a community. It helps to think of extreme cases where all subscribe to a norm. Technically put, for a strategy to be a social norm, it must be self-enforcing. A social norm is an equilibrium strategy. The kinds of social norms I have in mind here, such as norms of reciprocity, tend to be prevalent only among people who expect to encounter one another repeatedly in similar situations. However, if the chance of future encounters is reduced, norms that previously supported long-term relationships disintegrate; they cease being self-enforcing. Let us see why.[31]

Consider a group of far-sighted people who know one another and who prepare to interact indefinitely with one another. By a 'far-sighted' person I mean someone who applies a low rate to discount future costs and benefits of alternative courses of action. I assume as well that the parties in question are not separately mobile (although they could be collectively mobile, as in the case of nomads); otherwise the chance of future encounters with one another would be low and people (being far-sighted!) would discount heavily the future benefits of current cooperation.

The basic idea is this: if people are far-sighted and are not separately mobile, a credible threat by everyone that they would impose sufficiently stiff sanctions on anyone who broke the agreement would deter everyone from breaking it. But the threat of sanctions would cease to have potency if opportunistic behaviour became personally more attractive. This can happen if formal markets grow nearby and uncorrelated migration accompanies the growth of those markets. As opportunities outside the village improve, those with lesser ties (young men) are more likely to be able to take advantage of them and to make a break

---

[30] de Soto (2000) has argued that the process of globalization can leave the poor behind because frequently they don't have titles to the capital with which they work (i.e. land). They are unable to offer collaterals for loans. The example I have offered in the text is of a different kind from his. On international trade and the environment in optimizing economies, see Ulph (1997).

[31] The formal theory is reviewed in Fudenburg and Tirole (1991).

with those customary obligations that are enshrined in prevailing social norms. Those with greater domestic attachments would perceive this and infer that the expected benefits from complying with agreements are now lower. The chance of future 'encounters' falls. Either way, norms of reciprocity could be expected to break down, making certain groups of people (women, the old, the very young) worse off. This is a case where improved institutional performance elsewhere (growth of markets in the economy at large) has an adverse effect on the functioning of a local, non-market institution.

To the extent that social norms weaken, communal management systems deteriorate, as free-riding goes unpunished. So there can be a chain of events, leading from growth of markets elsewhere, through a deterioration of the local resource base, to greater hardship for those unable to take advantage of growing opportunities elsewhere (owing to an absence of roads to transport their produce, to a lack of human capital, or whatever). Freeing trade without considering safety-nets for those who are vulnerable to the erosion of communitarian practices is defective policy. It has sometimes been argued that, since safety-nets are the responsibility of governments, international agreements on trade expansion should be seen as a different matter. The antecedent clause is true, but the inference from it isn't right. In a dysfunctional world it matters very much who gets to move first. If there is no guarantee that governments will put in place the needed safety-nets, the consequences of trade expansion can be expected to be quite different from the consequences if there are guarantees that governments will do their job. Earlier in this essay I argued it is right and proper for the purposes of accountability that international organizations be given clear and distinct goals and tasks.[32] So it is proper that the WTO should be concerned with trade, and trade alone. But for citizens at large it is governance, not trade, that is at the heart of the matter.

---

[32] Introduction (Sect. I.3).

PART V

VALUING POTENTIAL LIVES

Prologue

In Part III a method was developed for valuing the allocation of resources among 'present' and 'future' people. In Part IV a method was developed for evaluating changes in resource allocations in terms of their impact on 'present' and 'future' people. 'Present' people are alive now; 'future' people aren't alive now, but will be alive in the future. Demographers refer to 'present' people when informing us that a country's population has passed the billion mark. They include 'future' people in their reckoning when issuing a forecast that the world's population will be 10 billion in 2050.

Discussions on economic policy usually presuppose a forecast of future numbers. This is obviously a simplification, for it is hard to imagine any economic policy that does not have an influence on reproductive behaviour; but since it is a good approximation in many cases to imagine this, much policy discussion is based on it. The chapters in Part IV were about policy evaluation in a world where the present and future demographic profile is given: we studied Same Numbers Problems there.

However, there are policies that affect reproductive behaviour, and thus future numbers, significantly. With advances in genetics, policies can also affect the quality of people who will be born. So we need a framework for including in our deliberations *potential* people and, so, potential lives. The inclusion of potential lives in policy discussions gives rise to Different Numbers Problems, and theories of optimum population emerge from them.[1]

Population is a controversial subject. Many are persuaded that the sheer size of today's world population is a prime cause of human misery and environmental destruction.[2] There are also those who infer over-population from evidence of widespread poverty in many parts of the globe. But there are others who do not see the world's population size as a problem at all. Some believe that poverty and high fertility are distributional or 'entitlement' failures, while others think that human inventiveness and ingenuity are capable of an indefinite enhancement of Earth's capacity to support our species, and to support it at a high standard of living.[3] In Chapters 8 and 9, I reviewed some of the reasons why ecologists are wary of the latter viewpoint. They emphasize the deleterious effects that a

---

[1] The term is due to Parfit (1982).   [2] See e.g. Ehrlich and Ehrlich (1990).

[3] Among well-known statements along these lines, see Bauer (1981; 2000), Kelley (1988), Simon (1989; 1990), and Sen (1994).

growing and increasingly affluent population would have on Earth's capacity to supply the ecosystem services upon which we depend. They are unconvinced that humanity can rely upon technological progress to limit the pressure our activities will impose upon Earth's ecosystems.[4] There is a tension here between ecologists and economists, one that is unlikely to ease in the foreseeable future.

However, as far as I am aware, no one regards population as an unimportant matter. Government attitudes towards schooling, family planning and reproductive health, old-age pension, and family allowances have an impact on the number of children people choose to have.[5] Policy reforms in these areas of government activity, as in any other area, need to be evaluated before they are undertaken. Recently, reproductive behaviour has been studied with an eye on a number of externalities with which the behaviour is likely to be associated.[6] Several arise because reproduction is a paradigm of non-market activity and its effects can ripple across non-market channels. But externalities reflect institutional failure. Their presence is a reason for instituting policy reforms. Contrary to what is sometimes assumed in popular writings, reproductive decisions are not an entirely private matter. You might therefore think there is an extensive literature on the ethical foundations of population policy. In fact there is little to appeal to, despite the fact that notable thinkers have periodically expressed views on the matter.

It could be countered that no extension of standard welfare economics is needed, because parents care about their children and considerate parents take into account the future welfare of the children they choose to have when deciding how many children to have and how much to save for them. If they are thoughtful parents, they know in addition that the welfare of the children they will have will depend upon the welfare of the children they *in turn* will have; that the welfare of the children they in turn will have will depend upon the welfare of the children *they* in turn will have; and so on. There is a recursion along a family line.[7]

But the recursion is built on the desires of those who are alive and on a forecast of the desires of people who will be born. To accept this as the sole basis

---

[4] See e.g. Ehrlich and Ehrlich (1981), Lubchenco *et al.* (1991), Wilson (1992), Matson *et al.* (1997), and Vitousek *et al.* (1997). The famous '$I = PAT$' equation of Ehrlich and Holdren (1971), that *I*mpact on the environment is a function of *P*opulation, *A*ffluence and *T*echnology, is the metaphor frequently used by ecologists to express this concern.

[5] See the essays in Rosenzweig and Stark (1997).   [6] Dasgupta (2000b,c).

[7] To formalize, consider a deterministic world. Imagine that the welfare of generation 0 of a dynasty depends on the consumption services the average member enjoys (which I write as C_0), the number of children each member produces (denote this as N_1) and the average welfare of each of the children (which I write as U_1). But U_1 in turn would be expected to depend upon the consumption services the average member of generation 1 enjoys (C_1), the average number of progeny they bear (N_2), and the average welfare of the progeny (U_2), and so on, down the generations. We may express U_0 as

$$U_0(C_0, N_1, U_1(C_1, N_2, U_2(C_2, N_3, U_3(\dots)))).$$

This is a recursive function.

for population ethics is to accept the view that all ethical thought ought to be based solely on actual desires. There is a voluminous literature on why that view should be rejected. In this essay I have built on that literature to develop a framework for valuing and evaluating in a world in which future numbers are given. In the chapters that follow I try to extend the framework and offer an outline of a theory that would enable us to value objects and evaluate policies when the policies influence future numbers and the characteristics of people who are born.

Children are both ends and means. The mix of the two motivations for having children depends on the institutional structure of society and the personal circumstances of the parents. Children substitute for capital assets in economies where markets are underdeveloped. Among poor households, who possess few labour-saving devices (electricity, tap water), children are also a source of labour for daily chores. Children mind their siblings, look after cattle, collect firewood and potable water, and provide old-age security for their parents. They begin work from as early an age as six. Caldwell (1981, 1982) has offered empirical evidence that the intergenerational transfer of resources is from children to their parents in societies experiencing high fertility and high mortality rates, but that it is from parents to their children when fertility and mortality rates are low.

Although children would appear to substitute for capital assets only in poor households in poor regions, child bearing and child rearing are everywhere a paradigm of non-market activities. The externalities associated with such complex patterns of reproductive motivation as I am alluding to go some way to explain the pro-natalist attitudes that prevail in the poor regions of the world (Dasgupta, 2000b,c). In Part V, however, I am concerned with developing an ethical framework for public policies. So, as in Chapter 6, I shall purge from consideration the myriad institutional failures with which households have to cope. The way they cope must, of course, be taken into account when policy reforms are evaluated in imperfect economies (Part IV). But the normative basis of the theory of policy evaluation is independent of the particular imperfections from which economies suffer.

In Chapters 13 and 14, I review two widely discussed theories of population ethics: Average and Classical Utilitarianism. However, it has been known for some time that each of these has serious weaknesses. In Chapter 15, I offer an outline of a theory, based on an especially strong conception of personhood, that performs well when put to work in a world facing environmental constraints. (This is confirmed in Chapter *15.) But I hasten to emphasize that the subject is controversial, and my treatment of it possibly even more so.[8]

---

[8] In thinking about the welfare economics of potential lives, I learnt much from the many discussions I had in the early 1970s with Simon Blackburn. Our joint article was, alas, never completed for publication. I have been stimulated greatly by the criticisms of my subsequent writings on the subject (Dasgupta, 1974b; 1988; 1989; 1994) by John Broome, both in correspondence and in publications (Broome, 1996; 1999: ch. 15). The following chapters are based on Dasgupta (1998b). Professor Broome will probably still not agree with what I write here, but I hope he will think I have expressed myself less incoherently.

13

Some Views

13.1. OLD THEORIES

Interest in the question of desirable numbers dates back well into the past. Plato, in Pythagorian fashion, concluded that the number of citizens in the ideal city-state is 5,040, arguing that it is divisible by every number up to ten (it is, in fact, the product of the first seven integers) and has as many as 59 divisors, which would allow for the population to 'suffice for purposes of war and every peacetime activity, all contracts for dealings, and for taxes and grants'.[1]

Rousseau (1946: 356–7) also admitted no difficulty with the idea of desirable population size. By a different route, he arrived at a concept akin to that of the mercantalists. For he wrote:

I am always amazed that one obvious mark should be consistently misconstrued, and that men should be of such faith as not to agree about it. What is the goal set by all political organizations?—Surely it is the maintenance and prosperity of their members. And what is the most certain sign that a people is being maintained and rendered prosperous?—the size of the population. There is no need to go further in our search. Other things being equal, the government under which . . . the citizens do most increase and multiply is infallibly the best.

Today Rousseau's sentiments would appear quaint to some, wild to many. However, there is the well-known thought that any curtailment in the birth rate may deprive the world of a Bach. One counter-argument is that, by symmetry, we may thus also protect ourselves from a Hitler. More important is the thought that, if they are to flower, potential geniuses, like everyone else, require resources, such as potable water, food, clothing, health care, and education. So it would seem that we cannot get very far with the idea of a desirable population size without considering resource constraints. Whether it be for a household or for an entire nation, population policy cannot be formulated without a concurrent saving and investment policy. This leads to modern formulations.

---

[1] Plato (1970).

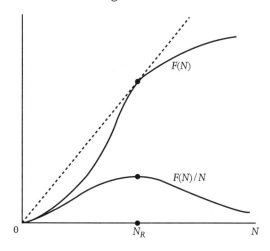

Figure 13.1. *Average Utilitarianism and productivity curves*

13.2. AVERAGE UTILITARIANISM

Edwin Cannan and Knut Wicksell are credited with having developed the modern concept of optimum population.[2] Their idea was to identify the stationary population at which output per head is maximized. Consider a closed economy, the natural illustration of which is the world as a whole. At any date there is a given stock of manufactured, environmental, and knowledge capital and a set of institutions the economy has inherited from the past. These comprise the economy's productive base. As this base is a given datum, it is exogenous to the analysis.

Let $F(N)$ denote net aggregate output if population size is N. By net output I mean gross output less the amount needed to replenish the depreciated capital. The existing productive base is an implicit parameter of F. One may imagine that, if the base were larger, $F(N)$ would be shifted upward, as in the model economy in the Appendix. But we are interested in the way F varies with N. I assume that $F(N)$ has the shape given in Figure 13.1, by which I mean that F increases with N at an increasing rate when N is small, but increases at a decreasing rate when N is large. This implies that average (net) output, $F(N)/N$, is bell-shaped, as in Figure 13.1. The assumption that average output is bell-shaped is instructive. It captures the idea that at low population sizes additional people have instrumental value (they add to average output), but that when population is large that particular value is lost.

---

[2] Gottlieb (1945) has an early survey of the history of optimum population theory.

As genuine investment is zero along a stationary state, net output equals consumption. It is now a simple matter to confirm that net output per head attains a maximum when population is N_R, the size at which

$$F'(N) = F(N)/N, \tag{13.1}$$

or, in other words, where marginal output equals average output (Figure 13.1).[3]

The sticking point in this account is that we have restricted ourselves not only to stationary programmes, but, more particularly, to stationary programmes associated with the productive base inherited from the past. The latter restriction is not only arbitrary, it is questionable: investment transforms the capital stock.[4] If England in the mid-eighteenth century had taken equation (13.1) seriously, its optimal policy would not have allowed for capital accumulation of any form: there would have been no Industrial Revolution.

The amount of income that ought to be invested today depends on future population size, and the desirable level of population in the future depends upon the future productive base, which in turn is affected by the amount invested today. A wider theory would require that investment and population be jointly determined.

Explorations into the twin problems within what may broadly be called Average Utilitarianism have been made by a number of authors. Ohlin (1967) asked what genuine investment and population growth would have to be in order that the rate of growth of national income per head is maximized. But he offered no ethical justification for the question. I don't know how one justifies a social purpose where earlier generations are seen as mere tools for preparing the productive base of the distant future. (How else would one arrive at the idea of maximizing the rate of growth of national income per head?) So we look elsewhere.

The problem is that it is not obvious what Average Utilitarianism amounts to in an intertemporal setting. One interpretation would have it that the objective should be to maximize the intertemporal sum of each generation's average level of well-being.[5] Since this interpretation has been explored by Pitchford (1974), we know theoretically what it implies in the way of policy. The problem is that the objective lacks philosophical foundations: it is *ad hoc*. Furthermore, as the criterion regards each generation as a unit of account, it is insensitive to differences in the numbers comprising the generations. If average well-being of two generations were to be the same, the criterion would regard the two on a par with each other, even if they differed greatly in numbers.

---

[3] $F'(N)$ is the differential coefficient of F.

[4] Genuine investment was the subject of discussion in Parts III and IV, as is also the Appendix.

[5] Letting U_t denote the well-being of the representative person of generation t, this criterion takes the form $\sum_0^\infty \beta^t U_t$, where $\beta(0 < \beta \leq 1)$ is the per-period discount factor (Ch. 6, expression (6.5)).

The more reasonable version of Average Utilitarianism would be to seek policies that would maximize the ratio of the intertemporal sum of each generation's aggregate well-being to the total number of all who are ever born.[6] As we observed in Chapter 6, this objective can be given a rationale: which island would you choose among islands of differing population sizes and levels of individual well-being, if you were not to know which person's shoes you would occupy in any island, and were to attribute 'equi-probability' to each such position?[7]

But there is a serious problem with the formulation. It is questionable whether the thought-experiment of choosing among islands can be the foundation for thinking about the problem in hand, which involves determining the desirable size of future population. When we think about the ethical foundations of population policies, Average Utilitarianism, whichever way we define 'average', would seem to have fundamental problems.[8]

---

[6] Letting N_t denote the size of generation t and U_t be the generation's average well-being, the criterion takes the form $\Sigma_0^\infty(\beta^t N_t U_t)/\Sigma_0^\infty(\beta^t N_t)$, where β is the per-period discount factor (Ch. 6, expression (6.7)).

[7] See Harsanyi (1955). I have qualified equi-probability in the text because it makes no sense when the future has no termination. To give it sense, we must suppose that the probability of extinction over the indefinite future is unity. We may then talk of equi-probability of conditionals. We discussed this is Ch. 6. See also Dasgupta and Heal (1979: ch. 9).

[8] See especially Hammond (1988) for a critique of Average Utilitarianism in the context of optimum population theory.

14

Classical Utilitarianism and
the Genesis Problem

14.1. FORMULATING THE THEORY

Unlike the average view, the total view is not so vulnerable to scrutiny. It has in any case an impeccable pedigree, namely Classical Utilitarianism:

For if we take Utilitarianism to prescribe, as the ultimate end of action, happiness as a whole, and not any individual's happiness, unless considered as an element of the whole, it would follow that, if the additional population enjoy on the whole positive happiness, we ought to weight the amount of happiness gained by the extra number against the amount lost by the remainder. So that, strictly conceived, the point up to which, on Utilitarian principles, population ought to be encouraged to increase, is not that at which average happiness is the greatest possible . . . but that at which the product formed by multiplying the number of persons living into the amount of average happiness reaches its maximum. (Sidgwick, 1907: 415–16)

Sidgwick's formulation was revived in the important work of Meade (1955) and was subsequently developed for an intertemporal economy by others.[1] It will pay to put the idea through its paces to see what it involves. In doing so I will deliberately misuse established classification schemes and regard Classical Utilitarianism to mean any theory that regards social well-being to be the sum of individual well-beings, whether or not well-being is interpreted as happiness.

It is simplest to consider a timeless economy with a fixed resource base, eschew production, and imagine that the base is an all-purpose 'consumption' good. Let the stock of the resource be K. If C is a person's consumption level, his well-being is $U(C)$. As in previous chapters, I take it that U is an increasing function of C ($U'(C) > 0$), but that it increases at a diminishing rate ($U''(C) < 0$). If C is large, life is good, which is to say that the person enjoys positive well-being. It would be better if a life of positive well-being were lived than if it were not. If C is small, life is not good, which is to say that well-being is negative. It would be better if a life of negative well-being were not lived than if it were.

---

[1] See Dasgupta (1969), Lane (1977), and Gigliotti (1983).

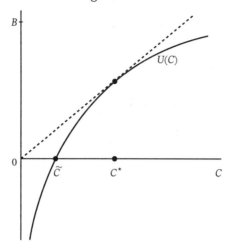

Figure 14.1. *Classical-Utilitarian optimum, C^**

By continuity, this means that there is a consumption level, call it $\tilde{C}$, at which well-being is zero. I will refer to $\tilde{C}$ as *well-being subsistence*. Figure 14.1 depicts a typical shape of $U(C)$.

Well-being subsistence is the living standard at which life is just good; it should not be identified with the standard of living at which life is just worth living for someone alive at well-being subsistence. We may presume that $\tilde{C}$ is higher than the living standard below which life is judged to be not worth living. (This is a point to which I return later.) $\tilde{C}$ offers a way of defining *carrying capacity*: given the resource base, $\tilde{C}$ yields the population size at which the best that can be achieved is a life for all that is neither positively bad nor positively good. If $\tilde{N}$ solves $K/\tilde{N} = C$, then $\tilde{N}$ is carrying capacity.[2]

It is tempting to think that $\tilde{C}$ can be arrived at through comparison with non-existence, but I am persuaded it would be a mistake to try. Comparison with non-existence is conceptually more than merely problematic. The unborn are not a class of people, nor is non-existence a state of being. It makes no sense to me to attribute a degree of well-being, low or high or nil, to the 'state of not being born'. Non-existence is like nothing for us, not even a very long night, because there is no *us* to imagine upon. One cannot be asked what it would be like to experience one's own non-existence, for there is no subject of experience in non-existence.

Well-being subsistence has to be tracked elsewhere. I can think of no other way to arrive at the calibration than through reflection on good and bad states of

---

[2] Cohen (1995) contains a wide-ranging discussion of Earth's carrying capacity and offers accounts of various estimates that have been made of it.

affair. The recognition that someone's level of well-being is positive or negative involves no more (and no less!) than comparison with the worst state such that it is not a positively bad thing that a person should live in such a state. That this is an immensely difficult judgement only goes to show that normative population theory is an immensely difficult subject: it does not offer a reason for avoiding such comparisons.[3]

Classical Utilitarianism poses the problem of optimum population as a Genesis Problem. We are to suppose that there are no people to begin with. Let N denote the number of people to be created. For simplicity, continue to assume that people will all be identical. Since marginal well-being declines as consumption increases (i.e., $U''(C)$ is negative), Classical Utilitarianism tells us that an equal distribution of K among all who are created is the ideal distribution. If N people are created, each should receive K/N units of the consumption good. Total well-being would then be $NU(K/N)$. We search for the value of N that maximizes this.

Routine arguments show that optimum N satisfies the condition[4]

$$(K/N)U'(K/N) = U(K/N). \tag{14.1}$$

Write $C \equiv K/N$. Since we know K, identifying optimum N is the same as identifying optimum C. The condition that yields optimum C is therefore a re-write of equation (14.1):

$$U'(C) = U(C)/C, \tag{14.2}$$

that is, the value of C at which marginal well-being of consumption equals average well-being per unit of consumption.

Equation (14.2) is fundamental to Classical Utilitarianism.[5] I shall call it the Sidgwick–Meade Rule here. Its intuitive basis is simple. At the optimum, neither a small increase in population nor a small decrease should alter aggregate well-being. Suppose that we were to consider a marginal increase. (The argument associated with a marginal decrease is analogous.) Then this additional person would share K equally with the population originally contemplated. The gain in introducing this additional person is her well-being, which is $U(C)$. But there

---

[3] If we return to the Ramsey–Koopmans theory of intergenerational well-being in Ch. 6, we would note that in that theory current well-being is measurable uniquely up to a positive affine transformation. (Thus, if $U(\cdot)$ is an admissible function, so is $aU(\cdot) + b$, where a and b are arbitrary constants and $a > 0$.) But in the Ramsey–Koopmans theory future population sizes are a given data. In contrast, future population sizes are a choice variable here. Identifying the zero level of current well-being is necessary. This makes current well-being unique up to a proportional transformation. (Thus, if $U(\cdot)$ is an admissible function, so is $aU(\cdot)$, where a is an arbitrary positive constant.) See Ch. *1.

[4] To arrive at (14.1), differentiate $NU(K/N)$ with respect to N, which yields the derivative $U(K/N) - (K/N)U'(K/N)$. Equate this to zero to obtain the condition.

[5] See Meade (1955) and Dasgupta (1969) for successive generalizations of this.

is also a loss, which is that each of the others being considered has slightly less consumption. The loss in well-being is $CU'(C)$. At the optimum this gain and loss must equal. The Sidgwick–Meade Rule asserts this. Figure 14.1 shows how we may locate optimum consumption per head with the help of the Sidgwick–Meade Rule. I denote the solution as C^*. The corresponding population size is denoted by N^*.[6]

14.2. OPTIMUM POPULATION SIZE

There is a problem with Classical Utilitarianism. It can recommend what could be regarded as overly large populations. Under Classical Utilitarianism, social well-being is the product of average well-being and the number of people who are born. The product gives us the trade-off between average well-being and the number of people who enjoy that average. Imagine now a world where average well-being declines slowly to zero when numbers increase. Classical Utilitarianism encourages numbers to increase indefinitely no matter how low the average has fallen, so long as it is positive.[7] But this means that the optimum standard of living, C^*, can be close to well-being subsistence $(\tilde{C})$, which is a way of saying that the theory can recommend overly large populations. Parfit (1984) found this conclusion of Classical Utilitarianism repugnant. So he has a term for it: the Repugnant Conclusion.[8]

One can argue, that, while the Conclusion is unappealing, it isn't 'repugnant'. Parfit found it repugnant because he interpreted well-being subsistence to be the standard of living below which it isn't worth living. In justifying his feelings, he described the Conclusion in the following terms:

For any possible population of at least ten billion people, all with a very high quality of life, there must be some much larger imaginable population whose existence, if other things are equal, would be better, even though its members have lives that are barely worth living. (Parfit, 1984: 388)

One would not contest that this is repugnant, but one would be forgiven for suggesting that the phrasing is more than a bit rigged. We are first tempted with a figure for world population that is almost certainly to be reached by

---

[6] In Ch. *14 the theory is illustrated with the help of an example. The example has been so chosen that we are able to determine an explicit solution of (14.2).

[7] See Dasgupta (1969: 307) and Rawls (1972: 162–3). The example developed in Ch. *14 reveals this feature explicitly.

[8] The Repugnant Conclusion has been the source of a number of further seeming paradoxes, much discussed in the recent philosophical literature. Parfit (1976, 1982, 1984, 1990) are the sources. Parfitian paradoxes have been discussed and added to by, among others, McMahan (1981), Hurka (1983), Sterba (1987), Temkin (1987), Cowen (1989), and Broome (1996).

the middle of this century, a figure that many people think can *in principle* be sustained at reasonable material comfort. This is followed at once by a picture of an overcrowded Earth, where people scramble for resources so as to eke out an existence, leading lives 'barely worth living'.

But the underlying logic in well-being subsistence is a far cry from this. Someone whose life is barely worth living has a very low, *negative*, level of well-being; their standard of living is below well-being subsistence. They are among the wretched of the Earth; and there are nearly a billion such people today, malnourished and prone to illness and disease, but surviving and tenaciously displaying that their lives are worth living by the fact that they persist in wishing to live. If you were to say that you would not wish the circumstances those people endure on anyone, I would not take you to mean that their lives aren't worth living: I would take you to be saying that their circumstances are so bad that you wouldn't wish them on even your worst enemy, that something ought to be done to improve their lives.

When the Conclusion is stated in the form Parfit adopts, it *is* repugnant. But it isn't repugnant if well-being subsistence is interpreted in the way it should be for the Genesis Problem. There is nothing repugnant about a very large imaginable population, all enjoying positive well-being. Their lives may not be *very* good, but as well-being is positive, their lives are good, in fact a good deal better than just worth living. There is nothing ethically repugnant about numbers compensating for living standards so long as well-being is positive, that is, so long as lives are good. In Chapter *14 I offer a simple model that illustrates Classical Utilitarianism's formulation of the value of potential lives and the numbers that ought to be born.

But there is a problem with Classical Utilitarianism. It doesn't lie where Parfit looked: it lies elsewhere. We turn to this in Chapter 15.

*14

Numbers and Well-Being under Classical Utilitarianism

Classical Utilitarianism can recommend what many would regard as overly large populations. I illustrate this by studying an example that is so simple that we are able to obtain an explicit solution.

Consider the following class of utility functions:

$$U(C) = B - C^{-\sigma}, \quad \text{where } B \text{ and } \sigma \text{ are positive constants.} \quad (\text{*}14.1)$$

The functional form (*14.1) is useful because it is defined by two parameters, B and σ. Ramsey (1928) called B 'bliss': B, the least upper bound of U, can be approached, but never attained. As $(1 + \sigma)$ is the elasticity of marginal well-being, it is also a measure of the extent to which individuals are averse to risk, in a world where decision under uncertainty is guided by expected utility maximization.[1] In Chapter 11 we noted that it is also an index measuring the extent to which social well-being is sensitive to equality in consumption: the larger is σ, the more equity-conscious is Classical Utilitarianism.

It is easy to check from (*14.1) that well-being subsistence is given by the expression

$$\tilde{C} = (1/B)^{1/\sigma}. \quad (\text{*}14.2)$$

As in Chapter 14, I consider a timeless world. There is a fixed stock of resources, of size K. The idea is to determine the number of people who should be created. To identify the optimum population, use (*14.2) in the Sidgwick–Meade Rule (equation (14.2) in Chapter 14) to obtain optimum consumption per head as

$$C^* = [(1 + \sigma)/B]^{1/\sigma}. \quad (\text{*}14.3)$$

Now use (*14.2) in (*14.1) to re-express (*14.3) as

$$C^*/\tilde{C} = (1 + \sigma)^{1/\sigma}. \quad (\text{*}14.4)$$

---

[1] See Pratt (1964). In Ch. 11 we noted that social discount rates on changes to future consumption depend on the elasticity of marginal well-being. In (11.3) the latter was denoted as η. In the notation adopted here, $\eta = 1 + \sigma$.

Equation (*14.4) is useful because it relates optimum consumption per head to well-being subsistence. For ecologists and demographers, however, it would prove more natural to recast the equation in terms of population size. So, let $N^* = K/C^*$ and, as earlier, $\tilde{N} = K/\tilde{C}$. N^* is optimum population for Classical Utilitarianism, and $\tilde{N}$ is the economy's carrying capacity. We may then re-express (*14.4) as

$$\tilde{N}/N^* = (1 + \sigma)^{1/\sigma}. \tag{*14.5}$$

σ is a positive number, and it is a well-known mathematical fact that when σ is positive, $(1 + \sigma)^{1/\sigma}$ is less than e (the base of natural logarithms), which in turn is approximately 2.74. I conclude that

$$C^*/\tilde{C} = \tilde{N}/N^* = (1 + \sigma)^{1/\sigma} < e \approx 2.74. \tag{*14.6}$$

Inequality (*14.6) is interesting. It says that Classical Utilitarianism favours a large population: optimum consumption per head is less than only 2.74 times the well-being subsistence rate. To put it another way, carrying capacity is less than only 2.74 times the optimum population size.

It is instructive to work with stylized numbers. Suppose $\sigma = 1$.[2] Then $C^*/\tilde{C} = \tilde{N}/N^* = 2$, which is to say that optimum consumption per head is only twice as large as well-being subsistence. Optimum population is therefore half the carrying capacity. If carrying capacity were, say, 10 billion people, optimum population would be 5 billion.

Notice, however, that the larger is σ, the closer is $C^*/\tilde{C}$ ($= \tilde{N}/N^*$) to unity, which is a way of saying that Classical Utilitarianism can advocate very large populations. In Chapter 6 we observed that applying concave transformations to well-being is a way of accommodating equity considerations in our conception of social well-being. Our present result says that the more sensitive is social well-being to equity, the greater is optimum population. If carrying capacity were, say, 10 billion people, and if σ were large, optimum population would be nearly 10 billion. I have known this result for a long time, but still find it puzzling that the idea of equality should play such an influential role in normative population theory. Admittedly, the theory I have invoked here instructs that all who are born are to be treated equally. Even so, it isn't obvious why the attitude *towards* equality influences the optimum number of lives.

---

[2] This choice is not *ad hoc*. Empirical studies of choice under uncertainty have consistently revealed that σ is only a little in excess of unity.

15

Actual versus Potential Lives

15.1. WHAT IS WRONG WITH THE
GENESIS PROBLEM?

As an exploration into a deep and difficult set of issues, Classical Utilitarianism has something to commend it, but it has only that to commend it. The theory's weakness is that it insists on casting the problem of desirable population and consumption as a Genesis Problem, not as an actual problem. I will now argue that the Genesis Problem is the wrong problem to study.

In the Genesis Problem there are no people actually present. All are potential. In its purest form, the Genesis Problem asks how many lives there ought ideally to be, enjoying what living standards.[1] This is the way ideas of optimum population were presented in Chapters 13–14. The problem is that the Genesis Problem may have been God's problem, but it is not the problem *we* face. This is because we are here. In contrast, the unconceived are not a class of people. The impossibility of imagining the unconceived (and thereby our own non-existence) gives spurious credence to the view that non-existence must be a long dismal night from which we must try to rescue people. We may feel grateful to the persons who created us for doing just that—not because they rescued us from anything, but because they are responsible for all this experience. To say that someone has a wretched life, for example a dismally low standard of living, isn't to say that the person would have been 'better off unconceived'. It is only to say that it is *bad* that her standard of living is what it is. No doubt it is enormously difficult to make such an assessment (where are we to draw the line separating positive and negative levels of well-being?) but that doesn't mean we can avoid making it, or that we ought to even if we could. Potential people are not present or future people, any more than clay by the river bank is a mud hut. Living people have feelings, aspirations, needs, claims, projects, and a sense of justice. And they have rights. Future people will have feelings, aspirations, needs, claims, projects, and a sense of justice, once they are here. They too will have rights. In earlier parts of this book I noted that their claims have to be accommodated now, otherwise

[1] Sidgwick (1907), Meade (1955), Dasgupta (1969), and Parfit (1984).

we could be in danger of leaving them a barren Earth. But it is hard to know what it even means to say that potential people have rights or claims. When we revere the memory of deceased persons, it is to persons, now deceased, that we show reverence. When we debate at what stage in the development of a foetus we ought to regard it as a person, we recognize that there is something akin to a discontinuity in the process of each person's creation. The debate no doubt shows the notion to be fuzzy—even more than, and intrinsically a good deal more important than, the notion of a heap of stones (how many stones are needed to form a heap?)—but this doesn't mean the notion is spurious, or that it depends upon mere convention. Social convention, possibly backed by formal legislation, dictates how in fact we resolve the issue of when a foetus becomes a person. This only means that we think there is something to resolve; it doesn't mean that the resolution is right. But in so thinking, we are right, for it offers room for the idea that a person's life has sanctity.

So there is a difference between present and future persons on the one hand, and potential persons on the other. Classical Utilitarianism would appear to conflate the two categories. I want to argue that this is a mistaken move and a reason why it should be rejected.

15.2. ACTUAL PROBLEMS

In an actual problem there are real persons, whom I shall for simplicity call the current generation, who deliberate over future population sizes and future living standards. They are by the nature of things the decision-makers. Thoughtful parents grapple with actual problems, not with the Genesis Problem. This leads us to a study of fertility decisions. The size of the current generation is given; it is a datum.

Consider the following problem.[2] A woman suffers from a medical problem. There is a large chance that, if she were to conceive now, the child would suffer from a disability, but would otherwise enjoy a good life. However, a minor medical treatment would cure the woman within a month. Once cured, any child she bears will be free of the disability and enjoy a life of high quality. The woman is somewhat impatient to conceive. Ought she to wait a month, or would it be reasonable to conceive now?

One can argue that it is reasonable she conceives now. After all, or so the argument could go, the woman's feelings matter and the child she conceives now can't complain later that she was unfair to him, that she should have waited and undertaken the medical treatment, that he would then have had

---

[2] It is taken from Parfit (1982).

a better life. The reason he would not have grounds for complaining is that, had she waited, the child she would have conceived wouldn't have been him. Nor, or so the argument may continue, can some unconceived child complain that the woman prevented him from being born by being hasty.

None the less, there is a strong intuition that the woman should wait. And the intuition is built on the thought that good lives are an intrinsic good, but that, while good lives are intrinsically good, better lives are intrinsically even better. I invoke this intuition presently.

Consider now another problem. A couple have a newly born daughter, whose lifetime well-being is firmly expected to be nil unless additional resources are diverted to her needs (e.g. additional health care and education in her early years). Option A_1 is to make available such resources as will raise her level of well-being to U^*. Option A_2 is for the couple to create an additional child, with the understanding that resources will be diverted to this new child sufficient to enable him to enjoy lifetime well-being equal to U^*; however, the little girl's lifetime well-being will be nil. Assume that in all other respects A_1 and A_2 have the same consequences. What should the couple do?

If, as Sidgwick would have it, pleasure or agreeable consciousness is the sole good, and if the fact that something good would be the result of one's action is the basic reason for doing anything (the ground of binding reasons), the couple in question should be indifferent between A_1 and A_2.[3] But there are many additional considerations the parents can legitimately bring to bear in choosing between A_1 and A_2. Would they *like* to have another child? How many children do they already have? What is the source of the additional resources under the two options? What are the implications of their decisions on the family? What is their motivation in having children? What about the claims the existing child may have on them? What about her rights as an individual? And so on.

One reason why A_1 may be the better thing to do than A_2 is that the newly born daughter is part of what constitutes the couple's family, whereas the unconceived child under option A_2 is not. A theory of obligation which invites the idea of a family, and more generally that of a community, to play a role will provide a reason to the couple for choosing A_1 over A_2. This reason does not of course settle the matter. (The little girl may be their only child; this may be the last opportunity to have another child; three may not conform to the couple's conception of a family; and so forth.) What the reason does is expose the fact that family members have a special claim upon one another. Unconceived people do not have this claim. They are not members of that community. In fact, they are not members of any community; they aren't anywhere.[4]

---

[3] I am assuming implicity at this point that well-being is a measure of agreeable consciousness.

[4] I am grateful to Paul Seabright for discussions on this point. He has developed it more fully in Seabright (1989).

Each of us, to be sure, belongs simultaneously to many communities, involving varying strengths of ties and commitments. Here I am thinking of the family as a nuclear community. But it is a community with so very many special properties that it is unlike any other community to which we belong.[5] Among other reasons, it is special in that a child is never a party to the decision leading to her birth. It is also special in that, assuming happy circumstances, her conception is the decision of a loving couple. Parents, by virtue of their act, acquire an obligation towards their offspring that no others have. People do not have an obligation to become parents, but they acquire an obligation if they choose to become parents. By the same token, children have a type of claim on their parents that no one else has.

This special claim of the little girl on her parents has a number of implications in our example. One implication is that thoughtful parents will not, and should not, attach the same weight to the potential well-being of an additional child as to their little girl's well-being. The special claim provides an argument for choosing A_1 over A_2. The argument is, of course, not decisive. But it must play a role in the couple's decision.

Another reason why there is a case for choosing A_1 over A_2 has to do with the *claim rights* of the new-born girl. She is a person; it is her well-being that is under discussion. In contrast, it makes no sense to talk of the claim rights of unconceived people. Someone could be experiencing a wretched existence (a low, negative level of well-being), and it is bad that she should be in such a state. Nevertheless, she has moral worth; her life has value because, if nothing else, it is *her* life. 'Better if you had not existed' is a different judgement from 'Better if an additional life is not created'. Other things the same, the little girl's claim rights would lead A_1 to trump A_2.[6]

This isn't to argue that good lives do not have intrinsic value: it is only to say that actual lives have a weight that potential lives do not. To say that A_1 is the better alternative is not to say that, other things the same, creating a good life isn't a good thing. Good lives are part of the intrinsic good; but, other things the same, an improvement in the quality of life of an actual person is better still.

One may put the matter more generally.

There are two reasons for benefiting a person: one is that her well-being is *good in itself* (this was the strong intuition that was referred to in the case of the woman with a medical problem); the other is that it is *good for her*.

---

[5] These properties include the close genetic linkage between members of the nuclear community.

[6] Neo-Utilitarians too have reached this conclusion of asymmetric treatment between actual and potential people, but by a different route: 'We are in favour of making people happy, but neutral about making happy people' (Narveson, 1973: 73). The pioneering paper on what we are calling 'actual problems' is Narveson (1967). He labelled the version of Utilitarianism that accommodates this asymmetry 'person-affecting Utilitarianism'. For a far-reaching critique of Classical Utilitarianism when applied to reproductive decisions, see Heyd (1992).

(I am including in the former indirect effects, such as the well-being others may enjoy from the well-being of a given person.) But there is only one reason for creating a person, which is that her life would be good in itself. (I am including in this the indirect effects, such as that an actual couple would like to have the child.)

To give an analogy, consider a different sort of problem: choice over product quality. Imagine a commodity possessing a single characteristic, G; and another that possesses an additional characteristic, H. Assume that both G and H are desirable characteristics. But now suppose that the two commodities are identical in terms of characteristic G. Clearly, we would value both commodities, but presumably we would value the latter commodity more, since it has an additional, desirable, characteristic, H. If, on the other hand, the first commodity were superior in terms of characteristic G, we would face a trade-off problem. And so forth.

Now return to the problem facing the couple. Suppose they were to subscribe to any of the many ethical theories that (a) regard good lives to be part of the intrinsic good and (b) insist that only present and future people have claims, rights, interests, or whatever. The couple could reasonably impute a positive weight to creating lives, even while awarding a lower weight to potential well-being than to the well-being of actual people. This means that it would be reasonable for them to regard A_1 as better than A_2.[7]

15.3. GENERATION-RELATIVE ETHICS

These arguments would seem to be at odds with the idea that ethical considerations must be impartial, an idea invoked in Chapter 6 in the Ramsey–Koopmans formulation of intergenerational well-being. But the notion of impartiality in social ethics, the idea that we should seek to peer at matters from no particular person's viewpoint (as in the notion of 'impartial preferences' in Harsanyi, 1955, and in the reasoning behind the 'veil of ignorance' in Rawls, 1972), has force

---

[7] In a move to avoid Parfit's Repugnant Conclusion, Blackorby and Donaldson (1985) have explored a modified version of Classical Utilitarianism. In their theory, potential lives have the same value as actual or future lives and, so, personhood has no special role to play in what is a Different Numbers Problem. But the authors posit that, other things the same, the creation of an additional person is good only if her lifetime utility exceeds some positive, 'critical' level, say w (> 0). Blackorby and Donaldson call their theory 'critical-level utilitarianism'. The language they use to motivate their condition suggests that they have in mind an actual problem, but they invoke it in order to avoid the seeming paradoxes of the Genesis Problem. The conflation of the two quite different settings puzzles me. For, suppose that each one of all existing people is firmly expected to enjoy a quality of life equal to $w/2$. This is a positive level, meaning that each person will enjoy a good life, and good lives are an intrinsic good. But, as I understand it, critical-level utilitarianism asks us to believe that, other things the same, adding an extra person who would enjoy a quality of life equal to $w/2$ would be a bad thing. I don't see why it would not be a good thing.

when future numbers are not subject to choice.[8] In those situations we, the present people, can deliberate over options affecting ourselves and future people. We can look at the world not only from our own perspective, but also from the perspective of future people as and when they appear. The veil of ignorance, for example, provides us with a reason for doing so.

The problem facing the couple is different. Future numbers are a matter of decision. Neither Harsanyi's nor Rawls's construct gets a grip on the matter being considered here. It isn't possible to assume the 'perspective' of potential people. The veil can be worn for a pure savings problem, in which future numbers are given. It can do no work for the joint saving and population problem. In the joint problem, an overall ethical ordering over alternatives can be conceived only for each generation of actual people. The ethical viewpoint is thereby *generation-relative*. As generations change with the appearance of newer and newer people, the ethical point of view inevitably changes.

The problem is then to tie the ethical viewpoints of succeeding generations as and when they come into being. This involves an intergenerational game. In Chapter 6 we noted that we should study equilibrium outcomes of such games. One possible outcome would involve a backward induction argument. It is simplest to conduct the argument if we know that the world will terminate at a known date. Assume then that the termination date is known. The size of the last generation and its well-being will depend on the size of the previous generation and the resources it left as bequest. Moreover, the size of the penultimate generation and its well-being will have depended on the size of the previous generation and the resources *it* had left as bequest. And so on. At each stage, starting with the penultimate generation, the size of the next generation is a decision of the current generation, as is the decision on what resources to leave as bequest. Backward induction enables each generation, when deciding, to take into account the consequences of its decisions for both the numbers and the quality of life of the generations that are to follow. The argument is completed by letting the terminal date go to infinity and computing each generation's policy in the limit.[9]

A simpler notion of equilibrium would involve each generation choosing the size of the next generation and the amount to bequeath to it on the basis of reasoned expectations about the consequences of its choice. The key point, however, is this: when considering what to choose, each generation would award a lower weight to potential well-being than to the well-being of actual

---

[8] Impartiality in this context is anonymity across people (see Ch. 1).

[9] The argument can be extended in a routine manner to the case where the termination date is not known with certainty, but is characterizable by a probability distribution. The idea would be to introduce the concept of 'probabilistic future people' (in the manner sketched in Ch. 11), pretend that the world will not terminate, but then discount future people's well-being at the hazard rates.

people, but with the proviso that resources are to be shared on the basis of a weighting system that reflects social discount rates on the well-beings of all who are born as a consequence of the choice made.

I have not been able to obtain an explicit characterization of policies the theory would recommend in models with durable capital. As in other areas of welfare economics, the possibility of accumulating capital makes for computational difficulties. But there are two very special models where the theory can be put through its paces easily. One is a world that captures the ethics of the theory in an impeccable manner, but is empirically audacious because capital accumulation is not a possibility in it. However, although simple to analyse, it involves a certain amount of formalism. So the model is developed in a starred chapter (Chapter *15). Among other things, I show there that the Genesis Problem in Classical Utilitarianism may be viewed as an extreme special case of Generation-Relative Utilitarianism.

The other special world is easier to describe, but it is ethically dubious. It involves the thought that *no* weight should be awarded to potential well-being. The viewpoint was explored by Enke (1966) in his study of social cost–benefit analysis of family planning programmes in poor countries. Enke sought ways of measuring the economic value of prevented births, which he took to be the discounted sum of the differences between an additional person's consumption and that person's output over their lifetime. This means that children, in Enke's theory, have value only if they pay their way. The weakness of the theory is that it does not accept that good lives have intrinsic value.

But Enke's is an extreme point of view, as is Classical Utilitarianism: one awards no weight to potential well-being, while the other awards the same weight to them as it does to the well-being of present or future people. The arguments I have offered imply that both points of view are questionable. Generation-Relative Utilitarianism is attractive because it lies between the two extremes and reflects the strength of each without giving in to the weaknesses of either. It prescribes neither a very large population nor a very small population. Instead, it offers a wide space in between, within which more detailed ethical considerations can be embedded. We should not expect an ethical theory to do more.

15.4. RATIONAL ENDS

Population ethics has for long been an underdeveloped branch of moral philosophy and welfare economics. That it has remained backward has much to do with the insistence on the part of philosophers writing on the subject to ignore the ethical relevance of parental desires, and the related question of what in our own lives gives meaning to us. That my neighbour is not as close to me as are my daughters and son is a genetic fact, but that is not quite the point here. Closer to the mark is the fact that my children provide me with a means of self-transcendence, the widest avenue open to me of living *through* time. Mortality threatens to render the achievements of our life transitory, and this threat is removed by procreation. The ability to leave descendants enables us to invest in projects that will not cease to have value once we are gone, projects that justify life rather than merely serve it. These projects include not only the creation of ideas and artefacts; more pervasively, they include the formation of personal values. Thus the questions, 'what kind of person ought I try to be? what should I value?' do not presume the questioner to own a specific set of talents, abilities, and resources (anyone can, and should, ask such questions); they presume only that they play a role in any reasoned answer.

Procreation is a means of making one's values durable. We imbue our children with values we cherish not merely because we think it is good for them, but also because we desire to see our values survive. It seems to me that our descendants do something supremely important for us here: they add a certain value to our lives which our mortality would otherwise deprive them of. Alexander Herzen's remark, that human development is a kind of chronological unfairness, since those who live later profit from the labour of their predecessors without paying the same price, and Kant's view, that it is disconcerting that earlier generations should carry their burdens only for the sake of the later ones, and that only the last should have the good fortune to dwell in the completed building, or in other words that we can do something for posterity but it can do nothing for us (Rawls, 1972: 291), are a reflection of an extreme form of alienation: alienation from one's own life.

This viewpoint, of seeing ourselves as part of a delegation of generations, has roots reaching far back, in many cultures, and in recent years it has found its deepest expression in Schell (1982) and Heyd (1992). We act upon this perspective most often with no explicit verbalization to accompany it. We assume parenthood quite naturally; we do not make a big intellectual meal of it. It is the sort of thing we take responsibility for in the normal course of events. Of course, special circumstances may deflect us; we may have more urgent projects and purposes. Here, the fact of a general assumption of parenthood is of importance. An artist may regard his work as far more important than parenting, but he is helped in this by the fact that there will be a next generation to bestow durability to the value of his work. The springs that motivate the general run of humankind to assume parenthood are deep and abiding. The genetic basis of the matter merely explains the existence of this motivation; it does not justify it. Justification has to be sought elsewhere, and any reasonable answer must come allied to the viewpoint that every generation is a trustee of the wide range of 'capital stocks' (be it cultural or moral, manufactured or natural) it has inherited from the past. Looking backward, it acknowledges an implicit contract with the previous generation, of receiving the capital in return for its transmission, modified suitably in the light of changing circumstances and increasing knowledge. Looking forward, it offers an implicit contract to the next generation, of bequeathing its stocks of capital that they in turn may be modified suitably by it and then passed on to the following generation. The idea of intergenerational exchange is embedded in the perspective of eternity. But the intellectual source of such exchange is a far cry from the conception that balked Herzen in his effort to locate mutually beneficial terms of trade.

Recent attempts by social thinkers in Western industrial countries at creating an environmental ethic draw their strength from something like this conception.[10] But it does not provide enough of an apparatus to do so. Finally, there is no avoiding the question, 'what should I value?' if we are to see ourselves living through time, rather than in time. It is a mistake to try to justify the protection of the giant redwoods, or the seemingly so trivial a species as the hawksbill turtles, or, more widely, the preservation of ecological diversity, solely on instrumental grounds, on grounds that we know they are useful to us, or may prove useful to our descendants. We noted in earlier chapters that such arguments have a role, but they are not the ultimate solution. Nor can the argument rely on the welfare of the members of such species (it does not account for the special role that species preservation plays in the argument), or on the 'rights' of animals. A full justification must base itself as well on how *we* see ourselves, on what kind of people we ought to try to be, on what our rational desires are. In examining our values, and thus our lives, we need to ask if the destruction of an entire species-habitat for some immediate gratification is something we can live with comfortably. The mistake is to see procreation and ecological preservation as matters of personal and political morality. It is at least as much a matter of personal and political ethics.

---

[10] Schell (1982) has a lucid discussion of this.

*15

Generation-Relative Ethics and Classical Utilitarianism: A Comparison

In Chapter 15 arguments were advanced in favour of a generation-relative ethics when future numbers are a matter of choice. Here I put the arguments to work in a simple economic environment.

Children are desired not only as ends in themselves: in poor countries they are also a means of help with household activities and of security and comfort in old age.[1] Average Utilitarianism, in the way the theory was formulated by its founders (Figure 13.1), stresses the instrumental worth of children: if the contribution of the next person to be born is expected to exceed average output now, the theory recommends an expansion of population, but not otherwise. The model I develop in this chapter purges the instrumental worth of children so as to concentrate on their intrinsic worth. Even in this regard, there are two aspects of potential children to be considered. One aspect is that of children as determinants of their parents' well-being, the other is that good lives are an intrinsic good. The model that follows picks up the latter feature so as to capture a tension that exists between present people's desires and needs and reproduction with a view to enabling good lives to be experienced.

We move beyond the timeless economy studied in Chapters 13 and 14 and take it that time is discrete ($t = 0, 1, 2, \ldots$). In each period the economy is provided, rather like manna from heaven, with K units of a non-storable, all-purpose consumption good. This means that there is no production activity in the economy. It also means that there is no possibility of investing or disinvesting. With some stretching of the imagination, one could think of K as the flow of ecological services the environment provides in each period. However, the 'stretching' lies only in the thought that the natural resource base cannot be destroyed. In other respects the model is sensible. For example, in not allowing for the possibility of capital accumulation as a way of increasing the productive base, the model draws attention to the constraints set by the natural environment: the parameter K captures environmental constraints.

---

[1] For a summary account, see Dasgupta (2000c).

People live for two periods. In the first period of their lives a generation consumes whatever it is given to consume by the older generation. In the second period, being now the older generation, they decide how many children to have and how to share the consumption good of amount K among themselves and the new generation.

Imagine that everyone who is born is identical. Also assume that the older generation will allocate K among all actual persons according to the dictates of Classical Utilitarianism. However, when choosing the number of people to create, they will award *potential* well-being, relative to the well-being of an actual person, a weight γ (<1). γ is not to be interpreted as a time discount factor. It may be that people do not discount the future. If they do not, γ is the weight they will award to potential well-being relative to their own well-being, regardless of the date at which such potential people are to appear. γ is the intrinsic worth of well-being relative to the well-being of an actual person.

If a person's consumption level at any date is C, her well-being is $U(C)$. As earlier, I suppose that $U'(C) > 0$ and $U''(C) < 0$. This means that in each period K is shared equally among all who happen to exist at that time.

We begin by considering the problem faced by the current generation. The date is $t = 0$. The current generation is beginning its second period of life. (They are the adults.) Suppose they number $\bar{N}_0$. They are to choose the size of the next generation. Imagine that the size they choose is N_1. The older cohort know that, once they choose thus, K will be shared equally among $(\bar{N}_0 + N_1)$ people. The cohort therefore recognize that each person will consume $K/(\bar{N}_0 + N_1)$ units of the consumption good. And so on for subsequent generations.

Let β (≤ 1) be the discount factor applied to the passage of time, say, because of the risk of extinction.[2] If $\{N_1, N_2, \ldots, N_t, \ldots\}$ is a possible demographic profile, social well-being, as viewed by the current generation is[3]

$$\bar{N}_0 U(K/(\bar{N}_0 + N_1)) + \gamma[N_1 U(K/(\bar{N}_0 + N_1))$$

$$+ \sum_{1}^{\infty} \left[\beta^t(N_t + N_{t+1})U(K/(N_t + N_{t+1}))\right]. \tag{*15.1}$$

It will be noticed that in (*15.1) all who are ever born are treated equally with all others alive at the time. (They share K equally.) The current generation chooses N_1 on the basis of a forecast of the demographic profile. We are interested in forecasts that are rationally arrived at, which in this context means that they should sustain a Nash equilibrium sequence of choices. This means that every

---

[2] Ch. 6.
[3] This formulation is identical to the one in Phelps and Pollak (1968), who had considered a pure saving problem. The one being discussed in the text is a pure population problem.

generation expects subsequent generations to go through the same kind of reasoning that they themselves are engaged in.

The way to compute an intergenerational equilibrium under Generation-Relative Utilitarianism goes like this. On the basis of a forecast of the demographic profile, say, $\{N_2, \ldots, N_t, \ldots\}$, generation $t = 0$ chooses N_1 so as to maximize (*15.1), and in each subsequent t the then existing generation chooses the size of the succeeding generation on the basis of a similar piece of reasoning.

I am now using the term 'Utilitarianism' in a loose way. I am using it as a peg on which to accommodate a wide range of ethical theories, not only the wide variety of consequentialist theories (barring Classical Utilitarianism, of course) that are on offer by philosophers, but also a number of deontological ones (see especially Section 15.4). However, for purposes of comparison with Classical Utilitarianism, in the remainder of this section I will interpret $U(\cdot)$ in the way the Classical Utilitarians did when they spoke about human well-being.

Assume that $\bar{N}_0$ is not so large that the optimum value of N_1 is zero. If this assumption doesn't hold, further ethical considerations arise, for example that the continuation of the human enterprise has intrinsic ethical value (Section 15.4). Let C_t denote consumption per head at t. To determine the optimum value of N_1, we differentiate (*15.1) with respect to N_1. The first-order condition is

$$\gamma U(C_0) + \gamma \beta U(C_1) = \frac{K(\bar{N}_0 + \gamma N_1)U'(C_0)}{(\bar{N}_0 + N_1)^2} + \frac{\gamma \beta K U'(C_1)}{N_1 + N_2}. \qquad (*15.2)$$

Let $\hat{N}_1$ be the solution of (*15.2). At $t = 1$ those $\hat{N}_1$ persons will choose N_2 using an identical type of reasoning. The first-order condition for them would be

$$\gamma U(C_1) + \gamma \beta U(C_2) = \frac{K(\hat{N}_1 + \gamma N_2)U'(C_1)}{(\hat{N}_1 + N_2)^2} + \frac{\gamma \beta K U'(C_2)}{N_2 + N_3}. \qquad (*15.3)$$

And so on for subsequent generations. A demographic profile $\{\hat{N}_1, \hat{N}_2, \ldots, \hat{N}_t, \ldots\}$ is a Nash equilibrium if it is an outcome of such a sequence of reasonings.

It is an interesting exercise to identify the stationary state associated with the repeated use of the first-order conditions. The assumption of stationarity enables us to solve for an equilibrium outcome. We are to imagine that past choices have converged to the point where, at $t = 0$, the size of the population is such that equilibrium behaviour involves replication in every period. Being stationary, the demographic profile will be sustainable, and we may drop the time subscript from the population and consumption variables. If the solution

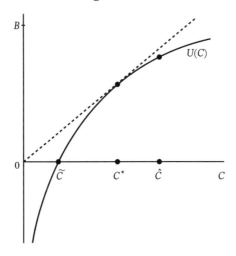

Figure *15.1. *Generation-relative Utilitarianism optimum consumption:* $\hat{C}$

is unique, there is a unique stationary state.[4] Let $\hat{N}$ be the size of a generation and $\hat{C}$ be per capita consumption in the stationary state. $\hat{C} = K/2\hat{N}$. Simple manipulation of (*15.2) then implies that $\hat{C}$ is the solution of

$$U'(C) = \frac{2\gamma(1+\beta)}{(1-\gamma)+2\gamma(1+\beta)} \frac{U(C)}{C}. \tag{*15.4}$$

Notice that if $\gamma = 1$, (*15.4) reduces to the stationary optimum under Classical Utilitarianism (compare Chapter 15, equation (15.1) with (*15.4)). Notice also that $U'(\hat{C}) < U(\hat{C})/\hat{C}$ if $\gamma < 1$. This means that stationary consumption per head under Generation-Relative Utilitarianism is greater than that under Classical Utilitarianism. Correspondingly, population is smaller (Figure *15.1).

By how much? To investigate this, consider once again the laboratory,

$$U(C) = B - C^{-\sigma}, \quad \text{where } B \text{ and } \sigma \text{ are positive constants.}$$

Well-being subsistence is $\tilde{C} = B^{-\sigma}$. Since two generations are alive in any given period, we should write carrying capacity as $2\tilde{N}$. Equation (*15.4) then yields

$$(\hat{C}/\tilde{C})^{\sigma} = (\tilde{N}/\hat{N})^{\sigma} = \frac{1+\Omega}{\Omega} > 1, \quad \text{where } \Omega = \frac{2\gamma(1+\beta)}{(1-\gamma)+2\gamma(1+\beta)} \tag{*15.5}$$

---

[4] Interested readers can test for the stability of the stationary state by studying (*15.2), (*15.3), and so on.

To obtain explicit numbers, let $\sigma = 1$, $\beta \approx 1$, and $\gamma = \frac{1}{9}$. Equation (*15.5) then implies

$$\hat{C}/\tilde{C} = \tilde{N}/\hat{N} = 4,$$

which means that optimum population size is a quarter of carrying capacity. If carrying capacity is 10 billion people, optimum population is 2.5 billion. Recall from the previous chapter that Classical Utilitarianism would advocate a population of 5 billion. (One can confirm this also from (*15.5) by setting $\beta = \sigma = \gamma = 1$.) With the parameter values being assumed here, Classical Utilitarianism advocates twice the population size recommended by Generation-Relative Utilitarianism.

It is informative too to consider the extreme values assumed in Enke's theory, which I described in the previous chapter. Enke (1966) assumed $\gamma = 0$. Equation (*15.5) implies that, if $\gamma \to 0$, then $\hat{C}/\tilde{C} \to \infty$ and, therefore, $\tilde{N}/\hat{N} \to \infty$. This is another way of saying that, the lower is the weight awarded to potential well-being, the smaller is optimum population. This too is consistent with intuition. In the limit, if no weight were to be awarded to potential well-being, optimum population would be vanishingly small.

Appendix[1]

In Parts III and IV I stated and made use of a number of technical results on valuation and evaluation in Kakotopia, the name introduced in the Preface for what can at best be called an *imperfect economy*. In this appendix I derive those results. Before doing that, though, it will pay to review what we know about valuation and evaluation in Utopia, or what economists refer to as *first-best economies*. In that way we can confirm that the results we derive for imperfect economies reduce to those that correspond to first-best economies as agreeable special cases.

For reasons that will become clear, it pays to divide first-best economies into two categories: convex and non-convex. So this appendix consists of three parts. After defining convex dynamical systems (Section A.1), I review what is achievable in first-best convex economies (Section A.2). The conditions that optimum economic programmes necessarily satisfy there are sketched, and are then applied to two simple model economies by way of illustration. The material on this is standard fare in environmental and resource economics.

The prevalence of non-convexities in Human–Nature interactions is discussed in Section A.3. I then present two proto-typical non-convex economies (Section A.4): one, a fishery; the other, a shallow freshwater lake, into which a pollutant (phosphorus) is discharged. The structural stability of the fishery under open access is studied in Section A.4.1. This is followed by an investigation into the dynamics of a lake when the pollutant discharge is constant over time (Section A.4.2). In Section A.5 the optimum discharge of phosphorus is characterized. The material in Sections A.4 and A.5 draws on relatively recent work and may well be novel to readers.

In Parts III and IV of this book I made use of a number of technical results on valuation and evaluation in non-convex, imperfect economies. From Section A.6 onward I prove and develop those results. The material there is of very recent origin.

The technical literature on intergenerational welfare economics has been mostly about convex Utopias.[2] Imperfections have frequently been introduced,

---

[1] In preparing this Appendix I have benefited greatly from the comments and suggestions made by Geir Asheim and John Hartwick.   [2] That literature is nicely summarized in Heal (1998).

but only piece by piece. In this book I have tried to develop intergenerational welfare economics for Kakotopia in a direct manner—and not as a series of foot-notes to standard welfare economics. The reason I have taken this approach is that, when I began work on intergenerational welfare economics for Kakotopia a few years ago, I found it far more helpful to view first-best economies as extreme special cases of imperfect economies than to regard the former as launching pads for investigations into various imperfections, piece by piece. So, even though this appendix is divided into three parts, it is the final part (Section A.6 and beyond) that is central to my concerns. I have prepared the material in such a way that readers, should they wish to do so, can translate the results on valuation and evaluation in imperfect economies for their use in the academically more familiar first-best economies.

The results collated here will, I hope, serve another purpose. It is salutary for economists to have at their disposal examples of the way ecologists have developed tractable models of very complicated processes. When modelling the world, ecologists are no different from economists in their search for simplicity. But there are differences in emphasis, and it is useful to know why and how the two groups differ. We will see that economists have had deep reasons for studying convex environments, while ecologists have discovered compelling reasons for shunning them.

A.1. ECONOMISTS' CONVEXITIES

The word 'convexity' is ubiquitous in economics. There is a reason for this. As prices are prominent in modern transactions, it is only natural that we would wish to uncover the ways in which the price system is capable of functioning as a resource allocation mechanism. In recent years economists have identified not only the way in which prices aggregate dispersed pieces of information, but also the sense in which they reflect the relative scarcities of goods and services. We now know that the price system can be an efficient allocation mechanism if transformation possibilities among goods and services—in and over time—constitute a *convex set*.[3] However, except in the case of partial economic systems, as in models of industrial organization (Tirole, 1993), or systems harbouring very specific forms of non-convexities, as in modern growth models (Jones, 1998) or in models of poverty traps based on the connection between nutritional status

---

[3] Koopmans (1957) and Debreu (1959) are the classic expositions of this. For completeness, here is the definition of convexity *of a set*:

A commodity vector, say z, is a *convex combination* of commodity vectors x and y if z is a weighted average of x and y, where the weights are non-negative and sum to unity (that is, where $z = \alpha x + (1 - \alpha)y$ for some $\alpha \in [0, 1]$). A set of commodity vectors is said to be *convex* if every convex combination of every pair of commodity vectors in the set is in the set. A set is *non-convex* if it is not convex.

and human productivity (Dasgupta and Ray, 1986, 1987; Dasgupta, 1997) or in models of spatial economies (Fugita, Krugman, and Venables, 1999), we still do not have a clear understanding of the mechanisms by which resources are allocated in non-convex environments. So, we economists continue to rely on the convexity assumption, always hoping that it is not an embarrassing simplification.

In traditional price theory, non-convexities are a reflection of atemporal scale economies (e.g. U-shaped average cost curves facing firms). In contrast, the non-convexities displayed by ecological processes manifest themselves across time. Nevertheless, there is a formal connection between the two. To see this, consider the economist's old stand-by, a one-commodity, constant-population economy, where the commodity in question is durable and non-deteriorating. Labour is supplied inelastically. Time is continuous and the economy is deterministic.[4] Let K_t (≥ 0) and C_t (≥ 0) be the capital stock and the flow of consumption, respectively, at time t (≥ 0). Output is assumed to be given by the production function $F(K)$, where $F(0) = 0$ and $F(K) > 0$ for some $K > 0$. An extreme assumption, much used in general equilibrium theory, is that output is *freely disposable*. Presently we will see what this assumption involves and why its violation is significant for environmental and resource economics ('ecological economics' for short).[5]

In this section, all arguments are conducted at $t = 0$, which we regard to be the present moment.[6] Let I_t denote investment at t. Since output is freely disposable, we may express the balance of flows at each date in the economy by the inequality,

$$I_t \leq F(K_t) - C_t, \qquad K_0 \ (>0) \text{ given,} \tag{A.1a}$$

which, without rigorous justification, we write as

$$dK_t/dt \leq F(K_t) - C_t, \qquad K_0 \ (>0) \text{ given.} \tag{A.1b}$$

An *economic programme* (*programme*, for short) is a complete forecast of the economy, from the present ($t = 0$) to infinity. An economic programme can be expressed as $\{K_t, C_t, dK_t/dt\}_0^\infty$. For simplicity of exposition, we suppose that *any* programme satisfying (A.1b) is feasible, which is to say that the economy is not subject to any other constraint. This is what we mean by a first-best economy.

The question is whether the set of feasible programmes is convex.

---

[4] As is well known, discrete- and continuous-time systems can differ fundamentally in regard to their stability properties. The decision to work in continuous time is therefore not an innocuous one. As may not be so well known, the global properties of 'non-linear' dynamical systems, even in continuous time, are currently understood best when the number of state variables does not exceed 2.

[5] Koopmans (1957) contains an especially thoughtful discussion of 'free disposability'.

[6] Later, we will find it useful to study the economy from an arbitrary date t.

The answer depends on whether F is *concave everywhere* (henceforth, *concave*). To confirm this, assume that F is concave (for a definition, see (A.7)). Consider any two feasible programmes, which we write as $\{K_t^*, C_t^*, dK_t^*/dt\}_0^\infty$ and $\{K_t', C_t', dK_t'/dt\}_0^\infty$. By definition, both satisfy (A.1b). Hence,

$$dK_t^*/dt \leq F(K_t^*) - C_t^*, \qquad \text{where } K_0^* = K_0, \tag{A.2}$$

and

$$dK_t'/dt \leq F(K_t') - C_t', \qquad \text{where } K_0' = K_0. \tag{A.3}$$

Now choose a number γ, where $0 \leq \gamma \leq 1$. Define

$$\bar{C}_t = \gamma C_t^* + (1 - \gamma)C_t' \qquad \text{and} \qquad \bar{K}_t = \gamma K_t^* + (1 - \gamma)K_t'. \tag{A.4}$$

We wish to confirm that $\{\bar{K}_t, \bar{C}_t, d\bar{K}_t/dt\}_0^\infty$ also satisfies (A.1b).
From (A.2) and (A.3), we have

$$\gamma \, dK_t^*/dt \leq \gamma F(K_t^*) - \gamma C_t^*, \qquad\qquad\qquad \text{where } K_0^* = K_0, \tag{A.5}$$

and

$$(1 - \gamma)dK_t'/dt \leq (1 - \gamma)F(K_t') - (1 - \gamma)C_t', \qquad \text{where } K_0' = K_0. \tag{A.6}$$

Since F is concave,

$$F(\bar{K}_t) = F(\gamma K_t^* + (1 - \gamma)K_t') \geq \gamma F(K_t^*) + (1 - \gamma)F(K_t'). \tag{A.7}$$

From (A.2)–(A.7) we conclude that

$$d\bar{K}_t/dt \leq F(\bar{K}_t) - \bar{C}_t, \qquad \text{where } \bar{K}_0 = K_0, \tag{A.8}$$

which means that the set of programmes satisfying (A.1b) is convex. We have therefore proved that, if the function $F(K)$ is concave, the set of feasible programmes is convex.

If $F(K)$ is not concave, the above argument does not work, because inequality (A.7) cannot be guaranteed. In fact, if $F(K)$ is not concave, it is possible to find a pair of programmes that satisfies inequality (A.1b) and a convex combination of the two that does not satisfy inequality (A.1b). This means that, if the function $F(K)$ is not concave, the set of feasible programmes is not convex.

CONVEX UTOPIAS

A.2. FIRST-BEST WELFARE
ECONOMICS IN A CONVEX WORLD

Let us review the character of optimum programmes in a first-best convex world. Since the arguments developed here generalize easily to economies with many goods, we study a parsimonious model that has a single manufactured capital good and one natural resource.

It pays to use a notation that will enable us to adopt any arbitrary future date as the point from which to view the further future. So, in what follows, time is denoted variously as t and τ ($\tau \geq t \geq 0$). Imagine that there is an all-purpose, non-deteriorating durable good, whose stock at t is K_t (≥ 0). The good can be consumed or reinvested for its own accumulation. Production of this good requires its own stock (K), labour, and the flow of a natural resource (R) as inputs. Labour is offered inelastically, so we can ignore it in macro-calculations. I write aggregate output as Y and assume that $Y = F(K, R)$. GNP at t is then $Y_t = F(K_t, R_t)$. F is taken to be an increasing and twice partially differentiable function of K and R. I also suppose that $F(K, 0) = F(0, R) = 0$ for all K and R. Finally, I assume that F is concave.

Let C_t (≥ 0) denote consumption at t. Assuming free disposal, and side-stepping rigour, we may express the net accumulation of manufactured capital as

$$dK_\tau/d\tau \leq F(K_\tau, R_\tau) - C_\tau, \qquad \tau \geq t \geq 0. \tag{A.9}$$

The stock of natural capital at t is denoted by S_t (≥ 0). It is assumed that the resource can be extracted costlessly. Let the resource's natural regeneration rate be $M(S_t)$, which we take to be a concave and twice differentiable function, bounded above, with $M(0) = 0$ and $M(S) > 0$ for some S.

Again assuming free disposal, the dynamics of the resource base can then be expressed as[7]

$$dS_\tau/d\tau \leq M(S_\tau) - R_\tau, \qquad \tau \geq t \geq 0. \tag{A.10}$$

An economic programme, or *programme* for short, can be expressed as $\{K_\tau, S_\tau, C_\tau, R_\tau, dK_\tau/d\tau, dS_\tau/d\tau\}_t^\infty$.

---

[7] The simplest example of $M(S)$ for an ecological resource, one that has been much used in the fisheries and forestry literature, is

$$M(S) = aS - bS^2, \qquad a, b > 0. \tag{A.10a}$$

Minerals and fossil fuels would be a limiting case ($a = b = 0$) of (A.10a). S_t would denote known reserves at t and we would have $M(S) = 0$ for all S. See below in the text.

Current well-being is taken to depend solely on consumption (but see Section A.5). I write this as $U(C)$, where $U(C)$ is an increasing, strictly concave, and twice differentiable function. In Chapter 6 I offered reasons why the Ramsey–Koopmans formulation of intergenerational well-being is the most compelling on offer. In continuous time, *social well-being* at t (≥ 0) in their formulation is

$$W_t = \int_t^\infty U(C_\tau) e^{-\delta(\tau - t)} d\tau, \tag{A.11}$$

where δ (>0), a constant, is the discount rate on future well-being.[8]

If generation t were to inherit K_t and S_t from the past, the utopian problem it would face would be to identify the feasible programme satisfying equations (A.9) and (A.10) that maximizes (A.11). Notice though that, because both assets are 'goods', and there are no bad byproducts from either production or consumption, it would be undesirable to dispose of any produced output or any extracted resource. This is another way of saying that accounting prices are positive. Moreover, in Section 6.1 we noted that, if (A.11) represents the ethical viewpoint of generation t, then the viewpoints of all generations are congruent with one another. This means that, from the available set of feasible programmes, each generation can be expected to choose the policy it deems optimum, aware that succeeding generations will choose in accordance with what it plans for them. Taken together, these two observations imply that we may as well locate the optimum programme once and for all at $t = 0$ and express the utopian problem—which I shall refer to as problem **P**—as

Choose $\{C_t, R_t\}_0^\infty$ so as to maximize $\int_0^\infty U(C_t) e^{-\delta t} dt$,

subject to

$$dK_t/dt = F(K_t, R_t) - C_t, \qquad K_0 \ (>0) \text{ given}, \tag{A.12}$$

and

$$dS_t/dt = M(S_t) - R_t, \qquad S_0 \ (>0) \text{ given}. \tag{A.13}$$

In what follows, I assume that **P** has a solution. Direct proofs of the existence of infinite-horizon optimum programmes, involving as they do Weierstrasse's Theorem in an infinite-dimensional space, are not very useful. The trick that economists have deployed over the years is to identify conditions on feasible

---

[8] Equation (A.11) is the continuous-time counterpart of (6.4) in Ch. 6.

programmes that are sufficient for optimality, these conditions enable one to characterize optimum programmes as well.

As is well known, **P** can be solved by using Pontryagin's Maximum Principle.[9] In the language of optimum control theory, K_t and S_t are the state variables, while C_t and R_t are the control variables. Choosing well-being as our numeraire, let $p_t e^{-\delta t}$ and $q_t e^{-\delta t}$ be the present-value accounting prices of manufactured capital and natural capital, respectively, and p_t and q_t be the co-state variables associated with equations (A.12) and (A.13), respectively.

Purely for expositional ease, I suppose that F_K (resp. F_R) is unbounded as K (resp. R) goes to zero, and that marginal well-being, $U'(C)$, is also unbounded as C tends to zero.[10]

Given this background, the present-value Hamiltonian of **P** can be expressed as

$$H_0 = U(C_t)e^{-\delta t} + p_t e^{-\delta t}[F(K_t, R_t) - C_t] + q_t e^{-\delta t}[M(S_t) - R_t]. \quad (A.14)$$

In view of the assumptions that have been made about F, U, and M, we know that H_0 is a concave function of K_t, S_t, C_t, and R_t. This means that the optimum can be implemented with the help of accounting prices in a decentralized economic environment. Let us confirm this.

Since C_t and R_t are the two control variables, the Maximum Principle states that, if they are chosen optimally, it must be that

$$\partial H_0/\partial C_t = \partial H_0/\partial R_t = 0,$$

which, applied to equation (A.14), yields the two conditions

$$U'(C_t) = p_t \quad (A.15)$$

and

$$p_t F_R = q_t. \quad (A.16)$$

Equation (A.15) is self-explanatory. Equation (A.16) is also easily interpretable. It says that the resource's accounting price should be set equal to the value of its marginal product.

---

[9] Kamien and Schwartz (1991) is a good introduction to the subject.

[10] F_K and F_R are the partial derivatives of F with respect to K and R, respectively. $U'(C)$ is the first derivative of U with respect to C. In economics such corner conditions on production functions and well-being functions are called Inada conditions. They ensure that optimum programmes never involve shutting down the economy or setting consumption equal to zero.

The Maximum Principle also states that

$$d(p_t e^{-\delta t})/dt = -\partial H_0/\partial K_t,$$ (A.17)

and

$$d(q_t e^{-\delta t})/dt = -\partial H_0/\partial S_t,$$ (A.18)

which, on using (A.13), yield

$$(dp_t/dt)/p_t = \delta - F_K,$$ (A.19)

and

$$(dq_t/dt)/q_t = \delta - M'(S_t).$$ (A.20)

Equations (A.19) and (A.20) are fundamental decentralization rules. They can be read as arbitrage conditions. They say that along an optimum programme it should be a matter of indifference whether the marginal 'dollar' is spent on manufactured capital or the natural resource: taking into account changes in their relative accounting prices, the rates of return on the two assets are the same at every instant.

Now, using (A.15) in (A.19) yields

$$\delta + \eta(C_t)(dC_t/dt)/C_t = F_K,$$ (A.21)

where $\eta(C_t) \equiv -C_t U''(C_t)/U'(C_t) > 0$, which is the elasticity of marginal well-being.[11]

In Chapter 11 (equation (11.3)) we deduced that the left-hand side of (A.21) is the consumption rate of interest. Moreover, it is a simple matter to check from (A.12) and (A.13) that F_K is the rate of return on investment in manufactured capital. Equation (A.21) says that along an optimum programme the consumption rate of interest equals the rate of return on investment. This is intuitive. If, say, the consumption rate of interest were less than the rate of return on investment, it would signal that there is under-investment: social well-being could be increased by marginally reducing consumption. Similarly, if the consumption rate of interest were greater than the rate of return on investment, it would signal that there is under-consumption: social well-being could be increased by marginally reducing investment. Equation (A.21) is the 'short-run' social cost–benefit rule governing the consumption–investment mix at each moment.

Having identified the conditions that an optimum programme must satisfy, I now state a proposition that locates conditions that are sufficient.

[11] $U''(C)$ is the second derivative of U with respect to C.

Proposition 1: A feasible programme satisfying equations (A.15)–(A.16) and (A.19)–(A.20) is an optimum if[12]

$$\lim_{t \to \infty} (p_t e^{-\delta t} K_t) = 0, \qquad\qquad\qquad\qquad (A.22)$$

and

$$\lim_{t \to \infty} (q_t e^{-\delta t} S_t) = 0. \qquad\qquad\qquad\qquad (A.23)$$

Equations (A.22) and (A.23) are the two transversality conditions for **P**. Together they ensure that there is no over-accumulation of manufactured capital and no under-use of natural capital. A feasible programme that satisfies the 'short-run' optimality conditions (A.15), (A.16) and (A.19)–(A.20), as well as the transversality conditions (A.22)–(A.23), solves P_1.

Let $\hat{C}_t$ be optimum consumption. We now denote optimum social well-being at t as

$$V(K_t, S_t) = W_t = \int_t^\infty U(\hat{C}_\tau) e^{-\delta(\tau - t)} d\tau.$$

In control theory V is called the *value function*.[13] Given that U, F, and M are assumed to be concave functions, $V(K, S)$ is a concave function. It is therefore differentiable almost everywhere. It is simple to confirm from the optimality conditions that, wherever V is differentiable,

$$p_t = \partial V_t / \partial K_t,$$

and

$$q_t = \partial V_t / \partial S_t.$$

We will find this relationship between accounting prices and the value function most suggestive when, in Section A.6, we come to develop an accounting price system for imperfect economies.

Do optimum programmes necessarily sustain social well-being? The answer is 'no'. To say that social well-being is sustained at t is to say that $dV_t/dt \geq 0$ (Chapter 9). But an optimum programme can violate that condition (see below). As 'optimality' is different from 'sustainability', neither implies the other.[14]

---

[12] For a proof, see Kamien and Schwartz (1991).

[13] Bellman (1957). In all this, we take it that V_t is well defined. The assumption that $\delta > 0$ is crucial for this.   [14] For further discussion on the differences, see Arrow, Dasgupta, Goulder, *et al.* (2003).

We now put *Proposition 1* to work on two special model economies. It is assumed in both examples that[15]

$$U(C) = -C^{(\eta-1)}, \qquad \eta > 1. \tag{A.24}$$

Example 1: (Manufactured Capital and Exhaustible Resources in an Unbounded Economy). Assume that

$$M(S) = 0, \tag{A.25}$$

which means that the natural resource is exhaustible. Assume also that

$$F(K, R) = K^\alpha R^\beta, \qquad \alpha, \beta, (\alpha - \beta), (1 - \alpha - \beta) > 0. \tag{A.26}$$

Using (A.25) in (A.20) gives us the famous Hotelling Rule, which says that along an optimum programme the present-value accounting price of an exhaustible resource is constant.

Dasgupta and Heal (1979: ch. 9) showed that the solution of P in an economy satisfying (A.24)–(A.26) tends to zero in the long run: $K_t, R_t, C_t \to 0$, as $t \to \infty$. Therefore, $dV_t/dt < 0$ for large t. This demonstrates that optimality is different from sustainability. However, this feature of an optimum programme is sensitive to the assumption that $\delta > 0$. Dasgupta and Heal (1979: ch. 9) showed that, if $\delta = 0$ and $\eta > (1 - \beta)/(\alpha - \beta) > 1$, then, no matter what the values of K_0 and S_0, $dC_t/dt > 0$ for all t along the optimum programme, meaning that $dV_t/dt > 0$ for all t. Optimality and sustainability are congruent notions in this case. It transpires also that $K_t, C_t \to \infty$ and $R_t \to 0$, as $t \to \infty$.[16]

Example 2: (Manufactured Capital and Renewable Resources in a Bounded Economy). By way of contrast to the previous example, assume that

$$M(S) = \alpha S - \beta S^2, \qquad \alpha > \delta, \qquad \beta > 0, \tag{A.27}$$

and,

$$\text{for all } R, \qquad \lim_{K \to \infty} F(K, R) < \infty. \tag{A.28}$$

Conditions (A.27) and (A.28) imply that production is bounded above. Using (A.24), (A.27), and (A.28) in (A.15)–(A.16) and (A.19)–(A.20), we arrive at the

---

[15] Estimates of the elasticity of $U'(C)$ obtained from consumer behaviour, or, alternatively, from consumer responses to questions have typically been in the range 1.5–2.5. The evidence thus acquired does not of course reflect what we mean by η here, but it is close enough for our purposes.

[16] An optimum programme does not exist if $\eta < (1 - \beta)/(\alpha - \beta)$, the point being that V_0 does not converge for any feasible programme.

following conditions:

$$(\eta - 1)C_t^{-\eta} = p_t, \tag{A.29}$$

$$p_t F_R = q_t, \tag{A.30}$$

$$(dp_t/dt)/p_t = \delta - F_K, \tag{A.31}$$

and

$$(dq_t/dt)/q_t = \delta - (\alpha - 2\beta S_t). \tag{A.32}$$

The dynamical system defined by (A.12)–(A.13) and (A.29)–(A.32) has a unique stationary point, which is the solution of

$$C = F(K, R), \tag{A.33}$$

$$R = \alpha S - \beta S^2, \tag{A.34}$$

$$(\eta - 1)C^{-\eta} = p, \tag{A.35}$$

$$pF_R = q, \tag{A.36}$$

$$\delta = F_K, \tag{A.37}$$

and

$$\delta = (\alpha - 2\beta S). \tag{A.38}$$

To solve equations (A.33)–(A.38), we obtain the (unique) value of S from (A.38), thereby R from (A.34), and thence K from (A.37), C from (A.33), p from (A.35), and, finally, q from (A.36). Taking a linear approximation of the dynamical system round the stationary point, it can be checked that the stationary point is (locally) stable. Given K_0 and S_0, there is a unique pair of values for p_0 and q_0 that lies on the stable arm of the system. The optimum programme is that arm. The transversality conditions are satisfied along the stable arm. In a decentralized environment, the planner's task would be to announce p_0 and q_0 and allow the optimum programme to be realized by a system of accounting prices satisfying (A.31)–(A.32).

NON-CONVEX ECONOMIES

A.3. THE PREVALENCE OF NON-CONVEXITIES

Unlike economists, ecologists have little desire to explore the structure of convex sets. Ecologists try to identify the pathways by which the constituents of an ecosystem interact with one another and with the external environment. A large body of empirical work has revealed that those pathways in many cases involve transformation possibilities among environmental goods and services that, together, constitute non-convex sets. Often the non-convexities reflect positive feedbacks in Human–Nature interactions. Mathematical ecologists therefore study the structural stability of ecosystems and the sizes and shapes of their basins of attraction for given sets of environmental parameters.[17] Such notions as the 'resilience' of ecosystems are expressions of this research interest.[18]

Earlier in this book we observed that the price mechanism is especially problematic in economic systems governed by positive feedback processes. In those systems it could prove impossible to decentralize an efficient allocation of resources exclusively by means of prices. Efficient mechanisms would typically involve additional social contrivances, such as (Pigouvian) taxes and subsidies, quantity controls, social norms of behaviour, and so forth. This was proved formally in a justly famous article by Starrett (1972), who showed that, for certain non-convexities associated with environmental pollution, a competitive equilibrium simply does not exist: markets for pollution are unable to equate demands to supplies. Starrett's non-convexities are present when losses traceable to environmental pollution are bounded. If the market price for pollution in such situations is negative (i.e., if the pollutor has to pay the pollutee), pollutees' demand will be unbounded, while supply will be bounded. On the other hand, if the price is non-negative, demand will be zero, while supply, presumably, will be positive.[19]

Starrett's finding implied that private property rights to environmental pollution are not capable of sustaining an efficient allocation of resources by means of the price system. In a subsequent note, Starrett (1973) demonstrated by means of an example that, if property rights are awarded to polluters, even such a non-price resource allocation mechanism as the core may not yield an outcome. But he showed (Starrett, 1972) that a suitably chosen set of pollution taxes, together with a system of competitive markets for other goods and services (assuming that the latter constitute a convex sector), would be capable of supporting an efficient allocation of resources. As there are no markets for pollution in such an allocation mechanism, the problem of equating supply to demand in pollution activities is bypassed. The moral would appear to be that social difficulties arising from the non-convexities can be overcome if the State assigns property rights

---

[17] Murray (1993) contains an illuminating account of both the mathematical and ecological reasoning.

[18] See Perrings *et al.* (1995), Levin, Barrett *et al.* (1998), and Gunderson and Holling (2002). We discuss these issues formally in Section A.4.

[19] In an earlier classic, Arrow (1971) had observed that markets for externalities will suffer from another problem: no matter whether the externalities are positive or negative, the markets will be 'thin'.

in a suitable way—permitting private rights to the convex sector, but reserving for itself the right to control emissions and discharges.[20]

Intuitively speaking, non-convexities arising from pollution activities mean that pollution ought ideally to be concentrated at certain locations, not spread evenly across space. Starrett's non-convexities provide a reason why communities create garbage dumps, locations where pollution is concentrated.

Despite the ecologist's strictures, we economists have remained ambivalent toward Nature's non-convexities. Often enough, that ambivalence reveals itself only indirectly. In Chapter 8 we noted that even today it is commonly thought that economic growth is good for the environment because countries need to put poverty behind them in order to care; or that trade improves the environment, because it raises incomes, and the richer people are, the more willing they are to devote resources to cleaning up their living space.

The view's origin can be traced to World Bank (1992), which observed an empirical relationship between GNP per head and atmospheric concentrations of industrial pollutants. Based on the historical experience of OECD countries, the authors of the document suggested that, when GNP per head is low, concentrations of such pollutants as the sulphur oxides increase as GNP per head increases, but that, when GNP per head is high, concentrations decrease as GNP per head increases further. Among economists this relationship has been christened the 'environmental Kuznets curve'.[21] The moral that would appear to have been drawn from the finding is that resource degradation is reversible: degrade all you want now, Earth can be relied upon to rejuvenate itself later if you require it.

The presumption is false. Nature's non-convexities are frequently a manifestation of positive feedback processes, which in turn often means the presence of ecological *thresholds*. But if much damage were to be inflicted on an ecosystem whose ability to function was conditional on its being above some threshold level (in size, composition, or whatever), the consequence would be irreversible. We confirm this below. The environmental Kuznets curve was detected for mobile pollutants. Mobility means that, so long as emissions decline, the stock at the site of the emissions declines. However, reversal is the last thing that would spring to mind if a grassland were to flip to become covered by shrubs, or the Atlantic gulf stream were to shift direction or come to a halt, or a source of water were to disappear, or an ocean fishery were to become a dead zone owing to overfishing. As a metaphor for the possibilities of substituting

[20] Over the past three decades much work has been done by economists to develop the theory of environmental policy. Baumol and Oates (1975) continues to be the outstanding treatise on the subject.

[21] It is, of course, a misnomer. The original Kuznets curve, which was an inverted U, related income inequality to real national income per head on the basis of historical cross-country evidence.

manufactured and human capital for natural capital, the relationship embodied in the environmental Kuznets curve has to be rejected.

Although non-convexities are prevalent in global ecosystems (e.g. ocean circulation, global climate), it is as well to emphasize the spatial character of many positive feedback processes. The latter have a direct bearing on the rural poor in the world's poorest regions. Eutrophication of ponds, or salinization of soil, or biodiversity loss in a forest patch involve crossing ecological thresholds at a spatially localized level. Similarly, the metabolic pathways between an individual's nutritional status and his or her capacity to work, and those between a person's nutritional and disease status, involve positive feedback.[22] Studies of extreme poverty based on aggregation at the regional or national level can therefore mislead greatly. The spatial confinement of many of the non-convexities inherent in Human–Nature interactions needs always to be kept in mind.

The connection between rural poverty in the world's poorest regions and the state of the local ecosystems should be self-evident. When wetlands, inland and coastal fisheries, woodlands, forests, ponds and lakes, and grazing fields are damaged (owing, say, to agricultural encroachment, or urban extensions, or the construction of large dams, or organizational failure at the village level), traditional dwellers suffer. For them—and they are among the poorest in society—there is frequently no alternative source of livelihood. In contrast, for rich eco-tourists or importers of primary products, there *is* something else, often somewhere else, which means that there are alternatives. Whether or not there are substitutes for a particular resource is therefore not only a technological matter, or a mere matter of consumer taste: among poor people location can matter too. The poorest of the poor experience non-convexities in a way the rich do not. As we noted in Section 8.2, even the range between a need and a luxury is context-ridden. The notion of genuine investment adopted in Chapter 9 (see Section A.6) is meant not only to be inclusive of various types of capital assets, but also to be sensitive to individual and locational differences. A pond in one village is a different asset from a pond in another village, in part because their ecological characteristics differ, and in part because the communities making use of them face different economic circumstances. For both reasons, seemingly identical ponds should have different accounting prices attributed to them. Of course, in practice such refinements may not be attainable. But it is always salutary to be reminded that macroeconomic reasoning glosses over the heterogeneity of Earth's resources and the diverse uses to which they are put—by people residing at the site and by those elsewhere. National income accounts reflect that reasoning by failing to record a wide array of our

---

[22] See Dasgupta (1993) for the relationship between nutritional status and human productivity, and for evidence on synergies between nutritional and disease status. An extensive set of references to the primary literature on these topics is also provided there.

transactions with Nature. In short, accounting prices depend not only on technology, consumer preferences, and the distribution of endowed capital assets, but also on institutions, and, ultimately, on their combined effect on people's lives.[23]

Despite their prevalence, we economists continue to show little interest in Nature's non-convexities. For example, the now enormous literature on 'green accounting' has been built largely on the backs of economic models in which non-convexities are safely out of sight.[24] However, the fact that regeneration functions of natural capital may not be concave was realised many years ago by fisheries experts. Denoting the biomass of a single-species fishery by K, it is commonly assumed that a fishery's regeneration function, $F(K)$, is *convex–concave*, that is, $F(K)$ *is convex at low values of K, but concave beyond some value of K*. As we noted in Section A.2, if F is convex–concave, feasible programmes do not constitute a convex set, even if catch is freely disposable. The price system is therefore generally not a viable avenue for implementing optimum programmes.

A.4. HUMAN INTERVENTION IN NON-CONVEX ECOSYSTEMS

Human intervention in an ecosystem takes the form of resource extraction or pollutant discharge. At a formal level, resource economics and environmental economics have identical underlying features.[25] It is not an exaggeration to say that one is a mirror image of the other: pollutants (economic 'bads') are discharged into ecosystems, thereby compromising the latter's ability to provide us with services (economic 'goods'). In positive, as opposed to normative, analysis the background institutional structure is postulated, the human intervention is inferred, and its consequences to the ecosystem are then studied. We illustrate this by considering, in turn, resource extraction and pollution discharge in the context of two simple models.

A.4.1. *Convex–Concave Growth Functions: Resource Extraction*

Dasgupta (1982b: ch. 6) constructed a model of an open access fishery. Denoting fish biomass by K, it was assumed that the fishery's growth function, $F(K)$, is

$$F(K) = -a + bK - cK^2, \qquad a, b, c, (b^2 - 4ac) > 0, \qquad \text{if } K > 0,$$

---

[23] See the interchange between Johnson (2001) and Dasgupta (2001c) on this. For a more detailed analysis of the connection between environmental and resource economics and the economics of poverty, see Dasgupta (1982b, 1993, 2000c, 2003). [24] See e.g. Lutz (1993), Heal (1998), and Weitzman (2000). [25] This thesis was elaborated by Dasgupta (1982b).

and

$$F(K) = 0 \qquad \text{if } K = 0. \tag{A.39}$$

$F(K)$, so defined, is convex–concave. (To confirm this, observe that $F(K)$ is discontinous at $K = 0$.) Notice also that $F(K) = 0$ at three values: $0, K_1 = [b - (b^2 - 4ac)^{1/2}]/2c$, and $K_2 = [b + (b^2 - 4ac)^{1/2}]/2c$. K_1 is a *threshold*: if biomass were to fall below it, the fishery would die.

If C is catch, the cost of harvest is taken to be $\beta K^{-\gamma} C^{\mu}$, where $\mu > 1$ and $\beta, \gamma > 0$. The idea here is that, while unit cost of harvest is an increasing function of harvest (there is crowding among fishermen), harvest cost is a decreasing function of stock (search costs decline if fish biomass increases).

Free entry (and exit) into the fishery is assumed to be an instantaneous adjustment process, resulting in zero profit at all times. This means that, if p is the market price of a unit of fish biomass,

$$p = \beta K_t^{-\gamma} C_t^{(\mu-1)}. \tag{A.40}$$

Writing $q \equiv p/\beta$ and using (A.39) and (A.40), the net growth rate of fish biomass (for $K_t > 0$) is

$$dK_t/dt = (-a + bK_t - cK_t^2) - q^{1/(\mu-1)} K_t^{\gamma/(\mu-1)}. \tag{A.41}$$

a, b, c, μ, γ, and q are parameters of the dynamical system. Since q reflects the fish market and an aspect of fishing technology, we shall vary q so as to study the qualitative properties of equation (A.41).

Figure A.1 is based on the right-hand side of equation (A.41). I have drawn the figure for the case where $\gamma > (\mu - 1)$. Observe that there is a critical value of q, call it q^*, such that, if $q = q^*$, the curves $(-a + bK - cK^2)$ and $q^{1/(\mu-1)} K^{\gamma/(\mu-1)}$ are tangential to each other.

If $q > q^*$, equation (A.41), allied to the second part of (A.39), has a unique stationary point: $K = 0$. This means that the fishery has a single basin of attraction and is doomed: there is overfishing to such an extent that, in finite time, the fishery becomes extinct. This is the case advanced by Hardin (1968), who claimed as a universal rule that freedom in the commons spells ruin. But the thesis is correct only if, relative to the harvesting technology, the resource is valuable ($q > q^*$). Even under open access, matters are different when $q < q^*$.

To confirm this, notice that, if $q < q^*$, the fishery has three stationary points, namely, $K = 0$ and the two stationary solutions of equation (A.41), which I

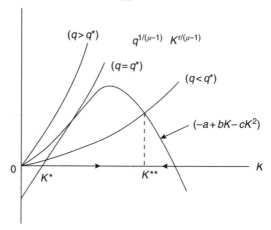

Figure A.1. *Open access fishery*

have denoted as K^* and K^{**} in Figure A.1. It is simple to infer from the figure that $K = 0$ and $K = K^{**}$ are (locally) stable, while K^* is unstable. K^* is thus a *separatrix*: it separates the two basins of attraction, each of which contains a stationary point ($K = 0$ and $K = K^{**}$, respectively). We conclude that, if $K_0 > K^*$, the fishery survives despite free entry. Hardin's analysis turns out to have been wrong for this case: if the value of fish relative to harvesting costs is low, there is not enough entry to pose a danger to the fishery. Because there is a qualitative break in the dynamical properties of the fishery under free entry at $q = q^*$, q^* is called a *bifurcation* point of the system.

A.4.2. *Convex–Concave Pollution Recycling Functions*

We now study a pollution problem that has been much analysed in recent years: phosphorus discharge into a shallow freshwater lake. I use the occasion also to develop a number of additional notions.[26]

The rate of phosphorus inflow into a lake is a byproduct of agriculture in the watershed (e.g. as fertilizer runoff from farms). Phosphorus is a key determinant of the state of a lake. It is a necessary nutrient for such ecological services as those that provide a habitat for fish populations, but at high levels of concentration phosphorus is a pollutant, causing increased plant growth, algae blooms, decrease in water transparency, bad odour, oxygen depletion, and fish kills. Thus, the state of a lake can be taken to be the quantity of phosphorus in the

---

[26] Each of the additional notions can also be developed by means of the fishery's model in the previous subsection.

water column, which I denote by K_t (≥ 0). Let C_t (≥ 0) be the phosphorus inflow into the system.

It would be absurd to assume that pollutants can be disposed of freely. In a well-known work, Kneese, Ayers, and d'Arge (1972) noted that mass has to be conserved, so that what is produced by society must eventually find a place of residence, in one form or another. This they formalized by requiring that economic activities satisfy a 'materials-balance condition'.[27] It is possible to go overboard with this thought, for in many cases there are ways to render pollutants harmless. But this involves costs (e.g. setting aside refuse places). But phosphorus seeps into lakes from the adjoining fields. This makes the problem of disposal very hard to solve. In what, follows, we therefore suppose that the dynamics of phosphorus in the lake's water column can be represented by the equation

$$dK_t/dt = F(K_t) + C_t, \qquad K_0\ (>0)\ \text{given.} \tag{A.42}$$

Assume for simplicity that $C_t = C$, a constant. Then equation (A.42) can be expressed as

$$dK_t/dt = F(K_t) + C, \qquad K_0\ (>0)\ \text{given.} \tag{A.43}$$

$F(K)$ represents the *net* recycling rate of phosphorus in the water column. Now, one of the services that ecosystems provide is the breaking-down of pollutants. (Organic pollutants are decomposed by microbes, atmospheric carbon dioxide gets absorbed by the oceans, and so forth.) In the present case, water does run off lakes. Such natural forms of pollution decay are included in $F(K)$. But in the case of phosphorus in a shallow freshwater lake, the pollutant has a limited ability to recycle between the lake bottom and the water column. So I assume that (i) F is twice differentiable, (ii) $F(0) = 0$, (iii) $F(K) > 0$ for some K, and (iv) $F(K) < 0$ for sufficiently large K.

The term *resilience* refers to the stability of ecosystems. It has been used alternatively to denote the size of the basin of attraction in which it currently resides and the speed of convergence back to its current state following a perturbation to it. In order to explore such problems, it pays first to study the dynamics of the lake when $C = 0$. In this case,

$$dK_t/dt = F(K_t), \qquad K_0\ (>0)\ \text{given.} \tag{A.44}$$

---

[27] Mäler (1974) contains a general equilibrium analysis of resource allocations subject to the materials-balance condition.

$K = 0$ is a stationary point of the system. How many other stationary points does the system possess?

If F is concave, there is precisely one other stationary point, and it is stable, while $K = 0$ is unstable. But if F is not concave, equation (A.44) can have any number of stationary points. In view of the conditions we have imposed on F, the function cannot be convex everywhere. So we look for convex–concave forms.

In the case of phosphorus in a shallow freshwater lake, it has been found that the following is a good approximation:[28]

$$F(K) = bK^2/(1 + K^2) - \gamma K, \qquad b, \gamma > 0. \tag{A.45}$$

The positive feedback governing the recycling of K is given by the first term on the right-hand side (RHS) of (A.45), which, as can be readily confirmed, is convex–concave, with an upper bound of b. The second term on the RHS of (A.45) is the rate at which the lake is cleansed of the pollutant. Combining (A.43) and (A.45), we have[29]

$$dK_t/dt = C + bK_t^2/(1 + K_t^2) - \gamma K_t, \qquad K_0\ (>0)\ \text{given}. \tag{A.46}$$

Equation (A.46) contains three parameters: C, b, and γ. We would like to know how the lake ecosystem's character depends on them. One expects that for

---

[28] Scheffer (1997) is a treatise on the subject. See also Carpenter, Ludwig, and Brock (1999), who provide a succinct account of the mathematical structure of the phenomenon discussed below.

[29] Close variants of (A.46) have been postulated for a number of natural systems. Here are three examples.

1. In order to explain periodic infestations of the spruce budworm in boreal forests, Ludwig, Jones, and Holling (1978) postulated that the budworm's population, K_t, changes in accordance with the equation

$$dK_t/dt = \alpha K_t - \beta K_t^2 - bK_t^2/(1 + K_t^2), \qquad (\alpha, \beta, b > 0), \tag{A.46a}$$

where the final, forcing term denotes predation by birds.

2. The account of the Atlantic thermohaline circulation in Rahmstorf (1995) can be formalized in terms of an equation not dissimilar to (A.46). Temperature and salt gradients across the North and South Atlantic give rise to the circulation. K_t is taken to be the North Atlantic deep water flow (travelling south) and C is the amount of freshwater entering, say, the surface of the North Atlantic (in part from ice melts). The circulation would come to a halt if C were too large.

3. Vegetation cover in the savannahs depends on rainfall, but rainfall in turn depends on vegetation cover. Denoting rainfall by C_t and vegetation (in biomass) by K_t, suppose, as a first approximation, that

$$C_t = \alpha K_t \text{ and } dK_t/dt = bC_t^2/(1 + C_t^2) - \gamma K_t, \qquad (\alpha, b, \gamma > 0). \tag{A.46b}$$

The pair of equations (A.46a,b) are variants of (A.46).

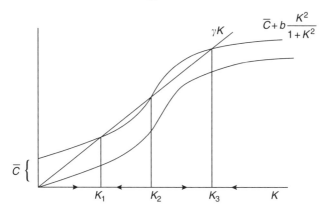

Figure A.2. *Pollution equilibria: the reversible case*

the most part the global properties of the ecosystem will vary continuously with the parameters. One should also expect that there are manifolds partitioning the parameter space into regions, such that the ecosystem's structure is the same at every point in any given region, but differs from the structure in the region adjacent to it. Such manifolds bifurcate the system's properties. To study the bifurcations, we take b and γ to be given and vary C. The reason we permit C to vary is that C denotes human intervention and it is in principle possible to control it.

So consider the equation

$$bK^2/(1 + K^2) = \gamma K. \tag{A.47}$$

Real solutions of (A.47) are the stationary points of (A.46) with $C = 0$.

We begin by assuming that $\gamma/b > 1/2$, which is to say that the pollutant decays rapidly. In this case (A.47) has only one real solution: it is $K = 0$. Simple graphics (Figure A.2) confirm, however, that there are values of C for which (A.46) has three (real) stationary points. Assuming one such value, $C = \bar{C}$, we label the stationary points as $K_1 \ (<) K_2 \ (<) K_3$, respectively. K_2 is unstable, while K_1 and K_3 are locally stable. K_2 is the separatrix of the system—the point that separates the two basins of attraction of the lake ecosystem.

A.4.2.1. *Ecosystem Flips*
Continuing to hold b and γ constant, let us now reduce C from $\bar{C}$. It is simple to confirm visually that the unstable stationary point (continue to label it K_2) and

the larger of the two locally stable stationary points (continue to label it K_3) get closer to each other continuously. It is simple to confirm as well that there is a critical value of C (call it C^*), for which K_2 and K_3 coincide to form a point that is stable from the right, but unstable from the left. C^* is a bifurcation point of the system: if $C < C^*$, the ecosystem possesses a unique (stable) stationary point, whereas if $C > C^*$ (but $C < C^{**}$—see below), it possesses three stationary points. In short, the system's structure changes discontinuously at C^*.[30]

In contrast, suppose C were to increase from $\bar{C}$. It is simple to confirm visually (Figure A.2) that the unstable stationary point (continue to label it K_2) and the smaller of the two locally stable stationary points (continue to label it K_1) would get closer to each other continuously, until, at a critical value of C (call it C^{**}), the two would coincide, to form a point that is unstable from the right but stable from the left. C^{**} is another bifurcation point of the system: if $C > C^{**}$, the ecosystem possesses a unique (stable) stationary point, whereas if $C < C^{**}$ (but $C > C^*$), it possesses three stationary points.

In Figure A.3 I have drawn the equilibrium values of K as a correspondence of C for a given pair of values of b and γ. Equilibrium K is unique when $C < C^*$. For C in the interval $[C^*, C^{**}]$, the curve depicting K as a correspondence of C bends back and then back again, to reflect the fact that equation (A.46) possesses three stationary points. The two upward sloping portions of the correspondence consist of (locally) stable stationary values of K, whereas the downward sloping portion consists of unstable stationary points.

We now conduct a thought experiment. Begin in a situation where $C < C^*$. We know that equilibrium K is small. We would like to discover how the system would change if C were to increase in a predictable way. Rather than try to integrate (A.46), we simplify by imagining that C increases slowly relative to the speed of adjustment of K_t. By 'slowly' we mean that at each C the ecosystem is able to equilibrate itself. If C were to increase under such conditions, K would increase continuously along the lower arm of the curve until $C = C^{**}$, at which point equilibrium K would 'flip' to the upper arm of the curve. The ecosystem therefore undergoes a discrete change at C^{**}. Further increases in C would lead to a continual increase in K along the upper arm of the curve in Figure A.3.

Ecosystem flips have been observed many times and on many scales. Shallow lakes have been known to flip from clear to turbid water in a matter of months, village tanks in a matter of weeks, garden ponds in a matter of hours. Insect populations have been known to crash or explode in a matter of days. Larger ecosystems generally take longer to flip at their bifurcation points

---

[30] Mathematicians call this a 'saddle-node bifurcation'.

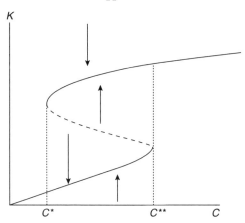

Figure A.3. *Lake dynamics for constant phosphorus inflow: the reversible case*

because the underlying processes operate over greater distances, and are therefore slower. Grasslands in sub-Saharan Africa can take more than a decade to change into shrublands. The 'salt conveyor' that drives global ocean circulation would probably take between decades and a century to shut down (or change direction) if the Greenland ice cover were to melt at rates estimated in current models of global warming.[31] The fossil records suggest that the interglacials and glacials of ice ages have appeared only occasionally, but have arrived and departed 'precipitously'—the flips occuring over several thousand years. And so on.

A.4.2.2. *Hysteresis in Ecosystem Dynamics*

Now suppose we were to reverse the process in our previous thought experiment. Start with $C > C^{**}$ and reduce it slowly. Figure A.3 shows that on the return journey K declines continuously along the upper arm so long as $C > C^*$. This means that, for C in the interval $[C^*, C^{**}]$, K remains higher than it had been on the onward journey. To put it another way, the ecosystem displays *hysteresis*. However, at $C = C^*$ the ecosystem 'flips' to the lower arm of the curve in Figure A.3. Further declines in K would occur continuously if C were reduced further. I conclude that, even though the ecosystem displays hysteresis, environmental degradation is *reversible*: given enough time, K can be made to

---

[31] Rahmstorf (1995).

be as small as we like if C is reduced sufficiently. This is the intellectual basis of the environmental Kuznets curve, mentioned earlier. As just confirmed, it would be a correct view of future possibilities if the pollutant's decay rate were sufficiently large.

A.4.2.3. *Irreversibility in Ecosystem Damage*

But now consider a less happy possibility. Suppose that $\gamma/b < 1/2$, which is to say that the pollutant decays slowly. In this case (A.47) possesses three real solutions. One is $K = 0$, while the other two are positive. Figure A.4, which is the counterpart of Figure A.2, depicts this case. We now use Figure A.4 to construct Figure A.5, which plots the equilibrium values of K as a correspondence of C. In contrast to Figure A.3, the curve bends backward to cut the vertical axis.

Let us conduct the thought experiment again. Suppose we begin in a situation where both C and K are low, which means that the system is on the lower arm of the curve in Figure A.5. As C increases, K increases continuously until the bifurcation point, $\hat{C}$, is reached. At this point the ecosystem flips to a higher value of K. However, once that happens, the system is incapable of reversing itself. Declines in C would certainly reduce K, but, as Figure A.5 shows, even if C were reduced to zero, the system would remain on the upper arm of the curve, at a higher value of K than it did to begin with. Not only does the ecosystem suffer from hysteresis, but in addition environmental degradation is now *irreversible*: the system is unable to return to where it was in the beginning.

We are used to the intuitive idea that the presence of thresholds in ecosystems means that large damages to them are irreversible. The above analysis has shown that large damages can be irreversible even if an ecosystem does not have

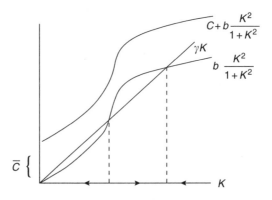

Figure A.4. *Pollution equilibria: the irreversible case*

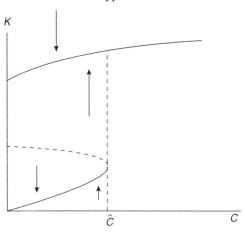

Figure A.5. *Lake dynamics for constant phosphorus inflow: the irreversible case*

thresholds. Positive feedback, allied to a slow decay rate for the pollutant in the ecosystem, is all that is needed.

A.5. OPTIMUM INTERVENTION

Particular interest lies in optimum intervention. As is well known, optimum programmes satisfy Pontryagin's Maximum Principle even in non-convex environments. The Maximum Principle gives us necessary conditions for optimality. The hard part is to find conditions that are sufficient.

In an interesting paper, Brock and Starrett (2003) have studied the optimum discharge of phosphorus into a shallow freshwater lake. As in the previous section, we are to imagine that the rate of phosphorus inflow into a lake is a byproduct of agriculture in the watershed. Imagine next for simplicity that phosphorus has a deleterious effect on the lake at all levels of concentration (not just at high levels of concentration). This latter assumption brings into sharp relief those economic problems where a produced good has positive social worth as a flow, even though it is a pollutant as a stock. Let the inflow of phosphorus into the lake be C_t. Current well-being is therefore taken to be a strictly concave and twice differentiable function $U(C_t, K_t)$, where U is an increasing function of C_t and a decreasing function of K_t.

For simplicity, we specialize and assume that

$$U(C_t, K_t) = \log C_t - hK_t^2, \quad h > 0. \tag{A.48}$$

Social well-being is given by

$$V_0 = \int_0^\infty U(C_t, K_t)e^{-\delta t}dt, \qquad \delta > 0. \tag{A.49}$$

Generalizing equation (A.46), Brock and Starrett (2003) assume that

$$dK_t/dt = C_t + bK_t^2/(1 + K_t^2) - \gamma K_t, \qquad K_0\ (>0)\ \text{given}. \tag{A.50}$$

The idea is to maximize (A.49) subject to equation (A.50), given that U satisfies (A.48).

Let p_t be the (spot) accounting price of phosphorus in the lake. It is easy to confirm that, for $\{C_t\}_0^\infty$ to be an optimum, C_t and K_t must satisfy not only equation (A.50), but also the Pontryagin conditions,

$$p_t = -U_C\ (<0), \tag{A.51}$$

and

$$(dp_t/dt)/p_t = \delta + \gamma - U_K/U_C - 2bK_t/(1 + K_t^2)^2, \tag{A.52}$$

where U satisfies (A.48).

The point is to select p_0 (equivalently, C_0) optimally and allow the dynamical system to evolve according to (A.50)–(A.52). On using equation (A.48), Brock and Starrett (2003) showed that, for a range of values of δ, h, γ, and b, (A.50)–(A.52) possess three stationary points. Two (call them K_1 and K_3, with $K_1 < K_3$, corresponding to what could be interpreted as the oligotrophic and eutrophic state, respectively) are saddle points, while the intermediate point (call it K_2) is a spiral source (i.e. it is unstable).[32] The authors noted that for any K_0, the two trajectories that asymptote to K_1 and K_3, respectively, satisfy not only the necessary conditions for optimality, but the transversality condition as well (namely, $\lim_{t\to\infty}(p_t e^{-\delta t}K_t) = 0$). This implies that, in order to judge which of the two is the correct trajectory, one would have to compute (A.49) for each trajectory and compare the two values—a tiresome requirement. However, Brock and Starrett have shown that there is a value of phosphorus stock, $\bar{K}$, such that if $K_0 > \bar{K}$ the optimum programme asymptotes to K_3, but that if $K_0 < \bar{K}$ it

---

[32] Although, for ease of exposition, we are using the same notation, the points K_1, K_2, and K_3 here are not the same as the points K_1, K_2, and K_3 in the previous section.

asymptotes to K_1. In other words, history matters.[33] They also confirmed that, if by fluke $K_0 = \bar{K}$, the two trajectories that asymptote to K_1 and K_3, respectively, are equally desirable. They call $\bar{K}$ a Skiba point, in recognition of Skiba (1978), who uncovered the existence of such points of indifference.[34]

Locating $\bar{K}$ is no easy matter. The disturbing conclusion is that, if the planner were by mistake to think that K_0 is greater than $\bar{K}$, the path he would choose would be the wrong one: the planner would regard the eutrophic state to be the optimal target, whereas he ought instead to aim for the oligotrophic state. It would seem that, in order to determine the optimum programme, there is no alternative to having to compute the value of (A.49) along both candidate trajectories.[35]

VALUATION AND EVALUATION IN IMPERFECT ECONOMIES[36]

Brock and Starrett (2003) is in the spirit of modern welfare economic theory. It is assumed there that policy analysis is conducted in an economy where the State (or the regulatory authority) selects those policies that maximize social well-being subject to technological, environmental, and institutional constraints. In modern welfare economics, what differentiates the 'first-best' from the plethora of 'second-best' policies, it is possible to envisage, is the inclusion of institutional constraints when deriving the latter. The State is assumed to act on behalf of its citizens even in second-best economies.

Earlier in this book I argued that this is a misleading approach to policy analysis in many societies today. It is hard to imagine the sense in which governments in what are demonstrably failed or predatory states may be said to be optimizing on behalf of their citizens. However, it is not absurd to imagine that even in the

---

[33] Skiba (1978) showed that in non-convex economies the optimality conditions may possess multiple stationary points even if the utility function is independent of stocks.

[34] To the best of my knowledge, Kurz (1968) was the first to note that, if U depends not only on C, but also on K (as is the case of the U postulated here), the Pontryagin optimality conditions may possess multiple stationary points, meaning that, in the space of K and its co-state variable, there are multiple basins of attraction. He showed that this can be even if the underlying production possibility set is convex. Kurz also showed that the long-run features of the optimum programme depend on K_0. Thus, even when the Hamiltonian of an optimization problem is concave in the state and the control variables, the Pontryagin optimality conditions can have multiple stationary points. See also Keeler, Spence, and Zeckhauser (1972).

[35] Brock and Starrett (2003) also showed that there is a range of parameter values for which the optimality conditions possess a single stationary point (a saddle point), so that there are no Skiba points. The set of parameter values that separate the two regions in the space of parameter values defines a bifurcation surface.

[36] The remainder of this Appendix is based on Dasgupta and Mäler (2000), Dasgupta (2001b), and Arrow, Dasgupta, and Mäler (2003b).

most corrupt and predatory of governments there are honest people. It can be safely assumed that such figures are only minor officials, involved in making marginal decisions (a road here, a local environmental protection plan there, and so on). What language does welfare economics have to speak to such people?

In what follows, I extend intergenerational welfare economics to such imperfect economies by determining rules that can be used to evaluate small perturbations to macroeconomic forecasts. A forecast is based on a reading of technological and environmental possibilities, and on the behaviour of households, firms, communities, and the State. A perturbation to the forecast is interpreted as a project (or, more generally, a small policy change) that is under the jurisdiction of the honest civil servant. I show that the required evaluation rule involves the use of accounting prices that can in principle be estimated by perturbing the forecast. The rule itself is to check whether the present discounted value of the flow of social profits generated by the perturbation is positive. In other words, the choice criterion is the one that has for long been advocated for social cost–benefit analysis in optimizing economies. *In our analysis we do not require the economy to be convex.*

I also develop a criterion for assessing whether or not social well-being is *sustained* along an economic forecast. In the context of a simple economic model with constant population, I confirm that the same accounting prices as those that can be used in social cost–benefit analysis can also be used to compute an index for assessing whether social well-being is being sustained. The index in question is shown to be a comprehensive measure of *wealth*, which is the social value of the entire stock of the economy's capital assets, inclusive of manufactured, human, and natural capital assets. *Our analysis does not require the economy to be convex.*[37]

To summarize, we are interested in three related questions here: (1) How should accounting prices be estimated? (2) How should policy changes in an imperfect economy be evaluated? (3) How can one check whether social well-being will be sustained along a projected economic programme?

---

[37] Pearce and Atkinson (1993) proved that an inclusive measure of wealth can be used to assess the sustainability of social well-being in a convex, optimizing world with constant population. Dasgupta and Mäler (2000) showed that an inclusive measure of wealth can be used to assess the sustainability of social well-being even in a non-convex, imperfect economy (Kakotopia, in our language here) with constant population. In the first edition of this book, conditions were identified in which an inclusive measure of per capita wealth could be used to assess the sustainability of social well-being in an imperfect economy with changing population (see Section A.17 below). It isn't clear what social well-being means when population is expected to change. Arrow, Dasgupta, and Mäler (2003a) and Asheim (2003) present alternatives, and for each alternative formulation identify an index that can be used to assess the sustainability of social well-being in an optimizing world.

For simplicity, we confine our analysis until Section A.18 to a deterministic world. In Section A.6 I develop the basic theory. It is proved that the same set of accounting prices should be used both for evaluating policies and for assessing whether or not social well-being will be sustained along a projected economic programme. In particular it is shown that a comprehensive measure of wealth, computed in terms of accounting prices, can be used as an index for problems (2) and (3) above. These results do not require that the economy be convex, nor do they depend on the assumption that the government optimizes on behalf of its citizens.

In Section A.7 the Ramsey–Solow model of national saving in a convex economy is used to illustrate the theory. In Section A.8 I return to the analysis of shallow lakes so as to confirm that the theory can be put to use in non-convex economies. The remainder of the appendix is concerned with rules for estimating the accounting prices of several specific natural resources, transacted in certain canonical economic institutions.

In order to make the findings easily accessible for empirical work, I report them as a catalogue of results. Rules for estimating accounting prices of exhaustible natural resources under both free and restricted entry are derived in Section A.9. Section A.10 shows how expenditure towards the discovery of new deposits ought to be incorporated in national accounts. In Section A.11 methods for including forest depletion are developed. Section A.12 shows how the production of human capital can be taken into account, and in Section A.13 I study the welfare economics of global public goods.

If an economy were to face exogenous movements in certain variables, its dynamics would not be autonomous in time. Non-autonomy in time introduces additional problems for constructing an index of social well-being, in that the wealth measure has to be augmented. Exogenous growth in total factor productivity, for example, is a potential reason for non-autonomous dynamics. In Chapter 9, however, I argued that, in growth accounting, production inputs (such as R&D expenditure and natural resource use) are often ignored, so that endogenous increases in total factor productivity are interpreted as exogenous. Section A.14 confirms that, by suitably introducing new variables, it is often possible to transform a non-autonomous economic system into an autonomous one.

But such helpful transformations are not possible in many other cases. In Section A.15 I show that the required index of social well-being can nevertheless be constructed. I do that by studying a small country exporting an exhaustible natural resource at a price that is time-dependent. The way in which defensive expenditure against pollution ought to be included in national accounts is discussed in Section A.16.

The theory developed up to and including Section A.16 assumes that population remains constant. In Section A.17 the theory is extended so as to cover population change. Section A.18 shows how future uncertainty in commodity transformation possibilities can be incorporated. I close in Sections A.19 and A.20 by showing why the analysis is particularly relevant for understanding extreme poverty.

A.6. THE BASIC MODEL

A.6.1. *General Resource Allocation Mechanisms*

We assume that the economy is closed and that population is constant. Time is continuous and is denoted variously by τ and t $(\tau, t \geq 0)$. The horizon is taken to be infinite. For simplicity of exposition, I aggregate consumption into a single consumption good, C, and let R denote a vector of resource flows (e.g. rates of extraction of natural resources, expenditure on education and health).

The state of the economy is represented by the vector K, where K is a comprehensive list of capital assets, including not only manufactured capital, knowledge and skills, but also natural capital. Certain types of natural capital are directly valuable as stocks in production and consumption (e.g. resources having intrinsic value). For expositional ease, I assume that such stock effects are absent (but see Section A.8). For simplicity of exposition, labour is assumed throughout to be supplied inelastically and is normalized to be unity. Current well-being is therefore taken to depend only on consumption. We write this as $U(C)$, where $U(C)$ is assumed to be strictly concave, twice differentiable, and monotonically increasing.[38] Social well-being at t (≥ 0) is

$$ W_t = \int_t^\infty U(C_\tau)e^{-\delta(\tau-t)}d\tau, \qquad \delta > 0. \tag{A.53} $$

I now formalize the concept of an imperfect economy (the economy of Kakotopia). In order to focus on the concept itself, in this section I do not specify the technological and ecological transformation possibilities among goods and services at a given moment of time and over time; nor do I specify the institutional structure of the economy.

The economy under study faces not only technological and ecological constraints, but also a wide variety of institutional constraints (sometimes called transaction and information constraints). By the economy's institutions I mean

---

[38] The following analysis does not require U to be concave. I assume concavity nonetheless for ethical reasons: (strict) concavity reflects concern for equity, both among people of the same generation and among people of different generations.

market structures, the structure of property rights, tax rates, non-market institutions (for credit, insurance, and common property resources), the character of various levels of government, and so forth. I do *not* assume that the government is bent on maximizing social well-being subject to constraints; it could be that the government is predatory, or is at best neglectful, and has objectives of its own that are not congruent with social well-being. Nor do I assume institutions to be unchanging over time. What I do assume is that institutions co-evolve with the state of the economy (K) in ways that are understood. It is no doubt a truism that social and political institutions influence the evolution of the state of an economy, but it has also been argued by political scientists (Lipset 1959, 1960) that the state of an economy (K) influences the evolution of social and political institutions. The theory I develop below accommodates this mutual influence.[39]

Let $\{C_\tau, R_\tau, K_\tau\}_t^\infty$ be an economic programme from t to ∞. (In Chapter 6 the consumption component of an economic programme was referred to as a consumption stream.) Given technological possibilities, resource availabilities, and the dynamics of the ecological–economic system, the decisions made by individual agents and consecutive governments from t onwards will determine C_τ, R_τ, and K_τ—for $\tau \geq t$—as functions of K_t, τ, and t. Thus if K_t is the vector of capital assets at t, let $f(K_t, \tau, t), g(K_t, \tau, t)$, and $h(K_t, \tau, t)$, respectively, be consumption, the vector of resource flows, and the vector of capital assets at date τ ($\geq t$). $\{C_\tau, R_\tau, K_\tau\}_t^\infty$ is, therefore, an *economic forecast* made at t. Now write

$$(\xi_\tau)_t^\infty \equiv \{C_\tau, R_\tau, K_\tau\}_t^\infty, \qquad t \geq 0. \tag{A.54}$$

Let $\{t, K_t\}$ denote the set of possible t and K_t pairs, and $\{(\xi_\tau)_t^\infty\}$ the set of economic programmes from t to infinity.

Definition 1: A resource allocation mechanism, α, is a (many-one) mapping

$$\alpha: \{t, K_t\} \rightarrow \{(\xi_\tau)_t^\infty\}. \tag{A.55}$$

It bears emphasizing that I do *not* assume that α maps $\{t, K_t\}$ into optimum economic programmes (starting at t), nor even that it maps $\{t, K_t\}$ into efficient programmes (starting at t). The following analysis is valid even if α is riddled with economic distortions and inequities. Nor do I assume, in defining α, that the economy's institutions are fixed. If institutions and the state of the economy were known to co-evolve, that co-evolution would be reflected in α. Note too that I do *not* assume commodity transformation possibility sets to be convex. The reason I am able to accommodate non-convex production structures is

---

[39] This observation owes much to a discussion I had with E. Somanathan, to whom I am most grateful.

that the economy is in Kakotopia: I assume that the government (rather, some honest agency in government) seeks only to institute a policy reform. For an optimizing government the matter would be different. As was showed earlier in this appendix, commodity transformation possibilities have to be convex if we are to guarantee that optimum programmes can be decentralized.

To make the dependence of the economic forecast on α explicit, let $\{C_t(\alpha), R_t(\alpha), K_t(\alpha)\}_0^\infty$ denote the forecast at $t = 0$. Consider date $t \ (\geq 0)$. We may now write (A.53) as

$$W_t \equiv \int_t^\infty U(C_\tau(\alpha))e^{-\delta(\tau - t)}d\tau. \tag{A.56}$$

Now W_t is a function of the state of the economy at t (K_t) and the resource allocation mechanism (α). So we can express it as a value function:

$$V(K_t, \alpha, t) \equiv W_t \equiv \int_t^\infty U(C_\tau(\alpha))e^{-\delta(\tau - t)}d\tau. \tag{A.57}$$

Before putting the concept of resource allocation mechanism to work, it is as well to discuss some examples. (In subsequent sections I illustrate the findings by means of formal models.) Imagine first that all capital assets are private property and that there is a complete set of competitive forward markets capable of sustaining a unique equilibrium (as in a special case discussed in Section A.7). In this case α would be defined in terms of this equilibrium. (If equilibrium were not unique, a selection rule among the multiple equilibria would have to be specified.) A great deal of modern macroeconomics is founded on this mechanism, as are many writings on the welfare economics of the environment.[40]

Of particular interest are situations where some of the assets are not private property. Consider, for example, the class of cases where manufactured capital is private property, but natural capital is common property (Section A.9). It may be that natural capital assets are local common property resources, not open to outsiders. If assets are managed efficiently, we are back to the case of a competitive equilibrium allocation, albeit one not entirely supported by market prices, but in part by, say, social norms.

On the other hand, it may be that local institutions are not functioning well (e.g. because social norms are breaking down and private benefits from using environmental natural resources exceed social benefits). Suppose in addition that decisions bearing on the accumulation of manufactured capital are guided by the profit motive. Then these behavioural rules together help to determine α. In a similar manner, we could (as we do in Section A.9) characterize α for the case where environmental natural resources are subject to open access (Chapter 7).

---

[40] Heal (1998) contains an account of the latter literature.

As noted earlier, institutional assumptions underlie the notion of resource allocation mechanism. Aspects of the concept of 'social capital' (R. D. Putnam, 1993) appear in our framework as part of the defining characteristics of α, as do ideas relating to 'social capability' (Adelman and Morris 1965; Abramovitz 1986), and 'social infrastructure' (Hall and Jones 1999). The prevalence (or absence) of trust and honest behaviour in the economy are embodied in α. Other aspects of the concept of social capital (personal networks) enter as components of human capital.[41]

Definition 2: α is time-autonomous (henceforth autonomous) if for all $\tau \geq t, \xi_\tau$ is a function solely of K_t and $(\tau - t)$.

If α is autonomous, economic variables at date τ ($\geq t$) are functions of K_t and $(\tau - t)$ only. So α would be non-autonomous if, say, knowledge or the terms of trade (for a trading economy) were to change exogenously over time. In certain cases exogenous changes in population size would mean that α is not autonomous. However, by suitably redefining state variables, non-autonomous resource allocation mechanisms can sometimes be mapped into autonomous mechanisms.[42]

Definition 3: α is time-consistent if

$$h(K_{\tau'}, \tau'', \tau') = h(K_t, \tau'', t), \qquad \text{for all } \tau'', \tau', \text{ and } t. \tag{A.58}$$

Time consistency implies a weak form of rationality. An autonomous resource allocation mechanism, however, has little to do with rationality; it has to do with the influence of external factors (e.g. whether trade prices are changing autonomously). In what follows, I assume that α is time consistent.

A.6.2. *Differentiability of the Value Function*

Let K_i be the ith capital stock. The crucial assumption I now make is that V is differentiable in K_i for all i. Unaided intuition is of little help for judging whether this is a strong assumption. The mathematical properties of V depend upon the mathematical properties of α. Problems are compounded because production and substitution possibilities in the economy are embedded in α, as is the economy's underlying institutional structure. Moreover, there are no obvious limits to the kinds of institution one can imagine. In many parts of the world the State has been known to act in bizarre and horrible ways. So one looks at what might be termed 'canonical' institutions. Analytically, the best

---

[41] See Ch. 9.
[42] Sections A.15 and A.17. See also Arrow, Dasgupta, and Mäler (2003a) for further examples.

understood are those that support optimum economic programmes. What do we know about them?[43]

If U is concave and commodity transformation possibility sets are convex, V is concave along optimum economic programmes and is therefore differentiable almost everywhere in each component of K. This property holds even in those circumstances where the optimum programme is chaotic. Thus, chaotic αs don't rule out differentiable Vs (almost everywhere).[44] However, if transformation possibilities are *not* convex, optimum economic programmes can have jumps at certain points on the space of Ks—the Skiba points (Section A.5). Skiba (1978) showed that, at those values of K where V is non-differentiable with respect to K (such points are, however, non-generic), V is continuous. But if V possesses right- and left-partial derivatives (and it does in the examples I have studied), social cost–benefit analysis of policy reforms can be conducted at the optimum with the aid of accounting prices, using the present discounted value of the flow of social profits as the criterion of choice (Section A.6.6). The same could be expected to be true for the case of market economies subject to fixed distortions, such as those considered by Little and Mirrlees (1968, 1974) in their account of social cost–benefit analysis.

Experience with dynamical systems suggests that, if α is *non*-optimal, V is discontinuous at certain values of K. Accounting prices would not be definable at such points (see equation (A.60) below).[45] It is as well to stress though that, in those αs that have been studied in the literature, discontinuities are non-generic (Section A.8). So, unless the economy is by fluke at a point of discontinuity, V would be differentiable within a sufficiently small neighbourhood of the initial capital stocks. It would seem then that the demand that V be differentiable does not rule out much of practical significance. The theory I offer here is valid for a substantially more general set of environments than is usual in writings on intertemporal welfare economics.

In Section A.7 I develop a convex model, based on Ramsey (1928) and Solow (1956), where the (imperfect) resource allocation mechanism has an explicit functional form. We confirm that V in that model is differentiable everywhere. In Section A.8 we revisit shallow lakes and confirm that V is differentiable almost everywhere. In what follows, I assume therefore that V is differentiable.

---

[43] Differentiability everywhere is a strong assumption. For practical purposes, however, it would suffice to assume that V is differentiable in K_i almost everywhere. The latter would appear to be a reasonable assumption even when production possibilities (including transformation possibility sets involving ecological processes) display plausible non-convexities. See Section A.8 below.

[44] See Majumdar and Mitra (2000) for a fine account. I am grateful to Mukul Majumdar for discussions on this point.

[45] However, if the location of these points on the space of capital stocks is uncertain and the uncertainty is a smooth probability distribution, the *expected value* of V would be continuous. I conjecture that in this case accounting prices exist.

A.6.3. *Measuring Current Well-Being*

In Part II practical methods for estimating current well-being were reviewed. Here I offer the theoretical reasoning underlying the methods.

Knowledge of α enables us to make an economic forecast. The forecast says that current well-being at t will be $U_t = U(C_t)$. So

$$dU_t/dt = U'(C_t)dC_t/dt. \tag{A.59}$$

$U'(C_t)$ is the social worth of consumption in well-being *numeraire*. Equation (A.59) gives us a way to judge whether or not current well-being is improving over time:

> *Proposition 2: If the accounting value of changes in the flow of consumption services is positive, current well-being can be said to be improving.*

International time series of the quality of life, such as those published annually in the World Bank's *World Development Report* and UNDP's *Human Development Report*, are based implicitly on Proposition 2. The reports include such indices as private consumption and life expectancy at birth, which serve as surrogates for key components of what we are calling consumption here.[46] But the reports veer away from Proposition 2 when they include gross national product (GNP). We noted in Chapters 4 and 5 that GNP is neither a measure of current well-being nor a measure of intergenerational well-being. This is why I dropped it in Chapter 5 when illustrating practical ways of measuring current well-being.

A.6.4. *Accounting Prices*

We now turn to intertemporal matters (developed informally in Parts III and IV). In Chapter 9 it was argued that substantive results on valuation and evaluation are independent of the numeraire: only relative prices matter. For the purposes of maintaining symmetry over goods and services, I continue to assume that the unit of account is well-being. As in the case of optimizing economies, accounting prices are useful in imperfect economies.

> *Definition 4: The accounting price, p_{it}, of the ith capital asset is defined as*
>
> $$p_{it} = \partial V_t/\partial K_{it} \equiv \partial V(K_t, \alpha, t)/\partial K_{it}. \tag{A.60}$$

Note that p_{it} is the spot price of K_{it}; it is the asset's social scarcity value. Note too that accounting prices are defined in terms of hypothetical perturbations to an economic forecast. Specifically, the accounting price of a capital asset is the present discounted value of the perturbations to U that would

---

[46] Ch. 5.

arise from a marginal increase in the quantity of that asset. It should be noted that accounting prices of private goods can be negative if property rights are dysfunctional, such as those that lead to the tragedy of the commons. Given the resource allocation mechanism, accounting prices at t are functions of $\mathbf{K}_t$ and, if α is non-autonomous, of t as well. Thus, $p_{it} = p_{it}(\mathbf{K}_t)$. The prices depend also on the extent to which various capital assets are substitutable for one another. If α is autonomous, accounting prices are not explicit functions of time, and so $p_{it} = p_i(\mathbf{K}_t)$. All future effects on the economy of changes in the structure of assets are reflected in accounting prices. That is why they are useful objects. Having stressed the functional dependence of accounting prices on α and $\mathbf{K}$ (and, possibly, t as well), we drop α and $\mathbf{K}$ from the formulae so as to save on notation.

A.6.5. *Marginal Rates of Substitution* vs *Market Observables*

Using equations (A.53) and (A.60), one can show that, if α is autonomous, p_{it} satisfies the equation

$$dp_{it}/dt = \delta p_{it} - U'(C_t)\partial C_t/\partial K_{it} - \sum_j p_{jt}\partial(dK_{jt}/dt)/\partial K_{it}. \qquad (A.61)$$

Equation (A.61) reduces to the Pontryagin equations for co-state variables in the case where α is an optimum resource allocation mechanism.[47] However, I show below that, in order to study the evolution of accounting prices under simple resource allocation mechanisms, it is easier to work directly with (A.60).

From (A.60) it also follows that accounting price ratios $(p_{it}/p_{jt}, p_{it'}/p_{it})$ and consumption discount rates (see below) are defined as marginal social rates of substitution between goods. In an economy where the government maximizes social well-being, marginal rates of substitution among goods and services equal their corresponding marginal rates of transformation. As the latter are observable in market economies (e.g. border prices for traded goods in an open economy), accounting prices are frequently defined in terms of marginal rates of transformation among goods and services. However, marginal rates of substitution in imperfect economies do not necessarily equal the corresponding marginal rates of transformation. This is why accounting prices are difficult to estimate in Kakotopia. A distinction needs to be made between the ingredients of social well-being and market observables. Using market observables to infer social well-being can be misleading in imperfect economies. That we may have to be explicit about well-being parameters (e.g. δ and the elasticity of U) in

---

[47] In Dasgupta and Mäler (2000) it was mistakenly claimed that it does so even in imperfect economies. I am most grateful to Geir Asheim for correcting the error in that article and deriving equation (A.61).

order to estimate marginal rates of substitution in imperfect economies is not an argument for pretending that the economies in question are not imperfect after all. In principle it could be hugely misleading to use the theory of optimum control to justify an exclusive interest in market observables.

A.6.6. *Wealth, Genuine Investment, and Sustainable Well-Being*

In Chapter 9 we noted that the notion of sustainable development invites us to seek a measure that would enable us to judge whether an economy's productive base is growing. However, our own analysis relied on an interpretation of sustainability that is based on the maintenence of social well-being, rather than on the maintainance of the productive base. Arguments were offered in Chapter 9 for adopting the following definition:

Definition 5: The economic programme $\{C_t, R_t, K_t)\}_0^\infty$ corresponds to a sustainable development path at t if $dV_t/dt \geq 0$.

Below we see that the requirement that economic development be sustainable implies, and is implied by, the requirement that the economy's productive base be maintained (Propositions 3–5). These results give intellectual support for the definition of sustainability we have adopted here.

Notice that the criterion for sustainability in Definition 5 does not identify a unique economic programme. In principle any number of technologically and ecologically feasible economic programmes could satisfy the criterion. On the other hand, if substitution possibilities among capital assets are severely limited and technological advances are unlikely to occur, it could be that there is no sustainable economic programme open to an economy. Furthermore, even if the government were bent on maximizing social well-being, the chosen pro-gramme would not correspond to a sustainable path if the well-being discount rate, δ, were too high.[48] Also, along an optimum path social well-being could decline for a period and then increase thereafter, in which case the optimum programme would not correspond to a sustainable path locally, but would do so in the long run.[49] Optimality and sustainability are thus different notions. The concept of sustainability helps us to understand better the character of economic programmes, and is particularly useful for judging the performance of imperfect economies.

Definition 6: Genuine investment, I_t, at t is $I_t = \sum_i p_{it} dK_{it}/dt$.

Differentiating (A.57) with respect to t, we have

---

[48] See Example 1 in Section A.4.
[49] Kenneth Arrow has produced an example of an optimum economic programme displaying such a feature.

Proposition 3:

$$dV_t/dt = \partial V_t/\partial t + \sum_i p_{it} dK_{it}/dt.$$

(A.62)

If α is autonomous, then $\partial V_t/\partial t = 0$, and we have

Proposition 4:

$$dV_t/dt = \sum_i p_{it} dK_{it}/dt = I_t.$$

(A.63)

Equation (A.63) states that, if α is autonomous, the rate of change of social well-being equals genuine investment.

Proposition 4 is a local measure of sustainability. Integrating (A.63) yields a non-local measure:

Proposition 5: If α is autonomous, then, for all $T \geq 0$,

$$V_T - V_0 = \sum_i (p_{iT} K_{iT} - p_{i0} K_{i0}) - \int_0^T \left[\sum_i (dp_{i\tau}/d\tau) K_{i\tau} \right] d\tau.$$

(A.64)

Equation (A.64) shows that, in assessing whether or not social well-being has increased between two dates, the capital gains on the assets that have accrued over the interval should be deducted from the difference in wealth between the dates.

Each of Propositions 3, 4, and 5 is an equivalence result. None of them says whether α gives rise to an economic programme along which social well-being is sustained. For example, it may be that an economy is incapable of achieving a sustainable development path, owing to scarcity of resources, limited substitution possibilities among capital assets, or whatever. Or it may be that, although the economy is in principle capable of achieving a sustainable development path, social well-being is unsustainable along the path that has been forecast because of bad government policies. Or it may be that α is optimal, but that, because the well-being discount rate has been chosen to be large, social well-being is not sustained along the optimum economic programme. Or it may be that along an optimum path social well-being declines for a period and then increases thereafter.

Imagine that substitution possibilities are limited, and that the resource allocation mechanism in place is profligate in the use of natural resources. Under these circumstances the quality of life will not be sustainable. At some date in the future accounting prices will assume such values as to make it impossible for genuine investment to be positive. As Proposition 4 shows, social well-being declines when genuine investment is negative.

A.6.7. *What Else Does Genuine Investment Measure?*

Imagine that the capital base at t is not K_t but $K_t + \Delta K_t$, where Δ is an operator signifying a small difference. In the obvious notation,

$$V(\alpha, K_t + \Delta K_t) - V(\alpha, K_t) \approx \int_t^\infty U'(C_\tau) \Delta C_\tau e^{-\delta(\tau - t)} d\tau. \qquad (A.65)$$

Now suppose that at t there is a small change in α, but only for a brief moment, Δt, after which the resource allocation mechanism reverts back to α. We write the increment in the capital base at $t + \Delta t$ consequent upon the brief increase in genuine investment as ΔK_t. So ΔK_t is the consequence of an increase in genuine investment at t and $(K_{t+\Delta t} + \Delta K_t)$ is the resulting capital base at $t + \Delta t$. Let Δt tend to zero. From equation (A.65) we obtain the following.

Proposition 6: Genuine investment measures the present discounted value of the changes to consumption brought about by it.[50]

A.6.8. *Policy Evaluation*

Proposition 6 gives us the tools required to develop a theory of policy evaluation in imperfect economies. Imagine that, even though the government does not optimize, it can bring about small changes to the economy by altering the existing resource allocation mechanism in minor ways. The perturbation in question could be small adjustments to the prevailing structure of taxes for a short while, or it could be minor alterations to the existing set of property rights for a brief period, or it could be a small public investment project. Call any such perturbation a *policy reform*.[51]

Consider as an example an investment project. It can be viewed as a perturbation to the resource allocation mechanism α for a brief period (the lifetime of the project), after which the mechanism reverts back to its earlier form. We consider projects that are small relative to the size of the economy. How should they be evaluated?

For simplicity of exposition, we suppose there is a single output (Y, which serves also as the consumption good), labour (L), a single manufactured capital good (K), and a single extractive natural resource (S). The rate of extraction is

---

[50] Proposition 6 is familiar for economies where the government maximizes social welfare (see Arrow and Kurz, 1970).

[51] Over the years economic evaluation of policy reform in imperfect economies has been discussed by a number of economists (e.g. Meade 1955; Dasgupta, Marglin, and Sen 1972; Mäler 1974; Starrett 1988; Ahmad and Stern 1990; and Dreze and Stern 1990), but they did not develop a formal account for intertemporal economies.

denoted by R. Let the project's lifetime be the period [0, T]. Denote the project's output and inputs at t by the vector $(\Delta Y_t, \Delta L_t, \Delta K_t, \Delta R_t)$.[52]

The project's acceptance would perturb consumption under α. Let the perturbation at t (≥ 0) be $\tilde{\Delta}C_t$. It would affect U_t by the amount $U'(C_t)\tilde{\Delta}C_t$. However, because the perturbation includes all 'general equilibrium effects', it would be tiresome if the project evaluator were required to estimate $\tilde{\Delta}C_t$ for every project that came up for consideration. Accounting prices are useful because they enable the evaluator to estimate $\tilde{\Delta}C_t$ indirectly. Now, it is most unlikely that consumption and investment have the same accounting price in an imperfect economy. So we divide ΔY_t into two parts: changes in consumption and in investment in manufactured capital. Denote them as ΔC_t and $\Delta(dK_t/dt)$, respectively.

U is the unit of account.[53] Let w_t denote the accounting wage rate. Next, let p_t be the accounting price of manufactured capital, q_t the accounting price of the extractive resource input of the project, and λ_t the social cost of borrowing capital (i.e. $\lambda_t = \delta - (dp_t/dt)/p_t$).[54]

From the definition of accounting prices, it follows that

$$\int_0^\infty U'(C_\tau)\tilde{\Delta}C_\tau e^{-\delta\tau} d\tau = \int_0^T (U'(C_\tau)\Delta C_\tau + p_\tau \Delta(dK_\tau/d\tau)$$
$$- w_\tau \Delta L_\tau - \lambda_\tau p_\tau \Delta K_\tau - q_\tau \Delta R_\tau)e^{-\delta\tau} d\tau.$$
$$(A.66)$$

But the RHS of equation (A.66) is the present discounted value of social profits from the project, in utility numeraire. Moreover, $\int_0^\infty U'(C_\tau)\tilde{\Delta}C_\tau e^{-\delta\tau} d\tau = \Delta V(0)$, the latter being the change in social well-being if the project is accepted.

---

[52] If the project has been designed efficiently, we would have:

$\Delta Y_t = (\partial F/\partial K)\Delta K_t + (\partial F/\partial L)\Delta L_t + (\partial F/\partial R)\Delta R_t,$

where F is an aggregate production function $(Y = F(K, L, R))$. The analysis that follows in the text does not require the project to have been designed efficiently. As we are imagining that aggregate labour supply is fixed, ΔL_t used in the project would be the same amount of labour displaced from elsewhere.

[53] Dasgupta, Marglin, and Sen (1972) and Little and Mirrlees (1974), respectively, developed their accounts of social cost–benefit analysis with consumption and government income as numeraires. Which numeraire one chooses is, ultimately, not a matter of principle, but one of practical convenience.

[54] Thus,

$q_t = \int_t^\infty U'(C_\tau)\partial C_\tau/\partial R_\tau e^{-\delta(\tau-t)}d\tau.$

Notice that, if manufactured capital were to depreciate at a constant rate, say γ, the social cost of borrowing capital would be $\lambda_t = \delta + \gamma - (dp_t/dt)/p_t$.

Let $\hat{q}_t$ be the accounting price of the resource *in situ*. At a full-optimum, $p_t\partial F/\partial R_t = q_t = \hat{q}_t$, and $U'(C_t) = p_t$.

We may therefore write (A.66) as

$$\Delta V_0 = \int_0^T (U'(C_\tau)\Delta C_\tau + p_\tau \Delta(dK_t/d\tau)$$
$$- w_\tau \Delta L_\tau - \lambda_\tau p_\tau \Delta K_\tau - q_\tau \Delta R_\tau)e^{-\delta\tau} d\tau. \tag{A.67}$$

Equation (A.67) leads to the well-known criterion for project evaluation.

Proposition 7: A project should be accepted if and only if the present discounted value of its social profits is positive.

Notice the connection between (A.63) and (A.67): they say the same thing. Proposition 7 brings out the connection between wealth as a measure of social well-being (Proposition 4) and the present discounted value of changes in consumption occasioned by a marginal change in genuine investment (Proposition 6). Proposition 7 says that the way to evaluate an investment project is to compare reductions in short-term well-being resulting from the project's investment outlay to the increase in wealth that the reductions help to create. I conclude that both valuation and evaluation involve wealth comparisons. This proves a central proposition in Parts III and IV.

In what follows, unless it is stated otherwise, we assume that α is autonomous.

A.6.9. *The Current-Value Hamiltonian*

The current-value Hamiltonian associated with α is defined as

$$H_t = U(C_t) + \sum_i p_{it}(dK_{it}/dt) = U(C_t) + I_t. \tag{A.68}$$

In the literature on green national accounts, much attention has been paid to the connection between the current-value Hamiltonian and net national product (NNP). In the economy being studied here, NNP at t is

$$\text{NNP}_t = U'(C_t)C_t + \sum_i p_{it}(dK_{it}/dt). \tag{A.69}$$

From (A.68) and (A.69), it follows that, unless U is linear in C, the current-value Hamiltonian is *not* NNP.

But it has been claimed otherwise. For example, M. L. Weitzman (1998: 1583) says:

it is assumed that, in effect, there is just one composite consumption good. It might be calculated as an index number with given price weights, or as a multiple of some fixed basket of goods, or, *more generally, as a cardinal utility-like aggregator function.* The important thing is that the consumption level in period t can always be registered unambiguously by the single number $C(t)$. (emphasis added)

There is a problem with this reasoning. Measuring non-linear utility functions for an entire economy involves estimating a battery of consumer surpluses. The practical appeal of such indices as NNP is that they are linear functions of quantities. We are being asked, however, to abandon practical advantages in order to accommodate a particular interpretation of the Hamiltonian. And we are asked to do it by simply renaming the 'utility of consumption' as 'consumption'. I know of no practical reason why we should do so. In view of Propositions 3 and 4, there are no theoretical advantages, either.[55]

What, then, does the current-value Hamiltonian measure? To answer this, we use (A.63) and (A.68) to obtain

$$\int_t^\infty H_\tau e^{-\delta(\tau-t)} d\tau = \int_t^\infty (U(C_\tau) + I_\tau) e^{-\delta(\tau-t)} d\tau$$

$$= V_t + \int_t^\infty I_\tau e^{-\delta(\tau-t)} d\tau$$

$$= V_t + \int_t^\infty (dV_\tau/d\tau) e^{-\delta(\tau-t)} d\tau. \qquad (A.70)$$

Integrating (A.70) by parts yields

$$\int_t^\infty H_\tau e^{-\delta(\tau-t)} d\tau = \int_t^\infty \delta V_\tau e^{-\delta(\tau-t)} d\tau. \qquad (A.71)$$

Since (A.71) holds for all t, we conclude that

$$H_t = \delta V_t. \qquad (A.72)$$

We have therefore proved the following proposition.

---

[55] If U is homogeneous of degree h $(0 < h < 1)$, one can construct a measure that looks like NNP and is proportional to the Hamiltonian. However, it involves using prices that do not reflect social scarcity values. To see how this can be done, notice that, for the case in hand, (A.68) can be written as

$$H_t \equiv hU'(C_t)C_t + \sum_i (p_{it} dK_{it}/dt).$$

Define $p_{it}^* = p_{it}/h$. Then

$$NNP_t = H_t/h \equiv U'(C_t)C_t + \sum_i (p_{it}^* dK_{it}/dt).$$

Notice though that in this expression the prices of investment goods relative to those of consumption goods do not reflect social scarcity values. This is why the result has no merit.

Proposition 8: The current-value Hamiltonian is the return on social well-being.

Now, $\delta\left[\int_t^\infty e^{-\delta(\tau-t)}d\tau\right] = 1$. So (A.72) can be written as

$$H_t = H_t\left[\delta\left(\int_t^\infty e^{-\delta(\tau-t)}d\tau\right)\right] = \delta\left[\int_t^\infty H_t e^{-\delta(\tau-t)}d\tau\right] = \delta V_t,$$

from which we have

$$H_t\left[\int_t^\infty e^{-\delta(\tau-t)}d\tau\right] = \int_t^\infty H_t e^{-\delta(\tau-t)}d\tau = V_t$$

$$\equiv \int_t^\infty U(C_\tau)e^{-\delta(\tau-t)}d\tau. \tag{A.73}$$

Equation (A.73) can be summarized as follows.

Proposition 9: The current-value Hamiltonian of an economic programme equals the constant-equivalent flow of well-being to which the programme gives rise.[56]

The version of this result that was proved by Weitzman (1976) was based on the assumption that U is linear. Since the Hamiltonian is NNP in such an economy, Weitzman argued that NNP is the constant-equivalent U. This interpretation of NNP is in wide usage today.

But a linear U is ethically flawed: it is insensitive to distributional issues. Furthermore, large bodies of evidence concerning household saving behaviour are at odds with linear Us. In response to this criticism, Weitzman (2000) has argued that a simple recalibration of U enables one to interpret NNP as the constant-equivalent rate of well-being. Recall that the ethical ordering of economic programmes represented by V is invariant under positive affine transformations of U. Thus, if U is a well-being function, one could as well use $(aU + b)$, where a and b are constants and $a > 0$. This means that there are two degrees of freedom when U is calibrated. Let us continue to assume that $U'(C) > 0$ and $U''(C) < 0$. Let α be the resource allocation mechanism and C_0 the initial rate of aggregate consumption resulting from it. Choose a and b so that $aU'(C_0) = 1$ and $(aU(C_0)+b) = C_0$. The idea therefore is so to calibrate U that initial well-being equals initial consumption (expressed in well-being numeraire) and initial marginal well-being equals one. This makes the Hamiltonian at $t = 0$ equal to NNP at $t = 0$. It follows from equation (A.68) that, at $t = 0$, NNP can indeed be interpreted as the constant-equivalent well-being associated with α.

[56] This generalizes Weitzman (1976), who proved the proposition for optimum economic programmes.

But there is a problem with this move, which makes it useless. Note that a high or low value of U in itself carries no significance (a and b are freely choosable, remember). So, to be told that today's NNP, expressed in well-being numeraire, is high (or low) because the constant-equivalent U is high (or low) in itself has no meaning. What *would* have meaning are *comparisons* of U (equivalently, V); across time, or space, or groups of people, or whatever. It would certainly be informative if we could be told, say, that because NNP is expected to be greater tomorrow than it is today, tomorrow's constant-equivalent U can be expected to be greater than what it is today. If we were to be told that, we would be able to infer that social well-being, V, tomorrow should be expected to be higher than what it is today. Unfortunately, we cannot in general be told that. The reason is that once U has been calibrated at $t = 0$, it must not be recalibrated ever again. To do so would be to alter the underlying ethical ordering of economic programmes, which would render intertemporal comparisons of V meaningless. But, unless U were to be constant over time, it would have to be recalibrated continuously if Weitzman's interpretation of NNP were to be preserved at each date. In short, Proposition 9 offers no normative interpretation of NNP.

A.6.10. *The Normative Significance of NNP*

There is another way to state Proposition 4. Equation (A.69) implies the following.

Proposition 10: $dV_t/dt \geq 0$ *if and only if* $U'(C_t)C_t \leq NNP_t$.

NNP is the sum of genuine investment and the accounting values of all consumption services (including direct consumption services from the natural environment and 'negative' consumptions arising from pollution (Nordhaus and Tobin 1972)). Proposition 10 says that, if social well-being is to increase, the value of consumption services must not exceed NNP. This is the sense in which NNP has normative significance.[57]

An alternative way to characterize sustainable development is to use (A.68), (A.72), and Proposition 8 to obtain the following proposition.

---

[57] Lindahl (1934), Hicks (1940), and Samuelson (1961). Dasgupta and Mäler (1991, 2000) and Mäler (1991) proved that the contribution that investment projects make to NNP (as defined in equation (A.68)) is the appropriate project evaluation criterion, *provided that projects are small and are of the briefest duration*. The intuition underlying the result is that accounting prices do not change if the period is short. But as investment projects are not of the briefest of durations, the result is of no practical interest. It is an easy matter to prove more generally that, if relative prices remain constant, NNP is an index of social well-being. So NNP is a measure of social well-being only when an economy is in a steady state.

Proposition 11: $dV_t/dt \geq 0$ *if and only if the value of net changes in the flow of consumption services plus the change in the value of net investment is positive.*[58]

A.6.11. *Numeraire*

So far we have taken current well-being (U) to be the unit of account. In applied welfare economics, however, it has been found useful to express benefits and costs in terms of current consumption. It will pay to review the way the theory being developed here can be recast in consumption numeraire. For simplicity of exposition, assume that there is a single commodity, that is, an all-purpose durable good that can be consumed or reinvested for its own accumulation. Assume too that current well-being is iso-elastic and that the elasticity of marginal well-being is η. Let p_t be the accounting price of the asset in well-being numeraire. Define $\bar{p}_t$ to be the accounting price of the asset in consumption numeraire. Then

$$\bar{p}_t = p_t/U'(C_t).$$

It follows that

$$(d\bar{p}_t/dt)/\bar{p}_t = (dp_t/dt)/p_t + \eta(dC_t/dt)/C_t. \tag{A.74}$$

Let ρ_t be the social rate of discount in consumption numeraire. In the text (Section 11.2), ρ_t was referred to as the consumption rate of interest. From (A.56) we have[59]

$$\rho_t = \delta + \eta(dC_t/dt)/C_t. \tag{A.75}$$

Using (A.75) in (A.74), we obtain the relationship between the asset's prices in the two units of account:[60]

$$(d\bar{p}_t/dt)/\bar{p}_t = (dp_t/dt)/p_t + \rho_t - \delta. \tag{A.76}$$

---

[58] This proposition is dependent on the numeraire. Asheim and Weitzman (2001) have shown that, if one were to use a Divisia consumption price index to estimate NNP in real prices, NNP can be used as a measure to check whether social well-being is sustainable along a given programme. The Divisia index is a construct that aggregates both the price and its rate of change in such a way as to make Proposition 11 read as saying that $dV_t/dt \geq 0$ if and only if the newly constructed NNP is non-declining.

[59] To prove equation (A.75), notice that, by definition, ρ_t satisfies the equation

$$U'(C_t) \exp(-\delta t) = U'(C_0) \exp\left(-\int_0^t (\rho_\tau) d\tau\right).$$

If we differentiate both sides of the above equation with respect to t, (A.75) follows.

[60] Notice that in imperfect economies δ and η may be unobservable. See Section A.6.5.

A.6.12. *Intragenerational Distribution*

The distribution of well-being within a generation has been ignored so far. Theoretically it is not difficult to include this in our account. If there are N people in each generation and person j consumes C_j, her well-being would be $U(C_j)$.[61] A simple way to express distributional considerations within each generation is to apply a concave transformation on U. The resulting function has greater curvature. It is therefore more sensitive to distributional concerns. So let G be a strictly concave, increasing function. We may then express intragenerational well-being as $\sum_j G(U(C_j))$. To be sure, some people would be well off, some others not so well off, while still others would be badly off. The formulation ensures that, at the margin, the well-being of someone who is badly off is awarded greater weight than that of someone who is well off. And so forth.

The social worth of consumption services (C) depends on who gets what. To accommodate this idea, we have to enlarge the set of commodities so as to distinguish, at the margin, a good consumed or supplied by one person from that same good consumed or supplied by another. Thus, in computing wealth, a piece of clothing worn by a poor person should be regarded as a different commodity from that same type of clothing worn by someone who is rich. With this reinterpretation of goods and services, the results we have obtained continue to hold.

A.7. ILLUSTRATION 1: A CONVEX ECONOMY

We begin illustrating the theory developed in the previous section with an example. As in Section A.1, imagine that there is an all-purpose durable good, whose stock at t is K_t. The good can be consumed or reinvested for its own accumulation. There are no other assets. Write output (GNP) as Y. Technology is linear; so $Y = \mu K$, where $\mu > 0$. Thus, μ is the output–wealth ratio. GNP at t is $Y_t = \mu K_t$.

Imagine that a constant proportion of GNP is saved at each moment. There is no presumption though that the saving rate is optimum; rather, it is a behavioural characteristic of consumers, reflecting their response to an imperfect credit market. Other than this imperfection, the economy is assumed to function well. At each moment expectations are fulfilled and all markets other than the credit market clear. This defines the resource allocation mechanism, α. Clearly, α is autonomous. We now characterize α explicitly.

[61] Person-specific factors (e.g. age, health status, gender) can be included. This is routinely done in applied economics.

Let the saving ratio be s ($0 < s < 1$). Write aggregate consumption as C_t. Therefore,

$$C_t = (1 - s)Y_t = (1 - s)\mu K_t. \tag{A.77}$$

Capital is assumed to depreciate at a constant rate γ (>0). Genuine investment is therefore,

$$dK_t/dt = (s\mu - \gamma)K_t. \tag{A.78}$$

K_0 is the initial capital stock. The economy grows if $s\mu > \gamma$, and shrinks if $s\mu < \gamma$. To obtain a feel for orders of magnitude, suppose $\gamma = 0.05$ and $\mu = 0.25$. The economy grows if $s > 0.2$, and shrinks if $s < 0.2$.

Integrating (A.78), we obtain

$$K_\tau = K_t e^{(s\mu - \gamma)(\tau - t)}, \qquad \tau \geq t \geq 0, \tag{A.79}$$

from which it follows that,

$$C_\tau = (1 - s)\mu K_\tau = (1 - s)\mu K_t e^{(s\mu - \gamma)(\tau - t)}, \qquad \tau \geq t \geq 0. \tag{A.80}$$

If the capital stock were chosen as numeraire, wealth would be K_t, and NNP would be $(\mu - \gamma)K_t$. Each of wealth, GNP, NNP, consumption, and genuine investment expands at the exponential rate $(s\mu - \gamma)$ if $s\mu > \gamma$, and contracts at the exponential rate $(\gamma - s\mu)$ if $s\mu < \gamma$. I have introduced capital depreciation into the example so as to provide a whiff (albeit an artificial whiff) of a key idea—that, even if consumption is less than GNP, wealth declines when genuine investment is negative. Wealth declines when consumption exceeds NNP (Proposition 10).

Current well-being is $U(C_t)$. Consider the iso-elastic form:

$$U(C) = -C^{-(\eta-1)}, \qquad \eta > 1. \tag{A.81}$$

δ is the social rate of discount if utility is numeraire. Let ρ_t be the social rate of discount if consumption is the unit of account. It follows that

$$\rho_t = \delta + \eta(dC_t/dt)/C_t = \delta + \eta(s\mu - \gamma). \tag{A.82}$$

The sign of ρ_t depends upon α. ρ_t can be negative. To see why, suppose the unit of time is a year, $\delta = 0.03$, $\gamma = 0.04$, $s = 0.10$, $\eta = 2$, and $\mu = 0.20$. Then $\eta(dC_t/dt)/C_t = -0.04$ per year, and (A.82) says that $\rho_t = -0.01$ per year.[62]

---

[62] These are not fanciful figures. Per capita consumption in a number of countries in sub-Saharan Africa declined over the past three decades at as high a rate as 1% per year, implying that, for small values of δ, the consumption rate of interest was negative.

Social well-being at t is

$$V_t = \int_t^\infty U(C_\tau)e^{-\delta(\tau-t)}d\tau. \tag{A.83}$$

Using (A.80) and (A.81) in (A.83), we have

$$V_t = -[(1-s)\mu K_t]^{-(\eta-1)} \int_t^\infty e^{-[(\eta-1)(s\mu-\gamma)+\delta](\tau-t)}d\tau,$$

or, assuming that $(\eta-1)(s\mu-\gamma)+\delta > 0$,

$$V_t = -[(1-s)\mu K_t]^{-(\eta-1)}/[(\eta-1)(s\mu-\gamma)+\delta]. \tag{A.84}$$

Notice that V is differentiable in K everywhere. Moreover, $\partial V_t/\partial t = 0$. Equations (A.79) and (A.84) confirm Proposition 4.

We turn now to accounting prices and consider in turn two numeraires in which to conduct the measurements.

A.7.1. *Utility Numeraire*

Begin by taking utility to be numeraire. Let p_t be the accounting price of capital. Now

$$p_t \equiv \partial V_t/\partial K_t = \int_t^\infty U'(C_\tau)(\partial C_\tau/\partial K_t)e^{-\delta(\tau-t)}d\tau. \tag{A.85}$$

Using (A.84) in (A.85), we have

$$p_t = (\eta-1)[(1-s)\mu]^{-(\eta-1)}K_t^{-\eta}/[(\eta-1)(s\mu-\gamma)+\delta]. \tag{A.86}$$

Notice that p_t is a declining function of μ. Given that U is bounded above but unbounded below (A.81), this is what one would expect: if the rate of return on investment is high, the accounting price of a unit of capital is low, other things being the same.[63]

Using (A.79), (A.80), (A.84), and (A.85), it can be shown that $p_t \neq U'(C_t)$, except when $s = (\mu + (\eta-1)\gamma - \delta)/\mu\eta$. Let s^* be the optimum saving rate. From (A.84) we find that

$$s^* = (\mu + (\eta-1)\gamma - \delta)/\mu\eta. \tag{A.87}$$

$p_t < U'(C_t)$ if $s > s^*$, which means there is excessive saving. Conversely, $p_t > U'(C_t)$ if $s < s^*$, which means there is excessive consumption.

---

[63] We will find this intuition useful in Section A.18, when we introduce uncertainty in μ.

A.7.2. *Consumption Numeraire*

Write $\bar{p}_t = p_t/U'(C_t)$. $\hspace{4cm}$ (A.88)

Using (A.60) in (A.88) yields

$$\bar{p}_t = \int_t^\infty [U'(C_\tau)/U'(C_t)](\partial C_\tau/\partial K_t)e^{-\delta(\tau-t)}d\tau. \qquad (A.89)$$

Now use (A.80), (A.81), and (A.82) to obtain

$$\bar{p}_t = \int_t^\infty (1-s)\mu e^{[-\rho+(s\mu-\gamma)](\tau-t)}d\tau, \qquad (A.90)$$

where $\rho = \delta + \eta(s\mu - \gamma)$.
Equation (A.90) simplifies to

$$\bar{p}_t = (1-s)\mu/[\rho - (s\mu - \gamma)]. \qquad (A.91)$$

Observe that $\bar{p}_t > 1$ (resp. < 1) if $s < s^*$ (resp. $> s^*$).[64]

In order to obtain a sense of orders of magnitude, suppose $\eta = 2$, $\mu = 0.20$, $\gamma = 0.05$, and $\delta = 0$. From (A.87) we have $s^* = 0.625$. Now imagine that $s = 0.40$. (By Ramsey's criterion, this is undersaving!) Using (A.82), we have $\rho = 0.06$ per unit of time. So (A.91) reduces to $\bar{p}_t = 4$. In other words, a saving rate that is approximately 30 per cent short of the optimum corresponds to a high figure for the accounting price of investment: investment should be valued at four times consumption.

Although intergenerational equity is nearly always discussed in terms of the rate at which future well-being is discounted (e.g. Portney and Weyant 1999), equity would be more appropriately discussed in terms of the curvature of U. Let the unit of time be a year. Suppose $\gamma = 0$, $\delta = 0.02$, and $\mu = 0.32$. Consider two alternative values of η: 25 and 50. Routine calculations show that $s^* = 0.038$ if $\eta = 25$ and $s^* = 0.019$ if $\eta = 50$. Intergenerational equity in both consumption and well-being (the latter is a concave function of the former) can be increased indefinitely by making η increasingly larger: C_t becomes 'flatter' as η is increased. In the limit, as η goes to infinity, s^* tends to γ/μ (A.87), which reflects the Rawlsian maxi-min consumption as applied to the intergenerational context.[65]

---

[64] A special case of equation (A.88) appears in Dasgupta, Marglin, and Sen (1972). However, unlike the present work, the earlier publication did not provide a rigorous welfare economic theory for imperfect economies.

[65] Solow (1974a) and Hartwick (1977) are the key articles on this limiting case.

A.8. ILLUSTRATION 2: A NON-CONVEX ECOSYSTEM

The Ramsey–Solow economy discussed above is convex. In this section we confirm that the theory presented in Section A.6 can be applied to non-convex economies. We do this by returning to the model of a shallow freshwater lake.

Let K_t be the stock of phosphorus in the water column of the lake and C_t the inflow of phosphorus from neighbouring farms. U is assumed to be of the form

$$U(C_t, K_t) = \log C_t - hK_t^2, \qquad h > 0$$

Social well-being is therefore,

$$V(K_t) = \int_t^{\infty} U(C_\tau, K_\tau) e^{-\delta(\tau - t)} d\tau. \tag{A.92}$$

We review in turn two resource allocation mechanisms—constant phosphorus flow and optimum phosphorus flow—which were studied in Sections A.4 and A.5.

A.8.1. *Constant Phosphorus Inflow*

Consider the case where the resource allocation mechanism for phosphorus inflow is such that $C_t = C$, a constant. Equation (A.46) gives the dynamics of phosphorus in the lake. We rewrite it here as

$$dK_t/dt = C + bK_t^2/(1 + K_t^2) - \gamma K_t. \tag{A.93}$$

It was shown in Section A.4 that, for a range of parameter values $C, b,$ and γ, the curves $[C + bK^2/(1 + K^2)]$ and γK intersect at three points (Figure A.2). The upper and lower intersects, K_3 and K_1, are stable stationary points of equation (A.93), whereas the intermediate intersect, K_2, is unstable. Thus, K_2 is the unique separatrix of the dynamical system. On using (A.93), the resource allocation mechanism α, governing the lake's quality, can be obtained from the equation

$$dK_\tau/d\tau = C + bK_\tau^2/(1 + K_\tau^2) - \gamma K_\tau, \qquad \tau \geq t \geq 0, \ K_0 \text{ given.} \tag{A.94}$$

α is autonomous and time consistent. One can confirm that $V(K)$ is differentiable in K everywhere except K_2. It is simple to confirm as well that $V(K)$ is discontinuous at K_2. However, it possesses both right- and left-hand derivatives at K_2. Therefore we can define the accounting price of the lake's quality to be $p(K) = \partial V/\partial K$ at all $K \neq K_2$, and we can apply the theory locally for the purposes of project evaluation and sustainability assessment. It should be noted that, because phosphorus is a pollutant in the lake, $p(K) < 0.$[66]

---

[66] Note too that, because the resource allocation mechanism is imperfect, $-U_C \neq \partial V/\partial S$.

A.8.2. *Optimum Phosphorus Inflow*

The resource allocation mechanism defined by (A.94) reflects an imperfect economy. In Section A.5 we studied the optimum resource allocation mechanism. There we noted that there is a range of values of δ, b, h, and γ for which the optimality conditions have three stationary solutions. Two of them (call them K_1 and K_3, where $K_1 < K_3$) are saddle points, while the intermediate point (call it K_2) is a spiral node (it is unstable).[67] We noted as well that there is a value of phosphorus stock, $\bar{K}$, such that, if $K_0 > \bar{K}$, the optimum programme asymptotes to K_3, but that, if $K_0 < \bar{K}$, it asymptotes to K_1. One can confirm that, if, by fluke, $K_0 = \bar{K}$, there are two equally desirable optimal programmes, one of which asymptotes to K_1, while the other asymptotes to K_3. This last property can be shown to imply that $V(K)$, although not differentiable at $\bar{K}$, is continuous at $\bar{K}$ and possesses both left and right derivatives. $\bar{K}$ is an endogenously determined separatrix. $\bar{K}$ is the Skiba point.

Let p be the accounting price of phosphorus. Since the optimum resource allocation mechanism is autonomous, $p = p(K)$. Let $V(K)$ be the value function. Then

$$p(K) = \partial V/\partial K \ (<0), \quad K \neq \bar{K}. \tag{A.95}$$

Denoting by $[p(K)]_{\bar{K}-0}$ (resp., $[p(K)]_{\bar{K}+0}$) the limit of $p(K)$ as K tends to $\bar{K}$ from the left (resp., right), and similarly for $[\partial V/\partial K]_{\bar{K}-0}$ and $[\partial V/\partial K]_{\bar{K}+0}$, it can be shown that $[p(K)]_{\bar{K}-0} = [\partial V/\partial K]_{\bar{K}-0}$ and $[p(K)]_{\bar{K}+0} = [\partial V/\partial K]_{\bar{K}+0}$. The theory presented in Section A.6 is thus applicable to the optimum resource allocation mechanism of this particular non-convex economy.

Having illustrated the theory by means of three examples, we now proceed to obtain rules for estimating accounting prices. We do this by focusing on specific categories of capital assets and several well-known institutional imperfections.

A.9. EXHAUSTIBLE RESOURCES: A CLOSED ECONOMY

Accounting prices of exhaustible resources when depletion rates are optimal have been much studied (e.g. Dasgupta and Heal 1979; see below). What is the structure of their accounting prices when resources are instead common pools?

Two property-rights regimes suggest themselves: open access and restricted entry. They in turn need to be compared to an optimum regime. It is simplest if we avoid a complete capital model. So we resort to a partial equilibrium world: income effects are assumed to be negligible. Let R_t be the quantity extracted at t.

---

[67] For values of δ, b, h, and γ not in that range, the optimality conditions have a single stationary solution.

Income is the numeraire. Let $U(R)$ be the area under the demand curve below R. So $U'(R)$ is the market demand function. U is assumed to be an increasing and strictly concave function of R for positive values of R. We take the consumption rate of interest to be an exogenously given constant, ρ. Let S_t be the stock. Then,

$$dS_t/dt = -R_t. \tag{A.96}$$

A.9.1. *The Optimum Regime*

In order to construct a benchmark against which imperfect economies can be evaluated, we first study an optimizing economy. Assume that extraction is costless. (Constant unit extraction cost can be introduced easily.) Social well-being at t is then

$$V_t = \int_t^\infty U(R_\tau)e^{-\rho(\tau-t)}d\tau. \tag{A.97}$$

Let p_t^* denote the accounting price of the resource underground. It is alternatively called the Hotelling rent, or the optimum depletion charge per unit extracted. We know that

$$dp_t^*/dt = \rho p_t^*. \tag{A.98}$$

This is the Hotelling Rule. It is the Pontryagin equation governing the co-state variable, p_t^*. Moreover, optimum extraction, R_t^*, must satisfy the condition

$$U'(R_t) = p_t^*. \tag{A.99}$$

Assume that $U'(R)$ is iso-elastic:

$$U(R) = -R^{-(\eta-1)}, \qquad \eta > 1. \tag{A.100}$$

Then

$$R_t^* = (\rho/\eta)S_0 e^{-\rho t/\eta}. \tag{A.101}$$

We next consider the two imperfect regimes.

A.9.2. *Restricted Entry*

Assume that there are N identical farmers ($i, j = 1, 2, \ldots, N$) drawing from an unrechargeable aquifer. Extraction is costless. We model the situation in the following way.[68]

---

[68] McKelvey (1980) has studied a special case of the model of diffusion developed below.

At t, farmer i owns a pool of size S_{it}. Each pool is separated from every other pool by a porous barrier. Water percolates from the pool that is larger to the one that is smaller. Let λ_{ij} (>0) be the rate at which water diffuses from pool i to pool j. We assume that $\lambda_{ij} = \lambda_{ji}$. Denote by R_{it} the rate at which farmer i draws from his pool. There are then N depletion equations:

$$dS_{it}/dt = \sum_{N-i}[\lambda_{ji}(S_{jt} - S_{it})] - R_{it}, \qquad (A.102)$$

where $\sum_{N-i}$ denotes summation over all j other than i.

The payoff function for farmer i at time t is

$$\int_t^\infty U(R_{i\tau})e^{-\rho(\tau-t)}d\tau. \qquad (A.103)$$

Farmers play non-cooperatively. This means that a distinction needs to be drawn between a farmer's personal accounting price for water and the social accounting price of water. The latter is what we wish to estimate, but to do so we have first to estimate the former. For tractablity, we study an open-loop solution, by which I mean that farmers are assumed to be naive: when computing his own optimum extraction rates, each takes the others' extraction rates as given.

Let p_{it} be the (spot) personal accounting price of a unit of i's own resource pool. The present-value Hamiltonian for i's optimization problem would then be

$$H_0 = U(R_{it})e^{-\rho t} + p_{it}\left[\sum_{N-i}(\lambda_{ji}(S_{jt} - S_{it})) - R_{it}\right]e^{-\rho t}. \qquad (A.104)$$

It follows from (A.104) that the co-state variable, p_{it}, obeys the equation

$$dp_{it}/dt = \left[\rho + \sum_{N-i}(\lambda_{ji})\right]p_{it}. \qquad (A.105)$$

For notational simplicity, assume now that $\lambda_{ij} = \lambda$ for all i, j. Then (A.105) reduces to

$$dp_{it}/dt = [\rho + (N-1)\lambda]p_{it}. \qquad (A.106)$$

Write $[\rho + (N-1)\lambda] \equiv \beta$. We conclude that the rush to extract because of insecure property rights amounts to each extractor using an implicit discount rate, β, which is in excess of the social discount rate, ρ.[69]

---

[69] In the limit, as λ tends to infinity, β tends to infinity, implying that depletion is instantaneous.

Assume now that the elasticity of demand is a constant, $\eta \, (>1)$. Using (A.101) and (A.106), we conclude that the extraction rate from the common pool is

$$R_\tau = (\beta/\eta)S_t e^{-\beta(\tau-t)/\eta}, \qquad \tau \geq t. \tag{A.107}$$

We now proceed to derive the (social) accounting price of the aquifer. In order to have a meaningful problem, we take it that $\beta/\eta > \beta - \rho$ (see below).

Let p_t be the resource's (social) accounting price. We know that $p = \partial V_t/\partial S_t$. Using (A.107), it follows that

$$p_t = \int_t^\infty U'(R_\tau)[\partial R_\tau/\partial S_t)]e^{-\rho(\tau-t)}d\tau. \tag{A.108}$$

Write $\bar{p}_t = p_t/U'(R_t)$. Then (A.107)–(A.108) imply

$$\bar{p}_t = (\beta/\eta) \int_t^\infty e^{-(\rho-\beta(\eta-1)/\eta)(\tau-t)}d\tau,$$

or

$$\bar{p}_t = \beta/[\beta - \eta(\beta - \rho)] > 1. \tag{A.109}$$

(Notice that $\bar{p}_t = 1$ if $\beta = \rho$.)

As a numerical illustration, consider the case where $\rho = 0.06$, $\beta = 0.10$, and $\eta = 2$. In this case, $\bar{p}_t = 5$, which reflects considerable imperfection in the resource allocation mechanism: the resource's accounting price is five times its market price.

A.9.3. *Open Access*

We next study an open-access pool. Assume therefore that the aquifer is homogeneous. For the problem to be meaningful, we assume too that extraction is costly. For simplicity, let the unit extraction cost be a constant $k \, (>0)$. Under open access, Hotelling rents are dissipated completely. Therefore, the equilibrium extraction rate, R_t, is the solution of the equation

$$U'(R_t) = k. \tag{A.110}$$

Equation (A.110) confirms that, irrespective of the size of the reserve, there is excessive extraction. Let $\bar{R}$ be the solution of (A.110). We then have

$$dS_t/dt = -\bar{R}.$$

Reserves remain positive for a period $T = S/\bar{R}$. Let us normalize well-being by setting $U(0) = 0$. It follows that

$$V_t = \int_t^{(t+S(t)/\bar{R})} [U(\bar{R}) - k\bar{R}]e^{-\rho(\tau-t)}d\tau. \tag{A.111}$$

Let p_t be the accounting price of the unextracted resource. Then

$$p_t = \partial V_t/\partial S_t = [(U(\bar{R}) - k\bar{R})/\bar{R}]e^{-\rho S_t/\bar{R}} > 0. \tag{A.112}$$

Write $\bar{p}_t = p_t/U'(\bar{R})$, which is the ratio of the accounting price to unit extraction cost. Then, from (A.111)–(A.112),

$$\bar{p}_t = [(U(\bar{R}) - k\bar{R})/k\bar{R}]e^{-\rho S_t/\bar{R}} > 0. \tag{A.113}$$

Equation (A.113) resembles a formula proposed by El Serafy (1989) for estimating depletion charges.[70] The charge is positive because an extra unit of water in the aquifer would extend the period of extraction. Notice that $\bar{p}_t$ is bounded above by the ratio of the Marshallian consumer surplus to total extraction cost. Furthermore, it increases as the aquifer is depleted and attains its upper bound at the date at which the pool is exhausted. If reserves are large, $\bar{p}_t$ is small, and free access involves no great loss—a familiar result.

What are plausible orders of magnitude? Consider the linear demand function. Assume therefore that

$$U(R) = aR - bR^2, \qquad a > k \text{ and } b > 0. \tag{A.114}$$

From (A.110) and (A.114),

$$\bar{R} = (a - k)/2b. \tag{A.115}$$

Substituting (A.114) and (A.115) in equation (A.113),

$$\bar{p}(t) = [(a - k)/2k]e^{-2b\rho S_t/(a-k)}. \tag{A.116}$$

Equation (A.116) says that

$$\bar{p} \geq 1 \text{ iff } \rho S \leq [(a - k)/2b]\ln[(a - k)/2k].$$

Equation (A.116) expresses $\bar{p}$ in terms of the parameters of the model. Suppose, for example, that $\rho = 0.02$ per year, $S/\bar{R} = 100$ years (i.e. at the current rate of extraction, the aquifer will be exhausted in 100 years), $(a - k)/2k = 20$ (e.g. $k = \$0.50$ and $(a - k) = \$20$). Then $\bar{p} = 20e^{-2} \approx 7$. We should conclude that the value to be attributed to water at the margin is high (about seven times extraction cost). As the date of exhaustion gets nearer, the accounting price rises to its upper bound, 20.

---

[70] See also Hartwick and Hageman (1993) for a fine discussion that links El Serafy's formula to Hicks's formulation of the concept of national income (Hicks 1942).

A.10. EXPLORATIONS AND DISCOVERIES

How should one account for expenditure on explorations of new deposits? Let the rate at which new reserves are discovered be denoted by N. We assume that N is an increasing function of current expenditure on explorations (E) and the accumulated expenditure on explorations (M), but is a declining function of accumulated extraction (Z). Let R_t be the extraction rate and let the discovery function be $N(E_t, M_t, Z_t)$, where

$$dM_t/dt = E_t, \qquad \qquad \text{(A.117)}$$

$$dZ_t/dt = R_t. \qquad \qquad \text{(A.118)}$$

Suppose there is one manufactured capital good (K) and an exhaustible natural resource (S). In the familiar notation, $Y = F(K, R)$ is taken to be the aggregate production function, where Y is GNP. The remaining equations of motion are

$$dK_t/dt = F(K_t, R_t) - C_t - E_t. \qquad \qquad \text{(A.119)}$$

$$dS_t/dt = N(E_t, M_t, Z_t) - R_t. \qquad \qquad \text{(A.120)}$$

The model has four capital assets: $K, S, M,$ and Z. Their accounting prices are denoted by p_K, p_S, p_M, and p_Z, respectively. Social well-being is given by equation (A.11). From Proposition 4, we have

$$dV_t/dt = p_K(F(K_t, R_t) - C_t - E_t) + p_S(N(E_t, M_t, Z_t) - R_t) + p_M E_t + p_Z R_t. \qquad \qquad \text{(A.121)}$$

There are two cases to consider.

(A) Assume that $\partial N/\partial M = 0$ (implying that $p_M = 0$) and $\partial N/\partial Z < 0$ (implying that $p_Z < 0$). Even in this case, genuine investment is not the sum of investment in manufactured capital and changes in proven reserves ($N_t - R_t$). This is because new reserves are valued differently from existing reserves. Note too that exploration costs should not be regarded as investment.

Consider now the special case where the mining industry optimizes.[71] Then $p_K = p_S \partial N/\partial E$. If, in addition, $p_S N_t$ can be approximated by $p_K E_t$, we would conclude from the RHS of (A.121) that discoveries of new reserves should be excluded from genuine investment, but that exploration costs should be regarded as part of that investment.

(B) Suppose $\partial N/\partial M > 0$. If the industry optimizes, we have $p_K = p_M + p_S \partial N/\partial E$, and so $p_K > p_M$. It follows that genuine investment should now

---

[71] That the industry optimizes does not mean that the economy is following an optimum programme.

include not only new discoveries and investment in manufactured capital (as in Case A), but also exploration costs, using an accounting price that is less than that of manufactured capital.

A.11. FORESTS AND TREES

As stocks, forests offer a multitude of services. Here we focus on forests as a source of timber. Hamilton and Clemens (1999) regard the accounting value of forest depletion to be the stumpage value (price minus logging costs) of the quantity of commercial timber and fuelwood harvested in excess of natural regeneration rates. This is an awkward move, since the authors do not say what is intended to happen to the land being deforested. For example, if the deforested land is converted into an urban sprawl, the new investment in the sprawl would be recorded in conventional accounting statistics.[72] But if it is intended to be transformed into farmland, matters would be different: the social worth of the land as a farm should be included as an addition to the economy's stock of capital assets. In what follows, I consider the simple case where the area is predicted to remain a forest.

I continue to suppose that income effects are negligible. Let the price of timber, in consumption numeraire, be unity and let ρ (assumed constant) be the social rate of discount. Holding all other assets constant, if B_t is the total forest land at t, we may express social well-being as $V(B_t)$. The accounting price of forest land is then $\partial V_t / \partial B_t$, which we write as p_t.

In the economics of forestry it has been common to assume that the growth function of a tree's biomass is concave. Denoting the biomass of a tree by S, it is typically assumed that S's growth function is quadratic. If trees are not harvested, biomass accumulates as

$$dS_t/dt = F(S_t) = aS_t - bS_t^2, \qquad a, b > 0, \text{ and } S_0 > 0. \tag{A.122}$$

Equation (A.122) possesses two stationary points: $K = 0$ and $K = a/b$. The former is unstable, while the latter is stable. The system therefore possesses a single basin of attraction. Starting with a seedling, a tree's biomass grows as a logistic function. Imagine now that logging is costless. It is then a simple matter to arrive at the famous Faustmann Rule for the age at which a synchronized forest should be felled for its timber and then reseeded immediately (see below). Underlying Faustmann's Rule is the assumption that a forest is valuable only for

---

[72] It should be noted though that the value of urban land would be more than just the new investment: there is a contribution to the value (which could be of either sign) arising from changes in population density—both in the newly developed property and in the places of origin of those who migrate to this area.

its timber, which means that tree biomass has no direct worth (say, for preserving biodiversity). Underlying the rule is another hidden assumption, which is that a tree cannot be trimmed continuously, but must be cut once and for all. This is a non-convexity, and it means that timber is harvested at a tree site periodically, not continuously.[73]

Consider a unit of land capable of supporting a single tree and its possible successors. If the land is virgin, if a seed is planted at $t = 0$, if $F(T)$ is the timber yield of a tree aged T, and if T is the rotation cycle, then the present discounted value of the land as a tree-bearer is

$$p_0(T) = F(T)e^{-\rho T}/(1 - e^{-\rho T}). \tag{A.123}$$

As $F(T)$ is logistic, it is a convex–concave function. Faustmann's Rule is the value of T that maximizes $p_0(T)$.

Suppose instead that at $t = 0$ the piece of land in question houses a tree aged τ. What is the value of the land?

If the cycle is expected to be maintained, we have

$$p_0 = F(T)e^{-\rho(T-\tau)}/(1 - e^{-\rho(T-\tau)}). \tag{A.124}$$

If instead the tree is logged now but the cycle is expected to be maintained, the value of the land after the tree has been felled is given by (A.123). Depreciation of the forest, as a capital asset, is the difference between (A.124) and (A.123).[74]

A.12. HUMAN CAPITAL

To develop an accounting framework for knowledge acquisition and skill formation, let us continue to suppose that labour hours are supplied inelastically and population is constant. Therefore, we may as well normalize by regarding the labour hours supplied to be unity. The resource allocation mechanism, α, is taken to be autonomous.

Production of a single all-purpose consumption good involves physical capital, K_{1t}, and human capital, H_{1t}. Here, H_{1t} is to be interpreted as the human capital embodied in those who work in the sector producing the consumption good. Thus, if Y is the output of the consumption good,

$$Y_t = F(K_{1t}, H_{1t}), \tag{A.125}$$

where F is an increasing function of its arguments.

[73] Of course, if a regular flow of timber is required, one should plant a non-synchronized forest. The non-convexity at each tree site would thereby be convexified by having trees of different ages in the forest. At each site, though, the Faustmann Rule would prevail.

[74] The economics of optimum forest management is well discussed in Johansson and Löfgren (1985).

Assume that human capital is produced with the help of physical capital, K_{2t}, and human capital, H_{2t}, and that, owing to mortality, it depreciates at a constant rate, γ. Output of human capital is given by the technology

$$G(K_{2t}, H_{2t}), \tag{A.126}$$

where G is an increasing function of its arguments. The input of 'students' is assumed to be constant. Imagine that all individuals at a given moment of time have the same amount of human capital. Then $H_{1t}/(H_{1t} + H_{2t})$ is the proportion of people employed in the sector producing the consumption good. Let the total quantity of human capital be H. It follows that

$$H_{1t} + H_{2t} = H_t. \tag{A.127}$$

Write

$$K_{1t} + K_{2t} = K_t. \tag{A.128}$$

Assume that physical capital does not depreciate. Using (A.125), the accumulation of physical capital can be expressed as

$$dK_t/dt = F(K_{1t}, H_{1t}) - C_t, \tag{A.129}$$

and, using (A.126), the accumulation of human capital can be expressed as

$$dH_t/dt = G(K_{2t}, H_{2t}) - \gamma H_t. \tag{A.130}$$

Since α is autonomous, we have, in the usual notation,

$$V_t = V(\alpha, K_{1t}, K_{2t}, H_{1t}, H_{2t}).$$

Let p_{1t} and p_{2t} be the accounting prices of physical capital and q_{1t} and q_{2t} the accounting prices of human capital in the two sectors, respectively (i.e. $p_{1t} = \partial V_t/\partial K_{1t}$, $q_{2t} = \partial V_t/\partial H_{2t}$, and so forth). Therefore, wealth can be expressed as

$$p_{1t}K_{1t} + p_{2t}K_{2t} + q_{1t}H_{1t} + q_{2t}H_{2t},$$

and genuine investment by

$$I_t = p_{1t}dK_{1t}/dt + p_{2t}dK_{2t}/dt + q_{1t}dH_{1t}/dt + q_{2t}dH_{2t}/dt.$$

Estimating q_{1t} and q_{2t} poses difficult problems in practice. It has been customary to identify human capital with education and to estimate its accounting price in terms of the market return on education (i.e. salaries over and above raw labour). But this supposes, as we have done here, that education does not contribute directly to well-being. If education does have that virtue (and it is widely acknowledged to do so), the market return on education is an underestimate of what we should ideally be after. Furthermore, human capital includes health, which is both a durable consumption good and a capital good.

An alternative procedure for estimating changes in human capital is to use estimates of expenditures on health and education. Such a procedure may be a reasonable approximation for poor societies, but it is in all probability too far off the mark for rich ones.

If α were an optimum resource allocation mechanism, we would have $p_{1t} = p_{2t} = p_t$, say, and $q_{1t} = q_{2t} = q_t$, say. On using (A.125)–(A.130), these prices would be related by the optimality conditions

$$U'(C_t) = p_t; p_t \partial F/\partial K_{1t} = q_t \partial G/\partial K_{2t}; \text{ and } p_t \partial F/\partial H_{1t} = q_t \partial G/\partial H_{2t}.$$

A.13. GLOBAL PUBLIC GOODS

Countries interact with one another not only through trade in international markets, but also via transnational externalities. Hamilton and Clemens (1999) included in their list of assets carbon dioxide in the atmosphere and regarded the accounting price (a negative number) of a country's emission to be the amount it would be required to pay the rest of the world if carbon emissions were the outcome of a fully cooperative agreement. Their procedure is, consequently, valid only if each country is engaged in maximizing global well-being, an unusual scenario. In what follows, we develop the required analysis.

Let G_t be the stock of a global common at t. Imagine that G is measured in terms of a quality index, which, to fix ideas, we shall regard as carbon dioxide concentration in the atmosphere. Being a global common, G is an argument in the value function V of every country. For simplicity of notation, we assume that there is a single private capital good. Let K_{jt} be the stock of the private asset owned by citizens of country j and let α_j be j's (autonomous) resource allocation mechanism and α the vector of resource allocation mechanisms. If V_j is j's value function, we have

$$V_{jt} = V_j(\boldsymbol{\alpha}, K_{jt}, G_t).$$

Define $p_{jt} = \partial V_{jt}/\partial K_{jt}$ and $g_{jt} = \partial V_{jt}/\partial G_t$. It may be that G is an economic good for some countries, while it is an economic 'bad' for others. For the former, $g_j > 0$; for the latter, $g_j < 0$. Let E_{it} be the emission rate from country i and let γ be the rate at which carbon in the atmosphere is sequestered. It follows that

$$dG_t/dt = \sum_i E_{it} - \gamma G_t. \tag{A.131}$$

Genuine investment in j is

$$I_t = dV_{jt}/dt = p_{jt}dK_{jt}/dt + g_{jt}dG_t/dt,$$

which, on using (A.131), can be expressed as

$$I_t = p_{jt}dK_{jt}/dt + g_{jt}\left(\sum_i E_{it} - \gamma G_t\right). \qquad (A.132)$$

Notice that the expression on the RHS of (A.132) is the same whether or not α is based on international cooperation. On the other hand, dK_{jt}/dt and dG_t/dt *do* depend on how the international resource allocation mechanisms are arrived at (e.g. whether they are cooperative or non-cooperative); and α also affects the accounting prices, p_{jt} and g_{jt}.[75]

A.14. TECHNOLOGICAL CHANGE AND GROWTH ACCOUNTING

How should technical change be incorporated in genuine investment? Assume there is an all-purpose non-deteriorating commodity, whose stock is denoted by K. Labour, as before, is supplied inelastically. Output (Y) can be consumed, or invested in the accumulation of K, or spent on research and development (R&D). We are to imagine that R&D expenditure leads to an outward shift in the production function for Y. Let E_t denote R&D expenditure. Define Z_t by the equation

$$dZ_t/dt = E_t. \qquad (A.133)$$

Z can be thought of as the stock of knowledge.

Output of the physical good is given by the production function

$$Y_t = e^{\lambda t}Q(Z_t)F(K_t), \qquad (A.134)$$

where $\lambda \geq 0$ and $Q'(Z) \geq 0$. Thus, technical progress appears as the term $e^{\lambda t}Q(Z_t)$. It combines exogenous factors (λ)—it is called the *residual* (see below)—with endogenous ones (Z). Accumulation of physical capital is then

---

[75] Social cost–benefit analysis, as sketched in Section A.6.7, would enable a country to estimate whether it ought to alter its emissions. Nordhaus and Yang (1996) have studied international carbon emissions as the outcome of a non-cooperative game among nations.

given by

$$dK_t/dt = e^{\lambda t}Q(Z_t)F(K_t) - C_t - E_t. \tag{A.135}$$

The economy's capital assets are K and Z. Stock adjustments are given by (A.133) and (A.135). I assume that the only source of non-autonomy of the underlying resource allocation mechanism α is exogenous technological change. It follows that $\partial V_t/\partial t > 0$ if $\lambda > 0$, but $\partial V_t/\partial t = 0$ if $\lambda = 0$. How plausible is it to assume that λ is not zero? In considering this, it is useful to identify the factors contributing to changes in GNP over time. Now GNP in our model economy is given by (A.134). Differentiating both sides of the equation with respect to time, rearranging terms, and dropping the time subscript from variables for the sake of notational simplicity, we obtain the following growth accounting identity:

$$(dY/dt)/Y = \lambda + (Q'(Z)dZ/dt)/Q(Z) + (F'(K)dK/dt)/F(K). \tag{A.136}$$

The first term on the RHS of (A.136) measures the percentage rate of change in total factor productivity (See Section 9.5), while the remaining two terms represent the contributions of changes in the two factors of production to the percentage rate of change in GNP. As λ is an exogenous factor, it is unexplained within the model; so it is often called the 'residual'. This residual is a determinant of $\partial V_t/\partial t$. (See Arrow, Dasgupta, Goulder *et al.*, 2003.)

In a famous article, Solow (1957) used a reduced form of the production function in (A.134) to estimate the contribution of changes in the factors of production to growth of non-farm GNP per man hour in the US economy over the period 1909–49, and discovered that it was a mere 12 per cent of the average annual rate of growth.[76] In other words, 88 per cent of the growth was attributable to the residual. (Solow's estimate of λ was 1.5 per cent per year.) A significant empirical literature since then has shown that, when K is better measured (e.g. by accounting for changes in the utilization of capacity and changes in what is embodied in capital) and when account is taken of human capital formation, the residual has been small in the US economy.[77]

This is congenial to intuition. As was argued in Chapter 9, it isn't prudent to imagine an everlasting growth in total factor productivity.[78] The residual is like manna from heaven. It is hard to believe that serendipity, unbacked by R&D effort and investment, can be a continual source of productivity growth. The assumption that total factor productivity can grow indefinitely would no doubt permit us to imagine that indefinite growth in consumption is sustainable. That indeed would be its attraction: it would enable us to assume away problems

---

[76] Solow assumed in particular that $Q'(Z) = 0$.

[77] Jorgenson (1995) contains a masterly account of this complex literature.

[78] These matters were discussed in Part III.

of environmental and resource constraints. But there are no theoretical or empirical grounds for presuming that it is a reasonable assumption. Recall too that most environmental resources go unrecorded in growth accounting. If the use of natural capital has in fact been growing, estimates of the residual would have an upward bias. At this point in our understanding of the process by which discoveries are made, it makes greater sense to set $\lambda = 0$ in (A.134). This would imply that $\partial V_t / \partial t = 0$.[79]

This is not to suggest that there is no such thing as technical change, but rather that, of the first two terms on the RHS of (A.136), it is the latter that is significant. It denotes the contribution of R&D to the growth in public knowledge, and thereby to growth in output.

The residual can have short bursts in imperfect economies. Imagine that a government reduces economic inefficiencies by improving the enforcement of property rights, or reducing centralized regulations (import quotas, price controls, and so forth). We would expect the factors of production to find better uses. As factors realign in a more productive fashion, total factor productivity would increase.

In the opposite vein, the residual could become negative for a period. Increased government corruption could be a cause; civil strife, which destroys capital assets and damages a country's institutions, could be another. When institutions deteriorate, assets are used even more inefficiently than before, and total factor productivity declines. This would appear to have happened in sub-Saharan Africa during the past forty years (Table 9.1).

A.15. EXHAUSTIBLE RESOURCES: THE EXPORTING ECONOMY

The export of natural resources at given world prices raises issues similar to those we have just encountered in our account of exogenous productivity change. World prices can be expected to change in ways that are, from the exporting

---

[79] Lau (1996) reports on a series of studies that have specified the aggregate production function to be of the form $Y_t = F(A_t K_t^a H_t^{(1-a)}, L_t)$, where K is manufactured capital, H is human capital, A is the augmentation factor of the composite capital, L is the number of labour hours, and $0 < a < 1$. The studies have uncovered that, since the end of the Second World War, the contribution of technical progress (i.e. the percentage rate of change in A_t) to growth in Y_t in today's newly industrialized countries has been negligible. He also reports that, if new knowledge is taken to be embodied in new capital equipment, the contribution of growth in the value of A_t to growth in Y_t among Western industrialized economies has been a mere 10%, that of growth in physical capital some 75%, while the contributions of growth in human capital and labour hours have each been some 7%. Lau also notes that the studies are silent on whether technical progress in Western industrialized economies has been exogenous or the fruit of expenditure on research and development.

country's perspective, exogenous. It follows that the drift term, $\partial V(t)/\partial t$, in (A.62) needs to be estimated.

Let S denote the stock of the resource. We take it that income effects are negligible. Assume that extraction is costless. Suppose that the world market price of an exhaustible resource is q_τ at τ. If R_τ is the volume of export, revenue is $q_\tau R_\tau$. Write

$$C_\tau = q_\tau R_\tau. \tag{A.137}$$

The country's export policy, being governed by the underlying α, can be expressed as $R_\tau(S_t, t)$ for $\tau \geq t$. From (A.137) it follows that

$$dC_\tau/dt = q_\tau dR_\tau/dt = (\partial C_\tau/\partial S_t)(dS_t/dt) + q_\tau \partial R_\tau/\partial t. \tag{A.138}$$

As before, we assume that social well-being at t is,

$$V_t = \int_t^\infty U(C_\tau) e^{-\rho(\tau-t)} d\tau. \tag{A.139}$$

Let p_t denote the resource's accounting price. Since the criterion for sustainable well-being is dV_t/dt, we differentiate both sides of (A.139) with respect to time to obtain

$$dV_t/dt = -U(C_t) + \rho V_t$$
$$+ \int_t^\infty U'(C_\tau)[(\partial C_\tau/\partial S_t)(dS_t/dt) + q_\tau \partial R_\tau/\partial t] e^{-\rho(\tau-t)} d\tau. \tag{A.140}$$

But $dS/dt = -R_t$.
Therefore, (A.140) reduces to

$$dV_t/dt = -U(C_t) + \rho V_t + p_t(dS_t/dt) + \int_t^\infty U'(C_\tau) e^{-\rho(\tau-t)} (\partial C_\tau/\partial t) d\tau. \tag{A.141}$$

Define

$$\mu(\tau, t) = \partial C_\tau/\partial \tau + \partial C_\tau/\partial t. \tag{A.142}$$

$\mu(\tau, t)$ can be regarded as an index of the extent to which the resource allocation mechanism is non-autonomous. Using (A.138), (A.139), and (A.142), (A.141) can be re-expressed as

$$dV_t/dt = -U(C_t) + \rho V_t + p_t(dS_t/dt) + \int_t^\infty U'(C_\tau)e^{-\rho(\tau-t)}\mu(\tau,t)d\tau$$

$$- \int_t^\infty U'(C_\tau)e^{-\rho(\tau-t)}(\partial C_\tau/\partial\tau)d\tau. \tag{A.143}$$

On partially integrating the last term on the RHS of (A.143) and cancelling terms, we obtain

$$dV_t/dt = p_t(dS_t/dt) + \int_t^\infty U'(C_\tau)e^{-\rho(\tau-t)}\mu(\tau,t)d\tau. \tag{A.144}$$

The integral on the RHS of (A.144) is the drift term $\partial V_t/\partial t$. The equation says that the index of sustainable well-being is the algebraic sum of genuine investment and the drift term. We now proceed to obtain simple rules for estimating the index in the case of two special resource allocation mechanisms.[80]

Suppose C is constant.[81] In this case, $\partial C_\tau/\partial\tau = \partial C_\tau/\partial t = 0$ and $\mu(\tau,t) = 0$. Therefore, the second term on the RHS of (A.144) is zero. It follows that genuine investment measures changes in social well-being.

Suppose instead R is constant. It follows that

$$\partial R_\tau/\partial\tau = \partial R_\tau/\partial t = 0, \tag{A.145}$$

and

$$\mu(\tau,t) = R_\tau \partial q_\tau/\partial\tau = q_\tau R_\tau(\partial q_\tau/\partial\tau)/q_\tau. \tag{A.146}$$

Using (A.145) and (A.146), we have

$$\int_t^\infty U'(C_\tau)e^{-\rho(\tau-t)}\mu(\tau,t)d\tau = \bar{\mu}_t/\rho, \tag{A.147}$$

where $\bar{\mu}_t$ is the average capital gains on the world market, as viewed from time t. On using (A.147), equation (A.144) can be rewritten as

$$dV/dt = p_t dS_t/dt + \bar{\mu}_t/\rho.$$

Thus $\bar{\mu}_t/\rho$ is the drift term.

[80] I leave it to readers to compute the drift term in (A.144) when the resource allocation mechanism is optimum.

[81] In this case the resource will be exhausted in finite time. For notational simplicity, I continue to present matters as though the horizon is infinite.

A.16. DEFENSIVE EXPENDITURE

How should defensive expenditure on pollution control appear in national accounts? Denote by Q_t the stock of defensive capital and X_t investment in its accumulation. Let P_t be the stock of pollutants and Y_t aggregate output. We are to imagine that the production of pollution, G, is an increasing function of Y and a declining function of Q. However, pollution depreciates exogenously at a fixed rate π. We may then write

$$dP_t/dt = G(Y_t, Q_t) - \pi P_t,$$

where $G(Y, Q) \geq 0$, $\partial G/\partial Y > 0$, and $\partial G/\partial Q < 0$.
Moreover, if defensive capital depreciates at the rate γ (>0), then

$$dQ_t/dt = X_t - \gamma Q_t.$$

In the usual notation, the accumulation equation is

$$dK_t/dt = F(K_t) - C_t - X_t.$$

Let p_t be the accounting price of K, m_t that of defensive capital, and r_t (<0) that of the pollutant. Wealth can then be expressed as

$$p_t K_t + m_t Q_t + r_t P_t,$$

and genuine investment as

$$I_t = p_t(dK_t/dt) + m_t(dQ_t/dt) + r_t(dP_t/dt). \tag{A.148}$$

Equation (A.148) says that defensive expenditure for pollution control ought to be included in the estimation of genuine investment ($m_t(dQ_t/dt)$). But (A.148) says that changes in the quality of the environment ($r_t(dP_t/dt)$) should also be included. To include the former, but not the latter, would be a mistake.

A.17. POPULATION CHANGE AND SUSTAINABLE DEVELOPMENT

A.17.1. *Basics*

How does demographic change affect the index of sustainable development? In Part V, I sketched a number of conceptual problems inherent in the welfare economics of reproductive behaviour. In growth accounting, however, such problems have typically been bypassed. Instead, it has been customary to regard changes in population as exogenously given. I follow that practice here.

We would like to determine how population change influences the drift term $(\partial V_t/\partial t)$ on the RHS of equation (A.62). Another way of casting the problem is to regard population as a capital asset. Once we do that, what might appear to be a non-autonomous model reduces to an autonomous one. To illustrate, I adopt a natural extension of Harsanyi (1955) by regarding social well-being as the average well-being of all who were ever born. I model this 'dynamic average utilitarianism' in the following way.[82]

Let N_t be population size at t and $n(N_t)$ the percentage rate of change of N_t.[83] For notational simplicity, I ignore intragenerational inequality and changes in the age composition of the population. Let c_t denote per capita consumption at t. If C_t is aggregate consumption, $c_t = C_t/N_t$. Assume as before that labour is supplied inelastically in each period. Current well-being of the representative person is $U(c_t)$ and social well-being is

$$V_t = \int_t^\infty N_\tau U(c_\tau) e^{-\delta(\tau-t)} d\tau \Big/ \int_t^\infty N_\tau e^{-\delta(\tau-t)} d\tau. \tag{A.149}$$

In order to ensure that V_t is well defined, we assume that $\delta > \int_0^t (n(N_\tau) d\tau)/t$ for large enough t. Let K_{it} denote the stock of the ith type of capital good and write $k_{it} = K_{it}/N_t$. We now let $\mathbf{k}_t$ be the vector of capital stocks per head. The state variables are therefore k_{it} and N_t. We take it that α is autonomous. Then (A.149) implies that

$$V_t = V(\mathbf{k}_t, N_t). \tag{A.150}$$

Let the numeraire be well-being. Define $v_t = \partial V_t/\partial N_t$. It is the contribution of an additional person at t to social well-being. v_t is the accounting price of a *person* (as distinct from the accounting price of a person's human capital). v_t can be of either sign. Let p_{it} denote the accounting price of k_{it}. Differentiating (A.150) with respect to t gives us

$$dV_t/dt = \sum_i p_{it} dk_{it}/dt + v_t dN_t/dt. \tag{A.151}$$

The RHS of (A.151) is genuine investment, inclusive of the change in the size of the population. It generalizes (A.62). I conclude that Proposition 4 remains valid so long as wealth comparisons mean comparisons of wealth per capita, *adjusted for demographic changes.*

[82] See equation (6.7). For an extensive discussion of demographic change and measures of sustainable development, see Arrow, Dasgupta, and Mäler (2003b) and Asheim (2003).
[83] If N_t is a logistic function, $n(N_t) = A(N^* - N_t)$, where A and N^* are positive constants.

I have been unable to identify circumstances where the adjustment term $(v_t(dN_t/dt))$ is not negligible, but at the same time can be estimated in a simple way. It is easy enough, however, to locate conditions under which the term vanishes. Suppose (i) $n(N_t)$ is independent of N_t; (ii) all the production processes are linear; and (iii) $c_t = c(k_t)$, which means that under α per capita consumption is not a function of population size. In such circumstances V_t is independent of N_t (i.e. $v_t = 0$), and so (A.151) reduces to

$$dV_t/dt = \sum_i p_{it} dk_{it}/dt. \qquad (A.152)$$

This finding can be summarized as

Proposition 12: If (i) $n(N_t)$ is independent of N_t, (ii) all the production processes are linear, and (iii) $c_t = c(k_t)$, then social well-being is sustained at a point in time if and only if the value of the changes in per capita capital assets at that instant is non-negative.

The conditions underlying Proposition 12 are overly strong. Nevertheless, it is tempting to use (A.152) as a first approximation to (A.151).

In Chapter 9 I invoked Proposition 12 to assess whether the world's poorest regions have experienced sustainable development in the recent past. In the following subsection I show how World Bank data were used for that purpose.

A.17.2. *Using World Bank Estimates of Genuine Investment*

Hamilton and Clemens (1999) offered cross-country estimates of the ratio of genuine investment (I_t in our earlier notation) to GNP (Y_t) over the period 1970–93. I converted their estimates for each region into figures for the average value of I_t/Y_t there during 1970–93. If we were now to regard the entire period as a moment in time, the ratio in question would be

$$I_t/Y_t = \sum_i (p_{it}(dK_{it}/dt))/Y_t. \qquad (A.153)$$

The first column of Table 9.2 consisted of my estimates of I_t/Y_t for the poorest regions of the world. I combined figures for population growth rates in these regions (column (2) in Table 9.2) with the figures in column (1) to arrive at estimates of $\sum_i (p_{it} dk_{it}/dt)/ \sum_i (p_{it} k_{it})$ in these regions. In what follows I show how this was done.

Let n be the constant rate of change of population size. Since $k_{it} = K_{it}/N_t$, we have

$$\mathrm{d}k_{it}/\mathrm{d}t = (\mathrm{d}K_{it}/\mathrm{d}t)/N_t - k_{it}(\mathrm{d}N_t/\mathrm{d}t)/N_t,$$

from which it follows that

$$\sum_i p_{it}(\mathrm{d}k_{it}/\mathrm{d}t) = \left[\sum_i p_{it}(\mathrm{d}K_{it}/\mathrm{d}t) - n\sum_i p_{it}K_{it}\right]/N_t. \qquad (\text{A.154})$$

Dividing both sides of (A.154) by $\sum_i p_{it}K_{it}/Y_t$ and writing $\sum_i p_{it}K_{it}/Y_t = \beta_t$ as the wealth–output ratio, we have

$$\sum_i (p_{it}(\mathrm{d}k_{it}/\mathrm{d}t))/\sum_i p_{it}k_{it} = I_t/\sum_i (p_{it}K_{it}) - n,$$

which may be written as

$$\sum_i (p_{it}(\mathrm{d}k_{it}/\mathrm{d}t))/\sum_i p_{it}k_{it} = I_t/\beta_t Y_t - n. \qquad (\text{A.155})$$

In Table 9.2 I assumed β_t during the 'instant of time' 1970–93 to be four years, a conservatively low figure. Despite the use of such a low figure, the RHS of (A.155) was found to be negative for all regions of the poor world, barring China.

In a critique of Dasgupta (2000c), Johnson (2001) questioned how a nation's wealth could decline while its GNP increases. It cannot of course happen indefinitely, but in this book I have shown how it can happen over an extended period of time. When it does, β_t declines, but analysts would not know this if their eyes were focused on GNP.[84]

Citizens of imperfect economies typically suffer injustice. They are also subjected to resource allocation mechanisms that are inefficient. In an inefficient economy there is room for raising the levels of both consumption and genuine investment. Table 9.2 suggests that people in the poorest countries today may well be consuming and (genuinely!) investing too little.

A.18. UNCERTAIN PRODUCTIVITY

How does future uncertainty in the productivity of capital assets influence accounting prices? In order to study this question in the simplest possible way,

[84] Johnson (2001) criticized much else in my paper (and, by implication, this book); see Dasgupta (2001c) for my response.

we revert to the Ramsey–Solow model of Section A.7 and assume that the productivity of the single asset is uncertain. Analytically it is easiest to imagine that the underlying stochastic process generates a return on investment that is independently and identically distributed (i.i.d.) in each period. For convenience we now assume that time is discrete ($t = 0, 1, 2, \ldots$). In what follows I indicate that a variable is random by placing a tilde over it. Thus, the uncertain productivity of investment at date t is denoted by $\tilde{\mu}_t$. I assume that $\tilde{\mu}_t$ is non-negative and that the distribution of $\tilde{\mu}_t$ is atomless.

Population is constant and aggregate saving is a constant proportion, s, of wealth, where $0 < s < 1$. At each t the size of the capital stock inherited from the previous period is a known quantity. Consumption is a fixed proportion, $1 - s$, of that inherited stock. Therefore, assuming that capital does not deteriorate, the discrete time, stochastic counterpart of the accumulation equation (A.78) is

$$\tilde{K}_{t+1} = (K_t - C_t)\tilde{\mu}_t,$$

from which we conclude that

$$\tilde{K}_{t+1} = s\tilde{\mu}_t K_t, \qquad t \geq 0,$$

and thus

$$\tilde{C}_\tau = (1 - s)K_t \left[\prod_t^{(\tau-1)} (s\tilde{\mu}_k) \right], \qquad \tau > t \geq 0. \tag{A.156}$$

Writing by $U(C)$ the utility of consumption, we take it that social well-being (V) is the expected value of the sum of the discounted flow of well-being over time. Letting E denote the expectation operator, this means that

$$V_t = E\left[\sum_t^\infty U(\tilde{C}_\tau)\beta^{(\tau-t)} \right], \qquad \beta \equiv 1/(1 + \delta) \text{ and } \delta > 0. \tag{A.157}$$

Suppose U is iso-elastic. Let η be the elasticity of $U'(C)$. We consider once again the empirically interesting case, where $\eta > 1$. So,

$$U(C) = C^{1-\eta}/(1 - \eta), \qquad \eta > 1. \tag{A.158}$$

Write $E(\tilde{\mu}_t^{(1-\eta)}) = E(\tilde{\mu}^{(1-\eta)})$. In order that V_t is well defined, we must suppose now that

$$\beta s^{(1-\eta)}E(\tilde{\mu}^{(1-\eta)}) < 1. \tag{A.159}$$

Using (A.156) and (A.158), and noting that the series in (A.157) is absolutely convergent, we can rewrite (A.157) as

$$V_t = -(1 - s)^{(1-\eta)}(K_t)^{(1-\eta)}/(\eta - 1)[1 - \beta s^{(1-\eta)}E(\tilde{\mu}^{(1-\eta)})],$$

and thereby deduce that the asset's accounting price is

$$p_t = \partial V_t/\partial K_t = (1 - s)^{(1-\eta)}(K_t)^{-\eta}/[1 - \beta s^{(1-\eta)}E(\tilde{\mu}^{(1-\eta)})]. \tag{A.160}$$

How would changes in the distribution of $\tilde{\mu}_\tau$ ($\tau \geq t$) affect p_t? To study this, imagine that $\log(\tilde{\mu}_\tau)$ is normally distributed with mean $m(>0)$ and variance σ^2. Denote the mean of $\tilde{\mu}_\tau$ by $\bar{\mu}$. In that case, we know that

$$\bar{\mu} = e^{m+\sigma^2/2}, \tag{A.161}$$

$$E(\tilde{\mu}^{(1-\eta)}) = \bar{\mu}^{(1-\eta)}e^{-\eta(1-\eta)\sigma^2/2}, \tag{A.162}$$

$$\text{var}(\tilde{\mu}) = \bar{\mu}^2[e^{\sigma^2} - 1]. \tag{A.163}$$

From (A.160)–(A.163) we confirm that, holding $\text{var}(\tilde{\mu})$ constant, $dp_t/d\bar{\mu} < 0$. To study the effect of an increase in $\text{var}(\tilde{\mu})$ on p_t, while keeping $\bar{\mu}$ constant, we must allow σ to increase in such a way that $(m + \sigma^2/2)$ remains unchanged. It is now a simple matter to confirm that $\partial p_t/\partial(\sigma^2) > 0$. And so, we have the next proposition.

Proposition 13: Other things being the same, (i) if the expected return on investment were to increase, the asset's accounting price would decrease, and (ii) if the underlying risk in the asset's productivity were to increase, so would its accounting price increase.

Part (i) of Proposition 13 is the extension of our finding in Section A.7.1, that an increase in the rate of return on investment will lead to a decrease in the asset's accounting price, other things being the same. But Part (ii) is also consistent with intuition. From (A.158) we know that U, while bounded above, is unbounded below. We would then expect V_t to be particularly sensitive to the downside risk in $\tilde{\mu}$. Part (ii) of Proposition 13 says that, if the risk in $\tilde{\mu}$ were to increase, the asset (at the margin) would become more valuable—other things being the same. The proposition's message should be even stronger if the underlying transformation possibilities among goods and services were to display thresholds or, more generally, ecological non-convexities of the kind that are present in the model of the shallow lake (Section A.8).[85]

---

[85] Readers can confirm that, if $0 < \eta < 1$ in (A.158), then $dp_t/d\bar{\mu} > 0$ and $dp_t/d\sigma^2 < 0$; and if $\eta = 1$ (i.e. if $U(C) = \log C$), then $dp_t/d\bar{\mu} = dp_t/d\sigma^2 = 0$. See the following footnote for an intuitive explanation for these results.

Of course, consumers could be expected to respond to an increase in the mean return on investment, or to an increase in uncertainty in the return. What would be their response? We cannot tell unless we are prepared to model the economic environment in which various parties make their saving decisions. The simplest place to look is an environment where the saving rate is optimal. There, people's response to a change in risk is also optimal. Levhari and Srinivasan (1969) have shown that, in the model economy studied here, optimum saving is a constant proportion of wealth; and that, if the distribution of $\log(\tilde{\mu}_t)$ is normal, the rate of saving declines with the expected return on investment and increases with increasing risk in that return. Specifically, they showed that the optimal saving ratio (s^*) is the solution of the equation

$$s^\eta = \beta E(\tilde{\mu}^{(1-\eta)}).$$
(A.164)

On using (A.161)–(A.163) in (A.160) and (A.164), we conclude that, if the saving rate is optimum, then, other things being the same, an increase in the expected return on investment leads to a decline in the accounting price of capital ($dp_t/d\bar{\mu} < 0$), and an increase in the riskyness of return leads to an increase in the accounting price ($dp_t/d\sigma^2 > 0$).[86]

Earlier we noted that accounting prices of capital assets (as opposed to their market prices) are rarely estimated. But when they *are* estimated, the estimates are made on the basis of economic models that eschew uncertainty. The general moral of Part (ii) of Proposition 13 is that such studies underestimate the social worth of those assets. In this book we have identified the many other reasons that give us cause to suspect that environmental capital is generally undervalued, and that materials and resources whose use generates pollution as byproducts are overvalued. The belief that humanity today is rapacious in its use of the natural resource base is therefore irresistible.

A.19. TIME AND SPACE

The welfare economics of environmental resources takes time seriously, but not space. And yet the spatial dimension is of the utmost importance. At the grandest scale, terrestrial ecosystems differ from marine ecosystems. But even within each there is a wide distribution, covering height, depth, and spread. Not only do individual members of a population interact with one another (involving

[86] Readers can confirm that if $0 < \eta < 1$ in (A.158) and (A.164), then $dp_t/d\bar{\mu} > 0$ and $dp_t/d\sigma^2 < 0$. To understand the result, note that, if $0 < \eta < 1$, then U is unbounded above, but bounded below. $\eta = 1$ corresponds to the case where $U(C) = \log C$. In this case s^* is independent of both $\bar{\mu}$ and σ^2, and so $dp_t/d\bar{\mu} = dp_t/d\sigma^2 = 0$. The opposite pulls arising from the unboundedness of U at both ends cancel each other. See Hahn (1970) for an intuitive explanation for the way η influences the relationship between σ and s^*.

both inter- and intra-species exchanges), but they affect and are in turn affected by the abiotic processes at different sites. The evolution of landscapes is modulated by such interactions. In any given patch, populations breed and die. They also disperse to other sites within and outside the patch. The physical, chemical, and biological processes at work operate on different scales, both spatially and temporally. Together they give rise to spatially structured populations and landscapes. What we observe is a system that is not only spatially and temporally patchy, but also modular.[87]

Despite the self-evident importance of the spatial aspect of Nature, the welfare economic theory of environmental natural resources is not yet spatially sensitive. If a community is to extract resources from its local ecosystem, then which patches should it harvest, what should it harvest, and when? Applied studies inform us of the harvesting strategies rural communities in the African savannahs, say, have adopted over time in response to the spatial and temporal character of their local ecosystems. Frequently enough, the rationale behind their strategies has been unearthed as well. But are the strategies optimal from the community's point of view? How would we know? As matters stand, even the mathematical tools that would be required to address those problems are not familiar in the economics literature. It is potentially a very fruitful area for future research.

A.20. GOOD AND BAD POSITIVE FEEDBACKS, AND RICH AND POOR PEOPLE

Contemporary models of economic growth are dismissive of the importance of Nature. In their extreme form, growth models contain an assumed positive link between the creation of ideas (technological progress) and population growth in a world where the natural resource base comprises a fixed, indestructible factor of production.[88] The models do involve positive feedback, but of a Panglossian kind.

The error in this literature lies in the fact that Nature is not fixed and indestructible; rather, it consists of degradable resources (agricultural soil, watersheds, fisheries, and sources of fresh water; more generally, ecological services). It may be logical to make the wrong assumption when studying a period when natural resource constraints did not bite, but it is not sensible when studying development possibilities in poor countries today. Such an assumption

---

[87] Levin (1999) has an excellent non-technical account of this.

[88] Kremer (1993) develops such a model to account for one million years of world economic history.

is especially suspect when no grounds are offered by growth theorists for supposing that technological progress can be depended upon indefinitely to more than substitute for an ever-increasing loss of the natural resource base. Moreover, as I argued in Section 7.6, ecological resources are frequently underpriced. This means that the direction of technological change is biased towards an excessive reliance on the natural resource base. As that base shrinks, it may prove harder and harder to find ways of substituting our way out of the problem of resource scarcity.

In any event, we should be sceptical of a theory that places such enormous burden on an experience not much more than 200 years old. Extrapolation into the past is a sobering exercise: over the long haul of history (a 5,000-year stretch, say, up to about 200 years ago), economic growth even in the currently rich countries was for most of the time not much above zero.[89]

Positive feedback in ecological and metabolic pathways are reasons why the prospects of economic betterment among the world's poorest are much bleaker than among the rich. For one thing, the poor in a poor economy have to operate on the boundary of the non-convex region of their nutrition-productivity possibilities, whereas people who possess sufficient assets are able to get onto the boundary of their convex region.[90] For another, the non-convexities the poor face can also be a reflection of their inability to obtain substitutes for depleted natural resources. As we noted earlier, resource depletion for the poor can be like crossing a threshold: their room for manœuvre is circumscribed hugely once they cross. In contrast, the rich can usually 'substitute' their way out of problems.

The simultaneous presence of two types of positive feedback—one enabling many to move up in their living standard, the other keeping many others in poverty—may explain the large-scale persistence of absolute poverty in a world that has been growing wealthier on average by substituting manufactured and human capital for natural capital. For human well-being, policies matter, as do institutions, but the local ecology matters too. If in this book I have stressed the positive feedback mechanisms that operate at the downside of life, it is because degradation of the natural resource base is felt first by the poor, not the rich.

[89] See Fogel (1994), Johnson (2000), and especially Maddison (2001). The claim holds even if the past 200 years were to be included. I offered a rough calculation in Chapter 8.

[90] Dasgupta and Ray (1986). To illustrate, the undernourished are at a severe disadvantage in their ability to obtain food: the quality of work they are able to offer is inadequate for obtaining the food they require if they are to improve their nutritional status. Over time, undernourishment can be both a cause and a consequence of someone falling into a poverty trap. Because undernourishment displays hysteresis, such poverty can be dynastic: once a household falls into a poverty trap, it can prove especially hard for descendents to emerge out of it. Many poverty studies involving econometric exercises (including many that explore nutrition and health) assume linear relationships among the stipulated variables. By construction they are incapable of detecting the non-convexities inherent in metabolic and ecological processes.

References

Abeygunawardena, P., B. H. Lohani, D. W. Bromley, and R. C. V. Barba, eds. (1999), *Environment and Economics in Project Preparation: Ten Asian Case Studies* (Manilla: Asian Development Bank).

Abramovitz, M. (1956), 'Resource and Output Trends in the United States Since 1870', *American Economic Review* (Papers & Proceedings) 46: 5–23.

—— (1986), 'Catching Up, Forging Ahead, and Falling Behind', *Journal of Economic History*, 56: 385–406.

Acheson, J. M. (1993), 'Capturing the Commons: Legal and Illegal Strategies', in T. L. Anderson and R. T. Simmons, eds., *The Political Economy of Customs and Culture: Informal Solutions to the Commons Problem* (Lanham: Rowman and Littlefield).

Adelman, I. (1979), *Redistribution before Growth* (Leiden: University of Leiden Press).

—— and C. T. Morris (1965), 'A Factor Analysis of the Interrelationship between Social and Political Variables and per Capita Gross National Product', *Quarterly Journal of Economics*, 79: 555–78.

—— and —— (1967), *Society, Politics and Economic Development* (Baltimore: Johns Hopkins University Press).

—— and S. Robinson (1989), 'Income Distribution and Development: A Survey', in H. Chenery and T. N. Srinivasan, eds., *Handbook of Development Economics* (Amsterdam: North-Holland).

Agarwal, A., and S. Narain (1989), *Towards Green Villages: A Strategy for Environmentally Sound and Participatory Rural Development* (New Delhi: Centre for Science and Development).

—— and —— (1996), *Dying Wisdom: Rise, Fall and Potential of India's Traditional Water Harvesting Systems* (New Delhi: Centre for Science and Development).

Agarwal, B. (1986), *Cold Hearths and Barren Slopes: The Woodfuel Crisis in the Third World* (New Delhi: Allied Publishers).

—— (1989), 'Rural Women, Poverty and Natural Resources: Sustenance, Sustainability and Struggle for Change', *Economic and Political Weekly*, 24(43): WS 46–65.

Aggarwal, R., S. Netanyahu, and C. Romano (2001), 'Access to Natural Resources and the Fertility Decision of Women: The Case of South Africa', *Environment and Development Economics*, 6: 209–36.

Aghion, P., E. Caroli, and C. Garcia-Peñalosa (1999), 'Inequality and Economic Growth: The Prespective of the New Growth Theories', *Journal of Economic Literature*, 37: 1615–60.

—— and P. Howitt (1996), *Endogenous Growth Theory* (Cambridge, Mass.: MIT Press).

Ahmad, E., and N. Stern (1990), *The Theory and Practice of Tax Reform for Developing Countries* (Cambridge: Cambridge University Press).

Alston, L. J., G. D. Libecap, and B. Mueller (1999a), 'Land Reform Policies, the Sources of Violent Conflict, and Implications for Deforestation in the Brazilian Amazon', mimeo, Department of Economics, University of Illinois.

—— —— and —— (1999b), *Titles, Conflict, and Land Use: The Development of Property Rights and Land Reform on the Brazilian Amazon* (Ann Arbor: University of Michigan Press).

Anderson, D. (1987), *The Economics of Afforestation* (Baltimore: Johns Hopkins University Press).

Appell, D. (2001), 'The New Uncertainty Principle', *Scientific American*, 284 (Jan.): 12–13.

Arnott, R., and J. E. Stiglitz (1991), 'Moral Hazard and Nonmarket Institutions: Dysfunctional Crowding Out of Peer Review?' *American Economic Review*, 81: 179–90.

Aronsson, T., and K.-G. Löfgren (1998a), 'Green Accounting in Imperfect Economies: A Summary of Recent Research', *Environmental and Resource Economics*, 11: 273–87.

Aronsson, T., and K.-G. Löfgren (1998b), 'Green Accounting: What do we Know and What do we Need to Know?' in T. Tietenberg and H. Folmer, eds., *International Yearbook of Environmental and Resource Economics 1998/1999* (Cheltenham, UK: Edward Elgar).

—— and —— (1999), 'Pollution Tax Design and "Green" National Accounting', *European Economic Review*, 43: 1457–74.

Aronsson, T., P.-O. Johansson, and K.-G. Löfgren (1997), *Welfare Measurement, Sustainability and Green National Accounting* (Cheltenham, UK: Edward Elgar).

Arrow, K. J. (1963a [1951]), *Social Choice and Individual Values*, 2nd edn. (New York: John Wiley).

—— (1963b), 'Uncertainty and the Economics of Medical Care'. *American Economic Review*, 53: 941–73.

—— (1971), 'Political and Economic Evaluation of Social Effects of Externalities', in M. Intriligator, ed., *Frontiers of Quantitative Economics*, Vol. I (Amsterdam: North-Holland).

—— (1974), *The Limits of Organization* (New York: W. W. Norton).

—— (1999), 'Discounting, Morality, and Gaming', in P. R. Portney and J. P. Weyant, eds., *Discounting and Intergenerational Equity* (Washington: Resources for the Future).

—— (2000), 'Observations on Social Capital', in P. Dasgupta, and I. Serageldin, eds., *Social Capital: A Multifaceted Perspective* (Washington: World Bank).

—— and A. Fisher (1974), 'Preservation, Uncertainty and Irreversibility', *Quarterly Journal of Economics*, 88: 312–19.

—— and L. Hurwicz (1958), 'Gradient Method for Concave Programming, III: Further Global Results and Applications to Resource Allocation', in K. J. Arrow, L. Hurwicz, and H. Uzawa, eds., *Studies in Linear and Non-linear Programming* (Stanford, Cal.: Stanford University Press).

—— and M. Kurz (1970), *Public Investment, the Rate of Return and Optimal Fiscal Policy* (Baltimore: Johns Hopkins University Press).

—— R. M. Solow, P. Portney, E. Leamer, R. Radner, and H. Schuman (1993), 'Report of NOAA Panel on Contingent Valuation', *Federal Register*, 58: 4601–14.

—— B. Bolin, R. Costanza, P. Dasgupta, C. Folke, C. H. Holling, B.-O. Jansson, S. A. Levin, K.-G. Mäler, C. Perrings, and D. Pimentel (1995), 'Economic Growth, Carrying Capacity, and the Environment', *Science*, 268: 520–1.

—— W. R. Cline, K.-G. Mäler, M. Munasinghe, R. Squitieri, and J. E. Stiglitz (1996), 'Intertemporal Equity, Discounting, and Economic Efficiency', in J. P. Bruce, H. Lee, and E. F. Haites, eds., *Climate Change 1995: Economic and Social Dimensions of Climate Change*, Contribution of Working Group III to the Second Assessment Report of the Intergovernmental Panel on Climate Change (Cambridge: Cambridge University Press).

—— G. Daily, P. Dasgupta, P. Ehrlich, L. Goulder, G. Heal, S. Levin, K.-G. Mäler, S. Schneider, D. Starrett, and B. Walker (2003), 'Are We Consuming Too Much?', forthcoming *Journal of Economic Perspectives*, 2004.

—— G. Daily, P. Dasgupta, P. Ehrlich, L. Goulder, G. M. Heal, S. Levin, K.-G. Mäler, S. Schneider, D. Starrett, and B. Walker (2003), 'Are We Consuming Too Much?', mimeo, Department of Economics, Stanford University; forthcoming, *Journal of Economic Perspectives*.

—— P. Dasgupta, and K.-G. Mäler (2003a), 'Evaluating Projects and Assessing Sustainable Development in Imperfect Economies', mimeo, Faculty of Economics, University of Cambridge; forthcoming, *Environmental and Resource Economics*.

—— P. Dasgupta, and K.-G. Mäler (2003b), 'The Genuine Savings Criterion and the Value of Population', *Economic Theory*, 21: 217–25.

Asheim, G. (1994), 'Net National Product as an Indicator of Sustainability', *Scandinavian Journal of Economics*, 96: 257–65.

—— (1997), 'Adjusting Green NNP to Measure Susainability', *Scandinavian Journal of Economics*, 99: 355–70.

—— (2000), 'Green National Accounting: Why and How?' *Environment and Development Economics*, 5: 25–48.

—— (2003), 'Green National Accounting with a Changing Population', mimeo, Department of Economics, University of Oslo; forthcoming, *Economic Theory*.

—— and M. L. Weitzman (2001), 'Does NNP Growth Indicate Welfare Improvement?' Mimeo, Department of Economics, Harvard University.

Atkinson, A. B. (1970), 'On the Measurement of Inequality', *Journal of Economic Theory*, 2: 244–63.

—— and J. E. Stiglitz (1980), *Lectures in Public Economics* (New York: McGraw-Hill).

Baland, J.-M., and J.-P. Platteau (1996), *Halting Degradation of Natural Resources: Is There a Role for Rural Communities?* (Oxford: Clarendon Press).

Banerjee, A., D. Mookherjee, K. Munshi, and D. Ray (2001), 'Inequality, Control Rights, and Rent Seeking: Sugar Cooperatives in Maharashtra', *Journal of Political Economy*, 109: 138–90.

Barbier, E. B., J. C. Burgess, and C. Folke (1994), *Paradise Lost? The Ecological Economics of Biodiversity* (London: Earthscan).

—— J. C. Burgees, T. Swanson, and D. W. Pearce (1990), *Elephants, Economics and Ivory* (London: Earthscan).

Bardhan, P. (1996), 'Research on Poverty and Development Twenty Years after Redistribution with Growth', *Proceedings of the Annual World Bank Conference on Development Economics, 1995* (Supplement to the *World Bank Economic Review* and the *World Bank Research Observer*): 59–72.

Barkow, J. H., L. Cosmides, and J. Tooby, eds. (1992), *The Adapted Mind: Evolutionary Psychology and the Generation of Culture* (Oxford: Oxford University Press).

Barnett, H., and C. Morse (1963), *Scarcity and Growth* (Baltimore: Johns Hopkins University Press).

Barrett, S. (1990), 'The Problem of Global Environmental Protection', *Oxford Review of Economic Policy*, 6: 68–79.

—— (1996), 'Comments on the 1995 Keynes Lecture', *Proceedings of the British Academy: 1995 Lectures and Memoirs* (London: British Academy).

—— (1997), 'Towards a Theory of International Environmental Cooperation', in C. Carraro and D. Siniscalco, eds., *New Directions in the Economic Theory of the Environment* (Cambridge: Cambridge University Press).

—— (1999), 'A Theory of Full International Cooperation', *Journal of Theoretical Politics*, 11: 519–41.

—— and K. Graddy (2000), 'Freedom, Growth and the Environment', *Environment and Development Economics*, 5: 433–56.

Barro, R. J. (1996), 'Democracy and Growth', *Journal of Economic Growth*, 1: 1–27.

—— (1999), 'Ramsey Meets Laibson in the Neoclassical Growth Model', *Quarterly Journal of Economics*, 114: 1125–52.

Barry, B. (1965), *Political Argument* (London: Routledge & Kegan Paul).

Bauer, P. (1981), 'The Population Explosion: Myths and Realities', in *Equality, the Third World and Economic Delusions* (London: Weidenfeld & Nicolson).

—— (2000), *From Subsistence to Exchange and Other Essays* (Princeton: Princeton University Press).

Baumol, W. M., and W. Oates (1975), *The Theory of Environmental Policy* (Englewood Cliffs, NJ: Prentice-Hall).

Beattie, A., and P. R. Ehrlich (2001), *Wild Solutions* (New Haven: Yale University Press).

Becker, G. (1983), *Human Capital: A Theoretical and Empirical Analysis, with Special Reference to Education* (Chicago: University of Chicago Press).

Becker, N., N. Zeitouni, and M. Shecter (1997), 'Employing Market Mechanisms to Encourage Efficient Use of Water in the Middle East', in D. D. Parker and Y. Tsur, eds., *Decentralization and Coordination of Water Resource Management* (Boston: Kluwer Academic).

Bell, D. E., H. Raiffa, and A. Tversky, eds. (1988), *Decision Making: Descriptive, Normative, and Prescriptive Interactions* (Cambridge: Cambridge University Press).

Bellman, R. (1957), *Dynamic Programming* (Oxford: Oxford University Press).

Beltratti, A. (1996), *Models of Economic Growth with Environmental Assets* (Dordrecht: Kluwer).

—— (1997), 'Growth with Natural and Environmental Resources', in C. Carraro and D. Siniscalco, eds., *New Directions in the Economic Theory of the Environment* (Cambridge: Cambridge University Press).

Berlin, I. (1959), 'Two Concepts of Liberty', in *Four Essays on Liberty* (Oxford: Oxford University Press).

Besley, T., and R. Burgess (2000), 'Land Reform, Poverty Reduction, and Growth: Evidence from India', *Quarterly Journal of Economics*, 115: 389–430.

Bewley, T. (1989), 'Market Innovation and Entrepreneurship: A Knightian View', Cowles Foundation Discussion Paper No. 905, Yale University.

Bhagwati, J. (1988), *Protectionism* (Cambridge, Mass.: MIT Press).

BIIEE (2001), *Essays on Property-Rights Structures and Environmental Resource Management*, by B. Adhikari, W. Akpalu, T. Bonger, P. Mukhopadhyay, D. Dore, M. Doss, M. I. Elfahal, T. S. Jeena, A. Jerome, W. Kosanayi, G. Kundhlande, L. Magagula, E. D. Mungatana, J. W. Mariara, C. Mutunga, R. Naguran, K. Nyikahadzoi, A. Paul, S. C. Sengupta, and G. Tesfay, mimeo, Beijer International Institute of Ecological Economics (BIIEE), Royal Swedish Academy of Sciences, Stockholm.

Binswanger, H. (1991), 'Brazilian Policies that Encourage Deforestation in the Amazon', *World Development*, 19: 821–9.

Birdsall, N., and A. Steer (1993), 'Act Now on Global Warming—But Don't Cook the Books', *Finance and Development*, March: 6–8.

Bjorndal, T. (1988), 'The Optimal Management of North Sea Herring', *Journal of Environmental Economics and Management*, 15: 9–29.

—— and G. R. Munroe (1998), 'The Economics of Fisheries Management: A Survey', in T. Tietenberg and H. Folmer, eds., *International Yearbook of Environmental and Resource Economics 1998/1999* (Cheltenham, UK: Edward Elgar).

Blackorby, C., and D. Donaldson (1985), 'Social Criteria for Evaluating Population Change', *Journal of Public Economics*, 28: 13–34.

Bockstael, N. E., and E. G. Irwin (2000), 'Economics and the Land Use–Environment Link', in T. Tietenberg and H. Folmer, eds., *Yearbook of Environmental and Resource Economics 2000/2001* (Cheltenham, UK: Edward Elgar).

Bohm, P. (1996), 'Environmental Taxation and the Double-Dividend: Fact or Fallacy?' GEC Working Paper Series No. 96-01, University College, London.

Bongaarts, J., and S. C. Watkins (1996), 'Social Interactions and Contemporary Fertility Transitions', *Population and Development Review*, 22: 639–82.

Bovenberg, A. L., and L. Goulder (1996), 'Optimal Environmental Taxation in the Presence of Other Taxes: General Equilibrium Analyses', *American Economic Review*, 86: 766–88.

—— and F. van der Ploeg (1994), 'Environmental Policy, Public Finance, and the Labour Market in a Second-Best World', *Journal of Public Economics*, 55: 349–90.

Boyle, K. J., and R. C. Bishop (1987), 'Valuing Wildlife in Benefit–Cost Analyses: A Case Study Involving Endangered Species', *Water Resources Research*, 23: 943–50.

Braden, J. B., and C. D. Kolstad, eds. (1991), *Measuring the Demand for Environmental Quality* (Amsterdam: North-Holland).

Brander, J. A., and M. S. Taylor (1998), 'The Simple Economics of Easter Island: A Ricardo–Malthus Model of Renewable Resource Use', *American Economic Review*, 88: 119–38.

Braverman, A., and J. E. Stiglitz (1989), 'Credit Rationing, Tenancy, Productivity, and the Dynamics of Inequality', in P. Bardhan, ed., *The Economic Theory of Agrarian Institutions* (Oxford: Oxford University Press).

Brock, W. A., and D. Starrett (2003), 'Non-Convexities in Ecological Management Problems', mimeo, Beijer International Institute of Ecological Economics, Stockholm; forthcoming, *Environmental and Resource Economics*.

—— K.-G. Mäler, and C. Perrings (1999), 'The Economic Analysis of Nonlinear Dynamic Systems', Discussion Paper, Beijer International Institute of Ecological Economics, Stockholm.

Bromeley, D. W. (1991), *Environment and Economy: Property Rights and Public Policy* (Oxford: Basil Blackwell).

—— et al., eds. (1992), *Making the Commons Work: Theory, Practice and Policy* (San Francisco: ICS Press).

Broome, J. (1992), *Counting the Cost of Global Warming* (London: White Horse Press).

—— (1996), 'The Welfare Economics of Population', *Oxford Economic Papers*, 48: 177–93.

—— (1999), *Ethics Out of Economics* (Cambridge: Cambridge University Press).

Brown, G., and C. B. McGuire (1967): 'A Socially Optimal Pricing Policy for a Public Water Agency', *Water Resources Research*, 3: 33–43.

Brown, K., and D. Pearce (1994), 'The Economic Value of Non-Market Benefits of Tropical Forests: Carbon Storage', in J. Weiss, ed., *The Economics of Project Appraisal and the Environment* (Cheltenham, UK: Edward Elgar).

Burk, A. (1938), 'A Reformulation of Certain Aspects of Welfare Economics', *Quarterly Journal of Economics*, 52: 310–34.

Burt, R. S. (1992), *Structural Holes: The Social Structure of Competition* (Cambridge: Cambridge University Press).

—— R. M. Hogarth, and C. Michaud (1998), 'The Social Capital of French and American Managers', mimeo, Graduate School of Business, University of Chicago.

Buvinic, M., and G. R. Gupta (1997), 'Female-Headed Households and Female-Maintained Families: Are They Worth Targeting to Reduce Poverty in Developing Countries?' *Economic Development and Cultural Change*, 45: 259–80.

Caldwell, J. C. (1981), 'The Mechanisms of Demographic Change in Historical Perspective', *Population Studies*, 35: 5–27.

—— (1982), *The Theory of Fertility Decline* (New York: Academic Press).

Carpenter, S. R. (2001), 'Alternate States of Ecosystems: Evidence and Its Implications', in M. C. Press, N. Huntly, and S. Levin, eds., *Ecology: Achievement and Challenge* (London: Basil Blackwell).

—— D. Ludwig, and W. A. Brock (1999), 'Management of Eutrophication for Lakes Subject to Potentially Irreversible Change', *Ecological Applications*, 9: 751–71.

Carraro, C. (2001), 'Institutions Design for Managing Global Commons', mimeo, Department of Economics, University of Venice.

—— and D. Siniscalco, eds. (1996), *Environmental Fiscal Reform and Unemployment* (Dordrecht: Kluwer).

—— and —— (1998), 'International Environmental Agreements: Incentives and Political Economy', *European Economic Review*, 42: 561–72.

Carson, R. T., and C. R. Mitchell (1993), 'The Value of Clean Water: The Public's Willingness to Pay for Boatable, Fishable, and Swimmable Quality Water', *Water Resources Research*, 29: 445–54.

Cass, D. (1965), 'Optimum Economic Growth in an Aggregative Model of Capital Accumulation', *Review of Economic Studies*, 32: 233–40.

Cavendish, W. (2000), 'Empirical Regularities in the Poverty–Environment Relationships of Rural Households: Evidence from Zimbabwe', *World Development*, 28: 1979–2003.

Chakravarty, S. (1969), *Capital and Development Planning* (Cambridge, Mass.: MIT Press).

Chenery, H., M. Ahluwalia, C. Bell, J. Duloy, and R. Jolly (1974), *Redistribution with Growth* (New York: Oxford University Press).

Chichilnisky, G. (1994), 'North–South Trade and the Global Environment', *American Economic Review*, 84: 851–74.

Chichilnisky, G. (1996), 'An Axiomatic Approach to Sustainable Development', *Social Choice and Welfare*, 13: 231–57.

—— and G. M. Heal (1998), 'Economic Returns from the Biosphere', *Nature*, 391: 629–30.

Chopra, K., and S. C. Gulati (1998), 'Environmental Degradation, Property Rights and Population Movements: Hypotheses and Evidence from Rajasthan (India)', *Environment and Development Economics*, 3: 35–57.

—— and —— (2001), *Migration, Common Property Resources and Environmental Degradation* (London: Sage).

—— G. K. Kadekodi, and M. N. Murty (1990), *Participatory Development: People and Common Property Resources* (New Delhi: Sage).

Clark, C. W. (1976), *Mathematical Bioeconomics: The Optimal Management of Renewable Resources* (New York: John Wiley).

Cleaver, K. M., and G. A. Schreiber (1994), *Reversing the Spiral: The Population, Agriculture, and Environment Nexus in Sub-Saharan Africa* (Washington: World Bank).

Cline, W. R. (1992), *The Economics of Global Warming* (Washington: Institute for International Economics).

Coase, R. (1960), 'The Problem of Social Cost', *Journal of Law and Economics*, 3: 1–44.

Cohen, J. (1995), *How Many People Can the Earth Support?* (New York: W. W. Norton).

Colchester, M. (1995), 'Sustaining the Forests: The Community-Based Approach in South and South-East Asia', *Development and Change*, 25: 69–100.

Coleman, J. S. (1988), 'Social Capital in the Creation of Human Capital', *American Journal of Sociology*, 94: 95–120.

Collier, P., and A. Hoeffler (1998), 'On Economic Causes of Civil War', *Oxford Economic Papers*, 50: 563–73.

Collins, S., and B. Bosworth (1996), 'Economic Growth in East Asia: Accumulation versus Assimilation', *Brookings Papers on Economic Activity*, 2: 135–91.

Cooper, C. (1981), *Economic Evaluation and the Environment* (London: Hodder & Stoughton).

Cooper, R. (1977), 'An Economist's View of the Oceans', *Journal of World Trade Law*, 9: 357–77.

Cosmides, L., and J. Tooby (1992), 'Cognitive Adaptations for Social Exchange', in J. H. Barkow, L. Cosmides, and J. Tooby, eds., *The Adapted Mind: Evolutionary Psychology and the Generation of Culture* (Oxford: Oxford University Press, 1992).

Costanza R. R., R. d'Arge, R. de Groot, S. Farber, M. Grasso, B. Hannon, K, Limburg, S. Naeem, R. V. O'Neill, J. Paruelo, R. G. Raskin, P. Sutton, and M. van den Belt (1997), 'The Value of the World's Ecosystem Services and Natural Capital', *Nature*, 387: 253–60.

Cowen, T. (1989), 'Normative Population Theory', *Social Choice and Welfare*, 6: 33–44.

Cropper, M. L., S. K. Aydede, and P. R. Portney (1994), 'Preferences for Life Saving Programs: How the Public Discounts Time and Age', *Journal of Risk and Uncertainty*, 8: 243–66.

—— and C. Griffiths (1994), 'The Interaction of Population Growth and Environmental Quality', *American Economic Review*, 84: 250–4.

—— and A. M. Freeman (1991), 'Valuing Environmental Health Effects', in J. B. Braden, and C. D. Kolstad, eds., *Measuring the Demand for Environmental Quality* (Amsterdam: Elsevier).

—— and W. Oates (1992), 'Environmental Economics: A Survey', *Journal of Economic Literature*, 30: 675–740.

Cruz, W., and R. Repetto (1992), *The Environmental Effects of Stabilization and Structural Adjustment Programmes: The Philippines Case* (Washington: World Resources Institute).

CSE (1990), *Human–Nature Interactions in a Central Himalayan Village: A Case Study of Village Bemru* (New Delhi: Centre for Science and Environment).

Dahl, R. (1989), *Democracy and its Critics* (New Haven: Yale University Press).

Daily, G, ed. (1997), *Nature's Services: Societal Dependence on Natural Ecosystems* (Washington: Island Press).

—— and S. Dasgupta (2001), 'Concept of Ecosystem Services', in S. Levin, ed., *Encyclopedia of Biodiversity*, Vol. 2 (New York: Academic Press).

—— and P. R. Ehrlich (1996), 'Impacts of Development and Global Change on the Epidemiological Environment', *Environment and Development Economics*, 1: 311–46.

—— P. Dasgupta, B. Bolin, P. Crosson, J. du Guerny, P. Ehrlich, C. Folke, A.-M. Jansson, B.-O. Jansson, N. Kautsky, A. Kinzig, S. Levin, K.-G. Mäler, P. Pinstrup-Andersen, and B. Walker (1998), 'Food Production, Population Growth, and Environmental Security', *Science*, 281: 1291–2.

Dales, J. H. (1968), *Pollution, Property and Prices* (Toronto: University of Toronto Press).

Dasgupta, A. (1975), *The Economics of Austerity* (Delhi: Oxford University Press).

Dasgupta, P. (1969), 'On the Concept of Optimum Population', *Review of Economic Studies*, 36: 294–318.

—— (1972), 'A Comparative Analysis of the UNIDO Guidelines and the OECD Manual', *Bulletin of the Oxford University Institute of Economics and Statistics*, 34: 33–51.

—— (1974), 'On Optimum Population Size', in A. Mitra, ed., *Economic Theory and Planning: Essays in Honour of A. K. Dasgupta* (New Delhi: Oxford University Press).

—— (1982a), 'Utilitarianism, Information and Rights', in A. Sen, and B. Williams, eds., *Utilitarianism and Beyond* (Cambridge: Cambridge University Press).

—— (1982b), *The Control of Resources* (Cambridge, Mass.: Harvard University Press).

—— (1988), 'Lives and Well-Being', *Social Choice and Welfare*, 5: 103–26.

—— (1989), 'Population Size and the Quality of Life', *Proceedings of the Aristotelian Society*, 58 (Suppl.): 23–40.

—— (1990a), 'Well-Being and the Extent of its Realization in Poor Countries', *Economic Journal*, 100 (Suppl.): 1–32.

—— (1990b), 'The Environment as a Commodity', *Oxford Review of Economic Policy*, 6: 51–67.

—— (1991), 'Nutrition, Non-Convexities and Redistributive Policies', *Economic Journal*, 101: 22–6.

—— (1992), 'Population, Resources and Poverty', *Ambio*, 21: 95–101.

—— (1993), *An Inquiry into Well-Being and Destitution* (Oxford: Clarendon Press).

—— (1994), 'Savings and Fertility: Ethical Issues', *Philosophy and Public Affairs*, 23: 99–127.

—— (1995), 'Population, Poverty, and the Local Environment', *Scientific American*, 272 (Feb.): 40–45.

—— (1996), 'The Economics of the Environment', *Environment and Development Economics*, 1: 387–428.

—— (1997), 'Nutritional Status, the Capacity for Work and Poverty Traps', *Journal of Econometrics*, 77: 5–38.

—— (1998a), 'The Economics of Poverty in Poor Countries', *Scandinavian Journal of Economics*, 100: 41–68.

—— (1998b), 'The Economics of Food', in J. C. Waterlow, D. G. Armstrong, L. Fowden, and R. Riley, eds., *Feeding a World Population of more than Eight Billion People: A Challenge to Science* (New York: Oxford University Press).

—— (1998c), 'Population, Consumption and Resources: Ethical Issues', *Ecological Economics*, 24: 139–52.

—— (2000a), 'Economic Progress and the Idea of Social Capital', in P. Dasgupta and I. Serageldin, eds., *Social Capital: A Multifaceted Perspective* (Washington: World Bank).

—— (2000b), 'Reproductive Externalities and Fertility Behaviour', *European Economic Review* (Papers & Proceedings), 44: 619–44.

—— (2000c), 'Population and Resources: An Exploration of Reproductive and Environmental Externalities', *Population and Development Review*, 26: 643–89.

—— (2001a), 'The Economic Value of Biodiversity, Overview', in S. Levin, ed., *Encyclopedia of Biodiversity*, Vol. 2 (New York: Academic Press).

—— (2001b), 'Valuing Objects and Evaluating Policies in Imperfect Economies', *Economic Journal* (Conference Issue), 111: 1–29.

—— (2001c), 'On Population and Resources: Reply', *Population and Development Review*, 26: 748–54.

—— (2003), 'World Poverty: Causes and Pathways', forthcoming in B. Pleskovic and N. H. Stern, eds., *Annual Bank Conference on Development Economics 2003* (Washington: World Bank).

—— and G. M. Heal (1974), 'The Optimal Depletion of Exhaustible Resources', *Review of Economic Studies* (Symposium Issue), 41: 3–28.

—— and —— (1979), *Economic Theory and Exhaustible Resources* (Cambridge: Cambridge University Press).

—— and K.-G. Mäler (1991), 'The Environment and Emerging Development Issues', *Proceedings of the Annual World Bank Conference on Development Economics 1990* (Supplement to the *World Bank Economic Review*): 101–32.

—— and —— (1995), 'Poverty, Institutions, and the Environmental Resource-Base', in J. Behrman and T. N. Srinivasan, eds., *Handbook of Development Economics*, Vol. IIIA (Amsterdam: North-Holland).

—— and —— (2000), 'Net National Product, Wealth, and Social Well-Being', *Environment and Development Economics*, 5: 69–93.

—— and E. Maskin (1999), 'Democracy and Other Goods', in I. Shapiro and C. Hacker-Cordon, eds., *Democracy's Value* (Cambridge: Cambridge University Press).

—— and D. Ray (1986), 'Inequality as a Determinant of Malnutrition and Unemployment,1: Theory', *Economic Journal*, 96: 1011–34.

—— and —— (1987), 'Inequality as a Determinant of Malnutrition and Unemployment,2: Policy', *Economic Journal*, 97: 177–88.

—— and I. Serageldin, eds. (2000), *Social Capital: A Multifaceted Perspective* (Washington: World Bank).

—— and M. Weale (1992), 'On Measuring the Quality of Life', *World Development*, 20: 119–31.

—— P. Hammond, and E. Maskin (1980), 'On Imperfect Information and Optimal Pollution Control', *Review of Economic Studies*, 47: 857–60.

—— B. Kriström, and K.-G. Mäler (1995), 'Current Issues in Resource Accounting', in P. O. Johansson, B. Kriström, and K. G. Mäler, eds., *Current Issues in Environmental Economics* (Manchester: Manchester University Press).

—— S. Levin, and J. Lubchenco (2000), 'Economic Pathways to Ecological Sustainability: Challenges for the New Millennium', *BioScience*, 50: 339–45.

—— K.-G. Mäler, and A. Vercelli, eds. (1997), *The Economics of Transnational Commons*. (Oxford: Clarendon Press).

—— S. Marglin, and A. Sen (1972), *Guidelines for Project Evaluation* (New York: United Nations).

—— A. Sen, and D. Starrett (1973), 'Notes on the Measurement of Inequality', *Journal of Economic Theory*, 6: 180–86.

Davidson, D. (1986), 'Judging Interpersonal Interests', in J. Elster and A. Hylland, eds., *Foundation of Social Choice Theory* (Cambridge: Cambridge University Press).

Deacon, R. T. (1994), 'Deforestation and the Rule of law in a Cross Section of Countries', *Land Economics*, 70: 414–30.

Debreu, G. (1959), *Theory of Value* (New York: John Wiley).

Deininger, K., and L. Squire (1997), 'Economic Growth and Income Inequality: Reexamining the Links', *Finance and Development*, 34: 38–41.

de Soto, H. (2000), *The Mystery of Capital* (New York: Basic Books).

Diamond, J. (1997), *Guns, Germs, and Steel: The Fates of Human Societies* (New York: W. W. Norton).

Diamond, P. A. (1965), 'The Evaluation of Infinite Utility Streams', *Econometrica*, 33: 170–77.

—— (1996), 'Testing the Internal Consistency of Contingent Valuation Surveys', *Journal of Environmental Economics and Management*, 30: 337–47.

—— and J. A. Mirrlees (1971), 'Optimal Taxation and Public Production: Parts 1 and 2', *American Economic Review*, 62: 8–27 and 261–78.

Dinar, A., ed. (2000), *The Political Economy of Water Pricing Reforms* (New York: Oxford University Press).

Dixon, J. A., and M. M. Hufschmidt, eds. (1986), *Economic Valuation Techniques for the Environment: A Case Study Workbook* (Baltimore: Johns Hopkins University Press).

—— D. E. James, and P. B. Sherman, eds. (1990), *Dryland Management: Economic Case Studies* (London: Earthscan).

—— and P. A. Lal (1997), 'The Management of Coastal Wetlands: Economic Analysis of Combined Ecological–Economic Systems', in P. Dasgupta and K.-G, Mäler, eds., *The Environment and Emerging Development Issues*, Vol. II (Oxford: Clarendon Press).

—— L. F. Scura, R. A. Carpenter, and P. B. Sherman (1994), *Economic Analysis of Environmental Impacts* (London: Earthscan).

Dollar, D., and A. Kraay (2000), 'Growth is Good for the Poor', Discussion Paper, World Bank, Washington.

—— and J. Svensson (2000), 'What Explains the Success or Failure of Structural Adjustment Programmes?' *Economic Journal*, 110: 894–917.

Douglas, M., and B. Isherwood (1996 [1979]), *The World of Goods: Towards an Anthropology of Consumption* (London: Routledge).

—— and S. Ney (1998), *Missing Persons: A Critique of Personhood in the Social Sciences* (Berkeley, Cal.: University of California Press).

Dreze, J., and A. Sen (1995), *India: Economic Development and Social Opportunity* (Oxford: Clarendon Press).

—— and P. V. Srinivasan (1997), 'Widowhood and Poverty in Rural India: Some Inferences from Household Survey Data', *Journal of Development Economics*, 54: 217–34.

—— and N. Stern (1990), 'Policy Reform, Shadow Prices, and Market Prices', *Journal of Public Economics*, 42: 1–45.

Dublin, H. T., A. R. E. Sinclair, and J. McGlade (1990), 'Elephants and Fire as Causes of Multiple Stable States in the Serengeti-Mara Woodlands', *Journal of Animal Ecology*, 59: 1147–64.

Duesenberry, J. S. (1949), *Income, Saving and the Theory of Consumer Behaviour* (Cambridge, Mass.: Harvard University Press).

Dutt, G., and M. Ravallion (1998), 'Why Have Some Indian States Done Better than Others at Reducing Poverty ?' *Economica*, 65: 17–38.

Dutta, J., J. Sefton, and M. Weale (1999), 'Education and Public Policy', *Fiscal Studies*, 20: 351–86.

Dworkin, R. (1978), *Taking Rights Seriously* (London: Duckworth).

References

Easterlin, R. (1974), 'Does Economic Growth Improve the Human Lot? Some Empirical Evidence', in P. A. David and M. Reder, eds., *Nations and Households in Economic Growth: Essays in Honor of Moses Abramowitz* (New York: Academic Press).

Eckstein, O. (1958), *Water Resource Development* (Cambridge, Mass.: Harvard University Press).

Edwards, J., and M. Keen (1996), 'Tax Competition and Leviathan', *European Economic Review*, 40: 113–34.

Ehrlich, P. R. (2000), *Human Natures: Genes, Cultures, and the Human Prospect* (Washington: Island Press).

—— and A. H. Ehrlich (1981), *Extinction: The Causes and Consequences of the Disappearance of Species* (New York: Random House).

—— and —— (1990), *The Population Explosion* (New York: Simon & Schuster).

—— and —— (1997), 'The Value of Biodiversity', in P. Dasgupta, K.-G. Mäler, and A. Vercelli, eds., *The Economics of Transnational Commons* (Oxford: Clarendon Press).

—— and J. Holdren (1971), 'Impact of Population Growth', *Science*, 171: 1212–17.

El Serafy, S. (1989), 'The Proper Calculation of Income from Depletable Natural Resources', in Y. Ahmad, S. El Serafy, and E. Lutz, eds., *Environmental Accounting for Sustainable Development* (Washington: World Bank).

Englin, J. and R. Mendelsohn (1991), 'A Hedonic Travel Cost Analysis for Valuation of Multiple Components of Site Quality: The Recreation Value of Forest Management', *Journal of Environmental Economics and Management*, 21: 275–90.

Enke, S. (1966), 'The Economic Aspects of Slowing Population Growth', *Economic Journal*, 76: 44–56.

Ensminger, J. (1990), 'Co-opting the Elders: The Political Economy of State Incorporation in Africa', *American Anthropologist*, 92: 662–75.

Falconer, J. (1990), *The Major Significance of 'Minor' Forest Products* (Rome: Food and Agricultural Organization).

Fankhauser, S. (1994), 'Evaluating the Social Costs of Greenhouse Gas Emissions', *Energy Journal*, 15: 157–84.

Farrell, J., and G. Saloner (1985), 'Standardization, Compatibility, and Innovation', *Rand Journal of Economics*, 16: 70–83.

Feder, E. (1977), 'Agribusiness and the Elimination of Latin America's Rural Proletariat', *World Development*, 5: 559–71.

—— (1979), 'Agricultural Resources in Underdeveloped Countries: Competition between Man and Animal', *Economic and Political Weekly*, 14(30–32): 1345–66.

—— and D. Feeny (1991), 'Land Tenure and Property Rights: Theory and Implications for Development Policy', *World Bank Economic Review*, 5: 135–53.

—— and R. Noronha (1987), 'Land Rights Systems and Agricultural Development in Sub-Saharan Africa', *World Bank Research Observer*, 2: 143–69.

Feeny, D., F. Berkes, B. J. McCay, and J. M. Acheson (1990), 'The Tragedy of the Commons: Twenty-two Years Later', *Human Ecology*, 18: 1–19.

Fehr, E., S. Gächter, and G. Kirchsteiger (1997), 'Reciprocity as a Contract Enforcement Device: Experimental Evidence', *Econometrica*, 65: 833–60.

—— G. Kirchsteiger, and A. Riedl (1998), 'Gift Exchange and Reciprocity in Competitive Experimental Situations', *European Economic Review*, 42: 1–34.

Feinberg, J. (1980), *Rights, Justice, and the Bounds of Liberty* (Princeton: Princeton University Press).

Filmer, D., and L. Pritchett (1996), 'Environmental Degradation and the Demand for Children', Policy Research Working Paper 1623, Policy Research Department, World Bank, Washington.

Fine, B., and K. Fine (1974), 'Social Choice and Individual Rankings, II', *Review of Economic Studies*, 44: 459–75.

Fisher, A., and W. M. Hanemann (1986), 'Option Value and the Extinction of Species', *Advances in Applied Microeconomics*, 4.

Floud, R., K. Wachter, and A. Gregory (1990), *Height, Health and History: Nutritional Status in the United Kingdom, 1750–1980* (Cambridge: Cambridge University Press).

Fogel, R. W. (1994), 'Economic Growth, Population Theory, and Physiology: The Bearing of Long-Term Processes on the Making of Economic Policy', *American Economic Review*, 84: 369–95.

—— S. L. Engerman, R. Margo, K. Sokoloff, R. Steckel, T. J. Trussell, G. Villaflor, and K. W. Wachter (1983), 'Secular Changes in American and British Stature and Nutrition', *Journal of Interdisciplinary History*, 14: 445–81.

Folmer, H., and P. von Mouche (2000), 'Transboundary Pollution and International Cooperation', in T. Tietenber and H. Folmer, eds., *Yearbook of Environmental and Resource Economics 2000/2001* (Cheltenham, UK: Edward Elgar).

—— and A. de Zeeuw (2000), 'International Environmental Problems and Policy', in H. Folmer, and L. Gabel, eds., *Principles of Environmental and Resource Economics: A Guide for Students and Decision-Makers* (Cheltenham, UK: Edward Elgar).

Freedman, R. (1995), 'Asia's Recent Fertility Decline and Prospects for Future Demographic Change', Asia–Pacific Population Research Report No. 1, East–West Center, Honolulu.

Freedom House (2000), *Annual Survey of Freedom: Country Ratings (1972–73 to 1999–00)* (Freedom House Web Page).

Freeman, A. M. III (1982), *Air and Water Pollution Control: A Benefit–Cost Assessment* (New York: John Wiley).

—— (1993), *The Measurement of Environmental and Resource Values: Theory and Methods* (Washington: Resources for the Future).

Frey, B., and A. Stutzer (1999), 'Measuring Preferences by Subjective Well-Being', *Journal of Institutional and Theoretical Economics*, 155.

—— and —— (2000), 'Happiness, Economy and Institutions', *Economic Journal*, 110: 918–38.

Fried, C. (1978), *Right and Wrong* (Cambridge, Mass.: Harvard University Press).

Friedman, M. (1962), *Capitalism and Freedom* (Chicago: University of Chicago Press).

Fudenberg, D., and J. Tirole (1991), *Game Theory* (Cambridge, Mass.: MIT Press).

Fugita, M., P. Krugman, and A. Venables (1999), *The Spatial Economy: Cities, Regions, and International Trade* (Cambridge, Mass.: MIT Press).

Fukuyama, F. (1995), *Trust: The Social Virtues and the Creation of Prosperity* (New York: Free Press).

—— (1999), *The Great Disruption: Human Nature and the Reconstitution of Social Order* (New York: Free Press).

Gadgil, M., and R. Guha (1992), *This Fissured Land: An Ecological History of India* (Delhi: Oxford University Press).

Gambetta, D., ed. (1988), *Trust: Making and Breaking Cooperative Relations* (Oxford: Basil Blackwell).

Gerking, S., and L. R. Stanley (1986), 'An Economic Analysis of Air Pollution and Health: The Case of St Louis', *Review of Economics and Statistics*, 68: 115–21.

Gewirth, A. (1981), 'Are There Any Absolute Rights?' *Philosophical Quarterly*, 31.

Giacomelli, A., C. Giupponi, and C. Paniconi (2001), 'Agricultural Impacts on Groundwater: Processes, Modelling and Decision Support', in C. Dosi, ed., *Agricultural Use of Groundwater* (Dordrecht: Kluwer).

Gigliotti, G. A. (1983), 'Total Utility, Overlapping Generations and Optimum Population', *Review of Economic Studies*, 50: 71–86.

Golding, P., and S. Middleton (1983), *Images of Welfare* (Oxford: Basil Blackwell).

Goodin, R. E. (1986), *Protecting the Vulnerable* (Chicago: University of Chicago Press).

Goodman, L. A., and H. Markowitz (1952), 'Social Welfare Functions based on Individual Rankings', *American Journal of Sociology*, 58.

Gordon, H. S. (1954), 'The Economic Theory of Common-Property Resources', *Journal of Political Economy*, 62: 124–42.

Gottlieb, M. (1945), 'The Theory of Optimum Population for a Closed Economy', *Journal of Political Economy*, 53: 289–316.

Goulder, L. (1995), 'Environmental Taxation and the Double Dividend: A Reader's Guide', *International Tax and Public Finance*, 2: 157–83.

Graff, J. de V. (1962), *Theoretical Welfare Economics* (Cambridge: Cambridge University Press).

Granovetter, M. S. (1978), 'Threshold Models of Collective Behaviour', *American Journal of Sociology*, 83: 1420–43.

Gren, I.-M., K. Turner, and F. Wulff, eds. (2000), *Managing a Sea: The Ecological Economics of the Baltic* (London: Earthscan).

Grossman, G. M., and A. B. Krueger (1995), 'Economic Growth and the Environment', *Quarterly Journal of Economics*, 110: 353–77.

Gunderson, L., and C. S. Holling (2002), *Panarchy* (Washington: Island Press).

Hahn, F. H. (1970), 'Savings and Uncertainty', *Review of Economic Studies*, 37: 21–4.

—— (1971), 'Equilibrium with Transactions Costs', *Econometrica*, 39: 417–40.

Hall, R. E., and C. I. Jones (1999), 'Why do Some Countries Produce So Much More Output per Worker than Others?' *Quarterly Journal of Economics*, 114: 83–116.

Hamilton, K., and M. Clemens (1999), 'Genuine Savings Rates in Developing Countries', *World Bank Economic Review*, 13: 333–56.

Hammond, P. (1976), 'Equity, Arrow's Conditions and Rawls' Difference Principle', *Econometrica*, 44: 793–804.

—— (1988), 'Consequentialist Demographic Norms and Parenting Rights', *Social Choice and Welfare*, 5: 127–46.

Hanemann, W. M. (1991), 'Willingness to Pay and Willingness to Accept: How Much Can They Differ?' *American Economic Review*, 81: 635–47.

—— (1994), 'Valuing the Environment through Contingent Evaluation', *Journal of Economic Perspective*, 8: 19–43.

Hardin, G. (1968), 'The Tragedy of the Commons', *Science*, 162: 1243–8.

Harrington, W., and P. R. Portney (1987), 'Valuing the Benefits of Health and Safety Regulations', *Journal of Urban Economics*, 22: 101–12.

Harrod, R. (1948), *Towards a Dynamic Economics* (London: Macmillan).

Harsanyi, J. C. (1955), 'Cardinal Welfare, Individualistic Ethics and Interpersonal Comparisons of Utility', *Journal of Political Economy*, 63: 309–21.

Hartwick, J. (1977), 'Intergenerational Equity and the Investing of Rents from Exhaustible Resources', *American Economic Review*, 66: 972–74.

—— (1990), 'Natural Resources, National Accounting, and Economic Depreciation', *Journal of Public Economics*, 43: 291–304.

—— (1994), 'National Wealth and Net National Product', *Scandinavian Journal of Economics*, 96: 253–6.

—— and A. Hageman (1993), 'Economic Depreciation of Mineral Stocks and the Contribution of El Serafy', in E. Lutz, ed., *Toward Improved Accounting for the Environment* (Washington: World Bank).

Hassan, R. (2000), 'Improved Measure of the Contribution of Cultivated Forests to National Income and Wealth in South Africa', *Environment and Development Economics*, 5: 157–76.

Hayek, F. (1945), 'The Use of Knowledge in Society', *American Economic Review*, 35: 519–30.

—— (1948), *Individualism and Economic Order* (Bloomington, Ind.: Indiana: Gateway edn).

—— (1960), *The Constitution of Liberty* (London: Routledge & Kegan Paul).

Hazilla, M., and R. J. Kopp (1990), 'The Social Cost of Environmental Quality Regulations: A General Equilibrium Analysis', *Journal of Political Economy*, 98: 853–73.

Heal, G. M. (1998), *Valuing the Future: Economic Theory and Sustainability* (New York: Columbia University Press).

Heath, J., and H. Binswanger (1996), 'Natural Resources Degradation Effects of Poverty and Population Growth are Largely Policy Induced: The Case of Colombia', *Environment and Development Economics*, 1: 65–84.

Hecht, S., A. B. Anderson, and P. May (1988), 'The Subsidy from Nature: Shifting Cultivation, Successional Palm Forests and Rural Development', *Human Organization*, 47: 25–35.

Heckman, J. J. (2000), 'Policies to Foster Human Capital', *Research in Economics*, 54: 3–56.

Hector, A., B. Schmid, C. Beierkuhnlein, M. C. Cladeira, M. Diemer, P. G. Dimitrakopoulos, J. A. Finn, H. Freitas, P. S. Giller, J. Good, R. Harris, P. Högberg, K. Huss-Danell, J. Joshi, A. Jumpponen, C. Körner, P. W. Leadley, M. Loreau, A. Minns, C. P. H. Mulder, G. O'Donovan, S. J. Otway, J. S. Pereira, A. Prinz, D. J. Read, M. Scherer-Lorenzen, E.-D. Schultze, A.-S. D. Siamantziouras, E. M. Spehn, A. C. Terry, A. Y. Troumbis, F. I. Woodward, S. Yachi, and J. H. Lawton (1999), 'Plant Diversity and Productivity Experiments in European Grasslands', *Science*, 286: 1123–7.

Henry, C. (1974), 'Investment Decisions under Uncertainty: The Irreversibility Effect', *American Economic Review*, 64: 1006–12.

Herfindahl, O. C., and A. V. Kneese (1965), *Quality of the Environment: An Economic Approach to Some Problems in Using Land, Water, and Air* (Washington: Resources for the Future).

Heyd, D. (1992), *Genethics: The Morality of Procreation* (Berkeley, Cal.: University of Calfornia Press).

Hicks, J. R. (1939), *Value and Capital* (Oxford: Clarendon Press).

—— (1940), 'The Valuation of Social Income', *Economica*, 7: 105–24.

—— (1942), 'Maintaining Capital Intact: A Further Suggestion', *Economica*, 9: 174–9.

Hinde, R. A. (1997), *Relationships: A Dielectical Perspective* (Hove, Brighton: Psychology Press).

Hirschman, A. (1991), *The Rhetoric of Reaction* (Cambridge, Mass.: Harvard University Press).

Hodgson, G., and J. Dixon (1992), 'Sedimentation Damage to Marine Resources: Environmental and Economic Analysis', in J. B. Marsh, ed., *Resources and Environment in Asia's Marine Sector* (London: Taylor & Francis).

Hoff, K., A. Braverman, and J. E. Stiglitz, eds. (1993), *The Economics of Rural Organizations: Theory, Practice and Policy* (New York: Oxford University Press).

Hogg, M. A., and G. M. Vaughan (1995), *Social Psychology: An Introduction* (London: Prentice-Hall/Harvester Wheatsheaf).

Holden, S. T., B. Shiferaw, and M. Wik (1998), 'Poverty, Market Imperfections and Time Preference: Of Relevance for Environmental Policy?' *Environment and Development Economics*, 3: 105–30.

Homer-Dixon, T. F. (1994), 'Environmental Scarcities and Violent Conflict: Evidence from Cases', *International Security*, 19: 5–40.

—— J. H. Boutwell, and G. W. Rathjens (1993), 'Environmental Change and Violent Conflict', *Scientific American*, 268: 16–23.

Howitt, R. E. (1995), 'Positive Mathematical Programming', *American Journal of Agriculture*, 77: 329–42.

Hurka, T. (1983), 'Value and Population Size', *Ethics*, 93: 497–507.

Hussain, A., N. Stern, and J. Stiglitz (2000), 'Chinese Reforms from a Comparative Perspective', in P. J. Hammond and G. D. Myles, eds., *Incentives, Organization, and Public Economics* (Oxford: Oxford University Press).

IUCN (1980), *The World Conservation Strategy: Living Resource Conservation for Sustainable Development* (Geneva: International Union for the Conservation of Nature and Natural Resources).

Iyer, S. (2000), *Religion and the Economics of Fertility in South India*, Ph.D. dissertation, Faculty of Economics, University of Cambridge.

Jodha, N. S. (1986), 'Common Property Resources and the Rural Poor', *Economic and Political Weekly*, 21: 1169–81.

—— (1995), 'Common Property Resources and the Environmental Context: Role of Biophysical versus Social Stress', *Economic and Political Weekly*, 30: 3278–83.

Johansson, P.-O., and K.-G. Löfgren (1985), *The Economics of Forestry and Natural Resources* (Oxford: Basil Blackwell).

—— and —— (1996), 'On the Interpretation of "Green" NNP Measures as Cost–Benefit Rules', *Environmental and Resource Economics*, 7: 243–50.

Johnson, D. G. (2000), 'Population, Food, and Knowledge', *American Economic Review*, 90: 1–14.

—— (2001), 'On Population and Resources: A Comment', *Population and Development Review*, 27: 739–47.

Jones, C. I. (1998), *Introduction to Economic Growth* (New York: W. W. Norton).

Jorgenson, D. (1995), *Productivity: Postwar US Economic Growth* (Cambridge, Mass.: MIT Press).

—— and B. M. Fraumeni (1989), 'The Accumulation of Human and Non-Human Capital, 1948–1984', in R. E. Lipsey and H. S. Tice, eds., *The Measurement of Income, Saving and Wealth* (Chicago: University of Chicago Press).

—— and —— (1992a), 'The Output of the Education Sector', in Z. Griliches, ed., *Output Measurement in the Services Sector* (Chicago: University of Chicago Press).

—— and —— (1992b), 'Investment in Education and US Economic Growth', *Scandinavian Journal of Economics*, 94: 51–70.

Kahneman, D., P. P. Wakker, and R. Sarin (1997), 'Back to Bentham? Exploration of Experienced Utility', *Quarterly Journal of Economics*, 112: 375–406.

Kamien, M. I., and N. L. Schwartz (1991), *Dynamic Optimization* (Amsterdam: North Holland).

Kaplow, L., and S. Shavell (2001), 'Any Non-Welfarist Method of Policy Assessment Violates the Pareto Principle', *Journal of Political Economy*, 109: 281–6.

Katz, M. L., and C. Shapiro (1985), 'Network Externalities, Competition, and Compatibility', *American Economic Review*, 75: 424–40.

Keeler, E., A. M. Spence, and R. Zeckhauser (1972), 'The Optimal Control of Pollution', *Journal of Economic Theory*, 4: 19–34.

Kelley, A. C. (1988), 'Economic Consequences of Population Changes in the Third World', *Journal of Economic Literature*, 26: 1685–1728.

Kneese, A. V., and B. T. Bower (1968), *Managing Water Quality: Economics, Technology and Institutions* (Baltimore: Johns Hopkins University Press).

—— R. U. Ayers, and R. C. d'Arge (1972), *Economics and the Environment: A Materials Balance Approach* (Washington: Resources for the Future).

Knowlton, N. (1992), 'Thresholds and Multiple Stable States in Coral Reef Community Dynamics', *American Zoologist*, 32: 674–82.

Kolm, S.-Ch. (1969),'The Optimal Production of Social Justice', in J. Margolis and H. Guitton, eds., *Public Economics* (London: Macmillan).

Koopmans, T. C. (1957), 'The Price System and the Allocation of Resources', in T. C. Koopmans, ed., *Three Essays on the State of Economic Science* (New York: McGraw-Hill).

—— (1960), 'Stationary Ordinal Utility and Impatience', *Econometrica*, 28: 287–309.

—— (1965), 'On the Concept of Optimal Economic Growth', *Pontificiae Academiae Scientiarum Scripta Varia*, 28; reprinted in T. C. Koopmans, ed., *The Econometric Approach to Development Planning*, 1966 (Amsterdam: North-Holland).

—— (1967), 'Objectives, Constraints and Outcomes in Optimal Growth Models', *Econometrica*, 35: 1–15.

—— (1972), 'Representation of Preference Orderings over Time', in C. B. McGuire and R. Radner eds., *Decision and Organization* (Amsterdam: North-Holland).

Kopp, R. J., and V. K. Smith, eds. (1993), *Valuing Natural Assets: The Economics of Natural Resource Damage Assessment* (Washington: Resources for the Future).

—— and J. B. Thatcher (2000), *The Weathervane Guide to Climate Policy* (Washington: Resources for the Future).

Kremer, M. (1993), 'Population Growth and Technological Change: One Million BC to 1990', *Quarterly Journal of Economics*, 108: 681–716.

—— (2000a), 'Creating Markets for New Vaccines, 1: Rationale', mimeo, Department of Economics, Harvard University.

—— (2000b), 'Creating Markets for New Vaccines, 2: Design Issues', mimeo, Department of Economics, Harvard University.

Krutilla, J. V. (1967), 'Conservation Reconsidered', *American Economic Review*, 57: 777–86.

—— and A. C. Fisher (1975), *The Economics of Natural Environments: Studies in the Valuation of Commodity and Amenity Resources* (Baltimore: Johns Hopkins University Press).

Kuper, A. (2000), 'Rawlsian Global Justice: Beyond *The Law of Peoples*', *Political Theory*, 28: 640–74.

Kurz, M. (1968), 'Optimal Economic Growth and Wealth Effects', *International Economic Review*, 9: 348–57.

Laibson, D. I. (1997), 'Golden Eggs and Hyperbolic Discounting', *Quarterly Journal of Economics*, 112: 443–77.

Lal, D. (1972), *Wells and Welfare* (Paris: OECD).

Landes, D. (1998), *The Wealth and Poverty of Nations* (New York: W. W. Norton).

Lane, J. (1977), *On Optimum Population Paths* (Berlin: Springer-Verlag).

Lau, L. (1996), 'The Sources of Long-Term Economic Growth: Observations from the Experiences of Developed and Developing Countries', in R. Landau, T. Taylor and G. Wright, eds., *The Mosaic of Economic Growth* (Stanford, Cal.: Stanford, University Press).

Laycock, W. A. (1991), 'Stable States and Thesholds of Range Condition on North American Grasslands – A Viewpoint', *Journal of Range Management*, 44: 427–33.

Ledyard, J. O. (1995), 'Public Goods: A Survey of Experimental Research', in J. H. Kagel and A. E. Roth, eds., *The Handbook of Experimental Economics* (Princeton: Princeton University Press).

Levhari, D., and T. N. Srinivasan (1969), 'Optimal Savings under Uncertainty', *Review of Economic Studies*, 36: 153–63.

Levin, S. (1999), *Fragile Dominion: Complexity and the Commons* (Reading, Mass.: Perseus Books).

—— ed. (2001), *Encyclopedia of Biodiversity* (New York: Academic Press).

—— S. Barrett, S. Aniyar, W. Baumol, C. Bliss, B. Bolin, P. Dasgupta, P. Ehrlich, C. Folke, I.-M. Gren, C. S. Holling, A.-M. Jansson, B.-O. Jansson, K.-G. Mäler, D. Martin, C. Perrings, and E. Sheshinski (1998), 'Resilience in Natural and Socioeconomic Systems', *Environment and Development Economics*, 3: 222–35.

Levi, M. (1988), *Of Rule and Revenue* (Berkeley, Cal.: University of California Press).

Lind, R. C., ed. (1982), *Discounting for Time and Risk in Energy Policy* (Baltimore: Johns Hopkins University Press).

Lindahl, E. R. (1934), 'The Concept of Income', in G. Bagge, ed., *Economic Essays in Honor of Gustaf Cassel* (London: George Allen & Unwin).

—— (1958), 'Some Controversial Questions in the Theory of Taxation', in R. A. Musgrave and A. T. Peacock, eds., *Classics in the Theory of Public Finance* (London: Macmillan); originally published in Swedish in 1928.

Lindbeck, A. (1995), 'Welfare State Disincentives with Endogenous Habits and Norms', *Scandinavian Journal of Economics*, 97: 477–94.

—— (1997), 'Incentives and Social Norms in Houshould Behaviour', *American Economic Review* (Papers & Proceedings), 87: 370–77.

—— S. Nyberg, and J. W. Weibull (1999), 'Social Norms and Economic Incentives in the Welfare State', *Quarterly Journal of Economics*, 114: 1–36.

Lipset, S. M. (1959), 'Some Social Requisites of Democracy: Economic Development and Political Legitimacy', *American Political Science Review*, 53: 69–105.

—— (1960), *Political Man* (Garden City, NY: Doubleday Anchor).

Little, I. M. D., and J. A. Mirrlees (1968), *Manual of Industrial Project Analysis in Developing Countries: Social Cost Benefit Analysis* (Paris: OECD).

—— and —— (1974), *Project Appraisal and Planning for Developing Countries* (London: Heinemann).

Loewenstein, G., and D. Prelec (1992), 'Anomalies in Intertemporal Choice: Evidence and Interpretation', *Quarterly Journal of Economics*, 107: 573–98.

Lomas, P. (1999), *Doing Good? Psychotherapy Out of its Depth* (Oxford: Oxford University Press).

Lopez, R. (1998), 'The Tragedy of the Commons in Cote d'Ivoire Agriculture: Empirical Evidence and Implications for Evaluating Trade Policies', *World Bank Economic Review*, 12: 105–32.

Loreau, M., and A. Hector (2001), 'Partitioning Selection and Complementarity in Biodiversity Experiments', *Nature*, 412: 72–6.

Lubchenco, J., A. M. Olson, L. B. Brubaker, S. R. Carpenter, M. M. Holland, S. Hubbell, S. A. Levin, J. A. MacMahon, P. A. Matson, J. M. Melillo, H. A. Mooney, C. H. Peterson, R. Pulliam, L. A. Real, P. J. Regal, and P. G. Risser (1991), 'The Sustainable Biosphere Initiative: An Ecological Research Agenda', *Ecology*, 72: 371–412.

Luce, R. D., and H. Raiffa (1957), *Games and Decisions* (New York: John Wiley).

Ludwig, D., D. D. Jones, and C. S. Holling (1978), 'Qualitative Analysis of Insect Outbreak Systems: The Spruce Budworm and Forest', *Journal of Animal Ecology*, 47: 315–32.

Lutz, E., ed. (1993), *Toward Improved Accounting for the Environment* (Washington: World Bank).

Lynne, G. D., P. Conroy, and F. J. Prochaska (1981), 'Economic Valuation of Marsh Areas for Marine Production Process', *Journal of Environmental Economics and Management*, 8: 175–86.

Maddison, A. (2001), *The World Economy: A Millennial Perspective* (Paris: OECD).

Magrath, W., and P. Arens (1989), 'The Costs of Soil Erosion in Java: A Natural Resource Accounting Approach', Environmental Department Working Paper No.18, World Bank, Washington.

Majumdar, M., and T. Mitra (2000), 'Periodic and Chaotic Programs of Optimal Intertemporal Allocation in an Aggregative Model with Wealth Effect', in M. Majumdar, T. Mitra, and K. Nishimura, eds., *Optimization and Chaos* (Berlin: Springer-Verlag).

Mäler, K.-G. (1974), *Environmental Economics: A Theoretical Enquiry* (Baltimore: Johns Hopkins University Press).

—— (1991), 'National Accounting and Environmental Resources', *Environmental and Resource Economics*, 1: 1–15.

—— (2000), 'Development, Ecological Resources and their Management: A study of Complex Dynamic Systems', *European Economic Review* (Papers & Proceedings), 44: 645–66.

—— and H. Uzawa (1995), 'Tradeable Emission Permits and the Stability of Lindahl Equilibrium', Discussion Paper, JDB Research Center on Global Warming, Japan Development Bank, Tokyo.

—— and R. E. Wyzga (1976), *Economic Measurement of Environmental Damage* (Paris: OECD).

—— A. Xepapadeas, and A. de Zeeuw (2000), 'Lake Model', Technical Report, Baijer International Institute of Ecological Economics, Stockholm.

—— and A. de Zeeuw (1998), 'The Acid-Rain Differential Game', *Environmental and Resource Economics*, 12: 167–84.

Marshall, T. H. (1964), *Class, Citizenship and Social Development* (Garden City, NY: Doubleday).

—— (1981), *The Right to Welfare and Other Essays* (New York: Free Press).

Martin, S., and N. Grube (2000), *Chronicles of the Maya Kings and Queens: Deciphering the Dynasties of the Ancient Maya* (London: Thames & Hudson).

Maskin, E. (1978), 'A Theorem on Utilitarianism', *Review of Economic Studies*, 44: 93–6.

Matson, P. A., W. J. Parton, A. G. Power, and M. J. Swift (1997), 'Agricultural Intensification and Ecosystem Properties', *Science*, 277: 504–9.

May, K. (1952), 'A Set of Necessary and Sufficient Conditions for Simple Majority Decisions', *Econometrica*, 20: 680–4.

May, R. M. (1977), 'Thresholds and Breakpoints in Ecosystems with a Multiplicity of Steady States', *Nature*, 269: 471–7.

Maynard Smith, J. (1982), *Evolution and the Theory of Games* (Cambridge: Cambridge University Press).

McConnell, K. E. (1985), 'The Economics of Outdoor Recreation', in A. V. Kneese, and J. L. Sweeney, eds., *Handbook of Natural Resource and Energy Economics*, Vol. 1 (Amsterdam: North-Holland).

McKean, M. (1992), 'Success on the Commons: A Comparative Examination of Institutions for Common Property Resource Management', *Journal of Theoretical Politics*, 4: 256–68.

McKelvey, R. (1980), 'Common Property and the Conservation of Natural Resources', in S. A. Levin, T. G. Hallam, and L. J. Gross, eds., *Applied Mathematical Ecology*, 18: *Biomathematics* (Berlin: Springer Verlag).

McMahan, J. A. (1981), 'Problems of Population Theory', *Ethics*, 91: 96–127.

McNeill, J. R. (2000), *Something New under the Sun: An Environmental History of the Twentieth-Century World* (New York: W. W. Norton).

Meade, J. E. (1955), *Trade and Welfare* (Oxford: Oxford University Press).

—— (1964), *Efficiency, Equality and the Ownership of Property* (London: George Allen & Unwin).

—— (1973), *The Theory of Externalities* (Geneva: Institute Universitaire de Hautes Etudes Internationales).

—— (1989), *Agathotopia: The Economics of Partnership* (Aberdeen: University of Aberdeen Press).

Meenakshi, J. V., R. Ray, and S. Gupta (2000), 'Estimates of Poverty for SC, ST and Female-Headed Households', *Economic and Political Weekly*, 35: 2748–54.

Milliman, J. W. (1956), 'Commodities and Price System and Use of Water Supplies', *Southern Economic Journal*, 22: 426–37.

Mirrlees, J. A. (1967), 'Optimum Growth when the Technology is Changing', *Review of Economic Studies* (Symposium Issue), 34: 95–124.

—— (1969), 'The Evaluation of National Income in an Imperfect Economy', *Pakistan Development Review*, 9: 1–13.

—— (1971), 'An Exploration in the Theory of Optimal Income Taxation', *Review of Economic Studies*, 38: 175–208.

Mitchell, R. C., and R. T. Carson (1989), *Using Surveys to Value Public Goods: The Contingent Valuation Method* (Washington: Resources for the Future).

Molians, J. R. (1998), 'The Impact of Inequality, Gender, External Assistance and Social Capital on Local-Level Collective Action', *World Development*, 26: 413–31.

Moore, M. J., and W. K. Viscusi (1988), 'The Quantity-Adjusted Value of Life', *Economic Enquiry*, 26: 369–88.

Morgenstern, R. D., ed. (1997), *Economic Analyses at EPA: Assessing Regulatory Impact* (Washington: Resources for the Future).

Murray, J. D. (1993), *Mathematical Biology* (Berlin: Springer-Verlag).

Musgrave, R. (1959), *Theory of Public Finance* (New York: McGraw-Hill).

Musu, I., and D. Siniscalco, eds. (1996), *National Accounts and the Environment* (Dordrecht: Kluwer).

Myers, N., and J. Kent (2000), *Perverse Subsidies: How Tax Dollars Undercut our Environment and our Economies* (Washington: Island Press).

—— and J. L. Simon (1994), *Scarcity or Abundance? A Debate on the Environment* (New York: W. W. Norton).

Myles, G. D. (1995), *Public Economics* (Cambridge: Cambridge University Press).

Myrdal, G. (1944), *An American Dilemma: The Negro Problem and Modern Democracy* (New York: Harper & Row).

Narayan, D., and L. Pritchett (1999), 'Cents and Sociability: Household Income and Social Capital in Rural Tanzania', *Economic Development and Cultural Change*, 47: 871–89.

—— R. Patel, K. Schafft, A. Rademacher, and S. Koch-Schulte (2000), *Voices of the Poor: Can Anyone Hear Us?* (Oxford: Oxford University Press).

Narveson, J. (1967), 'Utilitarianism and New Generations', *Mind*, 76: 62–72.

—— (1973), 'Moral Problems of Population', *Monist*, 57.

Nash, J. (1950), 'The Bargaining Problem', *Econometrica*, 18: 155–62.

Newcombe, K. (1989), 'An Economic Justification of Rural Afforestation: The Case of Ethiopia', in G. Schramm, and J. J. Warford, eds., *Environmental Management and Economic Development* (Baltimore: Johns Hopkins University Press).

Newell, R., and W. Pizer (2001), 'Discounting the Distant Future: How Much Do Uncertain Rates Increase Valuations?', Discussion Paper 00-45, Resources for the Future, Washington, DC.

Nordhaus, W. D. (1977), 'Economic Growth and Climate: The Carbon Dioxide Problem', *American Economic Review* (Papers & Proceedings), 67: 341–6.

—— (1994), *Managing the Global Commons: The Economics of Climate Change* (Cambridge, Mass.: MIT Press).

Nordhaus, W. D. and J. Tobin (1972), 'Is Economic Growth Obsolete?' in *Economic Growth: 5th Anniversary Colloquium of the NBER* (New York: Columbia University Press).

—— and Z. Yang (1996), 'A Regional Dynamic General-Equilibrium Model of Alternative Climate-Change Strategies', *American Economic Review*, 86: 741–65.

North, D., and R. P. Thomas (1973), *The Rise of the Western World: A New Economic History* (Cambridge: Cambridge University Press).

Nozick, R. (1974), *Anarchy, State and Utopia* (New York: Basic Books).

—— (1990), *The Examined Life* (New York: Simon & Schuster, Touchstone Books).

Ohlin, G. (1967), *Population Control and Economic Development* (Paris: OECD).

O'Neill, O. (1986), *Faces of Hunger: An Essay on Poverty, Justice and Development* (London: Allen & Unwin).

Ostrom, E. (1990), *Governing the Commons: The Evolution of Institutions for Collective Action* (Cambridge: Cambridge University Press).

—— (1996), 'Incentives, Rules of the Game, and Development', *Proceedings of the Annual World Bank Conference on Development Economics, 1995* (Supplement to the *World Bank Economic Review* and the *World Bank Research Observer*): 207–34.

—— and R. Gardner (1993), 'Coping with Asymmetries in the Commons: Self-Governing Irrigations Can Work', *Journal of Economic Perspectives*, 7: 93–112.

—— and E. Schlager (1996), 'The Formation of Property Rights', in S. S. Hanna, C. Folke, and K.-G. Mäler, eds., *Rights to Nature* (Washington: Island Press).

Oswald, A. J. (1997), 'Happiness and Economic Performance', *Economic Journal*, 107: 1815–31.

Parfit, D. (1976), 'On Doing the Best for our Children', in M. Bayles, ed., *Ethics and Population* (Cambridge, Mass.: Schenkman).

—— (1982), 'Future Generations: Further Problems', *Philosophy and Public Affairs*, 11: 113–72.

—— (1984), *Reasons and Persons* (Oxford: Oxford University Press).

—— (1990), 'Overpopulation and the Quality of Life', in J. Glover, ed., *Utilitarianism and its Critics* (London: Macmillan).

Pearce, D., and G. Atkinson (1993), 'Capital Theory and the Measurement of Sustainable Development: An Indicator of Weak Sustainability', *Ecological Economics*, 8: 103–8.

—— K. Hamilton, and G. Atkinson (1996), 'Measuring Sustainable Development: Progress on Indicators', *Environment and Development Economics*, 1: 85–101.

—— A. Markandya, and E. Barbier (1989), *Blueprint for a Green Economy* (London: Earthscan).

—— and D. Moran (1994), *The Economic Value of Biodiversity* (London: Earthscan).

Pearson, C. S. (2000), *Economics and the Global Environment* (Cambridge: Cambridge University Press).

Perrings, C., ed. (2000), *The Economics of Biodiversity Loss in Sub-Saharan Africa* (Cheltenham, UK: Edward Elgar).

—— and B. W. Walker (1995), 'Biodiversity Loss and the Economics of Discontinuous Change in Semi-arid Rangelands', in C. Perrings *et al.*, eds., *Biodiversity Loss: Economic and Ecological Issues* (Cambridge: Cambridge University Press).

—— K.-G. Mäler, C. Folke, C. S. Holling, and B.-O. Jansson, eds. (1994), *Biodiversity Conservation: Problems and Policies* (Dordrecht: Kluwer).

—— K.-G. Mäler, C. Folke, C. S. Holling, and B.-O. Jansson, eds. (1995), *Biodiversity Loss: Economic and Ecological Issues* (Cambridge: Cambridge University Press).

Persson, T., and G. Tabellini (2000), *Political Economics: Explaining Economic Policy* (Cambridge, Mass.: MIT Press).

Peterman, R. M. (1977), 'A Simple Mechanism that Causes Collapsing Stability Regions in Exploited Salmonid Populations', *Journal of the Fisheries Research Board of Canada*, 34: 1130–42.

Pezzey, J. (1992), 'Sustainable Development Concepts: An Economic Analysis', World Bank Environment Paper No. 2, World Bank, Washington.

—— and M. A. Toman (2002), 'Progress and Problems in the Economics of Sustainability', in T. Tietenberg and H. Folmer, eds., *The International Yearbook of Environmental and Resource Economics 2002/2003* (Cheltenham: Edward Elgar).

Phelps, E. S., and R. Pollak (1968), 'Second-Best National Savings and Game Equilibrium Growth', *Review of Economic Studies*, 35: 185–99.

Pigou, A. C. (1920), *The Economics of Welfare* (London: Macmillan).

Pitchford, J. D. (1974), *Population in Economic Growth* (Amsterdam: North-Holland).

Plato (1970), *Laws*, trans. T. J. Saunders (London: Penguin Classics).

Portney, P. R., and J. P. Weyant, eds. (1999), *Discounting and Intergenerational Equity* (Washington: Resources for the Future).

Postel, S. L., G. Daily, and P. R. Ehrlich (1996), 'Human Appropriation of Renewable Fresh Water', *Science*, 271: 785–8.

Pratt, J. (1964), 'Risk Aversion in the Small and in the Large', *Econometrica*, 32: 122–36.

Pritchett, L. (1997), 'Divergence, Big Time', *Journal and Economic Perspectives*, 11: 3–17.

Przeworski, A. (1991), *Democracy and the Market* (Cambridge: Cambridge University Press).

Putnam, H. (1993), 'Objectivity and the Science-Ethics Distinction', in M. C. Nussbaum and A. Sen, eds., *The Quality of Life* (Oxford: Clarendon Press).

Putnam, R. D. (with R. Leonardi and R. Y. Nanetti) (1993), *Making Democracy Work: Civic Traditions in Modern Italy* (Princeton: Princeton University Press).

Radner, R. (1967), 'Efficiency Prices for Infinite Horizon Production Programmes', *Review of Economic Studies*, 34: 51–66.

Rahmstorf, S. (1995), 'Bifurcations of the Atlantic Thermohaline Circulation in Response to the Change in the Hydrological Cycle', *Nature*, 378: 145–9.

Ramsey, F. P. (1928), 'A Mathematical Theory of Saving', *Economic Journal*, 38: 543–49.

Rawls, J. (1972), *A Theory of Justice* (Oxford: Oxford University Press).

Reardon, T., and S. A. Vosti (1995), 'Links between Rural Poverty and the Environment in Developing Countries: Asset Categories and Investment Poverty', *World Development*, 23: 1495–506.

Reed, D., ed. (1996), *Structural Adjustment, the Environment and Sustainable Development* (London: Earthscan).

Repetto, R., W. Magrath, M. Wells, C. Beer, and F. Rossini (1989), *Wasting Assets: Natural Resources and the National Income Accounts* (Washington: World Resources Institute).

Reutlinger, S., and H. Pellekaan (1986), *Poverty and Hunger: Issues and Options for Food Security in Developing Countries* (Washington: World Bank Publication).

Robbins, L. (1932), *An Essay on the Nature and Significance of Economic Science* (London: Allen & Unwin).

Robinson, J. (1964), *Economic Philosophy* (Harmondsworth, Middx: Penguin Books).

Rodrik, D. (2000), 'Participatory Politics, Social Cooperation, and Economic Stability', *American Economic Review* (Papers & Proceedings), 90: 140–4.

Roemer, J. (1999), 'Does Democracy Engender Justice?' in I. Shapiro and C. Hacker-Cordon, eds., *Democracy's Value* (Cambridge: Cambridge University Press).

Romer, D. (1996), *Advanced Macroeconomics* (New York: McGraw-Hill).

Rosenberg, N., and L. E. Birdzell, Jr (1986), *How the West Grew Rich: The Economic Transformation of the Industrial World* (New York: Basic Books).

Rosenstein-Rodan, P. (1943), 'Problems of Industrialization in Eastern and Southeastern Europe', *Economic Journal*, 53: 202–11.

Rosenzweig, M. R., and O. Stark, eds. (1997), *Handbook of Population and Family Economics*, Vols. 1A and 1B (Amsterdam: North-Holland).

Roughgarden, J., R. M. May, and S. A. Levin, eds. (1989), *Perspectives in Ecological Theory* (Princeton: Princeton University Press).

Roughgarden, T., and S. H. Schneider (1999), 'Climate Change Policy: Quantifying Uncertainties for Damages and Optimal Carbon Taxes', *Energy Policy*, 27: 415–29.

Rousseau, J.-J. (1946), *The Social Contract*, trans. E. Barker (Oxford: Oxford University Press).

Rudra, A. (1982), *Indian Agricultural Economics: Myths and Realities* (New Delhi: Allied Publishers).

—— (1984), 'Local Power and Farm-Level Decision-Making', in M. Desai, S. H. Rudolph, and A. Rudra, eds., *Agrarian Power and Agricultural Productivity in South Asia* (Berkeley, Cal.: University of California Press).

Ruitenbeek, J. (1989), *Social Benefit–Cost Analysis of the Korup Project, Cameroon* (London: World Wide Fund for Nature).

Sachs, J. D. (1999), 'Helping the World's Poorest', *Economist* (14 Aug.).

—— A. D. Mellinger, and J. L. Gallop (2001), 'The Geography of Poverty and Wealth', *Scientific American*, 284 (March): 62–7.

Samuelson, P. A. (1947), *Foundations of Economic Analysis* (Cambridge, Mass.: Harvard University Press).

—— (1961), 'The Evaluation of "Social Income": Capital Formation and Wealth', in F. A. Lutz and D. C. Hague, eds., *The Theory of Capital* (London: Macmillan).

Sandmo, A. (2000), *The Public Economics of the Environment* (Oxford: Oxford Univeristy Press).

Scanlon, T. M. (1978), 'Rights, Goals, and Fairness', in S. Hampshire, ed., *Public and Private Morality* (Cambridge: Cambridge University Press).

Schama, S. (1987), *The Embarrassment of Riches: An Interpretation of Dutch Culture in the Golden Age* (London: Collins).

Scheffer, M. (1997), *The Ecology of Shallow Lakes* (New York: Chapman Hall).

Schell, J. (1982), *The Fate of the Earth* (New York: Avon).

Schelling, T. (1978), *Micromotives and Macrobehaviour* (New York: W. W. Norton).

Schneider, R. R. (1992), 'Brazil: An Analysis of Environmental Problems in the Amazon', Report No. 9104-BR, World Bank, Washington.

—— (1995), 'Government and the Economy on the Amazon Frontier', World Bank Environment Paper No. 11, World Bank, Washington.

Schultz, T. W. (1974), *The Economics of the Family: Marriage, Children and Human Capital* (Chicago: University of Chicago Press).

Schumpeter, J. (1942), *Capitalism, Socialism and Democracy* (New York: Harper).

Scott, A. D. (1955), 'The Fishery: The Objectives and Sole Ownership', *Journal of Political Economy*, 63: 116–24.

Scott, M. F. G., J. D. MacArthur, and D. M. G. Newbery (1976), *Project Appraisal in Practice: The Little–Mirrlees Methods applied in Kenya* (London: Heinemann Educational Books).

Scrimshaw, N. C. (1970), 'Synergism of Malnutrition and Infection: Evidence from Field Studies in Guatemala', *Journal of the American Medical Association*, 212.

—— (1983), 'Importance of Infection and Immunity in Nutrition Intervention Programs and Priorities for Interventions', in B. A. Underwood, ed., *Nutrition Intervention Strategies National Development* (New York: Academic Press).

—— and M. B. Wallerstein, eds. (1982), *Nutrition Policy Implementation: Issues and Experience* (New York: Plenum Press).

Seabright, P. (1989), 'Creating Persons', *Proceedings of the Aristotelian Society*, 58 (Suppl.): 41–53.

—— (1993), 'Managing Local Commons: Theoretical Issues in Incentive Design', *Journal of Economic Perspectives*, 7: 113–34.

—— (1997), 'Is Cooperation Habit-forming?', in P. Dasgupta and K.-G. Mäler, eds., *The Environment and Emerging Development Issues*, Vol. II (Oxford: Clarendon Press).

—— ed. (2000), *The Vanishing Rouble: Barter Networks and Non-Monetary Transactions in Post-Soviet Societies* (Cambridge: Cambridge University Press).

Sefton, J., and M. Weale (1996), 'The Net National Product and Exhaustible Resources: The Effects of Foreign Trade', *Journal of Public Economics*, 61: 21–48.

Sen, A. (1970), *Collective Choice and Social Welfare* (San Francisco: Holden Day).

—— (1982), 'Approaches to the Choice of Discount Rates for Social Benefit–Cost Analysis', in R. C. Lind, ed., *Discounting for Time and Risk in Energy Policy* (Baltimore: Johns Hopkins University Press).

—— (1994), 'Population: Delusion and Reality', *New York Review of Books* (22 Sept.): 62–71.

—— (1999), *Development as Freedom* (Oxford: Oxford University Press).

Serageldin, I. (1995), 'Are We Saving Enough for the Future?' in *Monitoring Environmental Progress: Report on Work in Progress, Environmentally Sustainable Development*, World Bank, Washington.

Seroa Da Motta, R., and C. Ferraz (2000), 'Estimating Timber Depreciation in the Brazilian Amazon', *Environmental and Development Economics*, 5: 129–42.

Sethi, R. and E. Somanathan (1996), 'The Evolution of Social Norms in Common Property Resource Use', *American Economic Review*, 86: 766–788.

Seymour, F. J., and N. K. Dubash (2000), *The Right Conditions: The World Bank, Structural Adjustment, and Forest Policy Reform* (Washington: World Resources Institute).

Shapiro, I., and C. Hacker-Cordon, eds. (1999a), *Democracy's Value* (Cambridge: Cambridge University Press).

—— and C. Hacker-Cordon, eds. (1999b), *Democracy's Edges* (Cambridge: Cambridge University Press).

Shapiro, J. (2001), *Mao's War against Nature: Politics and the Environment in Revolutionary China* (Cambridge: Cambridge University Press).

Shove, G. (1942), 'The Place and Marshall's *Principles* in the Development of Economic Theory', *Economic Journal*, 52: 294–329.

Siamwalla, A., C. Pinthong, N. Poaponsakorn, P. Satsanguan, P. Nettayarak, W. Mingmaneenakin, and Y. Tubpun (1989), 'The Thai Rural Credit System: Public Subsidies, Private Information, and Segmented Markets', *World Bank Economic Review*, 4: 271–96.

Sidgwick, H. (1907), *The Methods of Ethics* (London: Macmillan).

Simon, J. L. (1989), 'On Population and Economic Development', *Population and Development Review*, 15: 323–32.

—— (1990), *Population Matters: People, Resources, Environment, Immigration* (New Brunswick, NJ: Transaction Press).

Singer, P. (1976), *Animal Liberation* (Cambridge: Cambridge University Press).

Skiba, A. K. (1978), 'Optimal Growth with a Convex–Concave Production Function', *Econometrica*, 46: 527–40.

Smith, P. B., and M. H. Bond (1993), *Social Psychology across Cultures; Analysis and Perspectives* (London: Harvester Wheatsheaf).

Smith, V. K., and W. H. Desvousges (1986), *Measuring Water Quality Benefits* (Norwell, Mass.: Kluwer-Nijhoff).

Solow, R. M. (1956), 'A Contribution to the Theory of Economic Growth', *Quarterly Journal of Economics*, 70: 65–94.

—— (1957), 'Technical Change and the Aggregate Production Function', *Review of Economics and Statistics*, 39: 312–20.

Solow, R. M. (1974a), 'The Economics of Resources and the Resources of Economics', *American Economic Review* (Papers & Proceedings), 64: 1–21.

—— (1974b), 'Intergenerational Equity and Exhaustible Resources', *Review of Economic Studies* (Symposium Issue), 41: 29–45.

Solow, R. M. (1986), 'On the Intergenerational Allocation of Exhaustible Resources', *Scandinavian Journal of Economics*, 88: 141–49.

—— (1992), 'An Almost Practical Step toward Sustainability', 40th Anniversary Lecture, Resources for the Future, Washington.

—— (2000), 'Notes on Social Capital and Economic Performance', in P. Dasgupta and I. Serageldin, eds., *Social Capital: A Multifaceted Perspective* (Washington: World Bank).

Somanathan, E. (1991), 'Deforestation, Property Rights and Incentives in Central Himalaya', *Economic and Political Weekly*, 26 (Special Issue: January 26): PE37–46.

Spence, A. M. (1974), 'Blue Whales and Optimal Control Theory', in H. Göttinger, ed., *System Approaches and Environmental Problems* (Gottingen: Vandenhoek and Ruprecht).

Squire, L., and H. Van der Taak (1975), *Economic Analysis of Projects* (Baltimore: Johns Hopkins University Press).

Srinivasan, T. N. (1994), 'Data Base for Development Analysis: An Overview', *Journal of Development Economics*, 44: 3–28.

Starrett, D. A. (1972), 'Fundamental Non-Convexities in the Theory of Externalities', *Journal of Economic Theory*, 4: 180–99.

—— (1973), 'A Note on Externalities and the Core', *Econometrica*, 41: 179–83.

—— (1988), *Foundations of Public Economics* (New York: Cambridge University Press).

Sterba, J. P. (1987), 'Explaining Asymmetry: A Problem for Parfit', *Philosophy and Public Affairs*, 16: 188–92.

Stern, N. (1991), 'Comments', in Roundtable Discussion on 'Development Strategies: The Role of the State and the Private Sector', *Proceedings of the World Bank Annual Conference on Development Economics 1990* (Supplement to the *World Bank Economic Review* and the *World Bank Economic Observer*).

Stiglitz, J. E. (1994), *Whither Socialism?* (Cambridge, Mass.: MIT Press).

Summers, R., and A. Heston (1988), 'A New Set of International Comparisons of Real Product and Prices: Estimates for 130 Countries, 1950–1985', *Review of Income and Wealth*, 34: 1–25.

Taylor, C. L., and D. A. Jodice (1983), *World Handbook of Political and Social Indicators*, Vol. 1 (New Haven: Yale University Press).

Taylor-Gooby, P. (1976), 'Rent Benefits and Tenant Attitudes', *Journal of Social Policy*, 5.

Temkin, L. S. (1987), 'Intransitivity and the Mere Addition Paradox', *Philosophy and Public Affairs*, 16: 138–87.

Temple, J. (1999), 'The New Growth Evidence', *Journal of Economic Literature*, 37: 112–56.

Thomas, V., M. Dailami, A. Dhareshwar, D. Kaufmann, N. Kishor, R. Lopez, and Y. Wang (2000), *The Quality of Growth* (Washington: World Bank).

Thomson, J. T., D. H. Feeny, and R. J. Oakerson (1986), 'Institutional Dynamics: The Evolution and Dissolution of Common Property Resource Management', in National Research Council, *Proceedings of a Conference on Common Property Resource Management* (Washington: US National Academy of Science Press).

Tietenberg, T. (1988), *Environmental and Natural Resource Economics*, 2nd edn (Glenview, Ill.: Scott, Forsman).

Tilman, D. (1997), 'Biodiversity and Ecosystem Functioning', in G. Daily, ed., *Nature's Services: Societal Dependence on Natural Ecosystems* (Washington: Island Press).

—— and J. A. Downing (1994), 'Biodiversity and Stability in Grasslands', *Nature*, 367: 363–7.

Tinbergen, J. (1954), *Centralization and Decentralization in Economic Policy* (Amsterdam: North-Holland).

Tirole, J. (1993), *The Theory of Industrial Organization* (Cambridge, Mass.: MIT Press).

Tversky, A., and D. Kahneman (1988), 'Rational Choice and the Framing of Decisions', in D. E. Bell, H. Raiffa, and A. Tversky, eds., *Decision Making: Descriptive, Normative, and Prescriptive Interactions* (Cambridge: Cambridge University Press).

Udry, C. (1993), 'Credit Markets in Northern Nigeria: Credit as Insurance in a Rural Economy', in K. Hoff, A. Braverman, and J. E. Stiglitz, eds. (1993), *The Economics of Rural Organizations: Theory, Practice and Policy* (New York: Oxford University Press).

—— (1994), 'Risk and Insurance in a Rural Credit Market: An Empirical Investigation in Northern Nigeria', *Review of Economic Studies*, 61: 495–526.

Ulph, A. (1997), 'International Trade and the Environment: A Survey of Recent Economic Analysis', in H. Folmer and T. Tietenberg, eds., *Yearbook of Environmental and Resource Economics 1997/1998* (Cheltenham, UK: Edward Elgar).

UNDP (United Nations Development Programme) (1990, 1994, 1998, 1999), *Human Development Report* (New York: Oxford University Press).

Uzawa, H. (1974a), 'Optimum Investment in Social Overhead Capital', in E. S. Mills, ed., *Economic Analysis of Environmental Problems* (Chicago: National Bureau of Economic Research).

—— (1974b), 'The Optimum Management of Social Overhead Capital', in J. Rothenberg and I. G. Heggie, eds., *The Management of Water Quality and the Environment* (London: Macmillan).

Vincent, J., R. M. Ali, and associates (1997), *Environment and Development in a Resource-Rich Economy: Malaysia under the New Economic* (Cambridge, Mass.: Harvard Institute for International Development).

Viscusi, W. K., and T. Gayer (2000), 'Quantifying and Valuing Environmental Health Risks', mimeo, Harvard Law Shool, Harvard University; forthcoming, in K.-G. Mäler and J. Vincent, eds., *Handbook of Environmental and Resource Economics* (Amsterdam: North-Holland).

—— W. A. Magat, and J. Huber (1991), 'Processing Health Risks: Survey Assessments of Risk–Risk and Risk–Dollar Tradeoffs', *Journal of Environmental Economics and Management* 21: 32–51.

Vitousek, P., P. R. Ehrlich, A. H. Ehrlich, and P. Matson (1986), 'Human Appropriation of the Product of Photosynthesis', *BioScience*, 36: 368–73.

—— H. A. Mooney, J. Lubchenco, and J. M. Melillo (1997), 'Human Domination of Earth's Ecosystem', *Science*, 277: 494–99.

Wade, R. (1988), *Village Republics: Economic Conditions for Collective Action in South India* (Cambridge: Cambridge University Press).

Waldron, J. (1984), 'Introduction', in J. Waldron, ed., *Theories of Rights* (Oxford: Oxford University Press).

Walker, B., A. Kinzig, and J. Langridge (1999), 'Plant Attribute Diversity, Resilience, and Ecosystem Function: The Nature and Significance of Dominant and Minor Species', *Ecosystems*, 2: 95–113.

Weibull, J. W. (1995), *Evolutionary Game Theory* (Cambridge, (Mass.: MIT Press).

Weisbrod, B. A. (1964), 'Collective Consumption Services of Individual Consumption Goods', *Quarterly Journal of Economics*, 77: 71–7.

Weiss, J., ed. (1994), *The Economics of Project Appraisal and the Environment* (Cheltenham, UK: Edward Elgar).

Weitzman, M. L. (1974), 'Prices vs. Quantities', *Review of Economic Studies*, 41, 477–91.

—— (1976), 'On the Welfare Significance of National Product in a Dynamic Economy', *Quarterly Journal of Economics*, 90: 156–62.

—— (1998), 'On the Welfare Significance of National Product under Interest Rate Uncertainty', *European Economic Review*, 42: 1581–94.

—— (2000), 'The Linearized Hamiltonian as Comprehensive NDP', *Environment and Development Economics*, 5: 55–68.

Weitzman, M. L. (2001), 'Gamma Discounting', *American Economic Review*, 91: 260–71.

Williams, B. (1976), 'Moral Luck', *Proceedings of the Aristotelian Society*, 50 (Suppl. Vol.): 115–35.

—— (1985), *Ethics and the Limits of Philosophy* (London: Fontana/Collins).

Wilson, E. O. (1992), *The Diversity of Life* (Cambridge, Mass.: Harvard University Press).

—— (1998), *Consilience* (New York: Knoff).

Wolfensohn, J. D. (1999), 'A Proposal for a Comprehensive Development Framework', World Bank, Washington.

World Bank (1982, 1983, 1986, 1992, 1995, 1999, 2001) *World Development Report* (New York: Oxford University Press).

—— (1989), *World Tables 1988–89* (Washington: World Bank).

—— (1997), *Expanding the Measure of Wealth: Indicators of Environmentally Sustainable Development* (Washington: World Bank).

—— (1998), *World Development Indicators* (Washington: World Bank).

World Commission (1987), *Our Common Future (Brundtland Report)* (New York: Oxford University Press).

Yaari, M. (1965), 'Uncertain Lifetime, Life Insurance, and the Theory of Consumer', *Review of Economic Studies*, 32: 137–58.

Name Index

Name Index

Subject Index

economy
  Kakotopia 260–5
  measurement of economic activity 27
ecosystem flips 255–6
ecosystem hysteresis 257
ecosystem stress 109, 248, 251, 258
  see also environment
Ecuador
  Borda ranking 61
  current well-being indicators 58
  improvements in living standards index 71
education 79*n*
  basic need 48, 49
  civic attitudes 52
  as constituent and determinant 33–4
  externalities 47–8
  social and human capital 144–5, 291–3
  student loans 49
  viewed as consumption 145
efficiency
  liberalism 25–6
  poor countries 198–9
Egypt
  Borda ranking 60
  current well-being indicators 58
  improvements in living standards index 71
elasticity, marginal well-being 181, 242, 244
elites, and democracy 67
embedding problem 135
enforcement, non-market transactions 194–5
enjoyment 89
environment
  biodiversity 125, 128, 129
  externalities 293–4
  genuine investment 154, 156–7, 271–2
  global and local problems 117–19, 293–4
  green accounts 154–6
  local community 110–14
  and markets 107–9
  necessities and luxuries, valuing 124–6
  pollutees' rights 19
  population growth 117–18, 300–3
  property rights 116–17
  protection
    accounting prices 131–8
    taxes and regulation 173–7
  State 114–15
  and structural adjustment programmes 200–2
  substitution 127–30

technological bias in society 119–21, 307
  see also biodiversity; geography; pollution
environmental Kuznets curve 125, 248–9, 257
environmental services, valuation 137–8
equality, and population size 221
equi-probability 214, 214*n*
equity
  and intergenerational well-being 245, 279–83
  poor countries 198–9
ethics
  accounting prices 177–8, 268–70
  agent-relative ethics 97
  Average Utilitarianism 213
  culture and facts 4–6
  generation-relative ethics 226–8, 231–5
  and human rights 16
  impartiality 226
  intergenerational saving 93
  intergenerational well-being 96–8
  social cost-benefit analysis 190
Ethiopia
  Borda ranking 60, 65
  current well-being indicators 58, 64
  improvements in living standards index 71
Eurasia, agriculture 76
European Union, agricultural subsidies 115*n*
eutrophic state 259–60
evaluation
  policy evaluation 195, 252
  project evaluation 168–71, 179–91, 272–4
  social cost-benefit analysis 30, 272–4
  and valuation 1–2, 260
    Kakotopia and Agathotopia 7–8, 236
  see also comparisons; measurement
expected-utility theory 101, 303–5
externalities
  environmental externalities 293–4
  institutional failure 195, 260
  markets and natural resources 107–8
  poor countries 202
  population growth 208
  project evaluation, social cost-benefit analysis 171, 261
  quality-of-life indices 47–8
Exxon Valdes, litigation 135*n*

facts
  and ethics 5–6
  and values 3–7
family 209, 224–5
famines 74*n*
Faustmann Rule 291–2

opulence, measurement of 146
ordering 95
  complete and partial 20–3
ordinal aggregator 55
ordinal indices 25
  and cardinal indices 54–5
output
  discounting future consumption 191
  per capita 130*n*
  see also consumption; GNP; NNP
ownership, property rights and the
  environment 116

Pakistan
  Borda ranking 60, 65
  current well-being indicators 58, 64
  genuine investment 157–9
  improvements in living standards index 71
Paraguay
  Borda ranking 61
  current well-being indicators 58
  improvements in living standards index 71
Paretianism, and continuity 95*n*
Pareto efficiency 26
partial ordering 24
pathogens, cost-benefit analysis of developing
  vaccines 172–3
personal well-being, and social well-being
  13–14
perturbation
  evaluation 169
  policy change as 167–8
Philippines
  Borda ranking 61
  current well-being indicators 58
  impact of logging 201*n*
  improvements in living standards index 71
  poverty, population growth and soil
    degradation 117*n*
  untreated waste 171
phosphorus discharge 176, 252–60
Pigovian taxes 157*n*, 173–4
  double dividend 175
plurality of measures, personal well-being
  30–2
Poisson rate 102
policy change
  evaluation 252
  growth and redistribution 196–9
  non-market interactions 191–6
  as perturbation 167–8
  policy evaluation in poor countries,
    accounting prices 195

project evaluation 168–71
  see also project evaluation
policy instruments, environmental protection
  175
policy reform 143
political citizenship 46
political instability 113
political rights *see* civil and political liberties
pollution
  accounting 155
  pollutants as bads 124–5
  pollutees' rights 201
  stock effects 259, 293–4
  see also environment
Pontryagin's equations 242–3, 259
Pontryagin's Maximum Principle 242–3,
  258–9
poor countries
  equity and efficiency 198–9
  and free trade 202
  see also common property; malnutrition;
    poverty; rural poor
population ethics 228
population growth
  deforestation 113
  and economic growth xxi
  environment 117–18
  genuine investment 157–8
  intergenerational well-being 98–101
  sustainable development 300–3
population size 207–8
  discounting future consumption 182–3, 188
  Genesis Problem 215–19
  genuine investment, Average Utilitarianism
    212–14
  inequality 231
  optimum population size
    Average Utilitarianism 212–14
    Classical Utilitarianism 218–19, 220–1
  theories concerning 211
  wealth and genuine investment 148–9
positive feedback 246, 249, 253–5, 258
poverty
  character of 3
  defined 1–2
  and destitution 37
  and environmental problems 117
  malnutrition 6, 78, 79
  mental health 37*n*
  and productivity 79
  social capital 40